LIVE AND WORK ABROAD

A GUIDE FOR MODERN NOMADS

Huw Francis
Michelyne Callan

Published by Vacation Work, 9 Park End Street, Oxford
www.vacationwork.co.uk

LIVE AND WORK ABROAD

A Guide for Modern Nomads

First Edition 2001

by Huw Francis and Michelyne Callan

Editor: Ian Collier

Cover design by Miller, Craig and Cocking Design Partnership

Typeset by Worldview Publishing Services (01865-201562)

Printed by William Clowes Ltd., Beccles, Suffolk, England.

Contents

LONG-TERM CONSIDERATIONS

HOW LONG WILL YOU REALLY STAY ABROAD?

RETURNING TO THE COUNTRY YOU USED TO CALL HOME

NOTE: While every effort has been made to ensure that the information contained in this book was correct at the time of going to press, some details are bound to change within the lifetime of this edition, and readers are strongly advised to check facts and credentials themselves. If you have any updated or new information that you feel would be of interest to readers of the next edition, please write to the author at Vacation Work, 9 Park End Street, Oxford OX1 1HJ. Contributors will be sent a free copy of the next edition, or a Vacation Work title of their choice.

INTRODUCING MODERN NOMADS

Mention the term Expatriate and most people think only of high-income oil workers in the Middle East, military families in Europe, or diplomats on glamorous assignment in Paris, New York or Bangkok. The spouse is always assumed to be female and often referred to as 'The Trailing Spouse', 'The Expatriate Spouse', or the 'Corporate Wife'. The children of these expatriates have been labelled anything from 'Global Nomads', through 'Expat Brats', to 'Third Culture Kids'.

The luxurious, all expenses paid expatriate lifestyle does still exist for some, but thousands of people live and work in a country other than their own on less extravagant incomes. Some have found a job through newspaper advertisements, recruitment fairs or recruitment agencies and moved abroad for professional advancement, improved lifestyle, or to experience a foreign culture. Some may have been sent by an employer without the resources to fund the stereotypical expatriate lifestyle. And others were backpackers who found jobs and changed from travelling abroad to living abroad.

Technically, these people are still 'expatriates', but many live abroad not necessarily for the money and the glamour, but because they enjoy the experience of meeting new people and learning from the different cultures they live in. Women now make up a large percentage of the employed expatriates, and in some international careers they seem to be in the majority. This trend has seen a corresponding rise in the number of men becoming the supporting partner.

There are numerous books on the market for people sent abroad by a company which organises their international relocation and provides the services of a relocation consultant. Vast numbers of people though, who organise a move themselves and then find their own niche after arrival, have to search for the information they require from diverse sources.

Much of the published literature aimed at people living overseas seems to assume that many expatriates do not really want to be living abroad, and their main aim is to reach the end of their difficult posting and return to normality.

Though there are many expatriates who view their life in this way, this concept is alien to the authors of *Live and Work Abroad — A Guide For Modern Nomads*, and many other expatriates too. The authors have chosen to live abroad with their families because of the fun, pleasure and wonderful experiences it offers, and the number of like-minded *Modern Nomads* is growing rapidly. No matter how any expatriate comes to be living abroad and how they currently feel about doing so, they too can learn to make their international experience a beneficial and enjoyable one as well.

So how can these Modern Nomads be defined?

1. **Modern** in the sense of a growing worldwide trend among educated, professional people who live abroad for an international renaissance education that can never be gained in a classroom or from books.
2. **Nomad** in the sense that a decision to move is frequently determined by a desire, or need, for new experiences and something 'different' and that a subsequent move (to another city, region, country, or back home) may happen some time in the future.

So, *Modern Nomads* are people who look forward to arriving in a new country and creating a new home for themselves, their family, their pets and their belongings, or any combination thereof (even if that anticipation is usually coupled with nervousness). A *Modern Nomad* may be a teacher, business executive, journalist, executive secretary, member of the armed forces, missionary, diplomat or entrepreneur; they may have found a new employer, been relocated by their employer, or be part of a country's political or governmental services. Despite the variety of reasons for living abroad, *Modern Nomads* have one common trait; whether they move one time or twelve, they look to gain from the experience.

Modern Nomads enjoy tasting new cultures, new cuisine and new climates. They move abroad looking for the exciting differences of the exotic and the foreign, and will happily convey their anticipation and enjoyment to those around them. *Modern Nomads* look to the horizon to find new homes, new experiences and new perspectives.

Whether you are a potential expatriate, an expatriate enjoying the lifestyle you have, or an unhappy expatriate looking to make your stay abroad a more enjoyable experience, you can be a *Modern Nomad* too. What you need is the view that it can be good to live abroad, good to experience different cultures and the recognition that though countries and cultures may not be identical to the one you call home, they still have much to offer.

Modern Nomads are people who acknowledge, accept and embrace the notion that there is something intrinsically wonderful in learning about different cultures, but they do not necessarily embrace those cultures as their own.

Modern Nomad is a term that can be applied to anyone who lives abroad. Becoming a *Modern Nomad* does not require membership of an exclusive club, race, religion or culture. Typically, it requires you to reconsider your own cultural preconceptions, so you can attempt to understand and accept those of others.

This book does not intend to tell you how to live your life abroad. It aims to give you ideas and help you develop a positive attitude so you can create a home away from home while you make new discoveries and expand your horizons. By developing a positive attitude you can enhance your stay abroad, helping to make it a worthwhile and beneficial time in your life.

Whether you go abroad for just one year or stay away for a few years, whether you decide to make your life abroad in one country or move to a number of different countries, this book has something to offer you!

Huw Francis and Michelyne Callan
Turkey, February 2001

Acknowledgements

As an expatriate, developing a support network from the people who live alongside you can go a long way towards making your time abroad happy and successful.

A good support network of host nationals and other expatriates can become a surrogate family and provide the emotional and practical advice that family and long-time friends would normally do at home.

The people listed below will appear throughout the book and have generously donated their time and the benefit of their experience to help shape this book and create a written pool of support and advice. Many others have assisted too and will make their own appearance elsewhere.

To all those who have offered advice, support and criticism, whether you are mentioned by name or not, thank you.

DRAMATIS PERSONAE

Phylis Adler is an American lawyer turned psychotherapist, who moved to London with her husband and three children. Her adjustment to expatriate life led her to found organisations, create workshops and write articles dedicated to easing the transition of expatriates from different countries. She works in private practice and with *Just Mediation Services* (tel ++44 (0) 7979 603 313; pajadler@aol.com).

Alison Albon, from South Africa, is currently living in the Netherlands as an equal partner to her husband who is in the Foreign Service. Alison and Mark have enjoyed postings in Transkei, Israel, and Switzerland. They have two children, Matthew and Meg. In her free time, Alison is the owner of the *Expat Moms Egroup* (www.egroups.com/files/expatmomsonline), which offers online discussion groups and an e-mail group service for expatriate mothers.

Mario Antognetti relocated from Canada to Turkey, accompanying his wife who taught at an international school; they returned to Canada after two years. Mario is a visual effects director and during his stay in Turkey found employment as a part-time university lecturer in a related field.

Frances Brown is a South African living in the UK, who works as an administrator at a local college. Her husband works for a franchised motor dealer. They are independent expats who have bought a home in a small village and plan to stay indefinitely. They have one daughter, Jenna.

Karron Combs is American and accompanied her spouse, Bill, to the UK where she is raising her granddaughter, Crystal. Bill is an independent expat who found his own job in the UK computer industry.

Bronwyn Davies, qualified as a lawyer in New Zealand before relocating to Hong Kong in 1990, with her husband, Mark, who is also a lawyer. Both found employment after they arrived, Bronwyn began lecturing at the University of Hong Kong and Mark started practising with a law firm. Both their children, Callum and Phoebe, were born in Hong Kong. Bronwyn has completed an MBA and started a PhD through distance education with an Australian Institution.

Barbara Davis, an American, is married to a Turkish national who originally expatriated to the US. Along with their teenage daughter, Barbara accompanied her husband on a posting to France. The family spent two years in Paris and has since then repatriated to the US, but they anticipate there will be opportunities for more international postings in the future, when their daughter has finished high school.

Harry Deelman, grew up in South Africa and England and worked as teacher and school administrator in Buenos Aires, Rome, Dubai and Bangkok. He is now director of the UK and International Baccalaureate branch of *Search Associates* (PO Box 168, Chiang Mai 50000, Thailand; deelman@loxinfo.co.th; www.search-associates.co.uk), an international teacher and school administrator placement agency.

Andrea DiSebastian is a Global Nomad who was brought up in England, Spain, Israel and Honduras, as well as her home country, the United States. Andrea repatriated to the US to attend university and gained an elementary teaching qualification. After having worked as a teacher in the US, Andrea moved to Germany and taught at an International School.

James DiSebastian is American. He has worked in the International School system since 1985. With his British wife and their two children he lived in England, Israel, Spain and Honduras. He is now in Turkey, with his wife, where he is Director of an International School.

Dell Harmsen, has had the pleasure of accompanying her Foreign Service husband from the USA to Greece. She is a qualified teacher and an aspiring writer currently chronicling her expatriate experiences.

Laura Herring is President and founder of the *IMPACT Group* (www.the-impact-group.com), a leading global spouse and family relocation transition firm, headquartered in St. Louis, Missouri, USA and serving over 4500 locations worldwide.

Jeri Hurd is an American international school teacher. After teaching in the US for over 10 years she accepted a teaching position in Turkey. Jeri admits to having gone through all of the facets and stages of culture shock.

Bill and Anne Jordan are American teachers. They have lived and worked in the Philippines, Norway and Turkey. They have one daughter, Natascha, who was born in Norway, and are expecting their second to arrive whilst this book is going to print.

Gillian Kerr, is originally from the UK, but moved to South Africa as a child. She returned to the UK with her husband, an IT consultant/programmer, initially to London, before moving on to Scotland and then Australia. Gillian is currently studying for her graduate diploma in Primary Education and works from home on her *Creative Memories* business. They have two children, Donald and Catherine.

Kelli Lambe, is an American from Alaska who has moved three times in the last two and a half years, to Oman, the Netherlands and Saudi, along with her three children.

Coleen McLeman, is Canadian and equal partner to Robert McLeman who works for Canadian Immigration. They have lived in Hong Kong, the USA and Austria. Coleen gained a teaching qualification whilst living in Hong Kong and usually finds at least part-time work in whatever country they move to. She has also co-authored a series of skill-based books for high school students.

Robert McLeman works as a Canadian Immigration Officer (Foreign Service) and has enjoyed postings with his wife, Coleen, in Hong Kong, the US, and most recently, Austria. He was also sent on a short term posting to India, on his own.

James Mistruzzi left Canada for Hong Kong in 1988 and is an International School principal. His wife, Wendy is also an International School teacher/administrator. They travel extensively throughout Asia, Australia and Europe from their base in Hong Kong.

Palma Pisciella spent two years in Turkey as a teacher at an International School. She returned to Canada, as planned, at the end of her contract.

Cindy Rothacker, an American equal partner currently lives in Belgium with her husband, a Chemical Engineer. They have two boys Markus (who is currently enrolled in the local school system) and Max.

Barbara F. Schaetti is Principal of *Transition Dynamics* (2448 NW 63rd Street, Seattle, WA 98107, USA; tel ++1 206-789-3290; fax ++1 206-781-2439; www.transition-dynamics.com), an independent consultancy serving the international expatriate community. She has been active in the field of intercultural and international training and consulting since 1985. Barbara herself is a Global Nomad and draws on this experience when helping families through an international transition. Barbara lived in ten countries on five continents by the time she was 18. In her business, Barbara coaches expatriate families on the practice of Personal Leadership throughout their expatriate life cycle. She works closely with international expatriate communities on the development and implementation of comprehensive transition programmes, consults with international employers and International Schools, coaches adolescent and adult Global Nomads, and offers a series of informational presentations and programmes on the expatriate and repatriate experience.

Dana Schwarzkopf, is a single American schoolteacher. She has lived and worked in Mexico, Germany, Turkey and Thailand and has spent a significant amount of time in Norway with her extended family.

Helena (Lonnie) Snedden was born in Scotland, but moved as a young child to England where she stayed for four years. Her family then moved to South Africa and she considers herself South African. After 26 years in South Africa Lonnie moved, with her husband and their daughter, Kaylee, back to Scotland. Lonnie's husband has since repatriated to South Africa, while she and Kaylee made a decision to stay in Scotland.

Tony Turton was formerly Personnel Director (International) for *Thames Water* in the UK, he now leads *Arnett Associates*, an International Human Resources Consultancy (www.btinternet.com/~arnettassoc/).

Peter van Buren is the author of *Traveling Internationally with your Kids* (www.travelwithyourkids.com). He and his wife, Mari, have two daughters who were born abroad. The family has lived abroad, in six countries, for most of the last 15 years and has travelled extensively.

Mike and Sarah van der Es are New Zealanders who started working abroad as nurses in 1985. They went to the Sudan and worked for one year with the nomads, for a non-profit organisation helping children. Further postings included Ecuador, Kenya, Burkina Faso and Nepal. Mike has also lived in New Zealand, Holland and now England. They have two children who travelled with them.

Bernadette van Houten, MA has lived abroad for many years, become proficient in five languages, and has much expertise in training for cultural and linguistic transitions. She is a former chair of the Cross Cultural Committee of the *European Council of International Schools* (ECIS) and has since created her own business, *Consultants Interculturele Communicatie* which has offices in the Netherlands (Marnixstraat 154 I, 1016 TE Amersterdam) and the USA (3601 Connecticut Avenue, NW #610, Washington DC 20008-2450).

Brennen Young is a Canadian Third Culture Kid (TCK). He moved to Belgium, Hong Kong, Al Ain (UAE) and Dubai (UAE) with his parents, and finally repatriated to Canada, alone, to finish high school and attend university.

Doug and Donna Young, are Canadian. They lived and worked in Belgium for two years, where Doug was a graduate student and Donna was busy raising three kids whilst being pregnant with a fourth. They repatriated to Canada for two years and then moved to Hong Kong where they both taught. After two years in Hong Kong they moved to Al Ain in the UAE and then on to Dubai where they currently reside.

THE NUTS AND BOLTS OF LIVING ABROAD

Why are you thinking of moving abroad? Be honest with yourself. You need to be realistic about why you are going and what you are expecting, because abroad will never be a replacement of your home country. France is only twenty-one miles from England, which shares a language with the USA, that has a land border with Mexico and yet the four countries are all unique destinations, with unique cultures that offer different experiences for their international residents. Deciding whether to move abroad at all and what the destination should be, is best made on informed contemplation, not blind enthusiasm, if the decision is to be the best one possible.

Are you going abroad because you have always nursed a dream to travel the world, or because you feel obligated to? There are many different reasons to move overseas, and your attitude towards the move can be a major determining factor in whether you enjoy your stay in the host country, or even if you manage to stay there and complete your contract. Barbara Schaetti, Principal of *Transition Dynamics* (2448 NW 63rd Street, Seattle, WA 98107, USA; tel ++1 206-789-3290; fax ++1 206-781-2439; www.transition-dynamics.com), an intercultural consultancy specialising in expatriate family services, states that, '...one's intention to succeed is a necessary ingredient when transferring abroad'.

Suzanne Stevens, an accompanying spouse on her first posting in Hong Kong, is more specific about the best approach to an international relocation and highlights one particular aspect of the necessary attitude. 'I would say that the best advice I received from our relocation counsellor was 'keep your sense of humour.' It is a *must.*'

Mike van der Es and his wife Sarah, are nurses who have lived on four continents, in eight different countries including Sudan, Ecuador, Kenya, Burkina Faso and Nepal concur with the sentiment. 'The most important thing to take is a positive attitude and a willingness to learn. That takes no space and costs nothing to ship.'

The fantasy of the traveller's dream is just that, a fantasy. Most dreams of international living omit the complications that accompany a normal life, let alone those that arise solely because you are living overseas. Jeri Hurd, a single American teacher who taught for many years in the US before relocating to Turkey, remembers hers:

In my dream of travelling, there was a sense of daring, of going out and trying new things and meeting new people, seeing new places and noting things being done differently from how I've ever seen them done before. It was the idea of difference. I liked the idea of chance encounters that turn into wonderful adventures, you know, getting lost and finding meaning.

Life without any challenges can be a life of boredom; an overseas life will certainly produce plenty of challenges. Meeting new challenges and deciding whether to side step them, ignore them, conquer them or shift the responsibility of them, and then learning from your choice is both the fun and frustration of living overseas.

Knowing about the many challenges (and planning for them) before a relocation will help to increase the enjoyment and lessen the frustration of being an expat. Though in some cases people will decide not to make a move abroad once they are aware of what the expat life is really like.

Expatlandia (www.expatlandia.com) is a company headquartered in Silicon Valley and founded in 1998 as a partnership between technologists and expatriates to provide a lifeline for expats and a winning model for their companies to succeed. Robert Smith, the President of Expatlandia who spent 26 years as an expat both as a child and working family man, agrees that collecting such pre-departure information is helpful in preparing expats for the challenges of an expatriate lifestyle. He and his team of experts offer education about living abroad through the Internet using virtual tours of expat housing and neighbourhoods and other technology-leveraged solutions. The Expatlandia team believe that two of the most overwhelming challenges, which can make or break a foreign assignment for corporate employees, are:

1. How to avoid being 'out-of-sight' without being 'out-of-mind' and,
2. Not being able to be 'in touch, anyplace, anytime'.

Robert suggests that by thoroughly investigating the expat world before you go, '...with technology-driven solutions such as virtual tours,' the '...expat unit (expat employee and their family) and the multinational firms employing expatriates are much better off'.

By knowing what you may encounter before, during and after the move you can begin to prepare yourself efficiently and effectively. You will be able to consider how to prevent problems from occurring, manage solutions for those that are unavoidable, and plan alternative methods of accomplishing potentially difficult tasks.

In the pages of this chapter you will read about the most common challenges and the corresponding benefits experienced by overseas residents. In considering these issues you will be able to decide for yourself whether you think the life of a *Modern Nomad* is for you. If the thought of meeting new challenges and working through them is too much for you to consider, then maybe you should decide to stay where you are. If, on the other hand you would like to take on the challenges and gain knowledge and pleasure in the process, then an international lifestyle will afford you these opportunities. There is no dishonour in deciding to be happy, whatever your choice.

Definitions

There are many styles of overseas life and a great variety of terms and conditions you may be employed under, some of which you may never even have heard of. International living and employment, like much of life, have their own phraseology, which can be obscure or unintelligible until they are explained. Below is a list of the most frequently used terms to help you through this chapter, the book and an international life:

1. **Expatriate**, or **expat**: A person living in a country other than the one they would call home, for reasons such as employment or retirement (e.g. an American living in Paris).
2. **Corporate Expatriate:** An expatriate employed by a large corporation (e.g. Shell, BP, Citibank) usually relocated from one corporate office to another. Corporate expatriates often move between countries frequently (every one-and-a-half to two years) and receive large compensation packages and relocation counselling.
3. **Independent Expatriate:** An expatriate usually employed by smaller companies, or self-employed. The postings/contracts tend to be longer (2 years or more) and the compensation packages smaller than those of corporate expats. Independent expatriates will often change employers every time they move. Relocation counselling can be seen as an unaffordable luxury. Independent expatriates often live abroad for the experience, rather than for purely professional, or monetary reasons.

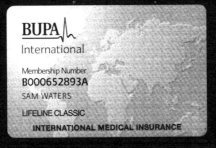

4. **Single Status:** No provision will be made for a spouse and children to accompany an employee. This can be for a variety of reasons and include: safety of the location, cost saving by the employer, lack of suitable accommodation; short length of the assignment.
5. **Married Status, without children:** A spouse can accompany the employee but not children. This can be for a variety of reasons and include: safety of the location, cost saving by the employer, lack of suitable accommodation and lack of suitable schooling.
6. **Married status, with children:** An employee may bring his family, but the employer might not cover the costs/expenses of relocating the family.
7. **Third Culture Kid (TCK):** A person who spends a significant part of their developmental years in a culture other than their parents' culture and develops a personal relationship to all of the cultures while not having full ownership in any (David Pollock, Director, *Interaction*, P.O. Box 158, Houghton, NY 145744; tel ++1 716-567-8774; fax ++1 716-567-4598; 75662.2070 @compuserve.com; www.tckinteract.net).
8. **Housing allowance:** A limited sum of money allocated to the employee to cover rental accommodation at the destination. The employee will often be expected to choose his or her own accommodation, though the employer may provide some assistance with the search.
9. **Housing provided:** The employee will be placed in accommodation, for the duration of the contract, by the employer and pay no, or subsidised, rent.
10. **Leave flight:** Return airline ticket to country of origin. The frequency of flights and the number of family members eligible for the flights vary from employer to employer.
11. **Medical insurance:** Private medical insurance paid for by the employer. The quality and scope can vary greatly and may not include dependants.
12. **Dental insurance:** Private dental insurance paid for by the employer. The quality and scope can vary greatly and may not include dependants. Usually separated from the medical insurance.
13. **Education allowance/schooling:** Financial assistance, for the schooling of employee's children, or a guaranteed (funded) place in a specific school. The allowance can vary in size and may cover only a part of a school's fees in Local Schools, International Schools, National Curriculum Schools (French, Pakistani, etc.), or Boarding Schools; details should be checked.
14. **Baggage allowance:** Allowance for excess baggage on the relocation flight at the start of the contract.
15. **Shipping allowance:** Allowance to cover the cost of using a shipping/moving company to transport your belongings. Can vary greatly in monetary value, as can the cost of shipments between various countries.
16. **Furnishing Allowance:** Allowance to cover the cost of purchasing essential items needed for you to live in an unfurnished apartment. Can vary greatly in value and what it can buy at local prices.
17. **Relocation Counselling:** Advice and support provided either by the employer (or HR Manager), or an outsourced relocation consultancy.
18. **Local terms:** Employment terms and conditions will be those that a local employee would be offered. Local terms of employment do not usually include housing, leave flights, medical or dental insurance, schooling costs or baggage/shipping allowances.
19. **Expat status/Foreign Hire Status:** Generally a better package than local terms, but the list of benefits included may not include all of those listed above.
20. **Home Office:** Headquarters of the employing company, and usually refers to an office in a country other than the one where you will be working.

Watching out for you from afar.

If you live abroad, or are intending to, then Brewin Dolphin Securities could be the investment house for you. Established in the 18th Century, we are one of the UK's leading independent firms of private client stockbrokers and fund managers, looking after 80,000 portfolios worth some £17 billion. Our service includes:

- Individually designed portfolios
- Global investment policy
- Continuity and flexibility
- Regular visits worldwide

However far away you may be, you can relax in the knowledge that we are taking care of your finances.

For further information, please contact Victoria Le Sueur.

BREWIN DOLPHIN

Complete Investment Management.

5 Giltspur Street, London EC1A 9BD.
Telephone +44 20 7246 1062, Facimile +44 20 7246 1093, Email: vlesueur@brewin.co.uk

21. Posting: An international assignment of variable (finite) length.
22. At post: Mostly used by US diplomatic personnel to describe their status when they are on a foreign assignment.

Personal and Family Considerations

First and foremost, moving overseas means leaving a lot behind. Unless you are running away from something specific, or searching for a more exciting life, the act of leaving can be painful. Immediate and extended family members, lifelong friends, the home you have lived in for years and many other sentimental attachments will be a long distance away when you move. However, they will usually still be there when you go back. Various ways of keeping in touch, cheaply, easily and on a daily basis if needs be, are discussed later in the book.

A move overseas will affect everyone you know socially and professionally. All your relationships will be affected in some way; even your relationships with the family members who accompany you will be affected. How you and the people affected approach the change in circumstances will determine how the relationships will develop after your move. It is not uncommon for overseas residents to say that their relationships with family members, both those staying at home and those travelling abroad, have strengthened since they relocated. Though there are families who say that their relationships suffer directly due to the stress of living abroad, especially where problems already exist.

However, moving overseas will introduce you to much that is new; new friends, new surroundings, new cultures, new foods, new languages and new opportunities. There is no doubt that you will miss what you have temporarily left, though realistically looking forward to the positive aspects of a move can make the transition a more valuable and enjoyable experience. Part way into her first overseas assignment Elaine Spooner, an experienced UK teacher who relocated to Turkey and later Egypt as an international schoolteacher, said:

> *...the first time abroad you are getting used to everything. Job, accommodation, culture, etc. Your closest friends and family seem a very long way away. It takes time to make new friends and learn to understand new cultures, but it will happen.*

Staying in Touch

When you are separated from family members by half the world you can be tempted to think they might as well be on another planet. Is that true?

International air travel has made it quicker to travel from continent to continent by plane than region to region by car within some countries. Daily flights are available to and from almost every corner of the globe and in many cases flights are available more than once a day. That being said, the physical separation from people and places can weigh heavily on your mind because it seems difficult to be emotionally close to someone so far away. But modern communications now mean you are not limited to the slow and old-fashioned surface mail of yesteryear to keep in touch with news from home. International telephone calls may be expensive, but faxes have the lasting benefits of letters, the immediacy of a telephone call and are much cheaper. Investing in a fax machine can save on telephone bills in the long-term, even if you buy two machines and give one to those you want to stay in touch with.

The Internet is the emerging communication tool of choice for overseas residents. With the click of a button, mail can be sent worldwide for very little money (many employers now provide personal e-mail facilities for their expatriate employees). Internet telephone services (both net-to-phone and net-to-net services) and real-time written conversations (Internet messaging) are becoming more

th**e**times
Now available on tap.

Not only is THE TIMES available
on the net, it's also constantly updated. So tap in and catch up.

Feed your mind [www.th**e**times.co.uk]

reliable and continually improving. Soon, intercontinental communication should be as easy and cheap as a local telephone call and maybe, one day, video-conferencing will transmit images just as easily over the Internet. If you have never used the Internet or e-mail try to learn, not only will it make communication easier if you move abroad, but carrying out essential research and making contacts before you go will be greatly simplified.

In some countries you may still find that international communication is an issue, because not all of the above services are available everywhere. One expat who went from Ghana to the US says:

*It sometimes becomes difficult to keep in touch with your family and even when you keep in touch, you may feel as if you have **nothing** to say. I usually use the telephone and sometimes e-mail to communicate with my family. Unfortunately, e-mails aren't always checked because of time constraints or slow ISPs. But the phone is usually a great, but expensive way, to keep in touch! Sometimes our phone bill runs as high as $500, even up to $1,000.*

Family Ties

Ties to your immediate and extended family can loosen, if they are allowed to, when you move to another country and they stay behind. It is possible that your absence from traditional holiday get-togethers may make you homesick while also making your family/friends resentful at your absence. At times like this the telephone bills tend to be larger, or your time spent on Internet communications can be greater. However, with careful words and some effort on your part, the competing emotions can be soothed.

Jeri Hurd remembers leaving her family behind and the emotional pangs she felt:

The first few months I actually felt very out of things. I was very worried about all the lives going on back home and me not being a part of them. I think I subconsciously worried that unless I was actually there, I'd trickle out of their lives event by event, until I was no more than a well-known friend who you look forward to seeing every few years, but never really think about much beyond that.

However, with the passing of time and the establishment of new routines Jeri settled down and realised that the separation from family would not ruin her experience abroad:

E-mail flew thick and fast during those first few months and I panicked if I didn't hear from someone for a few days, or if (horrors!) our server went down. It has now been months since I've heard from some people or written to them and I hardly even think about it. I don't care about them any less, but I need them less now to help me define who I am. I am more aware of my own ability to get along by myself.

The advantage of being abroad in this situation is that you have the option of starting new traditions of your own in your new home and new country. Enjoying traditional holidays in your own way can lead to a strengthening of ties among your immediate family who are abroad with you. In addition you can experience and enjoy the pleasure of alternative traditions with a family from your host culture, or the third culture of one of your overseas-resident colleagues.

While couples and families have their own built in support group, single people can find it better to join up with friends or families. Dana Schwarzkopf, a single teacher who has lived in Mexico, Germany, Norway, Turkey and Thailand has befriended many families and has been able to hook up with them during holiday times:

It is really nice to be able to be in a family situation when I want to. At Christmas my friends had a brunch for all the 'orphans', those of us who didn't go home for the holiday. For me, it was really nice to be with a family in a family setting on that day.

But aside from making friends with other expat families, Dana has had the pleasure of being accepted by a local family in Thailand:

I have Thai friends who own bungalows. I have spent so much time down there that we have developed a friendship as well. At this point, no matter when I arrive there, there is always a place to sleep. I have spent nights sleeping at their house, and eat many meals with them as well. They are friends who have accepted me into their lives and have helped me understand Thai culture. I can ask them anything. Being single allows me the opportunity to get up and go at anytime, but I think it is also easier to be accepted into a family situation. It is pretty easy to make room for one more, but one has to be open to it as well.

Effects on Children

Children may find an overseas relocation tougher to handle than adults. An explanation for a move might be logical and compelling to an adult and lead to an inevitable conclusion, but it still may not seem fair as far as your children are concerned. Alternatively, your children may accept an explanation without second thought, especially if it is not the first time you have moved, or they are too young to understand the implications of the changes. Though the two extremes are possible (and parents should be prepared for either) a middle route will probably be much more likely.

Andrea DiSebastian, an American veteran of numerous moves, who grew up in the US, England, Spain, Israel and Honduras and is now a single teacher living in Germany remembers her first move. 'I remember being excited and terrified at the same time.' She also remembers the transitions of subsequent moves, 'The more we moved, the easier it was to just 'pick up and go'. There was no fear anymore of the unknown. Packing up and changing homes didn't seem like such a project.'

Whatever their initial reaction, leaving behind everything that a child has ever known is bound to be stressful for them, let alone the fear of the unknowns that will follow. For children to enjoy a move to its fullest potential they need to become excited about it first. Parents need to foster enthusiasm for the idea of a move by providing their children with information and details about the destination that will make it attractive to the child and give them something to share with their friends. Giving them reasons to feel proud and happy about moving to a new country should help lessen the blow of acknowledging those things that they will leave behind. *Children and the Move* and *From Packing to Unpacking* both look at how an international move can affect children.

Education

As far as education is concerned, you want the best you can get; whether it is for your children, your partner, or yourself. What do you know about education in a country other than the one you went to school in? For most people the answer is likely to be, 'Not a lot'. The educational options available in any given country can be extensive to non-existent and all points in between. For your children, the school they attend can be one of the greatest determining factors on whether they settle and enjoy the change of lifestyle and the stay in their new country. After all, children make friends, acquire social lives and spend the majority of their time at school, or involved in school-related activities.

Researching the best option for your circumstances can be time consuming and confusing, unless you know where to look. The various schooling options of Local Schools, International Schools, Foreign Curriculum Schools (e.g. French, German, Australian, Pakistani), Religious Schools, Home Schools and Boarding Schools have differing advantages. It is, however, rare to find an impartial advisor to explain things so you can make up your mind without having to sort out the truth from the advertising.

James DiSebastian, the American Director of an International School in Turkey who has also taught in the US, England, Israel, Spain and Honduras says:

Check, check and check. You have to talk to your embassy for information. You have to check with the various international school associations or accreditation agencies, depending on how the school is accredited or recognised. You have to talk with the school people themselves: i.e. the administration. But if you also can, it's best to talk to some of the other parents of students that are already attending that school, and also teachers that work there; to find out what it's really like.

Harry Deelman, an experienced international teacher and administrator, who grew up in South Africa and England and has worked in Buenos Aires, Rome, Dubai and Bangkok, is now part of *Search Associates* (PO Box 168, Chiang Mai 50000, Thailand; deelman@loxinfo.co.th; www.search-associates.co.uk), an international teacher and school administrator placement agency. He says, 'Above all, try to find a way to communicate with some parents of children currently at each school'.

For further information on everything from understanding the options from kindergarten through secondary/high school and university education to continuing education for adults, please turn to *Education: Understanding the Options*.

Special Needs

Special needs, whether they are educational, physical, emotional or psychological, for you, your partner, or your children, can add a number of essential tasks to the planning of an overseas relocation, but should not have to prevent a move. Some destination countries will prove to offer better facilities, or be safer for people with certain special needs than the country of their birth.

The variation in cuisine around the world means some countries are better than others for people with food allergies. Some countries are more wheelchair friendly than others. Some societies are more open to accepting mental and physical impairment than others. There are many people who have not been prevented from travelling around the world by their special needs, and some have found their life improved with an international move.

The son of Michelyne Callan, one of the authors, has a fatal allergy to peanuts, which they discovered whilst living in Hong Kong, where peanuts and peanut products are a staple part of the diet. The family moved, but not back to their native Canada. She explains:

We have been lucky to find a comfortable home in Turkey, where peanuts are hardly used in the local cuisine or processed foods. In Hong Kong, it was much more dangerous given the amount of peanut oil, peanut flour and whole peanuts found everywhere. Everything from bakeries to restaurants to hawkers selling cooked foods on the streets posed a fatal threat to Liam. I feel it is much safer living in Turkey, probably even more so than in Canada where peanuts lurk in mislabelled food, and a higher percentage of processed foods.

Further resources and information about travelling with special needs can be found in the chapter *Special Needs*.

For How Long?

'How long are you staying there for?' is a question almost everyone will ask you, even if you do not ask it of yourself. How long you intend to live overseas is often related to the reason you are going. Your first thoughts regarding the length of your intended stay may well be defined by the contract under consideration. If you are not offered a fixed-term contract, then you will probably have a rough timescale of your own in mind. However, unless strictly bound by contract, there is a high likelihood that the actual time you live abroad will change from your initial estimate.

Many people have found that putting an initial timescale on the proposed relocation can ease making the decision to move overseas. However, many people who are living abroad seem to have set out with such a timescale in mind and subsequently changed their minds once they had relocated. The change in timescale can be to go home early, or stay longer. Those who really wanted to live abroad and knew what they were getting themselves into are more likely to be the ones who stay longer and even move to a third country after enjoying their first experience of living overseas.

Emanda Richards, a Canadian teacher who spent three years working at an International School in Turkey, accompanied by her IT specialist husband who worked in a local school as a support teacher, remembers when they made the decision to stay abroad for another year before returning to Canada:

Initially we planned to go for the duration of one contract that lasted two years. By the end of the first year, my husband and I decided we weren't going to be done experiencing living in this region, that there was so much else to see. So we decided to extend our time abroad by another year to make the most of the whole experience.

Those who made an impetuous or ill-prepared move are more likely to be the ones going home early, or staying under unhappy protest. Accompanying partners also have a large effect on the length of time spent overseas and many expatriate employers report a trend in failed assignments. A *Cendant Mobility* (Corporate Headquarters, 40 Apple Ridge Road, Danbury, CT 06810, USA; www.cendantmobility.com) survey attributes the main cause of assignment failure to be the cultural difficulties experienced by the assignee or their family. Quoting from the survey, an article on the *Mobility Services International* website (www.relojouranl.com) states:

*While more employers today are reporting failed international assignments (63% compared to 57% three years ago), the reasons why these assignments fail have changed little, according to a recent industry survey. Respondents to Cendant's **International Assignment Policies & Practices 1999 Survey** said the main causes of assignment failure continue to be cultural difficulties on the part of the assignee or family; personal or family problems; or poor candidate selection. The survey also revealed that while the majority (89%) of organisations formally assess a candidate's job skills prior to selection for an international posting, less than half (49%) formally assess his or her cultural suitability, and even fewer (41%) formally assess the suitability of the family.*

Effects on Partners

Socially, an international move can isolate a supporting partner, especially for those located in remote areas. Whereas, in most cases, the employed partner will be able to socialise with colleagues and associates during the day, a stay-at-home partner's social life can become limited to the same group of people if efforts are not made to expand the social circle. Some partners look forward to the time of day when the employed partner returns home with office gossip, and look forward to work-related social gatherings.

However, other partners can see this office-related social life as claustrophobically incestuous and boring as they listen to more work stories. In the worst case scenario, a work-dependent social life could lead the at-home partner to have feelings of worthlessness and resentment for being completely dependant on the working partner (not just financially, but socially) and for not having a 'real job' of their own.

The effect of a career hiatus on accompanying partners can also be a major component affecting the success of an overseas posting. If nothing is done to preclude it, the hiatus of the accompanying partner could be a black hole of wasted years on the career ladder. On the other hand, with planning, it could be the perfect opportunity to continue an education, pick up and complete a long awaited project, or be a wonderful chance to spend more time at home with the family.

Mario Antognetti, a Canadian visual effects director, who accompanied his schoolteacher wife to Turkey for two years prepared himself with project lists:

> *Before going, we spoke to some close friends who had the same experience. Two days after they were married, they jumped on a plane for Africa and lived there for two years. The wife worked as an engineer and the husband, like myself, was there to 'get away' for a while. His advice to me was, find something you always wanted to do and bring it with you. You don't want to be sitting around the apartment doing nothing because you'll start to feel you have no worth.*

Whichever partner has the primary source of income, the needs of the accompanying partner must also be considered. Aside from any assistance that an employer might offer to the accompanying partner, it is important that the employed partner provides support as well.

What may seem to be the subsidiary family role in your home country can become a major occupation abroad. The accompanying partner will be challenged with an endless list of new, previously unimagined set of issues to handle in a foreign country. Many expatriate partners cite their new role as 'domestic co-ordinator', because of all the tasks that must now be actively managed, though they were second nature in the home country. The accompanying partner should be considered an equal partner in a transition abroad. The accompanying partner will most likely be the family member who deals with all of the new domestic issues that the employed partner may often not have time to do, or even realise are being done. If this role, as domestic co-ordinator, is recognised it can give the at-home partner a sense of importance in the success of an overseas posting.

Shopping in a foreign language can be phenomenally frustrating, public transportation may run on confusingly illogical principles, and maintaining a home without the shopping resources you currently take for granted may seem impossible. Jeri Hurd remembers the frustration of daily domestic chores 'When you arrive you can't talk to anybody; you go to the store and you don't know what you're looking at; it takes you an hour to figure out the damned washer. Everything took so much more time.'

But just because things are different at first, does not mean there is no place for resourcefulness. A Ghanaian expatriate in the US remembers his mother finding that shopping for traditional foods was difficult. Yet with creativity and a flexible diet, the Ghanaian family was able to surpass this 'comfort block' and make a lot of rice and soup dishes that they were used to eating at home.

If a partner decides to invest in continuing education during the years overseas, there are many ways to do so. It can be the perfect time to study when you are a not restrained by the normal expectations of friends, family and work (see *Education: Understanding the Options*).

Overseas career options open to partners will undoubtedly be different from those at home; in some countries the options may appear to be non-existent, while in other countries the opportunities may be richer than in the home country. When considering a partner's overseas career options, you must expand your thinking into areas previously never considered. It will not be a simple case of lateral thinking, but rather a 3-D way of thinking. Overseas job opportunities for a partner are often not ones you would ever consider possible at home.

For example, one expatriate partner in Hong Kong had just finished graduate school in Canada and was hired by the University of Hong Kong as a PA, administrator and researcher, which she knows she would never have been considered eligible for in her home country. She reached out on a whim for something she did not think she would ever get, and won. By thinking as widely as you can, and through acquiring information, training and contacts before departure you can alter the balance between success and failure in a job search.

Which Country?

The number of independent countries that exist seems to change as often as the weather. The political stability of a country can be as important a consideration as the climatic conditions, economic development and congeniality of the population to your religion or ethnicity. These are the obvious components of a country to consider, but what about food, clothing, language, people, social customs, religion, historical rivalries, public services, medical care, internal travel and all the other components of daily life that only seem important when they are not as you would like them to be.

All of the above features of a country need to be considered to a greater or lesser extent, depending as much on their importance to you and your family as their importance to the nationals of the country you may be going to.

Running Away From Problems

Are you running overseas to escape from personal problems? Many of the day-to-day problems that you already encounter in your current country of residence will occur wherever you go, along with a whole lot more that are specific to the destination. If you are running because you cannot cope with certain aspects of your life, think closely about what you hope to achieve before you go and whether those problems are going to arise at the destination too.

Professional Considerations

Staying With the Same Employer

There are two ways to go overseas with your current employer:

1. You ask to go.
2. Your employer wants to send you.

If you ask to go, then hopefully you are excited about going and are eagerly planning your new life. But your new lifestyle will only be one part of the many changes to come. Professionally there will also be many considerations to be addressed to ensure that your secondment, sabbatical or relocation abroad is a successful step in your career.

Sometimes your request may coincide with your employer's decision to look for someone to send abroad as happened to Robert McLeman, a Canadian Foreign Service employee who has been posted to India, Hong Kong, the US and Austria:

Having been in Seattle for three years after having previously been overseas for four years, I was starting to get itchy feet — that is, I was looking forward to getting overseas again. I had made my thoughts known to the personnel section at our headquarters, and had suggested a number of cities where I would be willing to relocate. In making up this list of cities, my wife and I had decided we were willing and able to live in what could be considered 'hardship' conditions. These included such cities as Beijing, Delhi and Dhaka. My employer has traditionally found it difficult to staff offices in these cities with experienced managers, so the personnel office agreed to consider my wishes, and commended me on the shrewdness of my list. Several weeks later I was fortunate enough to have been offered a position. It was good timing.

If your employer has just announced an intention to send you overseas, then you probably have a mixed bag of emotions from excitement to anxiety and everything in between. You now need to consider both the personal and professional implications of such a move, possibly in a limited time-scale. If it is your employer's decision to transfer you to a foreign office, (as opposed to it being your decision to volunteer for the available position), you may have to make a concerted effort to be positive. You will need to take the right steps (including learning about the new culture, new language, and new professional expectations) to decide whether to go and to aid you in your professional success and adjustment if you do move abroad.

Whether you have requested a transfer abroad, or have been posted unexpectedly, your attitude to the country you are considering moving to and how you cope with the potentially huge differences in the working style could well be different. Robert McLeman remembers being absolutely shocked when he was told the posting he was being offered:

My personnel officer called me and said that she wanted to get my knee-jerk reaction to a position I had never mentioned in my wish list — Tehran. Even though my wife and I had never given any serious thought about living in the Middle East, I did not immediately reject it out of hand. I was too stunned — was this an opportunity or was it an offer they knew I would refuse and be thrown in my face in the future should I ask for another transfer abroad?

When employers send current employees overseas they usually only consider trusted, experienced and well-qualified personnel. A promotion often goes with an overseas posting, and if not an actual promotion then there is still likely to be more responsibility and greater autonomy due to the distance of the posting from the supervising office. Promotion and more responsibility are also likely to be promised for when return-time comes around.

As Robert relaxed after the initial shock he found out that the prospective move had built in advantages:

I eventually accepted the position, although not before my wife had done a great deal of research about the lifestyle and opportunities for Western women in Iran. (We actually only had Friday night, Saturday and Sunday to consider before I let my employer know on Monday morning). I learned shortly later that the assignment was offered to me because it was known that I was slated for an upcoming substantive promotion in salary and classification.

Over and above the professional reasons to go are the financial ones. Incentive packages including overseas cost of living bonuses, housing allowances, educational allowances, leave flights, entertainment allowances and cash bonuses may be offered. Of course, the personal satisfaction of being considered for the posting can be a boost to the ego too.

Robert also points out that:

For me, the position is a big step up the organisational ladder in terms of responsibility and reputation. The office in Tehran is smaller than the one in Seattle which I am leaving, but whereas I am the deputy manager of the office in Seattle, I will be the one and only manager in Tehran.

But why do some companies offer incentive packages? The answer is, 'Because working overseas can be tough'. Though she now enjoys living overseas and is looking forward to one day moving to another country Jeri Hurd says, 'People shouldn't kid themselves about the potential difficulties of adjusting'.

In his new posting in Iran, Robert knew he would...

be working in a challenging and completely alien cultural environment, with locally hired staff working in their second language. There would be unreliable telecommunications and the nearest counterpart would be literally 1000 miles away. While my array of responsibilities will be smaller, my personal level of accountability for the decisions made in my office will be 100%. Moreover, the scrutiny, which I will receive from my headquarters, will be intense — mistakes made in Seattle are much more easily rectified than those made in Tehran. In other words, there will be no safety net for me.

There are also numerous cases of employees who spend years in a company's overseas office ending up being out of sight, out of mind. Often, when the expatriate employee returns to the home office, someone else has filled the original job. The promised end-of-posting promotion may not actually be available upon return because everyone forgot it was already promised and someone who stayed behind was offered the job. 'This isn't just an occasional or even frequent issue — I believe it affects everyone,' says one legal professional posted in Asia:

It is easy to get pigeonholed as an overseas or country specialist if one goes overseas too early, shows too much enthusiasm for being in an outpost or if one stays out too long. For some, that is fine and even preferable (if one has a non-career draw to the expat arrangement). Still, others find that going overseas can break one out of a lockstep system and enable one to advance faster.

According to the newsletter *What's Happening? Stats and Info for Expats 1998*, put out by Mobility Services International, 'Most companies aren't prepared for the employee's return and make them wait up to a year for a new position. In the meantime, the expats get frustrated and quit, taking the knowledge they've gained (at the company's expense) straight to its competitors'. (Data and conclusion compiled by *HR Magazine*: Society for Human Resources Management, 1800 Duke Street, Alexandria, Virginia 22314, USA; tel ++1 703-548-3440; fax ++1 703-535-6490; shrm@shrm.org; www.shrm.org).

So accepting an international posting may not be just a temporary change until you return to your old life. It may be the start of a change in your career path that opens a whole new window of opportunities.

For expatriates who decide to move abroad themselves, the implications of leaving your professional field in your home country must be analysed as well. Making the decision to move abroad can make it difficult to return to your current way of life because once you are abroad you find that the professional field at home no longer offers what you want. Mike Callan, an International School Principal who has taught in Japan, Hong Kong and Turkey, but not his native Canada says, 'After 10 years of teaching in international educational institutions, I cannot imagine moving back home to work in the local system'.

Overseas postings can also come to an end with no prior notice at unscheduled times; contracts fall through or are cancelled altogether, or offices themselves fail to reach the position of economic viability. If you are single then the upheaval caused by the unexpected termination of the posting is less of a problem than if you have an accompanying partner and children. But if you are enjoying the posting, you may want to remain in your host country a little longer, which may or may not be possible. Balancing the potential for possible future disruption to your family and/or your professional life against the perceived benefits of a move abroad is important and turning down a posting may be the best option for some people.

Finally, bear in mind this bit of wisdom from one expat lawyer who has seen various movements within his own profession:

Like other career choices, going overseas involves a risk assessment — the key is for the prospective expat to clearly identify the impact of going on their prospects within their organisation and within their industry or field. Having the pros and cons match the experience is important to one's satisfaction overseas — people who fail to research well can get lucky but most end up bitter when unfounded expectations aren't met.

The *International Assignment Policies & Practices 1999 Survey*, carried out by Cendant Mobility produced some interesting results that are worth bearing in mind when making an international move for purely career considerations.

1. 16% of assignees leave their organisation within two years of returning home.
2. In companies of 10,000-30,000 employees 60% of boards have former expatriates as directors.
3. The data indicates that only 38% of assignees gain promotion following their assignments. Although a higher proportion than in some surveys, the majority of expatriates still do not appear to make career gains from their willingness to transfer overseas.

Going With a New Employer

Breaking away from an existing employer can be personally liberating and exciting; it can also be beneficial for your family and improve your career prospects. The main reasons for changing employer in your home country are often similar to the reasons for changing to a new employer with offices abroad; an improvement in career, lifestyle and finances.

A new employer can give you the chance to expand your skills, gain new practical experience as well as a new outlook within your professional field. Changing employers may mean promotion and pay increases. It could also mean a lateral move to a very similar job to your previous one or even a temporary step down. Often these kinds of changes will afford you more room for growth within the new company. You can feel less obligated to a new company than to one you have worked with for years, so the new employer will work harder to keep you. Of course, there will also be a greater number of employers available to you if you consider changing both employer and country.

Given enough drive and expertise in your field, you could also create your own employment and become a consultant or entrepreneur. This way, you have ultimate job freedom, though it will also entail the corresponding concerns of commercial success, income and employee responsibility.

John Barratt, a Canadian physiotherapist who has lived in Australia, repatriated back to Canada and then accompanied his employed wife to Hong Kong, where he started a business from scratch:

I knew that with my professional background and experiences as a physiotherapist I would be able to at least find part-time work. Upon arriving overseas obtaining full-time work was harder to secure than I expected. The salary was low and the work hours not enough. This dissatisfaction prompted a reassessment of our situation. With the support of my wife, I decided to start my own business. It was going to be hard due to our low cash flow, competition with established companies, and limited professional or social support network. I hit the challenge head-on and with an appropriate strategy, some long hours, budgeting, bit of luck and a lot of hard work I managed to gain a solid patient referral base. Four years later I have my own business, we have great friends and have not looked back.

The downsides of overseas employment can include different work ethics and business practices. Contractual obligations in some countries can be worth less than the fax paper they are sent on; so the terms and conditions of your contract may vary or even disappear without notice. International employment agencies operating from P.O. Boxes can be unregulated and unscrupulous, taking your money for empty promises. Foreign nationals may not always have the same legal protection as locals in harsh economic times; redundancy can come swiftly and harshly.

Once you have a new job with a new employer, the job can be less secure than you originally thought. As a new employee you might have less loyalty to a company than if you have been employed there for years. The same is true as far as the employer is concerned. Pay scales can be enticing on paper, but be sure to check if it is paid in a stable currency or the local one. High inflation can knock all value out of your salary in no time. For example, one expat living in Turkey has seen the exchange rate change from 17,000 Turkish Lira to the British Pound in 1993 to 985,000TL to the Pound in 2000.

So, do your research. Look for information on potential employers and employment agencies, contact Chambers of Commerce and other such organisations to collate information on working practices. Call your embassy or similar agency to ask if they have any information, good or bad, about the employer or general employment conditions within a country. Being prepared in advance for likely local complications can lessen the stress and smooth your stay.

Professional Culture Shock

What will working overseas be like? If anyone tells you that there is a generic style of overseas working practices, they are being optimistic. The differences will not just appear as you move countries, but will also appear between professions in the same country. For example, if you ask someone who once worked in Paris about what it is like to work in Santiago, they will have no idea. If you talk to someone who worked as a banker in Hong Kong, they will have no idea what it is really like to be a teacher in the same city.

Working overseas will be different from what you are used to; it may be easier or harder, or you may work longer or shorter hours.

In broad terms, people in Asia seem to work longer hours than those in Europe or North America, though some would say that long hours are no replacement for efficiency.

A Japanese teacher in a school where foreigners were employed once explained to a North American colleague that, 'In Japan we work very long hours — we don't always work hard in those hours — but we do work long hours'.

One expat who lived in Japan for a year noticed that all the teachers in his school remained after work until seven or eight o'clock at night, sometimes later, though the school day ended at three. They did not necessarily stay to finish work; many of them were reading the newspaper, or pretending they were doing paper work. The real issue was, however, the implicit rule that no one left until the boss left, and the boss could not leave until the teachers started to leave. It left everyone in a catch-22 situation. No one could leave until someone else left.

Six-day working weeks are standard for some professions in Hong Kong while Europe can be deceptively laid back in comparison; French business lunches tend not to include discussions about work, but can be more of a personal interview to see if the people involved can work together. In the Arab States, etiquette can demand an hour or more of polite social conversation before even the slightest mention of work is allowed.

Bureaucracy can dominate and strangle enterprise in some countries and let it flourish without hindrance in others. Whereas some countries embrace entrepreneurial enterprises from abroad to widen the spectrum of services, other countries close doors to foreign professionals in order to protect the employment prospects of their own nationals. Local attitudes to work and efficiency vary considerably around the world and can also vary within countries depending on the nationality of the boss.

Most people who have worked abroad will readily agree that learning to understand local working styles and attitudes is one of the most frustratingly important lessons they have to learn when trying to settle into the rigours of a new job. There can also be the cultural conflict between expats of different nationalities. Tessa Siebrits, a South African now teaching in Turkey has observed that, '...your personal outlook has a lot to do with how you cope with these situations at the work place'. She advises expats to bear in mind the following points when they find that differences in work styles are frustrating:

1. It is not home here and you should not expect it to be. Why should other people have the standards/attitudes/ways of doing things the way it is done 'back home'? It is a very arrogant thought to believe that your ways are better because of where you come from. Even though you may not outwardly say it, there can be a tendency to hold the thought that 'someday they'll learn how to do things properly'.
2. You are not owed anything in a different culture. Many people have an absolute sense that life owes them certain things and that they can expect to be treated certain ways. These are all preconceived ideas that may not necessarily fit in with the local culture.
3. Don't try to push your ideals of right/wrong and what is just on another culture. Some people try to force what they believe onto the local situation and battle to understand why things are different there.

Also, it is good to remember that frustration can go both ways, colleagues can be as frustrated with you as you are with them. Two-way communication and not criticism (active or passive) is the best way to improve the situation and all cultures can learn from each other, if they are willing to try.

Personnel employed from one country to work in another often seem to be given greater responsibility than they would ever receive at home at a similar age. For those who are ambitious this can be a wonderful way to progress.

However, experience gained overseas can be discounted as worthless if you return to your country of origin. Teachers, for example, can work around the world in high quality schools preparing children of multiple nationalities to enter universities in countries around the world, but Canadian public schools and UK state schools can often make it difficult for that experience to be recognised if the teacher returns home.

Despite the added responsibilities, the attitude of employees in a home office towards their counterparts in far-flung outposts can sometimes leave a lot to be desired. An ongoing complaint from overseas staff is that people in the home office have no idea that there is a time difference of eight hours or more between London, East Asia or America. This can be an ongoing problem for your private life when you have to stay in the office until all hours of the night, waiting for a telephone call from the big boss to discuss the outcome of the day's board meeting.

Another complaint is of the perception that work done abroad must be of a lower quality than that done at home. A lawyer based in a foreign office says that, '...one attitude occasionally encountered is that the work flowing into and out of the outpost offices is inferior in quality to that in the home office'. He says that, '...the attitude can make for somewhat condescending tones during those middle-of-the-night calls'.

Career Changing

Deciding to relocate your life and career overseas can open new worlds of employment opportunity, not just new worlds of culture. If an employer is going to hire a foreign worker it can be because there is a need for something other than practical skill and experience acquired through formal education. As a foreigner you may have skills and experience not necessarily available in a country other than your own. The skills can be as basic as native language ability, or as complex as a cultural attitude that can be applied to training and marketing for a company looking to expand internationally. In the international marketplace you have to re-evaluate what you can offer an employer to best market yourself, but once you have re-launched yourself, the potential careers you can contemplate entering will multiply.

Changing your career would be stressful in an environment you know well. Consider how much more so it will be in a country whose language and culture you may have no knowledge of. Of course, learning new skills on the job can be an exciting and rewarding challenge, which is why so many people do it.

It is possible to prepare for a career change while at the same time getting a taste of living abroad. The organisation *ITC Prague* offers prospective teachers of English with little or no previous experience 4-week TEFL training courses in Prague and Barcelona followed up by job-finding help for life: for details contact ITC at the address in the above advertisement.

In creating a new career abroad, you open a field of opportunity to yourself, which can include redesigning your professional profile. One professional, having moved from New Zealand to Hong Kong knows this herself, having moved her career from practising Law into teaching and training.

Professionally reinventing yourself can be an enormously satisfying process when you have to do it in an unfamiliar environment. I have found that a 'foreign' viewpoint is usually valued by organisations now that so many markets are globalising. This is not to say however that you can rest on your laurels. You do need to take stock of what skills you have to offer and what skills you will require in order to make an impact in your new market. This soul-searching exercise can be both a rewarding and a demoralising experience, but either way it should be highly motivating.

Research and Development

Whether it is in the academic world, the industrial or the commercial, there is always research going on somewhere. Different countries have reached different places on the research ladder and just about all of them want to reach higher.

A growing number of universities around the world are teaching and publishing research papers in languages other than the native language of their country, and they recruit foreign academics to boost their reputation. Whether your speciality is scientific, medical, social, anthropological, or some other field, some locales are better for your research than others.

Commercial organisations are also keen to develop their products, so they can compete on the world market, and will recruit specialists to develop their existing product lines, initiate new programs, or manage research programmes.

Unfortunately, even if you secure a research position in your ideal country, local bureaucracy, language difficulties and differences in the way research information is catalogued may make research more difficult on-site than it had been a continent away. Social attitudes can also make research more difficult in others countries; sexism, racism and xenophobia can rear their ugly heads anywhere in the world. While some places are prone to certain problems, others can be remarkably free of complications.

Unemployment Pressures

Facing unemployment can spur you on to new challenges, or stop you dead with depression. Either way it can be a stressful time. Avoiding unemployment by relocating internationally to a new job will also be stressful, but it can also kick-start your life and career again. One expatriate in Hong Kong was watching his company slowly go bankrupt, knowing he would find it very difficult to find work in a similar field just before the handover to China. So he and his wife looked for work elsewhere. His wife found a job halfway round the world in Turkey, he accompanied her and then successfully launched his own business in a country he had never been to before.

With thirty years experience in your profession you may be considered too old by many companies in your own country to be worth employing, but in other countries around the world your experience can be a considered a commodity well worth paying for. Training positions, management positions, specialist recruitment agencies and consultancy companies need people who know what they are talking about and have the ability to convey that knowledge to others. In fact, many people who would otherwise be retired in their home countries, go abroad and take on various senior positions within different companies, or simply carry on with similar employment in locations where their age can be positive factor in people's perception of their ability to do the job.

Practical skills can be translated into a marketing speciality. Maintenance skills can be turned into a training capability. University graduates, especially those with professional skills, can upgrade their qualifications to become specialist language instructors, teaching people from beginner level to advanced, subject specific classes.

The Practice of Being a Modern Nomad

Living the life of a Modern Nomad can be fun, exciting, exotic, stimulating and challenging. It can also be strenuous, frustrating and mundane if you let it be so. Your attitude and your approach to the expected and the unexpected challenges of your expatriate life will have a huge bearing on your happiness when living abroad.

If the challenges discussed above seem insurmountable, remember that many people have successfully followed this path before. Read through the charts at the end of this chapter to help you pinpoint the areas that you may find difficult. Then read the relevant chapters that follow to find ideas on how to smooth your way.

For those who are intrigued, tempted and excited by an overseas move and the challenges discussed above, read on too. The following chapters discuss the challenges you may face and the benefits you can gain in greater detail, which will help you work through them to increase the benefits of your time abroad.

Each chapter will prepare you for making the most of the many different aspects of living abroad while avoiding many of the potential drawbacks by quoting ideas, solutions and advice from people who have previously moved overseas and, have gained from their experience.

Every country is different and everyone who moves abroad is different, so it is important for you to find out about where you are going or thinking of going. How will the weather, accommodation, culture, food, transportation, communication, television, media, religion and all the other components of life impact on you. The chapters of this book aim to help you do that, no matter where you are going, by raising the many issues that need to be considered. They will assist you in making an informed decision as to what is best for you and/or your family.

In the final balance you might decide not to move abroad and Bernadette van Houten, a former Chair of the *Cross Cultural Committee of the European Council of International Schools* (www.ecis.org) who is now an International Communication and Training Consultant (*Consultants Interculturele Communicatie*, Marnixstraat 154 I, 1016 TE Amersterdam and 3601 Connecticut Avenue, NW #610, Washington DC 20008-2450) gives this advice:

Giving up the job, or postponing the transfer, might be a solution if a transfer is not seen as the best path within the whole context, which for young professionals includes the family. But giving up a job does not necessarily mean giving up the company, but it could.

On Balance, Should You Go?

The following balance sheet is intended to help you quantify your feelings and ideas as you contemplate the decision of becoming a *Modern Nomad*. Some sections you can complete now, while others will require some research before you can make an informed decision. Refer back to it often as you continue your research and read further through this book, so you can answer more questions. Expect some answers to change as you find new information too.

Personal Considerations

	Positive advantage	No problem	Minor problem	Definite problem	Not applicable
Distance from home country					
Separation from family					
Separation from friends					
Occurrence of homesickness					
Long distance communication					
Emotional separation from family					
Emotional separation from friends					
Absence from traditional family reunions					
Few traditional holidays in host country					
New national holidays					
New religious holidays					
Lifestyle change					
Schooling for the children					
Accommodation for the children					
Environment for the children					
Timescale of posting					
Relocation schedule					
Extended family objections & concerns					
Partner work options					
Partner social options					
Partner education options					
Partner career break					
Family commitments					
Host country economic stability					
Host country political stability					

Personal Considerations   *continued*

	Positive advantage	No problem	Minor problem	Definite problem	Not applicable
Host country social stability					
Host country wealth					
Host country wealth distribution					
Host country culture					
Host country religion					
Host country climate					
Host country diet					
Host country language					
Political disagreements					
Medical facilities					
Dental facilities					
Access to special needs facilities					

Resources

Print Resources
Vacation Work's *Live and Work* series: Australia & New Zealand; Belgium, Netherlands & Luxembourg; France; Germany; Italy; Japan; Russia & Eastern Europe; Saudi & The Gulf; Scandinavia; Scotland; Spain & Portugal; USA & Canada.

How to Books' *Living and Working Abroad* country specific series.

Online Resources
The World Factbook from the CIA, www.odci.gov/cia/publications/factbook providing political and statistical information about countries worldwide.

www.btinternet.com/~arnettassoc/index.html: website of international HR Consultant, Tony Turton, former Personnel Manager (International) of *Thames Water*.

www.escapeartist.com: contains information on living abroad, country profiles, finances, expat magazines and expat resources – including a comprehensive listing of embassies worldwide.

www.expataccess.com: provides country specific resource information for expats and those considering a move.

www.expatnetwork.co.uk: a UK based expat resources website that includes country information, bookshop and giftshop.

www.iagora.com: predominantly a discussion forum for expats, it contains useful firsthand information on living in many countries.

www.internationalliving.com: primarily aimed at people retiring abroad, but contains extensive links for expats.

www.kafeniocom.com: online European magazine.
www.liveabroad.com: companion site to the *Network for Living Abroad Newsletter.*
www.reloglobal.com: a partner site of expataccess.com for international HR managers.
www.suite101.com/welcome.cfm/expatriate_living: a series of articles on expatriate living from the author Huw Francis.
www.talesmag.com: the online version of the US Foreign Service spouses newsletter (though it is open to all expats), with personal accounts of living abroad.

Financial Considerations

	Positive advantage	No problem	Minor problem	Definite problem	Not applicable
Basic remuneration					
Cost of living in host country					
Cost of living allowance included in salary package					
Housing allowance or accommodation included					
Medical insurance included					
Schooling allowance included					
Cost of leave flights included					
Number of leave flights					
Leave flights included for partner & children					
Host country local travel facilities					
Host country taxes					
Home country taxes					
Loss of partner's salary					
Employer compensation to partner					
Dual taxation					
Pension funding					

Professional Considerations

	Positive advantage	No problem	Minor problem	Definite problem	Not applicable
Continuing with the same employer					
Changing employer					
You asked your employer to go					
Your employer asked you to go					
Your employer said you had to go					
You chose the destination					
Involves promotion					
Guarantee of continuing overseas work					
Guarantee of employment if overseas posting ends					
Employer support for partner					
Partner support for employee					
Host country attitude to your gender					
Host country attitude to your religion					
Host country attitude to your ethnicity					
Legal system of host country					
Reputation of employer in host country					
Reputation of employment agency					
Extended working hours					
Non-traditional holidays					
Non-standard working week					
Expected entertainment requirement of employee					
Expected entertainment requirement of partner					
Bureaucracy					
International communication and time zone differences					
Professional recognition of international work experience					
Career change opportunity					

GOING ALONE

Through Choice or Necessity

If you are going overseas on your own, whether because you are single or are on a single status posting, the prospect of having to re-establish your social circle can be one of the most daunting hurdles in view. Indeed, many solo overseas residents do say that getting past the initial loneliness and isolation was the single biggest obstacle they had to overcome the first time they made a move.

Jeri Hurd found:

The interesting thing about this is that, while I was worried about leaving friends behind, people on the international circuit actually do form friendships very quickly, because they're thrown into a somewhat intense situation, and bonds form through sharing that experience. However, because people come and go so quickly, the friendships aren't as strong, and often don't last beyond the two years of a contract, unless people stay several years. That's not true of everyone, of course, but of many.

Already having established a social circle once, most people find it less daunting and much easier to do on subsequent moves. Dana Schwarzkopf, with many moves under her belt says:

I think this is true for most people, but not for all. I am pretty outgoing and figure I will meet someone to be friends with, but it does always seem to be like those first few weeks in university when you spend a lot of time with the first people you meet. You all go through the orientation together so you have that one thing in common. It takes a while to then really figure out who you are truly compatible with. That is the hard part.

Moving overseas has many similarities to moving within your own country (mostly in the logistics area), but it also has many differences. When you move within your own country you usually retain the familiar basic cultural landmarks of language, currency, television, radio programming and food with which you retain much of your sense of identity. You are, of course, still within the psychologically safe cartographic borders of your home country. The social institutions and meeting places you grew up with usually exist in every town of your home country, so you know where to look when you begin re-establishing a social life.

Karron Combs, who is raising her granddaughter in the UK, having accompanied her husband there from the US after he secured a job in the computer industry, points out the difference between moving within a culture, and between cultures:

The most difficult part of moving abroad is the lack of cultural reference in your social life. In America, no matter where you go, there is a basis for your culture, regardless of your background. Overseas, that comfort zone is removed and you have to find other ways to rebuild your cultural reference and, in doing so, your comfort zone. I think one of the reasons many expats go to the nearest McDonalds is for the feeling of normalcy it gives in an often overwhelmingly different world. It is important to remember that you are no longer in Kansas, and so you should look beyond what is expected.

However, when you move abroad, the majority of the local social and cultural landmarks can be hidden behind a foreign language sometimes made worse by an unintelligible script, a differently styled bureaucracy and different cultural traditions. Trying to establish a social circle beyond your workplace can then seem to be an impossible hurdle to overcome. True, it will take more effort than at home, but with persistence and time you can form successful social circles almost anywhere. In setting up a social circle Dana Schwarzkopf advises, 'You want to be able to talk to others about all the things that are going on and that you are feeling. If nothing else just to check and see if you're 'normal', but you don't really know anyone well enough to do a lot of comparing. It is frustrating, but doesn't have to be bad'.

In many cases the loneliness suffered by expatriates is labelled simply as homesickness. This is an easy scapegoat that can be used far too much and much of the homesickness is likely to disappear once the person has established a satisfactory social network. Jeri remembers:

...during orientation week when we were all together visiting Ulus (the old city in Ankara, Turkey), going shopping or just being together, I always had a great time and felt very lucky to be here and very excited. The instant I was home by myself, I'd be sobbing into the pillow, and wondering if I was bipolar (manic-depressive). I realise in hindsight that the reaction was partly because, however much I enjoyed the other staff, those experiences were somewhat superficial. I was with people I'd known only a few days, when only a week before I'd been talking to people I'd known for ten years, where every glance and comment carries a history. I felt very cut off from my centre of support, a more significant loss than 'mere' homesickness.

The physical distance from home can be intimidating when looked at on the map, so try looking at it differently. In the UK you may have to drive for ten hours to travel from one end of the country to another and in Canada and the US it can take three days. From your current home to your international destination it may only be a seven-hour flight and while the distance is certainly further, the travelling time is often shorter.

Linguistically, countries may vary from north to south and east to west. Many Londoners find Glaswegians unintelligible, but they both speak English. In Belgium there are three official languages, Flemish, German and French. India has numerous languages and dialects. Despite these linguistic variations within the national borders, most nationals of these countries would find going to a foreign country more linguistically worrisome than travelling from one end of their own country to the other. The language barrier can be a problem, but it seems that few international residents learn to speak the host country's language, despite the many benefits that learning the language can bring. A common reason given for their failure is that so many locals speak English; one expat in Asia pointed this out. 'The frequent use of English has led me to be lazy. I have no real need to learn the local language as I can carry on all my personal admin, as well as my work in English. I feel pathetic at times but, it's the way it is.'

A lack of knowledge of the local language, though a handicap to full participation in everyday life, is not necessarily the overwhelming problem it is perceived to be. However, learning the language proficiently, or at least to the level where you can hold a reasonable conversation, will make it much easier to find friends in the local community.

Despite the potential causes for loneliness mentioned above, there is a major benefit of being a single overseas resident; you have the advantage of being able to decide where and when you want to go somewhere. Then, once you are there you can choose whom you socialise with, without having to worry about the potentially competing ideas of a partner and children. The situation of single parents will be discussed later in this chapter.

After arrival, many solo travellers find they are quickly welcomed into communities and families where they are able to experience the familial support and friendship which they were previously so frightened to be without. Dana Schwarzkopf points out that, 'As a single person you, more than a couple or family, need to have a support group of sorts'.

In reality, many singles overseas find great comfort in having a network of friends they have found abroad on which they can rely. Dana continues:

You need friends. You need people who at the very least speak a common language with you. In time, they do become a surrogate family. They are the nearest people to you when you want to share good or bad news. They can give you the hugs, pats on the back or beers when you need them the most. They don't take the place of your family, but they do become your support system. It's very important to have some kind of network.

Overseas residents who have moved a number of times use the lessons they learned on previous moves to help themselves on each new arrival. Even though they have freshly established themselves before and know they can do it again, they realise that they still have to put in the time and effort following each arrival.

Elizabeth Lanphier, a Canadian who lived in Hong Kong, Malta and Japan on single postings before she met and married her British husband in Japan, where they still live, prepares herself mentally before a move. 'Every time I move, I tell myself that I've done this before and I can do it again, that I know what to expect from the process, but there are always surprises and struggles on the arriving end.'

Most people agree that establishing themselves becomes easier each time. Moving countries then becomes less a depressing process of leaving something behind and more an exciting process of arriving somewhere new. For Elizabeth that is the reason she lives abroad, '...the very quality that I seek when I move on... the change, the unexpected, a new challenge, new experiences'.

New friends, cities and cultures are waiting to be discovered, while old friends do not have to fade away; they can be easily contacted and visited wherever they are in the world.

Networking

Starting the Process before You Depart

An effective way to begin the process of establishing your new social circle and ensuring that you arrive to at least one friendly face is to begin networking before you move. Knowing someone, or at least knowing of someone, at your intended destination will lessen the intimidating emptiness of your new address book.

Lorenza Fregni, now part way into her first job abroad, started contacting people in her destination city as soon as she was offered the position.

First of all I wrote generally to all the people that I could, about certain lifestyle questions. I wanted to get the sense that living abroad, as a single woman, was safe especially in a strange country. I really wanted a woman's point of view. After the first letter I just thought I'd keep writing to see how my new pen pals were. After writing back and forth for a while, I felt like I knew these people well. I wanted and needed a sense of familiarity when I did finally arrive. I'm glad that I contacted people in advance. It has made my transition here much smoother.

Contacts through a Current Employer

If your current employer is sending you to an existing overseas office, a ready-made resource bank of contacts is available. If you are replacing an existing international employee in the overseas office, then that person should be your primary source of information; even if you have to make contact with the person on your own time. If someone from your office was previously posted overseas, even if they went somewhere different from your destination, make contact with them. The majority of people who have lived overseas will be willing to talk about their experience and advise on what questions to ask about your specific destination; but beware of those who continuously complain, it is easy to follow them down the road to cynicism.

Depending on the size of the office you are being posted to, your contact options may be limited to the one person you are replacing, or stretch well into double figures; so ask your personnel office and your colleagues for the names of employees they know in the overseas office. In the unlikely event that you are asked why you want the information, you have the valid reason that you want to learn as much about the overseas office as you can before you leave, so that you will be able to be productive as soon as you arrive. If you do have any choice at all in whom you can contact, try to communicate with someone who is most likely to be in a similar personal situation as yourself and who will be able to make further introductions into a social life once you arrive.

Employers should recognise your need to build a contact network so that you can start to benefit immediately from your experience abroad. James Mistruzzi, Principal of the *Japanese International School* in Hong Kong where he has lived for ten years, believes everyone that he knows who has lived abroad has benefited in some way from the experience. As an employer he knows it is important for new staff to find a social circle where they can feel comfortable. However, he has seen many people who did not benefit as much as they could have from their overseas experience, because they were not happy at work and outside.

If part of the reason you are being posted abroad is to set up a new office you will not have the experience of those who have gone before you to draw on for your destination. Eric Nesme, a French design engineer previously posted to Turkey, was sent to Bucharest, Romania to start up the new office for his company. There was no one there to greet him. There were no previous employees there he could poll for information. He was however, offered the opportunity to fly to Bucharest, with his wife, for a three day 'look-see' visit to find a house where they would live. They found a housing agent who could speak French, and from there spent the three days looking at 30 different places. It was a taxing weekend, but it was important that he make this pre-visit. What remained to be seen was the location of the office and the resources Eric would have available when he actually started work three weeks after his initial visit.

If your employer is launching you into a new city with a previous network, use it. Ask whom the company has previously used as a local agent or a subcontractor at the destination, and then contact them, even if only for the personal help they will almost certainly be willing to offer you.

Trade Associations (Chambers of Commerce), Cultural Organisations (e.g. *The British Council*) and your country's Embassy can also serve the dual purpose of business and social introductions.

For an employee and an employer to benefit from an overseas assignment, the employee needs to be happy in both their work environment and their social life. James Mistruzzi has spent many years hiring many new teachers. He says he has:

...known some people who 'bury themselves' in their work and seem to have little or no interest in a social life. Anyone I've known on longer-term contracts has needed to be happy both inside and outside of the workplace. The most productive teachers I have are those with a variety of interests outside the school.

Contacts through a New Employer

Starting work with a new employer often means you will have fewer contacts within the company than if you have been working with them for years. Even so, when you accept a job offer ask for a contact name of someone at the overseas office you will be relocating to. If the company will not give you a name for reasons of confidentiality, ask if the company can send your contact details to the overseas office so someone can make contact with you. If needs be, you can point out to your employer that communicating directly with the overseas office prior to your departure means you are likely to settle in and become a productive employee quicker.

Contacts Independent of Your Employer

By establishing a line of communication before you depart for your new posting, you will at least know someone when you arrive, but only making contact with a work colleague can mean you limit the scope of your questions. There will probably be a tendency to ask only work-related questions and if you do branch out into other areas, the desire not to look silly can mean you never ask those questions you really want an answer to. One great question went something like, 'Do the apartments have baths or showers, and should I bring my shower curtain?'

But how many people would dare ask such an important question of a new boss?

How do you find people unrelated to your new office to communicate with? To start with, ask everyone you know if they know someone in the country you are going to, or if they know anyone who has ever lived there. 'I'm a friend of a friend', may seem like a weak introduction, but small beginnings can lead to great things. If the only contacts you make are with people living in a third country it can still be worth making contact; they will probably be able to answer general questions about living abroad and they are likely to know someone where you are going. Overseas residents are generally more than happy to help new arrivals with advice and information. Even if you do not end up being life-long friends with your pen pal, any initial introductions they make will speed up the rate at which you do meet the people who become your long-term friends.

Apart from personal introductions there are other sources that can generate great contacts before you depart for your foreign posting. Below are listed a number of sources and the contacts they may be able to provide. The list should not be considered complete, but it will give you ideas on where to look.

There can be a great temptation to limit your social circle to the immediate group of foreign residents you work and have daily contact with. This happens mainly because it is far easier to slot yourself into the first social playing field you come across, than to risk the potential strain and rejection of trying to break into new and uncharted territory.

Dana remembers the first year she was in Bangkok:

I went to all the farang (foreign) places to hang out. It was always the same old people, teachers from the various international schools, business people, old expats, etc. It was really no different than hanging out in a bar at home. The predominant language was English, and most people were western. It was western music, food, beer and atmosphere. The following year I met a Thai man whom I began dating. It was then that I saw the Thai side of Bangkok. I met and mingled with his friends. We went to Thai hangouts, places I would never have found on my own. I was often the only farang there. It really gave me a more complete picture of Bangkok. It is really important to meet and mix with the local people of the country and to meet other foreigners who do not work with you. There is a real threat when only mingling with co-workers, you never really leave work.

The result of this is twofold. First, you risk falling into a limited group of foreigners, which can become socially incestuous and can be like living in a goldfish bowl where everyone knows your business. Secondly, you can end up missing the rich cultural experience around you, which has the potential to be one of the highlights of living overseas and is often a driving force for moving overseas in the first place.

Contacts and Sources

Source	Type of contact
Embassy/consulate of destination country	1. Official contacts in destination country, administrative bureaucracies. 2. Friends/relatives of the diplomatic personnel in the destination city.
Home country Ministry of Foreign Affairs - regional dept.	Official/personal contacts in your country's embassy/consulate in your destination city/country.
Home country Chamber of Commerce	Business/personal contacts at your destination.
Rotary Club	Sister organisations exist in many countries worldwide; mostly with host national members.
Cultural Associations; e.g.: *Alliance Francais, Goethe Institute,* British Council	Personal contacts with expatriate staff and local nationals.
Religious Organisations	Overseas affiliate organisations and individual places of worship.
Sporting Associations	Overseas affiliate organisations and local clubs.
Relocation Consultants	Introductions to their extensive local contacts, both business and personal (probably fee charging).
Library/Bookshop	Guidebooks often contain addresses of local clubs, religious organisations and foreigner meeting places.
The Internet	Most of the above is often available through the Internet for those with access. There are also a growing number of web based expatriate support groups. (See resource list at the end of this chapter for useful website addresses).

What to Ask

Use any opportunity during your pre-departure communication to ask questions that only someone who lives in the destination can answer. For example, what social, sports or other special interest clubs are there, and what are the contact names and numbers of them. If you are talking with someone who is living overseas, or has in the past, but not at your destination, ask what information you should be trying to find out before you go. There will always be information that would be better to know in advance of the time when you find yourself in a situation you had not even thought of.

How to Make Contact

E-mail communication can be much less formal and much quicker than standard mail and is rapidly becoming the most popular method overseas residents use to keep in touch with their far-flung family and friends. This means that you will be able to contact many of the people already at your upcoming destination and short e-mails sent to your contacts can take on the character of conversations. Apart from the speed of message transfer, the other great benefit of e-mail is its low cost and many companies with expatriate employees are now providing personal e-mail facilities for their employees.

If you have never used e-mail, consider learning immediately. Being able to use e-mail can be a great benefit after your arrival as well as before you go. It makes communication much quicker, which will be helpful as the days before your departure speed by. It is also more personal than letters, cheaper than telephone calls and less formal than faxes. At this time it will be well worth the effort of collecting the e-mail addresses of everyone that you know, to make communication easier after your departure and lessen the feelings of impending separation.

If e-mail is not an option, a fax machine can be the next best thing. Faxes are cheaper than international telephone conversations and much faster than standard mail. Traditionalists and technophobes might also prefer this method of communication (rather than e-mail) and it can sometimes be more reliable than e-mail in less developed countries.

Telephone contact has the benefit of immediacy, but it also has the problem of putting people you do not know on the spot when you call asking for information. A high volume of international telephone calls can also become prohibitively expensive.

Post-arrival Contacts

Living overseas is a full-time lifestyle. You may not be able to return to your home country to meet up with old friends very often and you will almost certainly miss some of your traditional festivals and family get-togethers that have always been part of your culture and life so far.

Forming a social circle after arrival overseas can be more complex than forming one in a new town in your home country. In a new country you have to start from nothing and build up a social circle that can fulfil all your social, intellectual and emotional needs. There is more to consider than what you are going to do on an evening at the end of the week, and which friend you want to go to the cinema with. You need casual acquaintances you are happy to see occasionally as much as special friends whom you can trust in a crisis.

When you are meeting new people and deciding who will become friends and who will stay acquaintances, remember to consider not just what you are doing next weekend. It is also important to remember what you will want to be doing during long-weekend holidays, or cold winter nights when your bank balance is low. Who would you ask for help when you are ill and what do you want to be doing at Hanukkah, Diwali, Christmas or Eid?

Some people find that they make friends easier if the other residents know that they are there for a longer, as opposed to a shorter stay. Ellie Skeele, an independent entrepreneurial expat and single mother to two adopted children who lives in Kathmandu, points out how people perceive others by the length of how long they stay.

I've found that the composition of the expat community really makes a difference. Here in Kathmandu most are aid workers and are on two to three year assignments. There is only a very small private sector group, almost all entrepreneurial. We're all here for a longer period, basically indefinitely. In other cities, the private sector contingent can be huge, representing huge multinational companies. They're paid differently, have a different attitude etc. Anyway, those who are in a place for the long haul tend to shy away from 'short term' friendships. Once people learned that I was planning to stay for a long time I found doors opened up. People were willing to invest emotional energy in a friendship.

Beyond the immediate circle of people you work with, those you see on the way to work every morning, and the people who live near you, there may very well be a number of people who speak English nearby. What will almost certainly not happen is that those people come to find you; you will need to go and find them.

In the first few weeks after your arrival, despite the tiredness and culture shock you will undoubtedly feel, accept every reasonable invitation to a social event that you can. Even if you are invited somewhere you would not normally go, accept the invitation, unless the destination seems dubious or it is against your principles to go to such places. Holly Shaw remembers, 'I tried to stay open-minded. I didn't try to set up or find a little America. I didn't turn down any invitation from locals or foreigners and began learning as much as I could about the culture'.

On the other hand, Jeri Hurd recalls:

I'm cautious and it's one thing I kick myself for. I was in Istanbul one time (I was living in Ankara), and in my American way, I was barrelling down the street, with places to go, and also like most Americans, I'm friendly and smile at everybody, (which gets you into trouble some times). Anyway, I smiled at this one guy and he did a double take and looked at me, and I kind of did a double take on him, and he immediately started talking to me. 'Let me buy you tea', he said and I said 'Oh no'. He said, 'Oh come on, I'm an engineer, I live in Ankara'. He kept repeating himself and I thought well, good for you, you're an engineer. Why are you telling me this eight hundred times? Anyway I didn't go for tea. And as soon as I walked away, I thought, 'That was stupid; why didn't you just go for tea?'

The people you initially meet may not become close friends, but if you do not go out and meet them, you will never get the chance to choose. Additionally, the people you meet at social gatherings you would never normally go to and would never want to go to twice, may invite you to meet their friends, or tell you about the perfect club, association, religious group or sports club that you never even knew existed.

There are many places that you can go to meet people, some of which are unique to the overseas community and others which you would not normally consider in your home country (mainly because you have no need). Listed below are a number of institutions, associations and places where you can meet people and the sort of people you can meet there.

In your friendship-making forays always remember that there are more people than just other foreigners to meet; the local residents of your destination city will far out number the foreigners. It can be all to easy to limit your social life to the foreign community, and if you do you would be missing out on one of the best components of overseas living — the local culture.

Fiona Nicholls, who was initially an expat spouse and then began teaching at an international school, says, 'We try to meet people living nearby, especially locals who can speak some English, or other people who have been in the area a while, to get ideas of places to visit. We try to explore the local area and get some kind of feeling of being part of a community.' Another expatriate in Turkey says, 'Have a look. I mean a closer look. Do the cultural things preferably on your own,

Social Meeting Places

Type of meeting place	Style/Place of establishment	Clientele
Embassy social clubs	Often within embassy grounds and in the style of the country's normal social establishment. Usually for their own nationals, but sometimes open to non-nationals as well. Also a good source of information about other social clubs.	1. Diplomatic personnel 2. Non-diplomatic foreign residents of the country
Expatriate associations	1. Rented hotel facilities 2. Embassy social club 3. Bar/restaurant	Foreign residents of the country. E.g. Federation of American Women's Clubs Overseas, Foreign Wives Association, Caledonian Society.
Religious organisations	1. Hotel meeting room, or other rented facility 2. Own premises 3. Inside embassy	Variety of members usually grouped by religious denomination and language.
Sports clubs	Purpose built facilities of varying quality.	Active, middle class residents (local and foreign) of the city.
Language lessons	1. Local university/college 2. Private language schools 3. Private tuition at your home or tutors home	Foreign residents, probably recently arrived in the country.
Student cafes, restaurants and bars	In the local style of the country you are in.	Educated young local people who are likely to speak English, or are trying to learn.
Theatres, concerts	1. Purpose built facilities 2. General-purpose halls 3. Embassies 4. Schools	Local and foreign residents.
Cultural evenings	1. Hosted by tourist related groups in local restaurants, carpet shops, etc 2. Hosted by embassy clubs, expatriate associations and religious associations on their premises or in places similar to those organised by the tourism groups	Foreign residents of many nationalities and sometimes locals interested in learning more about specific subjects in their own culture.
Amateur dramatic groups	1. Schools 2. Embassies	Thespians.
The HASH, or Hash House Harriers	1. Embassy 2. Pub/bar 3. Restaurant	A mainly social group that organises walks, runs and outings. Originally a British club, but now definitely multi-cultural.

without the comfort of same-culture friends'.

Once you have established a social circle, always be open to making new friends and joining new social circles. Overseas residents move more frequently than those who stay in their own country and there always seems to be at least one of your friends who is excitedly looking forward to moving to a new and exotic destination. Being a new arrival in a city you will be constantly learning about new clubs, social groups, eating places and other places of entertainment, so you can continually enjoy new experiences as well as relax comfortably in a familiar group.

Settling In

What To Take With You

When you are preparing to move overseas for the first time there can be a temptation to treat the experience rather like an extended holiday; but one thing the experience is certainly not going to be is one long holiday. There are two components of life that you need to consider when deciding what to take with you.

First, even if you are lucky enough to be provided with a furnished apartment, your new accommodation is likely to feel as comfortable and welcoming as a hotel room until you can personalise the space. In remembering her first move overseas, Jeri Hurd recalled:

We came into these god-awful flats; you know, beige on beige. In a last minute panic, (this is something people do), I had freaked out because I thought I had too much luggage. So I took out the little homey bits that I had put in. The only things I brought were an afghan and Wendell (my stuffed monkey). So it was hard.

Secondly, you are moving not only to a new city and country, but also to a new lifestyle, where a whole host of cultural identifiers that we normally take for granted are going to be different, or missing. The outward signs of religion (mosques, synagogues, temples or churches) can be very different between Amman, Tel Aviv, Delhi and Rome. Personal habits can vary hugely between Beijing and Auckland. This can mean that expatriates lose their personal perspective, and in the worst cases behave in a manner that they, the local population and ultimately their employer find unacceptable.

Mike van der Es has this bit of advice regarding cultural expectations.

When you travel abroad for work alone, the unspoken rules on what is acceptable in terms of friendships, alcohol use, respect for authority or religion, relations with the opposite sex, and work commitment all alter. Often you may only receive guidance on half of these issues, if that. People working abroad alone face all the other issues mentioned in this book. But in addition to having to deal with loneliness, there may be no one to keep an eye on you or to warn you if your behaviour is unwise or even dangerous. Consequently an excess of alcohol intake or working can, over time, undermine the respect that locals have for the expatriate and lead to poor judgement or decisions. Frequently by the time more senior people discover this, a replacement expatriate is the only option. Such risks appear more common in isolated areas where you are the only expatriate, but the hothouse atmosphere of an expatriate compound seems to sometimes create this scenario as well.

Creating a New Home

Personalising your new space means more than hanging your clothes in the wardrobe and having your favourite coffee mug in the kitchen. Personalising your space means turning the square metres of space from utilitarian accommodation into a comfortable, pleasant home that you look forward to returning to at the end of a hard day at work to renew your batteries and reflect on what has happened around you.

If you have the luxury of an unlimited shipping allowance, or the money to pay your own costs, then shipping the entire contents of your current home to your new overseas living quarters can be a great way of helping you create a new home.

If you are limited in what you can transport to your new home, you need to start thinking as far in as advance as possible about what you really want to take with you. Knowing what you want to take with you is as much about your current lifestyle as about the new one you are going to be living after your move.

Climatic variation, cultural considerations, social sophistication, shopping options, accommodation standards and the work you will be doing all have an impact on what you take with you. Going to work with the Inuit people of northern Canada is going to be a physically different proposition to an assignment in Saudi Arabia, East Asia or Italy. Each possible destination will be different in endless ways.

No matter where they move in the world, there are very few people who can afford to buy the entire contents of a new home within the first few weeks of their arrival. And even if they can afford it, the shopping for and delivery of the new items might not be as easy as in your home country. You might be given a generous furnishing allowance by your employer, but the majority of people who receive one find it buys no more than the beds, chairs, tables and appliances you would class as essential items. There will be little money available for the items that would make your apartment hugely different from your neighbour's with the same allowance.

So what are the items that make your current home what it is? Take a good look around you, examine everything carefully and not just the items immediately in view. Look in your cupboards and in the storage room as well as on your shelves and at the pictures on the wall. Remember you are going for more than a month. Even if you are going for less than a year, you will still need to bring things with you that make you feel 'at home', things that you will turn to when you are missing the home you left behind. Do not fall into the trap of deciding that nine to eighteen months is not long enough to get homesick; think about how you might feel returning to an undecorated hotel room day after day for nine months.

Think about what you do at special times of year and if there is any special clothing or equipment you use, what music you listen to most, what music has special meaning for you, what books you frequently refer to. What picture cheers you up when you are depressed, what book always make you laugh and what music conjures up images of your favourite time and place? Look for the items that give you your happy thoughts. Seonaid Francis who has lived abroad for ten years, working in remote areas of China with *Voluntary Services Overseas (VSO)* and then Hong Kong and Turkey as a teacher says, 'I like to rearrange furniture and put out my own belongings, especially my books. Where I have books, I feel naturally safe'.

Look through your clothes and take your favourites, there is no point in leaving them at home to keep them safe; clothes give pleasure through the wearing. Sentimental items can cause agonies of indecision. Do you take them with you because they are of sentimental value, or do you ask a trusted friend to take care of them while you are away? Deciding what to leave behind and where to leave it can be a difficult decision. One expat said that she had left some paintings and various other bits of artwork with a friend for safe keeping until she and her family returned from abroad. The friend, over the three years she was babysitting them, decided that they were hers to keep, and refused to return them to the family. However, most expats who left their personal possessions with friends and family have had them safely returned. One way to avoid having to ask friends to look after your possessions is to place them in a commercial storage facility during your time abroad.

The final decisions have to be yours. It is what is important to you that creates your personal idea of home. Some people live happily with only the barest essentials in their accommodation, moving from country to country with the same two suitcases for years. Brian Meegan, an American college counsellor and school principal made such a decision and took the bare minimum of items on his first move abroad. 'I don't feel I need anything other than an established routine and new relationships when I move to a new country.' Others transport all their worldly possessions by the container load every time they move, no matter what the cost. However, most people seem to come somewhere in the middle and ship a few packing cases to their new destination.

Before making final decisions on what to take, refer to *From Packing to Unpacking* which discusses, in greater detail, the many aspects of choosing what to take, how to get it there and the bureaucracy you are likely to meet along the way.

Adjusting to a New Lifestyle

Apart from the physical variation of the destinations, you need to think about who you are going to be socialising with, what activities you are going to be doing inside and outside of work, and what you need to make you comfortable in a wide variety of situations. This is where it can be important to have done some research and asked questions of your contacts before you pack. If you know something of the social clubs, facilities and the social, cultural and climatic atmosphere of your destination before you move you are not going to be packing blindly.

However, even if you have been in contact with people at your destination, do not expect to have been told the full story. Everyone has a different perspective of overseas life. So keep an open mind and try to pack for most eventualities. Even if you are going to be an agricultural advisor in rural Africa, take a suit. If you are going to New York as a banker you still need your torn but comfortable jeans and your favourite threadbare shirt to slouch around the apartment in.

How Long Are You Going to Stay?

Although you may think you know exactly when you are leaving your overseas posting, it is not always a good idea to start talking about it as soon as you arrive. If you tell everyone you talk to that you are only staying for a year, eighteen months, or two years, why should they spend the time getting to know you? That does not mean nobody will talk to you, but some may question why they should put in the time and effort it takes to become really good friends with someone whose aim seems to be to reach the end of their assignment and leave. When asked, it can be a much better idea to answer with a non-committal, 'I don't know. A few years probably'.

If you are known as someone who will be around for a few years, not someone who is 'serving time', it can make a great difference to the quality of your social life for the time you are there. Then, if you do stay longer, you have not lost the previous years of friendship building.

Your own attitude can also be coloured by having a set length of stay carved into your mind. If you arrive at your destination city with a set date for departure firmly established and begin counting down the days, you can spend all your time working towards leaving and not give yourself the chance to stop and enjoy the delights around you. Worse still, if the length of your stay is then unavoidably extended, you can grow resentful and cynical about the country, your work and your lifestyle, which can make life very difficult for you and those around you.

Furthermore, if you tell your family and friends that you will be back home on a certain date, long-term relationship problems can arise if the date is postponed. The disappointment of a change in the length of your stay can renew any resentment, or sadness that some or all of your family/friends may have felt when you initially travelled overseas. The problems can then be compounded because you are so far away.

Having a contract in your hand with set dates can make you confident that you will return home on a certain date, but there are many reasons why you may not return when anticipated. For example, the task you were employed to do is not finished or else develops into something new. There may be no job for you to return to in your home country, or you are having such a good time overseas that you want to stay longer or move to another country and repeat your expatriate experience. For an extended discussion of this topic turn to the chapter *How Long For?*

Combating Homesickness

Homesickness is a fact of life when you travel half way round the world, or even to a country not far from home. No matter how much you enjoy living abroad there are times when you wish you could be back home, even if you left ten years ago.

Homesickness can manifest itself for many reasons and at unusual times. It can be cyclical with the weather or season. Illness is notorious for making people want to be at home. Stress at work, between members of your immediate family, or among your friends can have the same effect on some people. Some people find it hits them every year during a certain event such as Christmas, the end of a long winter, or a special anniversary.

Homesickness can also be a great catch-all in times of general unhappiness and stress, and when left unchecked can ruin your time overseas and may even mean that you never reach the end of your contract.

Though homesickness is a normal part of living away from your home country you can mitigate its effects by working towards preventing it from hitting too hard in the first place. By making friends and forming a large social circle you can go some way towards this. Additionally, by having a large social circle, you have people to help you overcome it when you do still become homesick.

When homesickness does hit it is not necessarily a negative thing to remember your home country and muse about the people and things you miss, as long as you do not let it become an obsession that ruins all your enjoyment of the host country. If your homesickness does become entrenched, try remembering the positive reasons why you came abroad and look for the good parts of your life. Phoning a friend at home, to catch up on what is happening, can also be very therapeutic too.

Fortunately, homesickness usually passes quickly, but it can recur. For some it will fade away completely as they realise that living abroad is the lifestyle they want and they can always return home for a visit if needs be. For others it may recur at the same time very year and they can prepare themselves for the process of working through it.

Expatriates who have lived in more than one foreign country also report feeling homesick for a country other than the one that they originally lived in, even countries where they were not actually happy when they lived there. Bad memories usually fade quicker than the good ones and this rose-tinted memory during times of change or stress is often the cause of homesickness. Having good memories of somewhere you previously lived is natural and should be enjoyed, but not to the exclusion of enjoying your current place of residence.

Holidays, Festivals and Beating the Blues

Special holidays and annual family reunions can be a great time when they are spent with your family and friends. However, when you are living in a different country and unable to return home to join in the festivities, what do you do?

You might think the easiest option would be to ignore the date and carry on as if nothing is going to happen. The trouble is that the closer you get to that special date, the harder it is to ignore. If there are other people around you who are going to be celebrating on the day, their talk and excitement can make things even harder to ignore. Among overseas residents who have previously tried ignoring their traditional holidays and festivals there seems to be a consensus that it was the wrong thing to do, as Seonaid Francis found:

It was my first Christmas away from home — I was living in China at the time — and I decided the best way to deal with it was to ignore it. It was an unmitigated disaster. We (the other people in Voluntary Services Overseas I was visiting at the time) were all depressed, although I suspect I was the most miserable, being new to this way of life. All I wanted to do was cry, go home to my family and experience my traditional Christmas.

The next year about 20 VSO teachers descended on a project and had the full works — roast chicken provided by the college, nut roast for the vegetarians, a decorated pot plant and even a Christmas day movie, 'Cabaret', that we all sang along to. We all exchanged gifts too — ear muffs, long johns, cheap music cassettes; it was all very cheerful and raucous — a real panacea to the previous year.

We all got merrily drunk on Chinese beer, and it even snowed. I was so happy that year — because all 20 of us tried to make it as traditional a day as possible, even in the middle of China.

The solution seems to be to do something special, even if it is not what you would normally do at home. There are many ways to mark a special day, not just those you are used to. You can invite friends and acquaintances that share your culture to join you for a meal; they would probably be as grateful as you would be if you were invited to someone's home. If there is no one of your culture or anyone who celebrates special occasions the same time as you, invite people to share your special day so they can learn more about your culture and you can learn more about theirs.

Nancy Kabisch Fredrickson, an independent expat and single mother originally from the US who lived in Mexico for six years before relocating to Taiwan, knows this is a situation that many expats face.

In some communities, groups of foreigners will get together to celebrate their own US style Thanksgiving dinner, for example. But, if the original decision to leave one's home country includes the idea that situations like these could be very different, then people find themselves open to celebrating or recognising special holidays in creative ways.

One woman I know celebrates a very traditional holiday with a family dinner in the middle of the summer, when all are available! It can even be memorable to say years later, 'We were so charmed by the Taj Mahal that we almost forgot it was Christmas Day!' People who choose to go overseas are typically adaptable and know how to make the best of a difficult situation.

If there is no one you are able to share the time with, or no one you want to share it with, do something, go somewhere; sitting at home on your own is a good way to sink into depression. Try taking a short holiday somewhere within your host country, or partaking of your favourite activity, but get out of your apartment and do it.

Jeri Hurd finally knew she had made the right decision to move abroad during Christmas:

Holiday time is not an issue now. It was that first Christmas, especially once everyone on campus left and it was just me. At the last minute I decided to go someplace cool with a friend, the Aegean. It was a most memorable adventure because it was an epiphanal experience. It made me realise why people go south for the winter. There we were sitting drinking freshly squeezed orange juice, dabbling our feet in the Aegean, with the bougainvillaea and the date palms and saying, 'God, look where we are'. I mean, who needs Christmas at home when you've got this?

Special Circumstances
Single Status Postings for Couples

Family members go abroad alone, not only because the job is a single status position, but because of personal reasons particular to the employee. There are many married people working in overseas locations away from their partner and children. Some couples and families find it works well, while others find it very difficult. Though most people agree that they only accept the arrangement out of necessity.

Single status positions exist primarily because the employer believes that the location of the employment would be too harsh for a spouse, or there are no facilities for housing and caring for a spouse. Cost can also be a factor, but an employer is unlikely to admit they are short of money. Steve Malone, is a British mining engineer who has worked on a number of single postings in Central Asia and Mexico, while his family have lived in the UK and Turkey. The reason? There were neither provision for family accommodation nor schooling for his three children and moving between mine sites made it impossible for the family to go along.

Unmarried couples are also likely to have the situation forced on them when a country will only issue a residence permit for a partner on production of a marriage certificate. If both partners can secure employment in the same place, and therefore residency on their own right, then they can get round these restrictions.

When a posting becomes single status through the employee's choice, the reasons can be many and various. The reasons can range through children being at a critical point in their education, the spouse's career is not portable and they cannot take a career break, or for personal reasons the spouse can either not leave their home country or could not live in the destination country.

Managing the separation successfully, so that the relationship and family members do not suffer too much requires constant hard work and a good level of understanding between the partners and family members as to why separation has occurred. Steve found that he had to explain his absence to his three children by being as simple as possible; it was necessary because of the location of where he was going. His children could not move around with him while he inspected mines.

Steve also found it particularly difficult to...

maintain strong relationships within the family unit. The different lifestyles that are lived complicate things; the working spouse has a hard-working environment and yet lives as a 'single' person with its freedoms. The 'stay-at-home' spouse must cope with all the family issues and subsequent stress, yet they are home and have a stable environment and friendships.

This is the story of one other separated family, trying to make the best out of a very hard situation:

My 45 year old husband, J.R. has been away from home for nine months working for an international contractor as an electrician. He is situated at an Army camp in Kosovo, near the Serbian border. Not unlike the military men with whom he eats and sleeps, the sacrifices and fears are many. This area of the Balkans continues to be very volatile, and until only recently had been under total camp 'lockdown'. Needless to say, this 'logging camp' environment in such an unsafe area, leaves little option for families.

Our decision to place my husband's life, faith, and mental health on the line was a serious one for us. Married 18 years with little to show for it other than credit card debt, the prospect of tripling our income and tax free status was more than we could afford to turn down. Short of winning the lottery, this seemed to be an OK option. After checking into the job description, we found that once accepted, JR would have 72 hours to secure three months supplies and report to Houston. Sure enough, just as described, and in five days he was actually in the Balkans. We could be accused of having a bit of 'blue collar snobbery', wanting more than we were affording; a little farmhouse outside the city on a couple of acres, and pay off the plastic. We had no idea what lay ahead.

Most of the men my husband works with are single/divorced, as this is not an ideal situation for a married couple. During one of my daily phone calls, my husband pauses, and later tells me of hearing a fellow employee crying to his wife not to divorce him. Another time he spoke of a military guy at the camp that had shot himself just to be shipped out of the area! Men exposed to this level of stress do well to maintain their own mental health much less preserve or nurture an existing relationship. This behoves a caring spouse to do all within one's power to provide both physical and emotional needs. It is critical to the survival of the mind, head and marriage.

Compared to the level of stress on my husband, along with the 14-hour workdays with no breaks even for holidays — my sacrifice is truly minimal. Our son, Cameron, and I are safe, secure and loved. My greatest anxiety being a missed daily phone call from our 'poppa'. Or maybe the day I received a call from a relative telling of a CNN report; a bombing at one of the camps in the Kosovo area claiming both military and civilian lives. How could I possibly tell this 'man's man' that the kitchen sink won't drain, or that the air-conditioning isn't cooling well? This devoted husband, and my 'hero' will be boarding a plane in two days and be in flight for 20 plus hours on four flights to be able to be with my son and me for nine days — fly back and do it all over again to provide for us our little slice of the American pie. Must be love!

Though life is difficult for Priscilla and her husband, she found that there can be positive aspects to the situation:

1. Confirmation of our commitment to each other and our goals.

2. In the ten months we've been able to pay off two credit cards and stash several thousand in seed money. (I personally could have enjoyed more of this part!)

3. Personal growth and awareness on both sides (if it doesn't break you, it makes you stronger).

4. New insight into family members and friends (the way some act, you would think we had won the lotto).

5. My husband, in particular, has been surprised during his visit home at the response of his male friends and ex-co-workers. He felt like some kind of celebrity or something. Some wanted him to speak some Albanian, others wanted to hear some of his famous stories. He found it baffling. (He also found it strange that his former boss was waiting in his office for JR to sit and speak to him, and was quick to offer him his job back if he should want to return. They never got along before.)

6. For myself, I learned a lot about me. I've always been very independent, and thought I could do it all, I've decided that I'm not so tough and even if I could divide and conquer, I'd rather not, thank you.

7. I've learned that my husband was right — that a 'single, family friend' turned out to be more than a family friend once my husband left to go overseas.

8. A very important thing I've learned is that our 17-year-old Downs Syndrome son is no doubt the one biggest blessing we have experienced. Cameron is a real man's man, just like his daddy. He is able to say anything he pleases (with slight difficulty), and through the entire ten months he has given us the thumbs up. He is fully aware of the situation and the purpose of his daddy's absence. I see to it that he remains informed of each and every decision. He is the consummate trooper.

9. Trips abroad every three months if one chooses. The men are given R&R's every three months and must leave the country during that time, (visa renewal). If a family chooses, it is a wonderful time to hook up with an expat in whatever country you may select for the prescribed period of time. We were able to join JR in London in February for a week. However, if changing one's financial situation is the focus, this can get into the pocket and negate the purpose of the entire project.

10. I learned much about my three older children (by prior marriage). I find it amazing how little we (I) really know about our children. The one I assumed would be most helpful generally and supportive wasn't, and the son that lives in Japan, and figured to be least available and supportive, was. You just never really know what you think you know.

11. Life is beautiful and there is always so much to learn!

Single Parents

Single parents live and work abroad too. They fall into a category of their own, somewhere between a single person and couples with children.

On the one hand they have the company of their children. But on the other hand the experience of loneliness can be enhanced because of the lack of a partner to come home to and the limitations imposed on their social life through having the responsibilities of looking after their children.

Single parents can also find that some employers are loathe to employ them because of the perceived greater conflicts between family and work that a single parent will face (during childhood illnesses, schooling commitments, etc.), because they have no partner to share the family responsibilities with. Nancy in Taiwan remarks that some employers are also nervous about employing single parents because of '...cultural limitations in parts of the world. What it might come down to is the fact that some countries are ultra-conservative, and single parents are shunned or not looked upon as doing the right thing.'

Moving overseas as a single parent requires more advance planning for childcare, schooling and emergency parenting jobs that always seem to crop up. As Nancy also points out, 'Language is typically the biggest barrier in this situation. It is difficult to be calm and confident when concerned or worried about the health and welfare of your child.'

If you are unable to communicate clearly with the childcare provider that you have organised, it can be an added stress that, in your home country, would never have been a problem. Good time-management and organisational skills will be necessary, which most single-parents are already likely to possess.

A longer settling-in period before starting work is probably a good idea, so that the children and the parent can finalise the childcare and/or schooling arrangements satisfactorily.

When children are of school age, the long holidays that international schools have (summer holidays are often two months long), also need to be taken into consideration. Parents and relatives will probably not be close enough to help out and many expatriate spouses who might normally help during the year also take extended holidays in the summer, so are unlikely to be available. Yet, some fortunate expats like Nancy are not hindered by the long vacation time, being teachers. Nancy has said that perhaps being an international teacher is a good job for a single parent. Not only would the parent have the same holidays as their child(ren) but also, the school age child(ren) would most likely be in the school where their parent works, and that can be comforting to the single parent.

The availability of summer schools and holiday clubs vary from country to country, though where they are less common it is likely that a national of your host country will be available to supervise children during the day.

While there are many difficulties involved in raising children internationally on your own, Nancy has stressed that she is doing it for the advantages it affords her children. 'There are positive benefits, especially for the children. For example, the facility that they will develop for picking up languages before the ages of 11 or 12 is an added bonus. They will also have the opportunity to learn about another culture by living it rather than reading about it in a book, and develop confidence through knowing they can adapt to different foods, smells, living conditions, languages etc.'

For more advice on your options refer to the chapter *Childcare Options*.

Gay and Going Abroad

As one expat pointed out, 'I'm not your average expat, I'm gay'. There are many gay expatriates in the global community, and though their situation is in many ways similar to that of single heterosexual expats, members of the gay expat community often have to deal with issues that other non-gay single expats do not.

The attitudes prevalent in the host country will have a large effect on the experiences of gay expats. Jim Aimers, a gay Canadian anthropologist and archaeologist currently living in the US, has also lived and worked in Japan, Honduras and Belize. Through his work he has learned much about homosexuality and how various cultures perceive it:

Archaeology and social anthropology have shown that homosexuality has long-existed and is cross-cultural. 'Gay', however, is a historically specific term and identity developed in the last century in the industrialised West, particularly the United States. Homosexuals are people who have sex with people of the same sex, often surreptitiously, while gay people are often 'out' and proud because gay denotes a political and social identity. Further, while there are two or sometimes three categories of sexual identity in the West (gay, straight, bisexual, as well as numerous gender identities such as transvestite and transsexual) there are often several more categories in other parts of the world.

Most notable here is the concept of the masculine homosexual man and the feminine homosexual man, who are expected to follow heterosexual behavioural norms in their homosexual activities. This is considered outdated, restrictive, and distasteful by the majority of men from Western countries, but it is common elsewhere. This in part explains the large number of very feminine men and transvestites in gay bars outside of the US and Europe. Similarly, in most parts of Latin America, a man can have sex with another man without being gay or even stigmatised socially as long as he is the 'top' during intercourse. In parts of Mexico, this type of man may be considered a hyper-masculine hombre hombre (man man or manly man) who can dominate not only women but men. These men may even publicly boast about their conquests and receive a measure of social approval for it, at least from other men.

Thus, gay men from Western countries are often frustrated by their experiences abroad. For gay men, the biggest long-term issue abroad is often not employment or overall social discrimination, but their relationships (in the general sense) with other men who have sex with men. Most gay Westerners are completely bewildered by the attitude of men who have sex with men but do not define themselves as gay or homosexual. These men in fact may be neither; they are simply looking for a good time with whomever and in fact whatever is available. Gay men can find this not only terribly insulting but also quite dangerous, since these types of men may be extremely homophobic and more likely to see the gay person as weak and worthy of poor treatment, especially robbery.

It is much safer and ultimately more satisfying for a gay man to be very cautious at first, and to understand as much as possible the mindset of the men he meets. A very masculine man in the West may be a turn-on; in other parts of the world he might be your worst first choice. In many parts of the world a gay identity is just emerging, and one truly gay friend or acquaintance can often open up a network of like-minded individuals, thus avoiding the masculine homosexual altogether. So, even if you don't drink and hate bars, a gay bar is the best place to start. Also, at the risk of stereotyping, transvestites tend to be trustworthy and are typically associated with the gayest men in any culture. There are few parts of the world where it is safe to meet men in parks or on the street, although these are the only options in many places. Obviously, extreme caution is needed, and never find yourself out of the public eye or at least out of shouting distance, ever. Sadly, it is probably best to expect that anyone you meet is a potential danger, and to behave accordingly.

An excellent cross-cultural indication of gayness is kissing. If he won't kiss, you can forget the monogrammed towels and honeymoon — he's more likely to be going home to the wife and kids.

In some parts of the world men who have sex with men may not be dangerous but will expect payment. You should try to research this beforehand because it varies greatly. In Cuba it is open and you may have to meet dozens of men before you find one who doesn't require money; in Honduras he'll just take your watch or clock, considering it not payment but a regalo (gift) for a good time. The fact that he took it while you were asleep or not looking makes little difference.

The Internet is an incredible resource. Key in the word 'gay' and the name of any large city in any country and you're likely to find information. Internet personal ads, although they may not help you to find the man of your dreams (unless you like them ten years older and 30 pounds heavier than their description) may put you on a one-to-one level with a gay man before you even leave home. And someone who has access to the Internet and an e-mail account is not likely to be desperately poor.

These varying cultural attitudes determine how open gay expats can be about their sexuality.

One Canadian who has travelled abroad to Japan, Singapore and Egypt was told outright at an orientation meeting for new employees in Japan that it was forbidden to be gay in Japan. They were all warned that if there were any gay members of the team, they should be as discrete as humanly possible, and not get 'found out' for fear of facing deportation.

Japan was the most isolating experience for me. I was living in a part of the country where there were almost no opportunities to meet other gay men. After working for a year, my employer suspected that I might be gay and in Japanese fashion asked a colleague about me. I found out and discussed it with her. She asked me not mention it to anyone because it jeopardised her business. I agreed, but I also grew to resent it. I felt like I was back in the closet. On a couple of occasions, I drove over two hours to find the nearest gay bar, but was always disappointed because the bars were so tiny and I was virtually ignored by the extremely shy Japanese men. I was only able to meet gay men when I was on vacation. In general, it was a difficult time for me as a homosexual person.

The non-gay community does not usually have to worry about being deported, or having their business shut down, because of their sexual preference. However, when making a decision to go abroad, gay members of the expat community must face this issue squarely, and honestly. Some countries are more tolerant of gay lifestyles. The same expat who was in Japan later moved to Singapore, which was more open than Japan, but still not entirely free from stress.

Singapore was a very different experience. I went there in a relationship. The entire staff knew that my partner and I were gay within a few weeks of arriving there. The staff was almost entirely Canadian and was very accepting. When the relationship ended, everyone knew about it and friends were supportive. It took me a while to find the bars shortly after the break-up. As a gay man, you learn quickly that the main meeting places are all bars. Finding them is sometimes hard. It's not the same for heterosexual expats; they have plenty more opportunities and resources than my community does. I was lucky that another member of staff was gay and took me to see the main gay bar in Singapore.

The government had closed gay bars in the past, but I had been told that they were relaxing their policy and allowing them to stay open. I was still concerned, on my first few visits, that I would be arrested in a bar and then face the embarrassment of being deported, but I slowly relaxed and realised that the government was changing its ways.

Sometimes it is difficult for gay members of the expat community to not feel pinpointed as a menace. Some feel instantly discriminated against for their chosen lifestyle. Some countries, though by no means all, have mandatory HIV testing, that the gay community may feel is aimed specifically at them. For example:

I was horrified to find out that in order to get a work visa, the Egyptian government requires a negative HIV test. Members of the administration called it an 'AIDS' test, which made me angry as well. I knew that I had to do the test to get my visa. However, my heart was pounding with the fear not only of possibly being the first staff member in the history of the school to test positive, but to have to face the embarrassment of having to leave and have people wonder how I had contracted it. Married female members of staff didn't even have to take a test, after all they never had been with anyone other than their husbands!

Unlike the ease with which the average single expat can find a niche, a club, or a social scene, the gay expats must dig harder to find their community abroad. One gay expat mentioned that:

...there must be places for gay men to go, but I have yet to do the research. I know that there must be other gay expatriates out there, but it will take some work to find out where they are. Until I do, I will feel very isolated. I will feel like I'm carrying a secret and that I just don't fit in with everyone. Perhaps when I find my community, I will feel a little less alien.

An expat Australian, however, found his experience much easier.

My experience of being a gay expat has been a positive one. Much of my experience has been in Asia (Indonesia, Thailand and Turkey), which is generally very gay friendly. In fact, all three countries have traditions of homosexuality and transvestitism. In all three countries it is acceptable for people to experiment with others of the same sex, especially since the traditions regarding relations with the opposite sex are generally rigid and proscriptive. In many Asian countries it is acceptable for people of the same sex to display affection in public.

I have found Thai and Indonesian gays to be more sharing — but this does not mean that Asian-European relationships are not subject to the same cross-cultural problems that straight couples experience.

Gay rights, funnily enough, is also an issue. I have found that in places like Bangkok, people of my sexual persuasion have bandied up together to the exclusion of others — both socially and professionally. I don't care what the person's predilection is — exclusion is exclusion.

Health is an issue too. Even in Bangkok where there are many gays — the community is still small enough that most people know each other.

As far as meeting people is concerned — I have found the Internet to be very useful. The chat lines on www.gay.com are a godsend. They offer a satisfactory alternative to noisy crowded bars. In any case, it is nice to go to a disco with a special someone. Such lines are also a valuable source of 'on the ground' information — and they cover most of the world!

Checklists

With so many things to do before you leave and after you arrive, it is easy to forget some and lose track of what you have done so far. On the next pages are lists that you should add to as needs be, to help you keep track of all those must-do jobs that will help you settle in to your new home country.

Resources

Print Resources

Dads at a Distance: An Activities Handbook for Strengthening Long Distance Relationships, by Aaron Larson

Moms Over Miles: An Activities Handbook for Strengthening Long Distance Relationships.

Women Travel, Rough Guides, ISBN: 1-85828-459-7.

Online Resources

Brits Abroad www.geocities.com/TheTropics/2865/index.htm, for those that miss home.

Federation of American Women's Clubs: www.fawco.org including a directory of their clubs around the world.

www.daads.com: Dads at a distance — to help fathers away from their children maintain and strengthen the relationships they have with their children.

www.dialpad.com: An Internet to phone service connecting to US numbers only (free apart from Internet dial-up costs).

www.expatexchange.com: an online community for expats, with associated expert to offer advice.

www.expatexpert.com: the website of expat writer, author and consultant, Robin Pascoe.

www.expatforum.com: host of numerous online chat groups, both general expat issues and country specific subjects.

www.net2phone.com: An Internet to phone service for most countries worldwide, charged at 'local' rates (on top of Internet dial-up costs).

www.xpats.com: community website for expats in Belgium, that contains much generally useful information.

Things To Do Before Departure

Task	Results	New task req'd?
Ask your employer for the contact details of people in the overseas office.	1. 2. 3.	
Ask your employer for the names of employees who have worked overseas and returned to your current office.	1. 2. 3.	
Ask your friends if they know anyone working in your destination country and how you can contact them.	1. 2. 3.	
Ask your friends if they know anyone who is, or has worked abroad, in any country, and how you can contact them.	1. 2. 3.	
Contact useful organisations: (a) Embassy/consulate of destination country (b) Home country Ministry of Foreign Affairs (c) Rotary Club (d) NGO Cultural Associations. E.g. *Alliance Francais, Goethe Institute*, British Council (e) Religious Organisations (f) Sporting Associations	1. 2. 3. 4.	
Visit the Library (public, university, school) for useful books & videos.	1. 2. 3.	
Check bookstores for useful books/videos.	1. 2. 3.	
Learn to use the Internet and e-mail, if necessary and possible.		
Check the Internet for useful websites and contacts.	1. 2. 3.	
Contact the people you found from the tasks above and ask them if they will help you. Then ask as many questions as they seem willing to answer.	1. 2. 3.	
Decide what personal items you have to take with you to create a new home.	1. 2. 3.	

Things To Do After Arrival

Task	Results	New task req'd?
Make your accommodation into a home: a) Buy furnishings b) Buy electronics c) Buy kitchen utensils d) Personalise your space e) Decorate f) Hang pictures g) h)		
Contact embassies to find out if they have a social club, and/or host any expatriate groups.	1. 2. 3. 4.	
Ask work colleagues for information about sports clubs, theatres, cinemas, cultural evenings or language lessons.	1. 2. 3. 4.	
List all the places you can go to make new friends according to the resources in your new city.	1. 2. 3. 4.	
Visit all the places you listed above.	1. 2. 3. 4.	

EQUAL PARTNERS

Personal Considerations

Couples move abroad most successfully if they do it together. Frances Brown, a South African independent expat living in the UK with her husband and daughter says:

Each couple is different but essentially the only advice I can give here is to be as close to one another (as you can be) before you leave. Your partner is going to be your only friend for a number of months so he/she may as well be your best friend! With us, we found that we got a lot closer, relied on one another more for entertainment and fun...no more South African boys' nights, Round Table, etc. It is tough going, everyone's mindset has to alter, you don't have the domestic help that you do in South Africa (necessarily) so your partner has to help a lot...this area has caused plenty of arguments but after two years, we work quite well side by side.

It may seem unnecessary to say that couples move best if they do it together, but the reality is that a non-working partner can easily become labelled as *The Trailing Spouse, The Corporate Wife* or *The Supporting Partner* and be relegated to the level where they feel they are nothing more than excess baggage. Simply because one partner earns less than the other, or even no money at all, does not mean their job or function is less important than the other's. What can happen though, if the importance of the non-employed partner's position is undervalued, is that the partner can become intellectually, socially and professionally frustrated, which can needlessly ruin the whole overseas experience.

Phyllis Adler, an American psychotherapist who lives and works in London, counselled in an article for the premiere issue of *Woman Abroad* magazine (1 Portsmouth Road, Guildford, Surrey GU2 4YB, England; www.womanabroad.com):

Being extra kind to each other is too easily overlooked but is as necessary as bubble wrap around crystal. If you don't want to endanger your marriage during a move, handle your partner with care, letting him or her know you value what they do. That's marital bubble wrap. Your marriage is fragile, look after it.

One expat who moved to Mexico City was upset that his wife was not coping well. Chris Smith indicated that the situation of living abroad was extremely stressful.

I speak the language and have some place to be every day, while she feels useless and stupid because she can't just jump in the car (we only have one car, she doesn't speak the language and she says she wouldn't drive even if she did have a car) and run to the store like she could back home. I look at it like it should be a great experience and while it's not perfect, it's not the end of the world. It seems though that she feels it is and she seems to resent me a little bit for it.

Traditionally, one partner usually secures a job before departure, and the accompanying partner secures a job after arrival, or does not become employed at all. From the beginning it is easy for the accompanying partner to fall into a submissive follow-on role, but this role should never be obligatory and the partner's position should certainly not be undervalued.

Once you arrive overseas, the initial post-arrival days are usually crammed full of the essential tasks of setting up home in a new country. Coleen McLeman is married to a Canadian Foreign Service employee and has moved with him to Hong Kong and the US, before starting a third posting in Vienna. Along the way she has qualified as a teacher in Hong Kong and co-authored a series of textbooks for high school students. She has learnt that:

The first two months are definitely trying and all of this running around is usually left up to the 'trailing spouse,' i.e. me. I've now been in my new home for six months and in retrospect, the settling in wasn't too bad. However, if you had asked while I was in the midst of these two months of settling in, I would have had a different story to tell.

The simple, but time-consuming and frustrating, tasks of battling bureaucracy, and finding your way around a new city have to be faced. Usually, all these tasks have to be done in a foreign language, broken English, or if you are lucky, with the help of a translator. Coleen found:

The paperwork, the deliveries, the bureaucracy, figuring out how things work and where to get the simplest things done...all in a foreign language is enough at times to make you want to pull your hair out. While struggling along through this settling in/homemaking stage you can feel that you will never be settled. And it is at this stage you start to question the wisdom of your decision to agree to this move. I know I started to ask myself why am I putting myself through this again. I've moved house every two years for the past eight years and enough is enough.

A sense of humour and patience can be a great help at this point, as can a good memory; recounting the experiences over a drink or dinner a few months down the line will have your friends in hysterics. Coleen advises that:

...the bright side is that these feelings do pass. This stage is temporary and once you are settled and into a routine the memory of the initial setting up stage fades immediately — and with your new accumulated knowledge of how things work around you — can actually seem really trivial (even though at the time these problems caused much grief).

Marriage on the Move

Moving is often listed as one of the most stressful things you can do. Add to that starting a new job and changing the country of your residence, which are also among the list of life's most stressful activities, even the strongest of marriages can begin to weaken at the seams unless it is protected, as Phyllis Adler counselled.

When the basic foundations of a marriage are changed, e.g. the home, an individual career, social status, leisure activities and financial contribution to the household, the personal inter-relationships of the partners can lose their footing.

A strong marriage may not suffer, but any dormant problems can be resuscitated and amplified.

Phyllis Adler also suggested in her *Woman Abroad* article that couples make an inventory of their marriage so they can discuss and resolve areas of potential conflict before they develop into serious problems.

Before you go make an inventory of your marriage. Not everyone handles moving, change and uncertainty with ease. Not everyone makes friends easily or is able to rough it in a different country. Not everyone can live in limbo. Knowing your own value and needs and the need to value the other, while always important, becomes even more so when we are jet lagged and move lagged. Consider for a moment:

1. What does your partner contribute to the good feelings you have about yourself and your life together?

2. What may you be leaving behind that will need to be replaced and how will you do that?

3. What and where are your support systems?

4. Be aware of how vulnerable you may become during the resettlement process and how long that feeling will last.

5. Find out all you can about the new location and the people who live there before you go.

For couples who take care of their marriage and family relationships, the expatriate experience can strengthen family bonds. Alison Albon has found that:

Not only has being an expat given us, as a family, so many wonderful experiences of meeting different people and learning of different cultures, but our nomadic lives have given us the greatest blessing, and that is a close spousal (and family) relationship. Together we discuss the kids' development, we plan for the future, we laugh together and cry together. We are the ultimate team. We've been through some really tough times together, and have come out together and for that I am eternally grateful. My husband and I often have people telling us what a great couple we make, and how seeing us, gives them hope for marriage in general. I'm proud of that, we've worked hard for it.

Once Work Begins

The employee usually starts work within days of arrival at the destination, but if you are lucky the settling in period may extend to one or two weeks. This limited settling in period will of course mean that the partner is left to manage all of the home and family related tasks that still need to be completed. However Coleen says:

...these setting up problems are superficial ones; they are merely annoyances, which will quickly pass, so to base any decision on how you like your new life in the new country on this frustrating time would not be wise. This is not to say that less superficial problems may not be lurking under the surface — but these should be differentiated from the temporary irritations.

Once the initial settling-in period (however brief) is over, the employee can disappear to the safety-zone of an office, with people to talk to and definite tasks to occupy their time; they have a specific reason for being in the country. Their job is often comfortingly normal, they will have many similarities to what they have always done, and they have the opportunity of learning the local language and customs when talking and mixing with their colleagues. Robert McLeman, Coleen's husband, admits this is true:

The employed partner has instantly, upon arrival, a support system of acquaintances, colleagues and people to turn to for advice, while the at-home partner is on his/her own. The employed partner has to realise this, and make the effort to seek social activities that include the accompanying partner which are not simply work-related social functions.

Business lunches and after work 'getting to know the staff' sessions mean the employee is likely to be taken to restaurants, shown the sights and welcomed to the country. International jobs can entail hours of business entertaining and socialising with clients every week, plus there is often an increased need to travel on visits to the home office or other regional bases on a regular basis. From his experiences Robert notes:

...when I have arrived at a new assignment there has always been a lot of pressure on me to get up and running at work as quickly as possible upon arrival. When I arrived at my present assignment, I went straight from the airport to the office, got the official introductions and formalities out of the way, and started working in earnest the following morning.

He continues by pointing out that if the outgoing staff member is still in town, it is fortunate for the new employee to be able to overlap with them, in the job, for a few days. However, this '...adds additional incentive to go straight into the office and start working, and to leave the home-making arrangements to the partner'.

Tied in with the drive to go straight to the office are the long hours and travel as Robert admits.

It's an undeniable fact that expats in my industry are expected to travel a lot, and often on short notice. Planning holidays can be frustrating, especially for the partner. It's essential that the employed partner be ruthless in blocking out time in her/her schedule to take time off with the partner and/or family.

The working week often seems to stretch on a foreign posting, due to the subtle (or not so subtle) pressure to become productive as quickly as possible in the new position. In some countries, especially in Asia, the amount of hours spent in the office is often perceived as an indicator of your performance and dedication, which stretches the hours further and can ferment frustration and resentment both for the employee and their partner. Saturday workdays can change from being a rarity in Europe and North America to being the norm for staff in Asia. Weekends can disappear, especially in places like the Middle East where Thursday and Friday are the weekend and Saturday and Sunday are normal working days. It can be particularly awkward since North American and European offices might still expect to be able to reach you on Fridays.

James Mistruzzi knows well:

...that in Asia, many companies expect employees to work at least a half day on Saturday. This most likely will be quite different from the five-day working week, which the family has planned around in the past. In many cases this also means that 'golf day' is now moved to Sunday thus leaving no full day when the working spouse is at home. I've seen this cause strife among couples.

Work Related Stress

Working practices also vary from country to country, which means that even the simplest task can take twice as long as you are used to, especially if you have a communication difficulty due to the language. Sometimes James finds the whole procedure for making decisions simply frustrating:

Decisions often take longer to make. There are pre-meetings before the pre-meeting before the planning meeting, which comes before the final Board Meeting. Not the style we're used to where decisions are often made much quicker with less consultation. It sometimes seems that everyone must be consulted before any decision is made on even the smallest thing. As well, the people who must be consulted are often away on business and decisions are not often made via e-mail, fax or phone. Face to face meetings are often required as part of the decision making process. This can sometimes seem to slow things down as everyone is waiting for someone to return from business. At my old school it was often, 'We must wait for Mr.—— to get back from his holidays/business trip/etc., before we can make a final decision on that.' Why the Chairman of the Board would care how many red pencils we have in the school was beyond me, but that was the way things were done!

Being in the office for extended periods of time can set the accompanying partner off to a lonely start. However, some expat employees know how important it is to help their accompanying partner with the adjustment process. As understood by Robert:

The stay-at-home spouse may not have the same opportunities to learn about the business world and culture as the working spouse does on a daily basis. Communication at home will go a long way to helping the accompanying spouse to understand the new environment in which the working spouse must operate. I'd say communication is the key both at work and at home to help minimise any misunderstandings.

Strategies for Accompanying Partners

Once the employee starts going to the office everyday, partners can find they are left to fend for themselves. As the employee is learning the ropes of their new position and cultural working environment, the partner will begin adjusting to the realities of living abroad, with no one expected to help them. With a longer working week and maybe more foreign travel for the employee, the partner is going to have to make many of their own decisions on how best settle into the new country, set up a new home and find things to do to fill their extra free time.

Yvonne McNulty and her husband moved themselves to the US from Australia when they found they could not go with his company. She suddenly had a lot of free time and had to find something to do with it.

My husband travels during the week and is home every weekend so we spend Saturday and Sunday together. I have taken the opportunity of free time alone to finish my undergraduate degree, which I have been slogging away at for the past six years. I had about two and a half years to go if I kept studying part time/working full-time so we decided I would finish the degree on a full-time basis externally via my university in Australia whilst I was here and unable to work. That takes up about two and a half days a week. The other two and a half days a week I am roller-blading, reading (belong to a book club), doing sewing lessons and volunteering at the Anti-Cruelty Society, PAWS and the Starlight Foundation.

By keeping busy with her weeks alone, Yvonne is able to make the best of their three-year contract abroad.

Being in a new country, with no ties other than your immediate family can be a great liberator. With no obligations to family, friends and acquaintances, the partners can build their lives as they want to. Whether they join a club, learn a language, renew their education, find employment, the options are many and varied.

Being in a new country with no ties other than your immediate family can also be a frightening and lonely experience. To minimise the likelihood of that happening, it is important to meet people and make friends. The employed partner will have better opportunities to meet people than their at-home partner will, but both can have trouble meeting people they really want to socialise with. The rest of this chapter specifically looks at ways a non-employed partner can create a lifestyle they are comfortable with in their new country. The previous chapter, despite being titled *Going Alone*, also offers invaluable advice about where and how both partners can make friends and form a successful and enjoyable social life away from the employed partner's workplace and workmates.

The non-employed partner will commonly assume responsibility for some tasks that would have seemed relatively easy in their home country, but in a foreign country these tasks can quickly become frighteningly impossible and hugely time consuming. However, try telling someone who has never lived abroad, or tried to do the tasks themselves, that an everyday task has suddenly become difficult and they look at you as if you are mad.

One spouse who moved to France tells of doing things in her new domestic role, and how 'accomplished' she felt.

It was the new custom in their household for the family to gather round the dinner table to discuss their various accomplishments for the day. The husband asked his very capable wife what she had done that day. She answered, 'I went to the post office'. He then asked what else she had done, to which she replied. 'That's it. I

> *went to the post office. I figured out* **where** *the post office is, I figured out* **what I** *had to mail, I prepared my questions in advance by studying the words for stamps, overseas, airmail, etc. Then I* **drove** *there,* **parked** *the car, and figured out whether or not it was necessary to plug the meter. Then, I stood in the* **correct** *line, asked for my stamps, translated the cashier's questions about which stamps, how many and so on. I had to figure out how much they cost, and count my change. It took all afternoon, and I'm tired, but feel like I accomplished brain surgery'.*

Shopping can usually be accomplished satisfactorily, once you have found the shops you need and learned to navigate around the new city. It will almost certainly take longer in a different language, when you have to translate the packets and labels and learn to ask for specific weights and volumes, but it can be done. You may not be able to get some essential staples, but searching for them in specialist shops is a great way to discover the delights of your new hometown. Though in some countries the variety and quality of foods will be larger, more exotic, or seasonal, and items that are hard to get at home will be readily available.

Paula McAuley took a break from work to accompany her husband abroad, (he came out of retirement to take a teaching job), for the experiences it could offer. She has had a number of adventures when out shopping for various items.

Shopping in a foreign country is a little like going to the circus...for me there is that excitement of actually preparing to go on the hunt for that special something. In my case I have to either take a bus (a big deal for me and I never used buses at home) or I can take a taxi...or I make a compromise with myself; I take the bus to town and a taxi home. After all, I will have all those packages to carry! Sometimes I have a specific item I want and have no idea whether it will be a problem to find or not. Where do I go to find it? This is not North America...this is another world. I leave the house equipped with a ten-word vocabulary, the address to get home, a dictionary and a calculator. I arrive at the store (found the merry-go-round!). The ride begins. The first thing I do is physically look for the item. If it is not there, out comes the limited vocabulary followed by the dictionary followed by gestures, pointing, smiling, all useless but amusing for both of us and then one of two things happen:

1. He does not have the item. Usually he will try to tell me where to get the item by pointing in the direction that I must go or sometimes he can find someone who can speak a little English and he will give directions. Sometimes this works but sometimes they don't know where, but want to be helpful so they give you directions to somewhere and off you go on a wild goose chase looking for the elusive location. (Trying to find the Ferris wheel!)

2. Thank God, he has the item. Tea? Coffee? Water? Sometimes if my mood is right I can settle into the ride and enjoy the trip. How much? Too much! Calculator please? He writes. I write. He writes again. I write. Yes, yes. Good, good. More calculator for him and for me. Yes it is wonderful. I buy the item at the agreed price and the ride is over. My purchase is made. Taxi please. On the other hand, sometimes there is not much time and I have to forget about the ride and just buy the cotton candy, no bargaining. Product is mine without negotiation.

Learning the local bus routes, to get to the shops, can be difficult; especially when there are no bus timetables, route plans or information offices. Persistence is definitely called for, plus a sense of humour and adventure; map-reading skills can also be useful for when you end up in some distant part of town you never even knew existed. But as you pore over your map trying to work out where you are, do not be surprised if a friendly local offers to help get you back on track and points you helpfully on your way.

Dell Harmsen, formerly a teacher who is now writing a book on her experiences in Greece, offers this advice for easing local travel.

Here's my approach to using public transportation: when I take off on some journey, I tell myself that it's sure to be difficult, and full of interesting, unforeseeable challenges, but, clever me, I will overcome every obstacle and reach my destination. When I get lost, I ask everyone on the street if they know the way. Half of these people are just as turned around as I am, but someone always points me to the right bus, or street, or direction. In a pinch, I remind myself that I have always made it back home again safely, the same day, at least so far.

Expat partner in Turkey, Mario Antognetti, frequently took the bus:

When we first arrived, I mostly took the bus to the city. One time I wanted to take the bus to a small area in town to do some shopping. I asked the bus driver and a group of cleaning guys if this was the bus that went to 'kutuphane' (library in Turkish). They all said 'evet' (yes). As I sat on the bus reading my book I noticed the driver wasn't exiting from our campus area and we headed towards the main campus. As we approached the University Library, he stopped the bus and kept repeating 'here, here'. 'No', I thought to myself, 'the downtown library!' Well, since I was there, I made the most of it and checked out the library.

Taxis are not always an easier option, because you have to know how to say your destination, or have it written in the local script, which you may not even recognise. Learning to pronounce destinations clearly enough for the taxi driver to understand correctly will take time, and in the meantime expect to end up at the wrong destination a few times and have to try again. Having said that, getting lost in a taxi may mean you find somewhere you never even thought to look for. Yet, Mario noted that taking taxis did not have to be especially difficult, as long as he was prepared. That meant knowing the name of where he was going, approximately where it would be in town, and its location on the map. 'I usually gave the driver an intersection or pointed to my destination on the map (I always carried the city map with me).'

Aside from the outside world which you must acquaint yourself with, there is the task of setting up your new home. If you want to have curtains made, furniture covered, or maintenance and repairs carried out, it is often the non-employed partner who will need to find someone to do the job. At the least you will have to be there to supervise the handyman who arrives if someone else has helpfully made the appointment for you. Once the handyman arrives you could very well find that you have no common language; this is when it is a great help if you are good with sign language and quick on the draw with a dictionary. But look on the positive side, using a dictionary to hold a conversation certainly means you are economic with words and it also means you are learning the language.

Barb Davis, from the US, moved to France with her Turkish husband and teenage daughter. She is now back in the US but hopes to relocate abroad again once their daughter finishes high school. In France she used a local handyman on a regular basis:

My handyman in France was a Monsieur Uno. He spoke not a word of English, and in fact spoke French with a heavy southern accent. He was my favourite person. He could fix anything, and was amazingly patient with my horrible French. We discovered that the French/English dictionary was helpful, but also full of funny words that neither of us had heard before. It didn't seem to matter. When he arrived, I always offered him a cup of coffee, and we chatted for about 15-20 minutes, then we set out to repair whatever it was he came for. I always looked forward to my visits with M. Uno, he made me feel so competent in French, since he always complimented my accent, or grammar, or at least my efforts.

Partners are often heard bemoaning the fact that, 'My partner (the employee) just has their job to do, but I have to do everything else'. A common response from the employed partner is, 'What's so hard about what you do?'

The reality is that the tasks of day-to-day life are no more difficult in themselves. But trying to get them done in a foreign language, in a foreign city, in a culture that may eat, socialise and conduct business in a totally different way from what you know can cause great difficulties for expats.

After a few moves abroad, Robert and Coleen have come to an agreement about the fact that theirs is an equal partnership, and that each has to help the other in their adjustment. Even though it is Robert that is the 'contracted' partner, he feels it is important to help with the domestic and set-up issues as well.

> *One way to deal with this initial pressure (put on the partner) is for the employed partner to go a couple of weeks in advance and get that initial flurry of workplace activity out of the way. That way, when the accompanying partner arrives, the employed partner is able to take a few days off and pitch in properly in setting up the household. It also means the employed partner will have already had a chance to scout out the grocery stores, transportation routes and such, so that s/he can play tour guide to their arriving partner.*

At the start of a posting, most expatriate partners have to learn how to complete their daily tasks without much help, guidance, or a friendly face, which always slows things down. This is where any pre-departure contacts that are made come into their own (see the previous chapter and further on in this one for ideas). A spouse of the working partner's colleagues, or a friend of a friend, whoever the contact, can be of great assistance in helping the non-employed partner to settle into a new country. Do not be afraid to ask questions, especially if you have a local contact. Most people are only too happy to help you feel comfortable and 'at home' in their country.

Once a partner (who has not lined up any kind of employment) has learnt to complete their essential tasks efficiently, they can find that life revolves around shopping, children and housework, with little intellectual stimulation to break the monotony. Finding the intellectual stimulation, at whatever level a particular partner needs, will be a large factor in determining whether the couple will be happy and consider the overseas experience a success.

Gillian Kerr mustered her courage and then went out and did for herself what she had neglected after an initial difficult period.

> *Before my husband got his first overseas contract, for which I had to give up my own work, I had had a very demanding stressful job that really challenged me to my limits. From that to nothing. I had my children then, thinking they would provide the stimulation I needed in life. Not true — I felt even more isolated with a mound of nappies and no adult conversation. I'm not designed to be a stay at home mother. I was bored to the point of depression, then decided to get busy.*

Among other things, Gillian continued her education and started her own business.

The partner's happiness has major implications on family harmony, the employee's performance at work and ultimately the success of an international posting as viewed by the employer, employee and the family. Many firms doing research on the subject have indicated that many international contracts are terminated early because of reasons associated with the partner's unhappiness (as mentioned in *The Nuts and Bolts of Living Abroad*).

There can be a danger that a partner will end up sitting around all day with other expatriate wives complaining about how boring or difficult a place is.

Currently, the vast majority of expatriate spouses are women, so there are not many men for the male partners to do the same thing with. Consequently, the male partners who stay at home can have an incentive to work harder to find something to do through lack of an alternative.

Sitting around complaining is a certain way of making sure that you are not going to enjoy your time overseas. Karron Combs believes that expats need to develop and maintain a positive nature when they move abroad.

> *Discontent feeds on discontent. Small problems can become huge, and niggly little annoyances become massive, insurmountable obstacles the longer one sits around and moans about them. Everyone who lives in your expat community knows exactly what you are suffering, so instead of sitting around and complaining, get out, start exploring, and stop sitting in each other's kitchens adding to the discontent.*

The increased spare time an expat partner does have, (if the employee's hours are long), can be spent pursuing productive and positive social interests, educational ambitions and career goals.

Barb Davis grasped her opportunities to the maximum and says. 'You may think about renaming the 'trailing spouse' to the 'lucky spouse'! I've never had so much fun, guilt-free! Since I was not allowed to work in France, I was free to enjoy everything about our expat experience, without the guilt associated with being a freeloader.'

Expat Spouse Organisations

In many cities around the world there are organisations, both formal and informal, for expatriate partners. Most of the organisations are for women, but the male partners are beginning to link up too. Your own embassy will be a good place to ask for information about expatriate organisations in your city; so will the embassies of other countries that speak your language(s). Many embassies keep lists of local organisations for their own staff and will happily supply the information to non-embassy expatriates of their own country, and sometimes nationals of 'friendly' countries too.

Despite the fact that she has not been able to work, Wendy Wilson has had a great time during her new life in Buenos Aires, in part, because of the expat groups in the city.

None of the expat wives work, between the language difficulties and protectionist Argentine employment policies it's just about impossible. Add that to the fact that most everyone has a live-in maid and you have a lot of people with an awful lot of time on their hands. What has sprung up are a wealth of 'groups', with options for filling time ranging from tennis and jogging groups, community service groups, book clubs, cards, playgroups for those with kids at home (like me), Spanish conversation groups, cooking groups — anything you can think of. It's kind of an interesting phenomenon, coming from the US where everyone bemoans the lack of time in their lives to be living in a place where everyone acknowledges way too much time on their hands. It's great for the school; I've never seen one where each class has so many volunteer parents. Most everyone here is here temporarily, two years is the average, and they kind of look at it as a break from work and real life, to take full advantage of, for the two or so years they can.

Even when a club or society is nominally country specific (i.e. The Caledonian Society), most will generally welcome all-comers; the number of nationalities you can meet at a Scottish Ceilidh in Asia is quite surprising. The Australian Embassy and Canadian Embassy Happy Hours in some countries invite many nationalities of expats, as long as you send in your passport number before the event. This allows people of many nationalities to meet up with people not only from a different country, but also a different professional field.

What is an Accompanying Partner Going to Do?

It is important that the partner decides as early as possible, preferably before the move, what they want to do once they are living in the new country. Mario Antognetti remembers that he had been advised by a friend to put together a list of projects that he longed to do, but never had time to do when he was employed full-time. He sat down and wrote a list of ten things he would really like to accomplish whilst his wife worked full time in Turkey. He found this not only rewarding in being able to do things he wanted to do, but he also found they helped him keep his sanity in an otherwise difficult adjustment period.

The decision making process is best started before moving overseas, as some decisions are easier to make in your home country where you will almost certainly have greater access to information, resources and advice in your own language. But what are the available options? Some (but by no means all) are listed below:

1. Continue a career.
2. Take a career break.
3. Change career track.
4. Retrain for a new career
5. Continue education.
6. Continue as primary childcarer.
7. Become primary childcarer.
8. Continue as homemaker.
9. Become a homemaker.
10. Work for a voluntary organisation.
11. Become involved in charity work.
12. Devote more time to a hobby.
13. Develop a hobby into a business.
14. Pursue your own personal ambition
    — whatever it is.

Partners Continuing a Career

Depending on what your current career is, working in the same field may or may not be an option at your destination. There are a number of reasons for this, including but not limited to:

1. Local legislation regarding professional regulation (e.g. some countries forbid foreign nationals to work as medical staff).
2. Local work permit regulations regarding spouses (can be totally forbidden).
3. Local social customs regarding working women (e.g. Saudi Arabia).
4. Local job availability (due to high local unemployment).
5. Language requirements (i.e. one you do not already know).
6. Physical location of employed partners work/accommodation (i.e. remote oil wells in Venezuela).

To ascertain whether working is an option and how to make sure you correctly follow the local regulations, it is essential that you begin researching as soon as you know which country you are going to.

Natascha Gaim-Marsoner, a South African married to a Brazilian, who has lived in Germany twice, separated by a stay in Sao Paulo, has a work permit for Germany already, though she does not currently work there. She says:

I would advise all women, with or without children, to explore the work situation before they move. In many countries the work permit is the first problem because the companies do not enforce spouses to work abroad (it makes the husband inflexible...) so the support is very poor. I have seen it with people from the UK and France here (they don't need a work permit in Germany), due to language problems and poor support they were very frustrated not to work, especially without children. Most of these expats return before their contract ends.

If the partner is absolutely determined to continue a specific career then it is essential that you determine which countries will allow foreign nationals to practice that profession before a move is finalised. Otherwise there are only two options, the partner does not work or the partner works in a different country.

Miles Wright, who accompanied her husband to Saudi Arabia and subsequently Turkey where she found work after they arrived says, 'I wish I knew how a person could check on jobs abroad before I left home. I had no idea so was left to find and figure out things for myself when I moved here. I had no idea, but I suppose I should have checked with the embassy'.

Lori de Ravello remembers struggling with her concerns before accompanying her husband to Hong Kong:

One of the issues between my husband and I about the impending move was that since I work in public health, I always knew that I would never make the 'big bucks.' Since he works in finance (in the private sector) I guess we both knew that at some point we would come to rely more on his career than mine for our economic well being. Still, now that the moment is upon us, it is hard for me to rationalise that I will give up a great job with my employer to follow him all over the world. I know that consulting is a possibility for me while there, but with two small children and living in a big, bustling, new city, I can foresee that I will be otherwise preoccupied.

Some countries require that a job and work permit be secured before arrival. Others allow a spouse to find a job and work as long as their partner possesses a work permit upon arrival. But it is essential to check as long before departure as possible, since every country is different and the rules continually change. Embassies and consulates are not the only source of information; trade and cultural associations can also be of help.

If you want to work at your destination it is probably true to say that if you can secure a job before your arrival, the pay is likely to be better than a locally secured job. On the other hand, not knowing who the employer is, and what the job and conditions entail can be a drawback, especially if the employer does not normally employ foreigners.

Venetra DeGraffenreid an American librarian, married to German lecturer specialising in American Culture and Literature, found employment after her husband secured an expatriate lecturing post at a university in Turkey. She says, '...contacting the employer before arriving, if it is possible, can ease some of the potential fears. When I was hired, I sent an e-mail full of questions about my job, and the head of Library Information Systems for the university herself called me in Cincinnati. I was still going into the virtual unknown, but as least I didn't feel so worried'.

Cendant Mobility Services International provides the following advice on their website (www.cendantmobility.com/moving/int_spouse.html), for spouse considering working in the host country.

Spouses or partners moving with an international assignee may want to continue or begin careers. In many cases, finding paid employment for the spouse or partner of an international assignee is challenging. Here are some tips for a spouse or partner who wishes to pursue paid employment:

Apply for a work permit at the same time as the international assignee.
Take copies of transcripts from all academic institutions attended.
Take plenty of copies of an up-to-date resume and business references/letters of introduction.
Investigate the tax implications in your particular destination country.
Contact companies in your home country that do business in the destination country, and attempt to arrange interviews before you leave.

Check with your current employer for useful customer or supplier contacts.
Ask if the embassy or consulate can provide a list of companies doing business in your new area.
Explore military installations that may hire local civilians (the possibilities for launching a new career are limited only by your imagination and the laws in your destination country).

Here are some ideas you may want to explore:

1. Teach your native language as a second language, either privately or in a commercial language school.
2. Offer translation services (if you are bilingual).
3. Export products from your new country to retailers back in your home country.
4. Start a co-operative to supply goods and/or services to the expatriate community in your new country.
5. Teach skills, such as painting, sewing, or photography.
6. Look for a tourism-related job in hotels and tourist-service companies.
7. Write for publications or other media.
8. Consider volunteer work.

Take a Career Break

Taking time-out from your existing career does not need to be a hiatus on your c.v. or résumé. Using a few years to fulfil a long held dream, that your busy schedule previously prevented, can do you the world of good. It can allow you an invigorated return to your career, present opportunities for a new career or starting your own business, or allow you to develop skills that will enhance your career prospects when you return to your job. All said, it could give you the time to decide what you really want to do with your life, without the pressures of work getting in the way.

John Barratt took advantage of his time off.

Moving overseas and then finding a job was a bit worrisome but I thought about the advantages of having some free time and indulging my hobbies. The previous year's work had been very stressful so the forced break was very welcome. Once overseas, the lack of pressure from the daily grind allowed me to focus on my goals and myself. Being a motivated person, I decided it would be good to set up my own business.

Initially, I began to work for some companies in town because they were offering work and I needed the finances but also the mental stimulation. I soon learned the ins-and-outs of the profession in a different land. It gave me the opportunity to network, find out about, identify the main players in the area, and research a strategy. I was optimistic that I could do this by myself. So, I used my free time, figured out a strategy, and then implemented it. The time off was beneficial in allowing me to take personal stock. This down time also rejuvenated my work ethic and outlook. The new challenge made me feel in control again.

What are the options for filling your time during an overseas career break? Look back at the list above for some ideas to start with. The list is not supposed to be all-inclusive, but it should give you ideas to help you decide what you want to do.

Change Career Track

As a foreigner working in a foreign country, there can be a variety of jobs open to you, which are not necessarily the same as that which you are currently pursuing. One of your most useful qualifications is likely to be your knowledge of a foreign language (i.e. one not normally spoken in the country you move to).

As an office assistant your native language ability may be indispensable to a businessman looking to expand his operations into your home country, where he needs to impress others with letters written in your first language and his second language. In international sales and marketing, your language skills could ensure the success of a corporate presentation or help an international deal to completion.

The options can be as wide as your imagination, though you will often have to sell your idea to an employer rather than wait for a job to fall into your lap. For example, co-author Huw Francis left an engineering job in the UK and secured a job (that was not advertised) in international sales, marketing and import-export of technical equipment in Hong Kong, primarily because he spoke English (as did all the clients) and he had technical knowledge of the products being sold. He had found the company listed in the local business directory and written directly to the manager asking for a job.

Retrain for a New Career

If you desire to move your career into a very different area from that which it is currently in, retraining may be required. A change of career can have great benefits, both personally and professionally. Gillian Kerr, commenting on her retraining from IT programmer and consultant to teacher after she moved from South Africa to Australia, feels, 'I have grown so much this year — in self confidence, in feeling that I actually can fit in here in Australia, in self esteem, in so many ways'.

Skills learnt in one career and taken into another field can be much sought after if coupled with some new training. For instance, engineering qualifications coupled with an MBA, or bilingual ability with secretarial skills. Gillian's previous skills were beneficial in her job hunt:

My computer knowledge from my years at South African Breweries is really valued in the teaching sphere where they are trying so hard to integrate the curricula with information technology. On my recent practicum placement I was asked to install software and train the teachers and students how to use Microsoft Publisher.

Studying will be hard work, especially in an unfamiliar field, so it is probably best to choose a subject you will enjoy, or are motivated to study for the benefits you will receive at the end.

The opportunity to retrain for a new career does not come easily for many people; family commitments, financial constraints and the psychological barrier of leaving a career to train for another one are difficult to overcome. But once you have moved to a foreign country and set up a new home, these difficulties can seem much smaller and easier to overcome. After Gillian sorted her family out, and realised she did not want to remain a stay-at-home-mother, she went on a mission to make herself happy.

I put the children in day-care and:
1. Began to train as a Billings teacher,
2. Enrolled full time for my Graduate diploma in primary education and,
3. Started my own Creative Memories business (scrapbooking and direct selling).
My kids are happier now that I am happier.

Retraining also requires the support of the employed partner. Studying for a new career will be demanding on time, energy and money. Obtaining new IT (information technology) skills or a good MBA does not come cheaply or easily, nor does the loss of a second income. Then finding your first job after re-qualifying can be just as stressful.

Bronwyn Davies retrained while in Hong Kong:

Finding the confidence to study at the Master's level, in a totally new subject discipline, was one of the most difficult things I have faced as an adult. Juggling all of my commitments was, at times, near impossible. I had to perform — we had invested almost all of our savings in paying the course fee. My husband had to take on a much greater domestic burden and my children hardly saw me. I had to commit enormous amounts of time to course attendance and self-study and had little time — not to mention energy — for much else. The course momentum was responsible in large part for getting me through. If I had had the choice to delay I probably would have — simply from sheer exhaustion. But without it I would not have the job I have today. I also have the respect of my spouse who, it seems, did not always think I would stick at it, and I also have an enormous sense of achievement. Professional confidence is not something I ever lacked but now I know I am 'current' and expanded and that my contributions to the workplace have improved as a result. Put simply, this was both the best and worst thing I have put myself through in recent years.

Choosing the subject(s), the level and the nationality of the course you study is an important decision. Research is important for you to find out as much as possible about what is available and help you determine what is realistically achievable in terms of career prospects, personal growth and family situation; before you sign up for a course. Gillian says, 'Facing a totally new career has made me feel as if I have a clean slate on which to base my new life in a new country'. Her decision to go into teaching was well thought out, and was an excellent addition to her already busy life. 'Teaching will fit in well with my lifestyle as a mother too. Getting back to university opened up my life to new friendships and acquaintances, and was surprisingly easy.'

The education options are discussed in the next section and the *Education: Understanding the Options* chapter includes reference sources for a wide range of training courses.

Continue/Become a Primary Childcarer

Just because you are moving overseas does not mean your life will change beyond recognition. Having the time and opportunity to stay at home with the children is something many parents wish they had, though the experience of being a stay-at-home parent is not the same for everyone.

Lori De Ravello said that in giving up her career to travel abroad with her husband she was a bit sceptical at her ability to stay home with the kids.

My friends who are stay at home moms, some who also gave up careers to stay at home, assure me that it will be more gratifying than I can ever imagine and that I will learn patience, etc. by being with them. Still, I can't help but fall into the trap of thinking that day-to-day child care may be better left up to someone besides me.

For other parents the idea of becoming a stay-at-home parent can be a real problem; some parents need their job to feel fulfilled and happy. One expat in Hong Kong admits, 'There's no way I could be a full-time mother. I would lose my wits. I feel more useful and effective in my working environment. Maybe it boils down to the fact that I'm afraid to be a full-time mother.'

Wendy Wilson, living in Buenos Aires with her husband who works for an international merchandising company, says she does not miss her career much and '...sees it as an opportunity to stay home with my kids and explore things I never would have before'.

Staying at home with the kids is not for everyone, as Gillian pointed out earlier in this chapter. Cindy Rothacker, accompanying her engineer husband in Belgium with their three children, found out what a great benefit school was for her young one:

To me, it depends on the age of your children. In most of Europe, starting at three (and sometimes two-and-a-half), your child can go to school for the day. I thought this idea was absurd until I sent my three-year-old who was driving me insane from boredom (his not mine). He absolutely loves school. He was going for half days at first. They are doing great things with young kids in the kindergarten school.

Some career parents find that they have no real choice in becoming a full-time childcarer. Natascha, in Germany, indicates that aside from the fact that she likes being with her kids, she has three specific reasons why she is a full-time mother:

1. Part-time work as a food engineer (my profession) is impossible...only low profile jobs offer some kind of part-time option,
2. The situation of childcare in Germany is extremely bad. If you are a single mother you have some chances to find day kindergarten or an afternoon group after school. But, the level of teachers is very poor so that you just take this option if you absolutely have to and,
3. Day-care workers are so expensive that about 80% of your net income goes to this person. It is more of an emergency option for mothers who need to prove that they are not so-called 'only mothers' and who do not really need the money.

Childcare options are addressed in more detail in *Childcare Options*.

Accompanying Male Partners

With an increasing number of women being employed as expatriates, there has been a parallel growth in the number of men accompanying their partners abroad in a supporting role. These men usually refer to themselves as 'trailing males'.

Though the percentage of trailing males is a sizeable percentage of all expats, the wide distribution of expats in general can mean that some trailing males know few, if any, of their counterparts. That is unless you are living somewhere like Brussels with a large number of trailing males. Alan Spencer, Membership Chairman of the STUDS group (*Spouses Trailing Under Duress Successfully:* tel ++32 2 649.83.55; alan.spencer@skynet.be; www.gamber.net/studs/) says, 'With the STUDS support group, current membership 60, it is relatively easy to find males in the same situation'.

In addition, because the majority of spouse support groups have been set up and run for women, trailing males may also find that they can not fit into the ready-made support networks when they arrive at their posting. Consequently they can have a tougher time establishing themselves and finding a peer group with which they can identify compared to their female counterparts.

Alan Spencer found that, 'Although Brussels is a small city and the number of trailing spouses is high, they are still widely distributed. This makes it difficult, especially with a young child, to socialise on a regular basis with other trailing spouses'.

By taking on the role of supporting partner, trailing males are also assuming many of the traditional female roles such as homemaker and childcarer. In the US and the UK an increasing number of men have assumed these roles over the years, though they are still something of a novelty and magazines run feature articles about them as they do other unusual news items.

Alan found that,

Yes, there is great media interest in STUDS as an organisation. We are regularly contacted by journalists who want to interview members for articles. We even had a Belgian national television station spend a whole day with one of our members. The most common question asked is do we do the cleaning and cooking. Another interesting conversation was with some Japanese journalists who asked how we had learned to keep house, males in Japan just don't do it.

Men acting as primary child-carers in their home country, as well as trailing male expats who take on the role, have reported that they sometimes face resistance and resentment from women (other than their partners) and their families to them taking on this function. One Australian study found that the majority of men taking on the role received negative reactions from their social group (Gbrich, 1992), though the frequency with which it happened decreased among professionals and semi-professionals.

This can mean that fathers can feel left out from the social groups of mothers in playgrounds, not be invited to coffee mornings and not feel welcome at women dominated Expat Wives Association meetings. Though whether that is from real or perceived reactions provokes debate. Alan recalls:

We heard about the BCT (Brussels Childcare Trust) group in Brussels and knew it had originated with the National Childbirth Trust in the UK. I confess to having had some misgivings about the organisation. Stereotypes sprang to mind, such as having to participate in intense discussions on what is **the** *Laura Ashley curtain pattern this year, and listen to how little Johnny is taking his GCSE's and he's only six months old. Just some of the questions that flitted through my mind were: would the BCT live up to these stereotypes? What if the mothers ostracise me as a man who is presuming on their territory? Would it be impolite to dunk the biscuits in my coffee?*

Though when he attended he found:

I was made very welcome by the mothers in attendance and once I had got used to the strange looks from the children (as it if to say, 'What's a dad doing here?') I came to the conclusion that it would be worth making this a regular event in my and Laurel's social calendar. And not one mention was made of Laura Ashley.

The attitude, or perceived attitudes, of people to the way they live has resulted in stay-at-home fathers in the UK and the US creating their own support groups, playgroups and social events as well as publishing a number of newsletters and dedicated websites.

In the Belgian capital, Brussels, the trailing males group, STUDS, was formed not because they felt ostracised, but because, 'There were a sufficient number of trailing spouses (male) that one of their wife's, a member of the American Women's club, suggested they formed a club of their own'. STUDS run playgroups, sports events and daytime activities, but this group is, unfortunately, a rare one. Even though there are 60 members, only three or four have children below school age who are not in crèche full-time.

The STUDS homepage explains who the members of this group are and why they formed:

Spouses Trailing Under Duress Successfully is an informal group of male trailing spouses — mostly expats who are in Belgium because of their wives' employment. The common language is English but the membership comes from many countries. Members range in age from 30's to 70's. Some are true househusbands, taking care of the children and other home chores while the wife is the main breadwinner. Others are retired, or not employed in Belgium because of local employment rules or lack of local languages. A few are employed on a schedule that provides free time during the week — including one airline pilot. A couple of members are not married.

Brussels is unusual in that it is home to a high number of international organisations and therefore has a very large number of expats; in many countries, however, trailing male expats face the real prospect of being the only stay-at-home father, or trailing male, around.

Some people find it strange that a man would want to take on the traditional woman's role of supporting partner, and not be the breadwinner, and their negative attitude towards stay-at-home fathers and trailing males can make socialising an uncomfortable experience. When co-author Huw Francis first began staying at home to look after his son, he and his wife were often asked, 'When is Huw going to get a real job?' or 'How long will he last before he starts looking for a job?' This condescension from other expats can be stressful for stay-at-home fathers/trailing males and make it difficult for them to feel part of the working male dominated social groups that they would normally join.

Fortunately, it is not an attitude that persists everywhere, Alan found that, 'In Brussels I'm asked, now that my daughter is in crèche, am I going to look for a job When I say, 'No. It's better for our quality of life for me to stay at home,' it's accepted'.

Trailing males without children to look after can find that they are even more isolated than fathers, who usually have at least some contact with other parents (mothers) during the day, even if they do not feel overly welcome. For them it is important to develop interests and activities to keep them occupied both mentally and physically so they do not lapse into boredom and depression, especially if it is impossible for them to work due to the host country regulations.

Alan recalls, 'From the time before my daughter was born I found it took discipline to maintain my motivation and prevent myself from becoming bored. In this respect the Internet is a very useful tool as it allows you to maintain contact with friends at home as well as research projects'.

There can be internal stress on couples too. Some mothers can be struck by the competing pulls of a need to work and maternal guilt at being away from their children for the longer work hours that are common for expats. Men and women often have different expectations on the amount of housework that needs to be done and the loss of a second income can cause money worries.

The reasons why you decide that the man should stay at home need to be clear and well thought through. When Huw Francis and his wife moved from Hong Kong to Turkey they accepted a drop in income of 80%, but consider that their increased standard and quality of life was well worth the financial cost.

Arranging the competing aspects of work and home life, like for traditional expat couples, is therefore important. Alan reports that, 'Most of the trailing spouses I know have partners in senior positions, and have good wages, so employ a cleaner. My wife also strictly limits the time she works so that she sees our daughter in the morning and evening'.

The trailing male may also find that not earning a wage can lead him to feel guilty about not paying his way, especially when he really enjoys being at home with the children, without having to deal with the stress of working (often for the first time in his adult life).

Alex Johnson, a journalist and writer has been a trailing male in both his home country (England) and Spain. He is currently writing a book about the trailing male experience, due to be published in the summer of 2001 by *Expatriate Press*. It is the first major attempt to document and analyse the trailing male spouse experience, offer advice to those men who find themselves with nowhere and nobody else to turn to and look at how everybody can make the best of a growing minority in the expatriate community. Here he reports his view of the trailing male experience.

A recent major report into expatriate trends, which surveyed 65,000 expatriates from PricewaterhouseCooper, starts off with the bullish assertion that, 'the traditional expatriate is alive and well'. On the assumption that this stereotype is probably white, likely to be middle-aged and almost certainly male, PWC is probably pretty close to the mark. But while the report notes certain key trends in the expatriate working world (shorter assignments, lack of growth in central and eastern Europe, a failure by companies to understand the reason for the failure of assignments), it makes barely a mention of one of the biggest changes: the increasing number of expatriated women.

One major consequence of this shift in working patterns is that there are far fewer 'international travelling wives', women who follow their male partners around the globe wherever his work takes them. Instead, the last few years have seen the birth of a new creature, variously called the trailing male spouse, the accompanying male spouse or even 'Stud' (spouse travelling under duress). Whatever you call them, more men are deciding that if her career takes them abroad, then so be it.

I am one of them (trailing male), breaking the concept of the traditional expatriate assignment. We're hardly wild-eyed revolutionaries but we are the very visible heralds of revolution in what is one of the last bastions of male dominance.

I have been a trailing male, first nationally and then internationally, since my wife left law school. When she started work as a city solicitor seven years ago, we moved from the north of England, where I was a news journalist for a large regional newspaper, to London where I worked as a freelance writer. After three years, my wife's firm asked if she would like to relocate to Madrid to help open up a Spanish office. It seemed too good an opportunity to turn down; she was born and brought up in Spain and was pleased at the idea of seeing her family more regularly and returning to a country where summers lasted more than one afternoon, while I was ready for a new challenge after several years of freelancing. We took them up on the offer and moved to Madrid in the autumn of 1998. I had no job (and received no career assistance from her firm in finding one) and nothing remotely resembling a 'support network', spoke Spanish very badly and knew nobody in the country (let alone the capital).

Over the last two years, I've been patronised, congratulated, wondered at, ignored and generally regarded as something a bit odd. I've wanted to pack it all in and go home and I've wanted to stay abroad permanently. I've missed friends, family and the comfort of a familiar culture. I've also managed to find a job, learn the language and get to know plenty of new people. I've also met other trailing males and talked to them about every aspect of their brave new worlds: what reaction they receive to their status, the effects of new technology, how the move has affected their marriage and the relationship with their children. In short, what their lives are like as trailing spouses.

Spouses of expatriates generally get ignored, whatever their sex. Politely ignored, but ignored (except of course when they're expected to drop everything and work as an unpaid member of the company's staff — oh yes, this happens to trailing male spouses just as much as international travelling wives).

In the same PWC report mentioned above, when assessing a candidate's suitability for an international assignment, the five least important criteria for a company are headed up by 'intercultural adaptability of the spouse/partner'. 'It is revealing to see', concludes the report, 'that these are also the most common reasons for assignment failure'. Companies are starting to learn that they ignore the expatriate spouse at their peril but learning why is one thing and understanding why still seems to be quite another.

Helping them get there are a growing number of active expatriate spouses and spouse support groups. However almost all, of these are female. The voice of the lesser-spotted male is seldom heard and, arguably, even less frequently considered.

The new internal and external pressures on any role-swap arrangement require hard work, communication, discussion and ultimately understanding between the partners for them to be overcome. The arrangement will not work for everyone, but successfully renegotiating household and childcare responsibilities and finding friends who are supportive can go a long way towards smoothing the path.

And as Alan says, 'Accepting an overseas secondment imposes stresses no matter who is employed. I think all relationships need to engage in constant communication to overcome those pressures'.

Resources

Print Resources

A Career in Your Suitcase, by Joanna Parfitt, Summertime Publishing, ISBN 0952945304

Culture Shock: A Wife's Guide, Robin Pascoe, Graphic Arts Center Pub C, ISBN: 155868123X, $13.95.

Woman Abroad, a monthly magazine available from: Postmark Publishing, Woman Abroad Subscriptions, 1 Portsmouth Road, Guildford, Surrey GU2 4YB, UK (fax +44 (0)1483-577284, www.womanabroad.com).

Online Resources (Personal)

Brits Abroad www.geocities.com/TheTropics/2865/index.htm.

Federation of American Women's Clubs: www.fawco.org.

Spouses Travelling Under Duress Successfully: www.xpats.com/STUDS homepage of the Brussels based expat group for trailing males.

www.expatexchange.com: an online community for expats, with associated expert to offer advice.

www.expatexpert.com: the website of expat writer, author and consultant, Robin Pascoe.

www.expatforum.com: host of numerous online chat groups, both general expat issues and country specific subjects.

www.expatspouse.com: a free service providing information from expats, for expats, under the auspices of Windham International, the Relocation Consultancy.

www.expat-moms.com: a forum for mothers to swap tips, also has a bi-weekly newsletter.

http://members.nbci.com/househusband: aimed at US househusbands, but useful for expats too.

www.outpostexpat.nl: for Royal Dutch Shell expat employees, but open to all and containing local information on many countries.

www.womanabroad.com: website of the excellent print magazine with the same name. Edited by Joanna Parfitt, author of *A Career in Your Suitcase*.

www.xpats.com: for expats in Belgium.

Online Resources (Professional)

www.escapeartist.com/jobs/postings.htm: Job vacancies listed by country.

www.jobsite.co.uk: Employment opportunities in the UK and throughout Europe.

www.jobs-overseas.net: US based portal offering links to employment websites and agencies in the US and around the world.

www.jobzone.com: A German language employment service.

www.monsterboard.com: Job-search site with resources in 13 countries.

www.overseasjob.com: Database of international employment opportunities.

CHILDREN AND THE MOVE

Before the Move

The prospect of an international move can raise competing emotions between parents and children.

On the one hand there are the positive benefits of spending time abroad, including learning about new cultures and new foods, making new friends and the chance to learn new languages. The prospect of your children growing up bilingual and international in their outlook can be very appealing.

On the other hand there are bound to be concerns about the standard of education available in a foreign country, the health risks, leaving current friends and making new ones and the general disruption to a life that is stable and familiar. There will also be the intangible, but nevertheless worrying, aspects of unknown situations that will always arise when you move somewhere new. Some children also have the worry that they will be left behind.

Accepting that these competing emotions exist and addressing the issues that cause them, both with your children and personally, is important. Barbara Schaetti of *Transition Dynamics* points out:

The children may like where they are or hate it, be excited to leave or angry —
all at the same time. Remember that how someone feels about the move one day
may change and change again over time. (Schaetti, B. (1995) Families on the
Move: Working Together to Meet the Challenge. Inter-Ed, 23(75)).

Phyllis Adler, an American Psychotherapist based in London (pajadler@aol.com, tel ++44-(0)7979-603 313) who specialises in working with expatriates, has found that parents can approach a child's fears in inappropriate ways.

Many parents feel they must be strong and trouble free in order to set an
example. It is often more helpful to admit nerves and sadness at leaving while at
the same time expressing excitement and confidence that whatever obstacles
there may be will be manageable. Much of the value of the move lies in the
shared and supported experience of conquering what may be negative and
discovering that it was worth the effort.

Apart from the immediate effects of moving abroad, parents will also worry about the long-term affects that living abroad will have on their children. Margie Markram, a mother of three admits: 'We enjoy travelling around and getting to know each culture of the countries we land in. The disadvantage is that as the children have got older the more reluctant they are to move as friends etc. and the thought of starting a new school always plays a role. The experiences they gain are something that they will only appreciate as they get older'. These long-term affects of international living, which are generally very positive, are addressed separately in *The Long Term Considerations*.

Phyllis Adler points out that there are some instances when moving a child is not a good idea.

Some children do not take to change well. Their personality may not be flexible
enough to deal with quick and unplanned changes that are part of the
experience. They may not be socially graceful and disturbing a comfortable
position that they may currently enjoy could be hurtful.

Some children may have learning needs that are not as well provided for overseas. In that instance specific questions need to be asked if the child is to flourish (see Education: Understanding the Options). Less apparent are the children who rely on specific activities such as football or music for their 'position'. Consideration need to be given to how those activities are viewed in the new location and the effect loss of status may have.

The potential for a child to become anxious during the process of a family's international move is similar to that when the move is from one city to another in the home country. When a family moves within one country the prospect of leaving friends, relatives, school and the comforting familiarity and security of an established home can be hard on children. Add to these the concerns of moving to a new country with a different language, culture, customs, food and what will almost certainly be a change in lifestyle, then a child can quickly become overwhelmed by the negative aspects.

In the article mentioned above, Barbara Schaetti also outlined the context within which an expatriating family often views the changes in their lives.

Whether you're happy to go or sad to leave, whether it's your first transfer or only the latest of many, everything you do now suddenly takes place within the context of the upcoming move. One moment you're living with a sense of relative permanence as you plan for next week, next month, even — daringly — next year. The next moment, every thought and action is accompanied by the sharp realisation that you're only here a few more weeks — at best, a few more months. It's time to finish projects, organise logistics, say goodbye. Your life as you know it has become temporary; your future vague.

Preparing the Children

Children are well known for overhearing their parent's conversations when they are not supposed to, and when the overheard discussion revolves around an upcoming move the children may not like what they hear, or completely misunderstand the entire situation. An innocent joke or throwaway comment, that you make very casually, could also make a child unnecessarily anxious and upset before, during and after a move.

Parents should also be aware of the problems that can be caused by children first hearing about a possible move from third parties. When parents talk to their adult friends, who have children that are friends with their children, the gossip chain can work extremely quickly. If children learn about a move this way they can misunderstand what they hear, or the content of what has been relayed to them may have been distorted.

The best way to make sure your children hear the news from you is to involve the children in the process of a potential move as early as possible. By doing so you can put your own perspectives on the move and assure the children that they will be an integral part of the move. As the parent, you will have to evaluate at what age your child(ren) are able to understand the concepts and implications of moving. However, even two-year-olds can understand much of what is said to them and around them and can become anxious if they see their toys being packed and removed for no apparent reason. The older children are, the more they can be involved in the process of moving and even discussions about where a move should be to, or whether a move should take place at all.

The inclusion of the children in the process can go a long way towards limiting the subconscious worries of being left behind (at home, or abroad), that the move will be permanent and that life as they know it will never be the same again. In her previously mentioned article, Barbara Schaetti advocates involving children in the discussion process from the beginning and continuing that involvement throughout the whole expatriate experience.

Have regular family discussions in which everybody gets to talk about the move, what they're looking forward to and what they're anxious about. Get everybody's burning issues on the table. This is a good family practice even if you're not about to move...(Parents should) honour feelings and encourage all family members to express them freely and without judgement. Don't try to fix someone else's grief. Deal with emotions by recognising and acknowledging them.

Diane Clayton and her husband Mark have three boys aged 11 and 8 (the latter two are twins). They decided that with older children it was not a good idea to keep secrets from them. They openly talked about leaving and worked towards the move as a unit.

We all worked together, as the move was a big step for all of us. We all enjoyed the adventures and excitements that living in a new country brings and discovered that if school is fine, bed is warm, food is on the table, clothes are provided, Mom and Dad happy, then so are the kids. I think the biggest issue that helped was that I talked to the kids about my difficulties, and the differences I was coping with, as did their father. The fact that we all coped together was the biggest, best factor.

Barbara Schaetti further advises that communication within the family unit is important at all times. But with explanations to children in the family Barbara warns:

Be careful especially about what your children may be misunderstanding. One mother told me about her young son's sudden panic when they gave away the family's pet. In that child's reasoning, the pet was part of the family. What family member were they going to give away next? Be explicit about what you're doing and why.

Though that particular family did not take their pet, it is possible to do so and further information on shipping your pet can be found in *From Packing to Unpacking*.

One expatriate father remembers calculating how he was going to initiate the thought process of an international move to his young children:

My wife and I started with the propaganda campaign several months before we told our children we were moving to Japan. We tried to find as many videos of day-to-day life in Japan to give the children the clearest mental picture we could, of what their lives would be like once they got off the plane. We tried to identify the things in Tokyo that the children would like and would rely on for comfort, and then we introduced those things to them in a way that let them discover that life in Tokyo is not only survivable for children there but also fun. We talked about the kind of things they liked to do at our own home and helped them to see that children in Tokyo do them also. When we told them we were moving, one of my children hugged me with gratitude and the others were able to be excited because they knew what to expect and had confidence that they could be happy there.

Generally, children are resilient and adaptable, and with the right encouragement from their parents can usually make a successful transition to a country and culture that is markedly different from what they are used to. A good way to help them through the transition period is to clearly mark a calendar with all the important upcoming dates, including packing, shipping, moving out of your current home, hotel stays, flights, moving into your new accommodation and starting school at the destination.

Though some parents will find it difficult to encourage their children to look positively toward an international move, some parents will find that their children actually relish a new move, and look forward to it with an air of adventure.

Moving around did not particularly bother Brennen Young, a third culture kid who has made numerous moves in his young life:

For me, the best thing about moving to another country was the newness of it all. It was like going for a vacation to a place I'd never been before, but with the knowledge that I'd be spending more than two weeks there. That was a sort of conscious realisation, and the emotional realisation only hit me after we had done the tourist bit and finally moved into our house or flat, and I had to start cleaning my room again.

Yet not everyone who makes an international move is as confident as Brennen. Much of the stress generated by an international move, on both adults and children, can be caused not by what they know, but by what they do not know. Barbara Schaetti believes that the experience of moving into the unknown is something that families (children included) must be ready to face honestly.

Anybody who has experienced an international move, even one ardently sought and eagerly engaged, knows that it is an inherently stressful experience. It can also be a very isolating experience. The process of transition requires that those moving and those staying disengage from one another. Colleagues and friends can empathise with all that's to be done, farewell parties can be thrown in your honour, but ultimately it's you and your family alone who get on that airplane, who leave behind all that has become familiar and head off for the once-known or unknown. It's you and your family alone. (Families on the Move: Working Together to Meet the Challenge. Inter-Ed, 23(75)).

Common fears expressed by children of various ages prior to making their first international move are that:

1. They will be left behind.
2. They do not understand how the move will take place.
3. They do not know exactly when the move will take place.
4. Their toys/books will be left behind.
5. They do not know which members of their immediate family are making the move.
6. They will never see their friends and relatives again.
7. They will never come home again.
8. They will not have anywhere to live once they are abroad.
9. They will not be going to school anymore.
10. They will have no friends at the destination.
11. They will have to eat 'strange' food.
12. There will be nothing familiar (shops, food, TV, etc.) at the destination.
13. No one will speak their language.
14. They will be abandoned at the destination.

The number and intensity of the fears vary with the age and personality of every child, but older children are just as likely to have difficulty overcoming them as younger children.

A number of expatriate children have identified that the single biggest fear of moving to a new country was the establishment of new friends. While they often talked about leaving their old friends behind, they are most often worried about creating and fitting into a new social circle at their new school. It is a fear that they have to live up to every day until things start moving along and they realise they are able to make friends.

Phyllis Adler offers the following advice on helping children make friends in the host country.

One of the most difficult obstacles for almost everyone is how to make the first move toward a person who seems so busy and settled in their own life. If it possible, children often find that having classmate's telephone numbers in advance is helpful. Also, calling for a reason, such as a homework assignment, is an icebreaker that has been used successfully. Older children may enjoy a calling card with their own number on it that they can casually give to someone else if an opportunity arises in a conversation. It is always important however to remember that each child is unique and each relationship is unique. What may seem a sound and helpful idea to one may sound like a vote of no confidence to another.

The second most frequent comment about their fears was the anger they felt resulting from the fact that they had no control over the situation and that their family was going to move no matter how they felt.

Expatriate children who move from one international home to another often respond that though they were nervous about adjusting to a new school and making new friends, they also add that they were excited about the prospect of meeting new people and getting to know their new temporary home. Some even saw it as a 'clean break'. One such expat teen, Michael Hedge, indicated quite frankly that he was always happy to leave a country for a new one because he could start all over. If anything got uncomfortable, or did not go the way he wanted, he was be able to relax in the knowledge that he would be able to pack up his bags in the near future and make a clean break. He saw it as a positive element in his nomadic life.

Not all expatriate children feel the same way however. The attachment that they grow to their new home is hard to get over when they leave. And though they may enjoy moving to a new country, they can find that they are sad about leaving behind a significant chunk of their lives to create a new one. Yet, the more often they move with their families, the easier it seems to be. Andrea DiSebastian learned that the more she moved, the easier it got. 'The more we moved the easier it was to just 'pick up and go'. There was not as much fear of the unknown. Packing up and changing homes didn't seem like such a project.'

Older children can also build up a certain amount of resentment and anger about a move, some of which arise from the fears and concerns listed above, but also from those below:

1. Nobody seems to care about what they think of the move.
2. The move is only about a parent's money and career and the family does not matter.
3. Their life will be ruined because they are being taken away from their school and their friends.
4. Life will be boring in the destination country because it lacks the sophistication of home.
5. They are being treated like a 'child' and not being told anything, or consulted, about the move and why it is happening.

Parents who have involved the children as much as possible in the whole process of the move have found that it helped reduce the fear and resentment of their children and they believe it helped smooth the family's transition to a new home. Parents will, however, have to consider the age and maturity of their children before they make decisions on how to involve the children in a move.

Helena Snedden, a South African in Scotland moved with her three-and-a-half-year-old daughter, and her fiancé. Being so young, it was not really an issue on how to allay her daughter's fears, but how to smoothly work her through the moving process.

*I don't think she understood much of what was happening. We took it one step at
a time, talking about the airplane trip. She was excited about this and actually
enjoyed it. We brought many of her toys with her so she had familiar things
about her when she got here.*

*We tried to make each new experience something special and she does not
seem to have been unduly traumatised. It was close to Christmas so there was
the excitement of presents. Then there was the snow that she experienced for the
first time. There were too many new things to think about and not much time to
dwell on strangeness, I think. Also, we established routines again as quickly as
possible. I got her into a nursery as soon as possible, she had been going in
South Africa and she seemed to enjoy going here as well. It was a case of most
of the children were new there so she couldn't really feel the odd one out.*

In contrast, Diane and Mark Clayton sat down with their boys and expected
them to help make important decisions about things that affected them directly.

Parents who have only told their children a short time before a move what is
going to happen have said that in the long run they believe it made the move more
difficult and they wished they had raised the subject earlier.

Barbara Schaetti further advises in her article mentioned above, 'Give your
children whatever control and planning responsibility you can. Older children can
take an active role in packing their own toys and books and then in unpacking
them at the end'.

Parents usually know their child best and careful consideration needs to be
given to how and when to involve children in the process of moving abroad. The
amount of child involvement that is practical will vary for every family and
circumstance, but there will almost always be activities and decisions that children
can be involved with.

Helping children gather information at the outset can help prepare them for the
whole moving process. Many of the suggestions elsewhere in this book for
making contacts, learning about the destination and planning the logistics of
moving apply equally as well to children as they do to adults. Watching videos,
looking at travel brochures, surfing the Internet, writing to children already at the
destination, meeting children who have visited the country and meeting nationals
of the country and eating their food will help lessen the mystique about where the
child is going.

One expatriate mother took her children to the library in the capital city where
they lived and did a search on the city they were moving to in the Middle East. Since
the children were very unfamiliar with the area they were moving to it was important
to them that they see where they were going. Picture books, a video and various other
books on Middle Eastern ways of life (including lots of fun stuff on desert camping
and camel riding) got them interested and less scared about their new home.

Phyllis Adler counsels:

*Part of the planning can focus on activities the child will want to continue after
the move and their availability in the new location. Advance research can be
done to organise little league, dance classes, music lessons, scouts, etc. The
faster a child can be helped to fit in and find new friends the easier the
adjustment will be. Children dread not knowing anyone in a school where
everyone else seems to have a friend.*

*Younger children may have fears about finding their way around or knowing
where the facilities are. Advance tours or photos can help provide information
about the layout and school culture such as clothing style, etc. While carrying
the wrong type of book-bag may seem of little matter to an adult, to a child it
can feel like a major social debacle.*

Discussing the process of the move, which family members are going to make the move and what you are taking with you, can mitigate the concerns (as listed above) that children have about moving.

The three stages of a move that you can consider directly involving your children in (as opposed to being spectators) are:

1. The reasons why a move needs to be made and where you will go.
2. The planning and execution of 'The Move'.
3. Arrival and settling in.

Promoting the positive aspects of a move and discussing the negative aspects to find ways to mitigate them can go a long way to helping children enjoy an international move. Potential problems and concerns can rarely be swept under the carpet for long and finding solutions to the problems, or preparing alternative plans, in advance, can reduce their impact when they do arise.

By giving your children something exciting to look forward to and allowing them time to prepare for the new situations and experiences they will encounter, their fears, anxieties and resentments can lessen and a sense of excitement created.

However, some sense of realism and sensitivity to your child's personality is needed as you present a move. An unrealistically positive attitude and a denial that there will be any problems at all can lead children to disbelieve everything you say. That is why communication is so important between family members in a move. By maintaining a realistic approach and being frank about what awaits you and not painting the picture as an ideal situation will help the children face the differences they are about to encounter.

According to Barbara Schaetti (in her article listed earlier), '*Open and honest communication is the backbone of all relationships, especially so in a family. It becomes of paramount importance when preparing for a move.*' By being honest with your child about what to expect, you better help them to prepare for the impending changes.

Children may also resent your imposition of an 'everything will be all right, don't worry about a thing' attitude, because you are trying to control their emotions (good and bad), fears and concerns.

It is highly unlikely that the fears and resentments will be eliminated, but by discussing them and making the experience a shared one, your children should at least feel that they have someone to turn to for help when they need it. Hopefully, this will give them the confidence to make the most of what can be the opportunity of a lifetime.

Andrea DiSebastian remembers having many family meetings to discuss the many moves they made internationally. Even with these meetings, there were times that she still felt resentment at her parents, especially when they moved to Spain:

When I was sixteen and living in Madrid I was having a rough time. The students that went to the school that I attended were not easy to get along with. I took my sadness and frustrations out on my father. He was working too much back then and I felt like I didn't have him around me (and the family) enough. I was also going through a teenage phase. We discussed things. I remember my father and I taking a walk around our neighbourhood in Madrid and him trying to cheer me up. It didn't work very well and I started crying. I remember crying a lot and I also remember my father being angry with me and vice versa many times that year. The next year was better.

There are many ways to involve children in the decision making process of a move and the practicalities of a relocation. By involving your children as much as you can in any move you can learn their fears and concerns and work towards reducing them and at the same reassuring your children that you are there to help them. Families that have moved a number of times believe that the shared experience of planning and executing an international move has brought them closer as a family and helped their children develop independence, confidence and adaptability.

How Children's Needs Can Factor into Making the Decision to Move

Whether your employer has decided that you are the perfect choice for representing the company abroad, or you have decided that the job you want is in a foreign country, making the decision to actually go will directly affect your family as much as you.

Depending on the age of your children, how much you involve them in the decision to relocate will vary. Your personal employment situation will also affect how much choice and freedom you have in whether or not to go.

In an article for *HR Magazine* (www.shrm.org), Laura Herring, identified three age levels and the differing issues of each.

The younger the children (younger than eight), the less information they need. The basic information they need is that they will be moving as a family and will be safe and secure.

The biggest issue for children in the 8-11 age group is maintaining their friendships, which can be done through letters, e-mails, telephone calls, or even visits. Sports and other activities are also important, and parents should investigate what activities the new location offers before even telling children about the move.

Teenagers are 'much more challenging' according to Herring. It is necessary to acknowledge up front that the move will not be easy, and explain why the move is taking place. Parents should also research the new area beforehand so they can point out its similarities and benefits.

Barbara Schaetti believes it is important to involve your children in the decision to move on a collaborative process, but in the same breath warns to be realistic. 'Don't tell a fifteen-year old that she doesn't have to move unless you're really prepared to consider other options.'

When you are planning on discussing the move with your child(ren), you might want to bear in mind the reason for your move, and try to work it into the explanation and discussion you will have with them. There are a number of scenarios that are likely to arise among people considering an international move.

1. Your employer has decided to send you.
2. You have decided that you want a promotion or career change, which involves moving abroad.
3. You have decided you want to move abroad for the personal benefits you perceive will arise (social, lifestyle, environmental, financial, etc.).
4. You are unemployed and moving abroad offers you the chance of a good job.

With a large percentage of the international contracts that are broken, the predominant reason given is family problems. *Cendant Mobility*'s recent survey *International Assignment Policies and Practices 1999* indicates that at least 56% of respondents fail in their assignments due to family related issues. When you bear in mind that many of these overseas assignees have children, the successful relocation of the children is an important factor which must be handled properly.

Older children are more likely to raise serious vocal objections to a move than younger ones, but both can be stressed by the prospect.

When Barbara Davis and her husband mentioned the prospect of moving abroad again after only having just returned from a previous posting in France, their daughter was outraged. She flatly said she would not join them abroad, and that it would mess up her life:

> *Her protestations were in spite of the fact that she had objected to moving to France, ended up loving it, crying to go back because she missed her friends there. She was unable to transfer that experience to another move. The possibility that she would again make new friends, and have a wonderful time didn't occur to her. I guess only time and multiple experiences teach us these things.*

Barbara and her husband weighed the pros and cons of insisting their daughter accompany them against her will. Finally, the family decided that their daughter's protestations were significant enough to wait out her completion of high school before pursuing the opportunity to accept another posting abroad.

When younger children might have difficulty with the concept of moving country it is probably better to introduce them to the idea slowly, once you know where you are going. By talking to them generally about what other countries are like, where people come from, why people might move from one place to another you can ease into the idea that your family is making one of these kinds of moves for a little while.

The older children get though, the more likely they are to want to have some say in whether the family should move, or not. How much opportunity you give them to voice their opinions and influence your decision will have to vary. If you are in situation four above (unemployed) and you are offered a job abroad that will rescue you from debt, how much choice do you really have in whether or not to accept?

If, on the other hand, you are in situation three and have decided you want to move somewhere for better weather, can you really justify the move if your child has one year left at school before important exams?

For families in situation one or two, the decision can be much more subjective and the arguments can become the cause of much upset and strife in a household.

Some families decide not to tell their children about a move until the day it happens, working on the basis that the less time they have to worry about it the better. Others work up to announcing a move slowly (especially with younger children) by asking the children what they think about the concept of moving abroad (by the beach, in the jungle, in the mountains) and where they would like to go.

To help you devise the best strategy for helping your child move abroad, answer the questions below.

Involving the Children in the Move

Once you know you are definitely moving and also where you are going to, there are many ways to build both your own anticipation and that of your children. By searching for the exciting and positive benefits of a move (and finding them) the magnitude of the negative aspects can be reduced. When you do find negative aspects of a move, looking for solutions and alternatives to work through them can also be beneficial in making the transition smoother and more successful.

Peter van Buren, veteran traveller and author of the website *Travelling Internationally With Your Kids* (www.travelwithyourkids.com), always keeps the topic of moving open in his family. He firmly advocates that involving your children, appropriately, is a most important point. Depending on the age, he says that kids can help to sort the household stuff by labelling things into sea, air, storage, give away and luggage piles. Letting the children organise their own toys for packing gives them the added reassurance that their stuff is equally important. Little tools like letting the children label their own boxes, or drawing pictures of what room their stuff is to be sent to in the new abode can also help turn over some of the control to the kids.

How Will The Move Affect Your Children

Is your child old enough to notice the move?	
What differences will the child notice?	1. 2. 3.
Is your child old enough to comprehend the concept of moving abroad?	
Is your child sensible enough (old enough) to logically think through the implications of a move on their own, or should you talk them through it?	
What reasons are there, from your child's point of view, why you should not move? (Schooling, social interaction, health, local culture, etc.).	1. 2. 3. 4.
What reasons are there from your point of view why your child should not relocate abroad?	1. 2. 3.
What reasons are there, from your child's point of view, why you should relocate abroad?	1. 2. 3.
What reasons are there, from your point of view, why you should relocate abroad? (So you can tell them to your child if applicable).	1. 2. 3.
What are the implications for your child, good and bad, of moving abroad? (School, friends, lifestyle, skills, opportunities, etc.).	1. 2. 3. 4.
What can you do to lessen the impact of the negative implications on your child?	1. 2. 3.
What can you do to increase the benefits of the positive implications on your child?	1. 2. 3.
Where can you find the resources to allow you to do the above?	1. 2. 3.

Barbara Schaetti agrees, in her previously mentioned article, that collaboration in the transition process is something that must be practised and be done openly.

Give your children whatever control and planning responsibility you can. Older children can take an active role in packing their own toys and books and then in unpacking them at the other end. My sisters and I used to serve as ground staff when the movers were packing, helped to label boxes appropriately and then directed boxes to the right locations upon delivery at the other end.

While the packers are actually in your home Peter warns about the dangers that lurk. Packers are not well known to be 'kid-friendly'. They have a job to do and it must be done quickly and efficiently. Having children run around playing with the cardboard boxes and styrofoam packing is not necessarily going to make the packers happy. In addition, they often have sharp knives that they use to cut cardboard/tape/packing paper, which get thrown around and left lying about on packing day. It is a good idea to have one parent designated as the one who deals with the professional packers, and the other parent who entertains and keeps the children out of harms way.

Peter and his wife have learned from experience that it is not a good idea to take children out of the house whilst it is being packed up. For children who are not involved in the process (either actively by pre-packing their own things and labelling them, or passively by witnessing the professionals pack up) leaving the home and returning to it when it is empty can cause undue stress and fear that their things are gone forever. If opportunity affords it, have the children outside watching the movers put the boxes in the truck. It puts an ending to their long day of watching everything be boxed up, much like the conclusion to a move when the boxes emerge at the destination.

Some parents have found it helpful to leave the home once all their belongings have been cleared out. A number find it helps with the transition to put a 'holiday' feel to the beginning of the move by moving into a hotel for the time between the emptying of the house and the time of the flight. One family recommends renting or borrowing a television and video machine to bridge the gap and give the kids something fun to look forward to instead of returning to a house that echoes. When Michelyne Callan, one of the authors, left Hong Kong with her family, they had eight days between the time that the flat was emptied and the departure of their flight taking them back to Canada. They opted to stay in a nearby hotel, so that they were in the same neighbourhood, thereby providing their nearly two-year-old son with a little familiarity, while at the same time providing the convenience of furnished surroundings. They realised it would have done no good to take their almost two-year-old back to an apartment void of personal effects. The move to the hotel was enough to confirm that the journey had begun, but offered enough stability so as not to shock the family with change.

From the beginning of the journey to your new home, Peter van Buren further recommends getting your children involved in packing their own things (if they are old enough) as it is an important place to start. When the move is on, and the travelling starts, get the kids to carry something. In the end it should make them happy and will involve them in the process in a very practical way. The older they are, the more they can carry. Peter remembers that even their three-year-old daughter went on the plane with a small back-pack stuffed with her own equipment (change of clothes, toys etc.). By allowing her to carry her own things on the plane ride, Peter said it gave her a sense of empowerment.

An expatriate father moving to Tokyo remembers trying to hand over whatever control he and his wife possibly could to their children, and why:

We let them choose what toys they wanted to bring with them on the plane and to help pack their suitcases. The goal was to give them control; even if our son brings a game boy and plays it non-stop between castle visits, he'll have got more exposure, and felt better about the trip, than if he was too scared to go at all, or too scared to relax and enjoy what's around him.

Some shipping agents have special information packs and shipping containers for children, so they learn about what the moving company will do and can pack their own belongings and tick off special items as they are packed. When looking for a shipper, if you have young children involved in the move, you should remember to ask what special services they offer to their young clientele.

There are also a few books written especially for children, in cartoon form, that deal with moving house, and in some cases they deal with moving abroad. Reading these books and explaining to your children the processes involved in moving, and confirming that their favourite toys, games and books and other family members will be going too, will alleviate some of their fears.

Reputable international removal agencies, with experience of relocating families, recommend that when it comes time to pack, that the children are encouraged to either do their own packing, or watch their belongings being packed and placed on the lorry. This way they are sure everything has been sent to their new home.

For children that are of school age it would help them make the transition by having them keep a sense of connection to the place they are leaving. By buying them a personal address book where they can record the mail/e-mail addresses of their best friends and compiling a scrapbook of their favourite places and friends, you can help them to feel they are able to stay in contact with the place and their friends. Purchasing a stack of postcards in advance of departure gives them something to do on the plane and in the first few weeks of arrival at the destination. For older children who are more likely to want an avenue to vent their concerns, frustrations and feelings, a journal or diary can be a good idea. Some adults who did this when they were children have now published their journals, the contents of which may help parents and children smooth their own transitions now.

After the Move

Arrival and Settling-In: Getting on with Life Abroad

Children suffer culture shock as much as adults do, but they are usually less well equipped to deal with the emotional issues. School aged children will also have the added complication of adjusting to a school system that may be alien to them. As discussed in *Education: Understanding the Options*, expatriate children are often educated in an 'International School', where the predominant nationality of the students may be as foreign as the country you are living in. North Americans are by far the largest group of expatriates around the world and a European student can find American children as foreign as someone from Asia, and vice versa. Though by placing a child in an International School there will be aspects that are familiar and provide continuity.

Bernadette van Houten of *Consultants Interculturele Communicatie*, based in the Netherlands agrees with Barbara Schaetti that continuity is important for children.

It would be so much easier to be back home with your old neighbourhood and there's only one language, (and everything is familiar). But it's not that way. You have to remember that if you think you are going to be moving frequently, it is very nice for the children to recognise the same textbooks and the same ideas.

When considering the education options at your new destination, bear in mind the effect that a similarly based education system may have to the easement of culture shock in your school-aged children. Something as simple as a common language, or recognised text books might make the difference between a child who is unsettled and miserable at school (and therefore the country) and one who adjusts quickly to the new surroundings.

Expatriate parents have two immediate jobs once they arrive at a new destination:

1. Settling themselves into the destination,
2. Settling their children into the destination.

If you have introduced children to the destination culture before you move, the effects of culture shock can be reduced, as they would be with you. A pre-relocation 'look-see' visit can go a long way towards accelerating this process as both you and the children will have had a chance to see at first hand what the destination will be like, then go away and think about it before you actually have to live there.

Schools, estate agents, sports and social clubs that are open to expatriates will usually be more than happy for you to visit and look around if you are on a pre-relocation visit. Some may even be willing to give you temporary membership or a few days trial during your stay.

A parent's attitude to the local culture and the change in environment will colour a child's attitude too. It can be difficult enough adapting to a new country yourself, but when you have to consider the differences through the eyes of a child too, so as to help them understand the immediate changes, it can be even more complicated. A negative view from a parent can not only create a negative attitude in a child but can also be embarrassing, when your child repeats, in public, a comment you made in private.

The chapter *Culture Shock* discusses the matter in greater detail, and you can adapt many of the suggestions there for dealing with the culture shock of your children. Living abroad will be different in many ways to what you are used and it will take time for your children to adjust, but many expatriate parents see these differences and the knowledge their children gain from experiencing them as one of the main reasons for living abroad.

There are many ways of smoothing the transition, and as a parent, while you are busy sorting yourself out, it is important to find the time to talk to your children about their feelings and not just find activities for them to do.

As an adult you may very well be able to cope well with the differences in your lifestyle, but children are often a lot happier if they have at least a few places and activities that are comfortingly similar to home. A meal at a favourite fast food restaurant, or a certain breakfast cereal every day can be enough to reassure a child that the life they have known has not disappeared all together.

Barbara Schaetti suggests keeping the family routines of meals, household duties, bedtimes and celebrations consistent and not relaxing household rules just because you have moved. Though they should be relaxed if doing so will ease a certain aspect of the family's adjustment.

Ieuan Francis, who is nominally British though he was born in Hong Kong, considered Turkey to be his home after living there for all but eight months of his first five years. He found visits to the UK stressful because of the many differences he encountered. He often asked for apricot juice and *köfte* (Turkish meatballs) when on holiday, because it was what he liked best in Ankara. His parents had to search obscure shops to find his favourite foods, but his joy at having them again made the time spent in the UK much easier.

Continuity comes from many things, not just the country of residence, and can include personal belongings, family traditions (bedtime stories, phoning the grandparents every Saturday, etc.) and favourite foods.

Expat parents continually talk about their children's cravings for home-country foods. Americans and Canadians often want the children's staple Kraft Dinner and Australians crave Vegemite. Though these can be hard to find in some countries, a care package sent from family or friends at home, or a suitcase filled with various treats to come out at special occasions can reaffirm to your children that not all from their past is lost. Though when mail deliveries are unreliable this might not be an option.

Even if the local cinema only shows dubbed movies, it does not mean that your children cannot go anymore. To a young child a film is a film regardless of the language it is presented in. Younger children especially do not seem to notice a different language if their favourite cartoon is on the screen. Ieuan Francis quite happily watches French, English, Polish and Turkish cartoons, even though he only understands the English and Turkish.

As a teenager, Brennen Young found settling into a routine after arriving in a new country very difficult. The establishment of a sense of continuity for him was important, and something he had to work at to achieve:

One of the hardest things to get used to in a new country was getting back into a daily rhythm of life. Everything was new, and there were certain things, such as groceries, that you are used to having and being able to use, but are no longer available. We would usually laugh at the new rules (or lack of them) — we all knew that we had no choice but to accept them, and complaining about them did us no good.

To help your child settle into their new life you can find familiar places and items from diverse sources. As you find these sources, before and after the move, note them overleaf.

Resources

Print Resources
Footsteps Around the World: Relocation Tips for Teens, by Beverly D. Roman, BR Anchor, ISBN 188889119.

Let's Move Overseas: The International Edition of Let's Make A Move!, by Beverly D. Roman, published by BR Anchor.

Missionary Children: Caught Between Cultures, by Dr Doris L. Walters, self-published, ISBN 0-533-08960-3.

Moving Your Family Overseas, by Rosalind Kalb and Penelope Welch, Intercultural Press, ISBN 1-877864-14-5.

We Are Moving, Victoria House Publishing, ISBN 1-85724-242-2.

Where in the World Are you Going?, by Judith M. Blohm, Overseas Briefing Center US Dept. of State, ISBN 1-877864-44-7.

Online Resources
www.travelwithyourkids.com: advice and suggestions on travelling with children from longtime expat, Peter van Buren.

Counselling
Just Mediation Services: Diorama Arts, 34 Osnaburgh Street, London NW1 3ND, England; tel ++44 (0)20-7916 7917; info.please@justmediation; www.justmediation.com. Provide counselling and mediation services for personal and business relationships, especially those with an international aspect. JMS principals are qualified in law, medicine, psychotherapy, mediation, stress management and relocation counselling.

Information Sources for Children

Children's resources	Local source	Alternative provider
Video store	1. 2. 3.	1. Online video supplier 2. Embassy social club 3. British Council Library 4. 5.
Cinema (with English soundtrack or subtitles)	1 2. 3.	1 2 3.
Theatre	1. 2. 3.	1. 2. 3.
Swimming pool	1. 2. 3.	1. 2. 3.
Bookshops	1. 2. 3.	1. 2. 3.
Clothes shops	1. 2. 3.	1. 2. 3.
Shoe shops	1. 2. 3.	1. 2. 3.
Toy shops	1. 2. 3.	1. 2. 3.
Children friendly activity centres	1. 2. 3.	1. 2. 3.
Favourite restaurants	1. 2. 3.	1. 2. 3.
Favourite food/drink	1. 2. 3.	1. 2. 3.
Social clubs	1. 2. 3.	1. 2. 3.
Sports teams	1. 2. 3.	1. 2. 3.
Sports facilities	1. 2. 3.	1. 2. 3.
Magazines	1. 2. 3.	1. 2. 3.

FROM PACKING TO UNPACKING

The basic logistics of moving overseas are not much different from moving across town.

If you only have a few possessions to move, you can pack your bags, pile them into your transport and move to your new home and hope you do not lose anything on the way.

If you have a lot of belongings you want to take with you, a removal company can come to your current home, pack your belongings, transport them to your new home and then unpack them for you. No matter how far the distance, you hope the company will arrange everything smoothly, transport your belongings without damage and deliver the shipment to your new home soon after your arrival.

However, if you are unlucky, or plan badly, you can experience a nightmare. The removal company may turn up a day late, on the morning the new occupants are supposed to move in to your home. The workmen may leave removing your belongings so late that your relocation flight happens only hours later. The company may also put your belongings in a warehouse and forget to ship them for three months, or they may neglect to tell you that you have to pay a customs bond in the destination country, before you can collect the shipment from a bonded warehouse. Finally, the company that is supposed to deliver your belongings to your new home may tell you that they have not been paid by the original shipper, who you paid, up-front, for door-to-door service.

The above difficulties can and do happen, causing stress, adding cost and spoiling what should be an exciting arrival in your new home. However, there are ways to help make the shipping go more smoothly.

Deciding What You Want to Take

Apart from how to pack and which way to get your belongings to your destination, there is also the decision-making process regarding what to take.

When moving overseas for the first time there can be a temptation to take only the necessities, as you would for your summer vacation. But it is important to remember that you are going to live overseas and not just be on holiday. Your new accommodation will be your new home for an extended period of time, not just somewhere to sleep for a few weeks.

When you have settled into your new home overseas, much of your daily life will be the same as it is already. You will go to work, go food shopping and invite friends and colleagues to your home. A non-employed partner may spend long periods of time alone at home and if you have children they will need to have things to keep them busy when they are not at school. Creating a real home where you can relax, feel safe and look forward to returning to at the end of a long day, will go a long way towards helping you enjoy and succeed in your new overseas lifestyle and international career.

Seonaid Francis, who has lived abroad for over ten years, believes that home is where your family is, and where it is happy. Everything else is just an added advantage, but pets, books, photos, and mementos of places etc. are good to take with you to make settling in easier. She firmly believes that home is not a place, it is an attitude.

Everyone's idea of how to create the attitude that the accommodation is your home will be different, but can you define what makes your current building a home?

Jeri Hurd believes that it is important to make yourself a small nest and build yourself an emotional home away from your historical home to give you a place to be yourself, without worry or stress from the culture around you.

Julie Lane, who has lived in the UK, Germany, Nigeria and Turkey believes that having your own house/flat is important, as well as having your belongings, e.g. pictures, toys, kitchen stuff — so that life is normal and not like camping out.

Lori Mickle takes a more philosophical approach:

The concerns of what to take and leave behind for me, at least, were addressing the bigger issues. It's trying to take enough familiar items with you that you feel secure, can stand up for your identity and can have some comfort out of things or food that are familiar. At the same time, even if you set costs of shipping aside, you don't want to show up being the gluttonous American with no desire to even venture out of your own safety zone.

Barbara Schaetti, Principal of *Transition Dynamics*, an intercultural consultancy based in the US specialising in expatriate family services, believes one of the important elements of moving is continuity. With respect to families she says:

Continuity is a psychological necessity for those living a discontinuous life. This is especially true of the multi-mover family who relocates to a new posting every two or three years. It is also true of the first-time mover. Constants are psychological necessities for those living a discontinuous lifestyle. (Families On The Move: Working Together to Meet the Challenge).

If you do have a relocation allowance, use it to its maximum. Move as much as you can (or want to) from one country to the next despite the nuisance and the risk of breakage or loss, or having to pay some of the cost yourself. Families continually report that familiar furniture and personal items contribute greatly to the making of a home.

For children, belongings and family are often the only continuity in their mobile lives.

Barabara also said in her article mentioned above:

Encourage all family members to identify their 'sacred object', those few items which remind them of home, family and friendship wherever they are. Take those with you on the plane instead of shipping them with the rest of the household goods. Having the family's 'portable roots' with you when you first arrive in your new posting can ease the chaos of transition.

There are a number of short questionnaires below to help you define your personal idea of home. Involving all members of your family in the process will help them feel like they are an integral part of the move. By involving your children they can be reassured that their needs and concerns are being considered, and their own possessions are important enough to come along too. This can reduce the direct and indirect opposition that the children may feel to your move.

Now look at your belongings, furnishings and keepsakes, and note the items you want and need to take with you in the table below. When you have finished compiling the list, go through it again and prioritise the items on a must have basis (1 = must have; 5 = want but do not need) to help you with your packing.

Different people have different needs. Some lists may overflow the tables above, others may leave them bare. Do not expect these charts to be filled out completely the first time you work on them; it can be difficult to sit and think about what you will need in the course of your time abroad. Some items you may be able to cross off later when you learn from your international contacts what you can get at your destination, others will have to be added if you learn they are unobtainable.

What Makes Your Current Home?

What makes you smile or feel happy? 1. 2. 3.
What is it that makes you feel comfortable in your home? 1. 2. 3.
What is it that allows you to relax in your home? 1. 2. 3.
What do you like to do when you are at home in the evening? 1. 2. 3.
What do you like to do when you are at home at the weekend? 1. 2. 3.
What is your favourite picture(s)? 1. 2. 3.
When you are sad or depressed what comfort item (e.g. book, video, cuddly toy) do you reach for? 1. 2. 3.
Can you sit in any chair, or do you need a special one?
Can you sleep in any bed, or do you need a special mattress?
What items do you use everyday? 1. 2. 3.
What items do you use regularly? 1. 2. 3.
What books and videos do you look at regularly? 1. 2. 3.
What cook books do you use that do not rely on packaged sauces or ingredients? (You may only be able to find raw ingredients at your destination.) 1. 2. 3.

What Will Your New Home Be Like?

Will your accommodation be a hotel room, apartment, or house?
Will you have storage space at the destination? How much?
Will there be a secure outside play area for your children and/or a storage area for their toys?
Will the accommodation be furnished, partly furnished, or unfurnished?
What are the local definitions of furnished and partly furnished, and what items are likely to be supplied? 1.   4. 2.   5. 3.   6.
How large will the accommodation be? (Is it bigger or smaller than where you are now?)
What local products will you be able to buy at the destination? Carpets, curtains, furniture, artwork, etc. and will you want to? 1.   4. 2.   5. 3.   6.

As people start making second, third and more international moves their ideas of what to take develop. For example, Doug and Donna Young with their four children are seasoned independent expats. They have gone through a growth process in deciding what to take with them when they move. They have moved five times so far and have this to say about how they now decide on what to take with them:

Anything related to cooking or entertainment is important to us, so those things always come with us. Depending on the distance of the moves and the expat package at the other end, we were able to determine what we brought with us. In Belgium, we basically brought nothing except clothing and a few pots and pans which was a big mistake. We needed much more. As it turned out, we ended up buying everything at IKEA and even then we were definitely camping out for the year.

In Hong Kong, we knew for sure that the flats were furnished. But even so, we brought much more with us, e.g. all the kids' toys, kitchen utensils — including dishes, cook books, bedding, a lot of teaching materials — but not many

What Do You Want To Take With You?

Favourite Item			Priority
Favourite books 1. 2. 3.			
Favourite videos 1. 2. 3.			
Favourite games and sports equipment 1. 2. 3.			
Essential items of furniture and linens 1. 2. 3.			
Essential leisure/playtime items 1. 2. 3.			
Frequently-used utensils (cooking, sewing, toolbox, etc.) 1. 2. 3.			
Frequently-worn clothes 1. 2. 3.			
Formal-wear clothes (for all seasons and over-air-conditioned rooms) 1. 2. 3.			
Other essential items 1. 2. 3.			

electrical appliances. Keeping in mind the size of the Hong Kong flats, we did keep things on a small scale. We didn't bring any big, bulky items, other than the bed quilts. Everything was brought over in 12 big cardboard boxes as part of our luggage allowance on the airplane.

The move to the UAE was on a much bigger scale as we had accumulated a lot of junk (valuable possessions to us!). We had excellent movers who coped beautifully at both ends and absolutely nothing was damaged in transit. We were getting a substantial furniture allowance here, so any furniture items we'd bought in HK were sold. We'd picked up a few Hong Kong souvenirs that came with us and even more dishes, cookbooks, small electrical appliances and a few Chinese pictures for the wall.

Al Ain to Dubai was the major move as everything we owned in this part of the world came with us. We moved it ourselves with help from some hired workers and our friend who works with a big company who supplied us with the truck.

What Can and Should You Take?

Once you have decided what you want to take, you need to determine if you can, or should, take it. Bureaucratic, climatic, cultural, political and religious reasons may preclude or prescribe what can be imported, or used, in different countries.

Research about your destination is important when deciding what to take, Donna Young made the mistake of thinking Hong Kong was always hot. 'We actually did not anticipate just how cold Hong Kong was in the winter and ended up having to buy some jackets when that cold wind arrived.'

Importing items that are banned, or incorrectly importing restricted items, can get you and your employer in serious trouble. Your shipment may be delayed, or you may be fined, forbidden entry, or jailed and the items concerned may be confiscated too. Many countries restrict the import of organic material, especially plants. Some countries have banned the importation of alcohol. Firearms are illegal in others. Many just have bureaucratic rules that are best found out about before you ship your belongings. One expat resident in Saudi Arabia reports:

The guidelines about importing sensitive material into Saudi Arabia are not clearly stated in an English translation. Many travel/business books comment on the topic but these comments are based more upon personal experiences rather than official information. It can be said that in general the systematic search of each piece of baggage that was quite common four years ago is becoming rare, especially for the western traveller and that occurrences of confiscation and/or more serious consequences are not increasing. Nevertheless, travellers to the Kingdom are advised to discreetly pack any items that make reference to a religion other than Islam, fitness books or magazines depicting women in exercise clothing and video tapes, especially those that are 'home-made' copies. These items may be inspected and withheld until customs officers view them or 'cleanse' them with a black marker. You may be given a receipt that you must use to collect the items at a later date or with serious infractions, the item will simply be confiscated.

One new development reveals an increased understanding of modern technology on the part of customs officials. Recently, travellers have had difficulty importing CD's because of the rise of recordable discs that can store data and music. As well, 'enhanced' music CD's incorporate video clips that may be deemed unsuitable in the Kingdom. The message, I believe, is to become more creative in packing questionable items in your suitcases.

But open countries can also have awkward import regulations as Lori Mickle remembers from her move to France.

We had to decide what was to be stored, shipped by air, and surface shipped (along with what was to be trashed, given to family, and given to charity). Our relocation people didn't spell out how customs works. In France, they very rarely open a surface shipment but air shipments are gone through with a fine-toothed comb. I blew it by shipping a computer via air. It was hung up in customs for weeks while we supplied copies of receipts proving we had owned it a while and it was actually a personal piece of equipment. It ended up arriving about the same time as the surface shipment. You might want to ask your shipper directly if any similar things might go on with getting your stuff through the red tape. Some destinations are also notorious for containers that arrive empty or looted. You might want to check into that too.

Information Regarding International Shipments

Source	Answer received?
The local Embassy/Consul of the destination country.	
Your own country's Embassy in the destination country.	
Your own country's Foreign Ministry.	
Shipping Agencies where you are now.	
Shipping Agencies at the destination.	
Colleagues/friends already in the destination country.	
Chambers of Commerce.	

Mike van der Es and his wife Sarah, working for a non-profit organisation, had an unfortunate experience on a move to Kenya in 1989.

Yes, we lost about a quarter of our clothes on arrival in Kenya. It was a quaint but irritating story. My wife had purchased clothes for the next 18 months for our children of toddler age as they were cheaper and better in Ecuador than in Kenya, where we were going.

When our shipment arrived at the end of our first week in Kenya I met it at the airport to sign off. The removal company then took all the boxes up from Nairobi to Meru, our home to be, a ride of four hours in a lorry. When we arrived we were asked to sign for the full number of 56 boxes and the staff were in a hurry to go. Some of the boxes seemed emptier than when we left, but it is hard to remember what the boxes looked like and we assumed that things had settled in the box (it is hard to see what is not there). Only the next morning, when we had opened all the boxes, were we sure what had happened. The removals guys had opened all the boxes in the lorry, taken out the good stuff and put the rest back, then neatly taped down each box again with their packing tape machine.

When we complained, their boss said it must have gone missing while we were in Ecuador (impossible because of the locked container). The insurance company did not pay out more than a third of the value because we had no receipts for the clothes (the last thing you expect to keep, sort and take in hand-baggage) or photos of the gear. Sarah was furious and a bit depressed as she had gone to so much trouble.

Always check the current rules and practices of the country you are going to and remember that rules change continually. Always ask as many sources as you can for the information and check each against the other for variations.

Questions To Ask at the Different Offices

What items are banned?
1.
2.
3.
What items are restricted?
1.
2.
3.
What are the restrictions/penalties for bringing in such items?
1.
2.
3.
What is the cost and process for importing restricted items?
1.
2.
3.

Bureaucracy

Even if you are allowed to take the items you want, it may not be a simple process to do so. There may be customs duties to be paid, on some or all personal belongings. These charges can vary on whether the items arrive with the owner, by air, or by surface shipment. Sometimes there may be a customs bond instead, which is returned when the items leave the country. Bill Jordan, an American teacher who has lived in the Philippines, Norway and Turkey and maintains a website for international teachers (www.wwteach.com), advises being prepared for extraneous charges like:

...bribes or fixes such as in the Philippines. There may be a large bond to pay such as in Turkey. We had to put up a $1,000 US bond plus fees upon coming to Turkey with our shipment. We have also had trouble with shippers that include extra charges. This has happened every time we have moved. It has varied from $100 to US$500, the worse being an air freight charge of US$500 with our shipment to Norway. We were under the weight allowance but exceeded the volume allowance by 11 cubic feet. We were unaware of the volume allowance and were charged for an extra container. We were informed of this after arriving in Norway and were given the choice to pay the extra or to make arrangements for storage and pick up of the items we did not want shipped. I have now come to expect that extra fees will be charged to me whenever I ship things. I also try to get very specific contracts in writing to minimise or eliminate these charges.

The main sources for information on the bureaucracy of the destination country are the same as those listed earlier, but the best sources are definitely other non-nationals who have recently imported personal belongings, or shipping agents who have done so.

What Bureaucratic Procedures Are Involved With Your Shipment?

What items will have customs duties or bonds imposed? 1 2. 3.
Is the duty/bond the same for each item? If not, what are the different rates? 1. 2. 3.
If the duties/bonds are percentages, how are they calculated? (Percentage of declared value, percentage of estimated value, etc.) 1. 2. 3.
When is the duty paid? Before, or after delivery?
Who completes the paperwork? Can an agent be designated to sign all paperwork?
How much does the paperwork cost?
Is all paperwork included in the shipping fee?
Does the paperwork ever have to be renewed? (e.g. annually, or at the same time as work permits or residence permits)

Will the Items be Usable at the Destination?

Electrical Items

Different countries use different electrical voltages; some use 110V and others use 220/240V. Voltage converters can be used, but where the local electricity supply is unreliable or unstable, equipment run on voltage converters seems more likely to suffer critical damage than equipment that is properly rated. It is possible to have equipment re-rated for use with different electrical voltage, but it can be more cost effective to buy new electrical items locally and sell them when you leave. Bill Jordan warns too:

Do not ship many electronics even if the voltage is similar. You can still have problems with other factors such as plugs and current frequency. Our 220-volt microwave from the Philippines blew up in Norway that also uses 220 volts but on a different hertz rating (50 versus 60hz).

Different countries use different video formats. North America uses the NTSC format, while the UK uses PAL and France uses a third format. Multi-system video machines offer the best solution to varying formats and allow you to watch local videos, videos from home and the videos of expatriate friends from around the world.

Getting expert advice before moving does not always prove to be the help it appears. One expat who moved from the US to France was not given the complete picture. 'We made the mistake of going through *Appliances Overseas* to get a TV & VCR only to find out that multi-format machines were available here (France) at about the same cost and could receive a TV signal (we got really bad advice and ended up buying a French VCR anyway).' Though she does admit that, 'Dealing with a firm like that for transformers and adapters would be a good idea'.

Clothes

Check out the weather, cultural/religious attitudes, social activities and the popular holiday areas of your destination country before you pack your clothes. What style of clothes you wear can also be an important factor in determining how comfortable you are in the host country.

Countries, cities and even districts within cities vary greatly in their tolerance of foreign dress styles. Social and professional dress codes are very rigid in some countries or professions, whilst non-existent in others. Different climates also demand different clothes, materials and dress-styles. Blending the requirements of culture, profession and climate can sometimes be difficult for new residents.

Donna Young experienced differences within the United Arab Emirates (UAE), before moving to the conservative city of Al Ain.

I pitched all the short skirts, but kept all the sleeveless dresses as they were quite wearable as long as I had a short sleeved jacket covering my shoulders. I seldom wore shorts unless I was going to a function where I likely would not encounter any locals. There was no change for the boys or Doug (my husband) though there are few occasions where a suit is mandatory in the UAE, likely due to the heat and to the varied style of dress throughout the country. Locals wear dishdashas, Pakistanis wear the trouser/tunic combination and Indians also have their own local dress. So, a suit is no longer the norm for being appropriately dressed.

Whereas in nearby Dubai,

Pretty well anything goes in Dubai, though to maintain my own level of comfort I dress with a certain mode of decorum. If you go out in a tiny top and shorts you have to expect to be stared at rather intensely by the male workers who haven't seen their wives in two or three years.

Take advice from expatriates who have lived and worked not only in the destination country, but also in the area where you will be living; local knowledge is very important. Women often need to be especially careful in how they dress, as the status and expectations for women vary much more than they do for men.

Though you need to consider how you dress outside the home, remember to pack your most comfortable and favourite clothes for when you are relaxing at home. However, you also need to consider more than the country you are going to be living in. You will undoubtedly be travelling for work and pleasure whilst you are away, so pack for those destinations too.

Medication

Much of the medicine you are likely to require is often readily available around the world and what would be prescription-only medicines in some countries are available over the counter in others. What can be difficult though, is trying to identify what the medicine on the shelf really is.

Lori Mickle advises taking essential supplies with you for one very good reason:

Depending on where you move makes a difference to what you take. For us, just about everything we could need is available, but reading the labels is tough. We moved to France and while they'll label most things in multiple languages, English isn't usually one of them. I would suggest buying a supply of over the counter medications that you use in the course of a year (to take with you). That way when you need them, they'll be on your shelf and you can make it easier learning to read those labels (on local medicines). I have been thankful for having Nyquil, kids Tylenol, and that sort of stuff.

Though she does add, 'It's weird as to what is easy to find and what is not'.

How to Get it There

Depending on how much you decide to move to your new home, you have a number of options on how to transport everything.

1. International Postal Service.
2. Airline luggage.
3. Air courier (unaccompanied luggage) using an agent based at the airport departure terminal.
4. Air cargo using an international shipping agency.
5. Surface cargo using an international shipping agency.

How Much Are You Taking and When Does It Need To Be There?

How will you travel to your destination (air, surface, or sea)?
How long do you intend to stay there?
How many of your personal possessions will you take?
Will you need more than a few suitcases?
Approximately how much will your shipment weigh? (20kg, 100kg, more than 100kg.)
Can you carry your shipment yourself, or will you need a car, a van or a transport truck?
How much of the expense will your employer cover and how much extra can you afford to spend?
How long prior to your departure can you send the shipment?
How quickly after you arrive must you receive the shipment? (for either personal reasons or customs regulations at the destination country or port of entry)
How long will the shipment take to reach your accommodation (which, at times, can be much longer than reaching the country)?

Postal Service

If you send items by regular mail you have two basic options:

1. Surface Mail.
2. Air Mail.

Within these two options, you have further options, whose availability and reliability depend as much on the destination country as to where you send the package from. Registered, insured, priority post/speedpost, first class and second class are some of the options that various national mail systems offer. Registering and insuring your mail usually improves the chances of the package arriving undamaged, though the added cost can mean that potential savings over other methods of shipment are reduced.

Sending bulky, but lightweight, items by post can be a cheap option, especially for surface post. If you get the timing right you can send a parcel on ahead of yourself and collect it when you arrive at your destination. In many large cities the main post offices also have *Poste Restante* facilities (where mail will be held for a limited time until you arrive at the post office to collect it), which can be good if you do not have an address you can send the package to directly. However, surface mail can be slow, taking up to six months to reach some parts of the world, and can be very unreliable.

Ask at major Post Offices for details and rates of the various options, though a Post Office in one country is unlikely to be able to competently vouch for the services at the other end. If you can contact someone at the destination in advance who might know about the postal services on the receiving end, this may help in making your decision whether it is cost effective or even safe to send your things through the post.

Airline Luggage (Accompanied)

Most airlines allow Economy Class passengers 20kg of checked in luggage and 5kg of carry-on luggage per person. Business Class and First Class passengers are often allowed 30kg of checked in luggage and 10kg of carry-on luggage per person. Some airlines enforce shape and size restrictions as well as weight limits and the number of pieces allowed per person. Adult and child tickets have associated luggage allowance, but infant tickets generally have no associated luggage allowance and the extra cost of buying a child ticket can be worth it for the additional luggage allowance (rather than paying excess baggage or reducing the amount you take with you).

However, different airlines have different allowances, and some airlines vary the luggage allowances between domestic and international flights and even between long-haul and short-haul international flights. It is therefore important to check the luggage allowances of all the flights in your journey, especially if you will be connecting between a domestic flight and an international flight, or changing airlines, anywhere during your route. Problems are especially likely to occur if you have to collect your bags somewhere en route and check them in for a second time.

One baby carrier, per child, will usually be allowed free of charge, in excess of the standard allowance for all class of passengers. The carrier will be tagged at the check-in desk and you can often keep it until you reach the aircraft. An airline employee will then take the carrier and usually put it in the cargo hold, though sometimes the carrier may stay in the cabin, especially if the flight is sparsely booked. The baby-carrier will be returned to you at your destination. Sometimes you may be allowed to use the carrier at transit stops.

Baggage limits and allowances do vary between airlines and can be flexible, but the amount of flexibility can depend on the individual airline employee, the number of passengers on any particular flight, the airline in question and the destination. If an airline does charge for excess weight, the fees can be large, especially on long-haul flights. Airlines also reserve the right to refuse excessively heavy, very large, or unusually shaped items. In addition, they sometimes insist that the excess payment be made in cash and do not necessarily accept credit card payment.

Excess baggage fees can be expensive (though they do vary between airlines and routes) and should be checked in advance if you are worried about the charges. One airline charges, '1% of a one-way C class (First Class) fare on the route flown, for every extra kilogram.'

Excess Baggage (Unaccompanied)

At some international airports there are companies who will arrange for your excess baggage to be flown to your destination, on a different flight. This can be a cheaper method of getting it to your destination than paying an airline directly for the luggage to accompany you on your flight. However, it is always best to determine in advance if your luggage can be sent to your destination, the rates applicable and the opening hours of the offices. Most excess baggage couriers impose 'handling charges' or 'per item charges', in addition to charging a 'per kilo' rate and this can make an 'Air Cargo' shipment cheaper. As unaccompanied luggage will be assigned to a shipping agent, or cargo department, at the destination airport, there may be additional charges if you want it delivered to your home. What is more likely is that you will be required to return to the airport to collect it yourself. Unaccompanied luggage can take up to a week to arrive.

Bronwyn Davies in Hong Kong found she had to transport her shipment to the airport, which was hard work, plus it was expensive.

Though Doug and Donna Young had the reverse experience when they moved from Canada to Hong Kong with their four children, they sent everything in 12 large cardboard boxes. They paid the fee, picked up the stuff from the airport when it arrived (undamaged) and had their things organised in their flat within the first three days of arriving. Travelling with four kids it was important for them to have a few essential things for every member of the family, but with six lists of essential things, they discovered they would need many boxes. For them, it was the perfect decision.

It is very much a personal decision whether the inconvenience of returning to the airport to collect the baggage outweighs the need to have, quickly, what is inside the baggage, and how the costs for unaccompanied baggage weigh against shipping costs. Do your research.

Air Cargo

The cost of an air cargo shipment is primarily calculated by weight. The rates are usually lower than they are for airline excess baggage. Small air cargo shipments can be cheaper than surface cargo shipments, which can specify larger, minimum volume shipments.

Most international shipping companies will arrange air cargo shipments, but it can sometimes be cheaper, though more complicated, to deal direct with the cargo department of an airline flying to the required destination.

Shipping companies usually provide packing, collection and delivery services if needed. When dealing directly with an airline cargo department you may have to arrange the packing and the delivery of the shipment to, and collection of it from the cargo terminals yourself. If lucky, you may only have to co-ordinate the delivery of the item directly to your home.

Bronwyn has also sent a number of items by Air Cargo and found it much better than sending a shipment as unaccompanied luggage.

Airfreight is cheaper than unaccompanied baggage — in my case less than one-third the price. The freight guys were amazing — took delivery of a large number of disparate items from several different merchants, packed them all and transported them without incident. Would even have arranged collection of the items if I'd wanted them to. They gave me the option of having their own agent do the collection and deliver to the door here (i.e. through customs etc) at my end. The last shipment was over one metric ton (1000kg), so I let them do all the hard work and was amazed at how cheap it was to get them to deliver. A couple of other times, I have done it myself and, although a bit time consuming, it is actually very straightforward.

Surface Cargo

For very bulky and/or heavy shipments, land and sea shipments are usually the most cost-effective method of transportation. Surface shipments are generally charged by volume, though a maximum weight may be specified.

However, surface shipments will be much slower than air cargo, sometimes taking weeks or months, depending on how far away you are from your destination and how often boats or transport trucks leave for your destination. If a sea shipment is necessary, but your final destination is not on the coast (thereby necessitating transhipment to surface transport), the time scale can be extended further and add a significant cost element too.

When co-author Michelyne Callan and her family moved their apartment full of belongings from Hong Kong to Turkey, they were told that the process would take longer than usual because ships did not frequently travel between Hong Kong and Turkey. This meant that their belongings sat on the docks in Hong Kong for a lot longer than was good for some parts of the shipment (e.g. electronic goods). In addition, because their destination city was not a port city, the shipment took some time to reach Ankara after it had arrived in Turkey. It took almost four months for the shipment to reach their new home.

International shipping companies often specify a minimum volume for less popular destinations of approximately 10 cubic metres and maximum weight (depending on local regulations) for surface shipments. The shipper will usually be constrained by having to send one complete container (by boat), or long distance transport (by land) no matter how much is shipped; though sea containers and transport trucks do come in different sizes.

How small the minimum shipment allowed by the shipper will be is dependent on how often they send containers to your destination, and how likely they will be able to 'consolidate' your small shipment with one or more other shipments that do not fill a complete container. Handling, customs and transhipment fees are usually fixed per shipment and may therefore be the same for the standard volumes of 'half-size' and 'full-size' sea containers.

The cost of cargo shipments can be made up of any or all of the following:

1. Terminal handling fees (paperwork at the port).
2. Customs/port fees (inspections and import authorisations at the point of import and export).
3. Transhipment fees (moving the container on/off ships and lorries along the route).
4. Shipping fees (the cost of the transportation on the ship or lorry).

Door-to-door services should mean that the shipping agent arranges for the packing of your belongings and delivery of them to your new home, where they will be unpacked. However, be sure to read the small print and ask what charges are specifically excluded from the invoice and what other charges you will have to cover. Insurance rates across shipping agents are generally similar and charged at a percentage of the insured/declared value of a shipment. 'All risks insurance' is the standard cover offered by reputable agents, though it is worth asking if the insurance company has an office or agent in the destination country. Valuables such as antiques, jewellery and special artefacts may have larger insurance premiums and the number of special items per shipment may be limited. Be sure to enquire about their coverage as 'valuable items' before choosing the shipper.

Picking a Shipping Agent

Choosing an agent you can trust with your precious belongings, whether they have financial or sentimental value, can be tough.

Though the horror stories recounted above are worrying, bear in mind that many more people have successfully shipped their belongings halfway round the world to many disparate destinations. Mike van der Es reports, 'I only lost stuff once in six moves. Even then it was only about a quarter of what we shipped — clothes mainly.'

One international removals agency suggests that the best way to find a removal agent in a country where you do not recognise any of the companies is to contact a company in your home country (or any company you are familiar with) and ask them to arrange one via their local agent. If a large and established international company arranges it you are likely to receive a better service because the local agent will not want to upset its overseas contact. Some companies, such as *Transeuro Worldwide Movers* (www.transeuro.com), have a section of their company (*Avalon* in the case of Transeuro) that works especially with independent expatriates to facilitate this process.

To further protect himself and his belongings when making a move, Mike van der Es, of *PLAN International*, a child-focussed international charity, has developed a checklist over the years.

1. Use a big, reliable insurance company with representation where you are and where you are going if possible.
2. Take photos of the things you are freighting and taking in hand baggage before you pack.
3. Keep lists of what you are taking, outside the freight itself - your inventory should be itemised.
4. Take your most valuable stuff like jewellery in your hand luggage.
5. If in any doubt put your own loyal person on the truck from the moment of receipt of the goods (I did that in my next country after Kenya).

And if something is lost, stolen or damaged Mike suggests, 'Focus on the people in your family and do not breakdown if someone steals a few of your replaceable possessions. Their need is probably much greater than ours'.

To provide a reliable estimate of the cost of a shipment the agent should come to your home to look at what is to be sent. They should examine what you want sent to determine what is valuable, what is hard to pack and what is fragile. If you can, make a list of items to mention to them when they come.

If your shipment is not complicated, the shipping agent should be able to sit down for five quiet minutes, with a calculator, and come up with a rough estimate. If not, then it should not take more than a day for an estimate to be reached.

Before the shippers arrive to calculate your estimate, try to separate what you will be taking and what you will not be taking. You do not want them to include the items you will be selling in a garage sale, putting away in storage or just throwing out. If you cannot separate the items, clearly point out what you want to go, a bright coloured piece of paper tacked to items might help them see what is going and what is not.

On his website (www.travelwithyourkids.com) Peter van Buren, a seasoned expat who has travelled extensively, with and without his family, makes a helpful suggestion for when you have received the estimate. He says that some companies actually do not include the cost of the packing materials in the estimate of the cost to ship your stuff. To be on the safe side, ask the agent if the cost he has quoted you includes all of the packing materials. Sometimes the weight of the packing materials/crates is figured into the weight of your shipment, and sometimes it is not. Find out in advance of agreeing to use their services.

Peter van Buren also warns on his website that, when picking a shipper be wary of one that does not have up to date information on the regulations for the country the shipment is going to. If they have to look it up and get back to you at a later date, it might mean they are not up to the job. In addition, if they have to subcontract it out to another company you might want to take this as a hint to talk to someone else. He suggests that you find an established company, since a new company may be using your shipment to learn from and you most definitely do not want a company to consider your consignment to be a practice run. He also points out one other thing to watch out for is multiple links in the shipping line. For example, avoid a shipping company that uses one contractor to pack and another to move it to port, while yet another to actually move it internationally.

Peter van Buren also mentions that you have the option to find a shipper that allows you to pack yourself; the acronym for this is PBO (packed by owner). If you want this option, because it is cheaper than having the company do it for you when you are paying the bill, then look for the small print on the shipping contract to check whether there will be insurance cover for a PBO shipment.

Is the Shipping Agent Reputable?

Is the point of origin agent a member of the International Federation of Removal Companies?
Is the destination agent a member of the International Federation of Removal Companies?
What international companies use this agent to move their personnel? 1. 2.
What do the international companies say about the quality of service of this shipping agency? 1. 2.
Does the local agent at your destination have a good reputation? (Ask expatriates already there.)
Has the agent ever sent a shipment to the destination before? How many? When/how frequently?
Does the agent have experience with personal shipments (not commercial ones)? How many non-commercial/smaller shipments do they ship every year? 1. 2.

Inclusions, Exclusions and Restrictions

Item	Included/excluded/restricted
Customs fees	
Port fees	
Delivery charges	
Restriction on which floor the delivering company will carry items to if there is no service elevator	

The Packing

When the time arrives for a shipper to pack your belongings there are still a few things that you can do to smooth the process.

Make sure you are there to supervise the process, to ensure the packing is done carefully and the correct items are packed. This also means that when your shipment arrives at your destination, you will have some idea of what is packed with what, so that you can know which boxes to unpack first.

If you have a few precious things that you want to pack, do it in a small box, and then have the packers pack them into a larger box. You might be able to get around the PBO label that way, and therefore the items will be included on the insurance list.

If you are taking any electrical equipment in your shipment, write down the serial number and make of the equipment and keep it in a safe place with the shipping contract and carry the list with you as carry-on luggage when you travel. Some countries that impose bonds on electrical equipment require the serial number for inspection when the shipment arrives and will not let the shipment be opened for someone to read them. If you do not have them you may end up paying stiff fines/bribes, before they will release your shipment.

Shipping Pets

You can often take your pet with you when you move abroad, especially cats and dogs. For many people their pet is part of the family. Children especially, will miss a pet terribly if they have to leave it behind. Before ruling out the possibility of taking your pet with you, investigate how cumbersome, or not, the paperwork would be. Many expats have said in the past that they are happy to have gone through the paperwork and medical procedures to bring 'a member of their family' overseas with them.

Chris Chew, Manager of *Jet Pets* in Hong Kong says that almost any animal can be shipped as long as they are not protected wild animals. Though you should check with the local Agriculture and Fisheries Department and the Customs Office of the importing country to find out whether your pet is an exotic pet, or whether it is on an endangered species list of that country.

You should also check what the scientific name of your animal is so that you can relay this name to the Agriculture & Fisheries department when checking on the status of your animal.

Shipping your pet overseas with you can have a number of advantages:

1. Your pet may be happier staying with you than being given away.
2. Your family will be happier and settle quicker in their new home (especially children) if the family pet is with you.
3. Dog walking is a good way to make friends and meet people in your new country, and birds make great conversation pieces with new neighbours.

Though cats and dogs are the most common pets to be transported around the world, some people take parrots and even horses. The paperwork can be relatively simple, if time-consuming, and your pet may be able to travel with you on the same aircraft.

Meridith Goldsmith, a university lecturer who took her parrot from the US to Turkey and then back again, initially encountered bureaucratic difficulties, but in the end found it was all very easy. There was a lot of paperwork, but it was do-able.

Most countries usually have very strict, but not necessarily onerous, rules you must comply with to import an animal, yet every country seems to be different. Chris Chew has found, that there is really no consistency, or no formula to measure the degree of difficulties and hassles, but has found that the developing countries are more difficult to deal with than their developed counterparts.

If you know that you will be returning to your home country at some point with your pet, it is important to determine the re-import rules before you leave; the rules may be stricter for bringing the pet back to the country than taking it out in the first place. For some animals or birds you may also have to prove that you are returning the animal to the country, not importing it for the first time.

Examples of Strict Rules for Animal Importation

1. Some parrots are on the endangered species list and so can only be returned to the point of origin, and not imported.
2. The UK imposes quarantine laws that apply to animals returning or entering for a first time from countries outside of Europe.
3. Many island countries impose quarantine on animals entering the country (e.g. Australia).

Chris Chew says that the basic rules are generally similar whichever country you are shipping an animal to, and in general you need the following documentation:

1. A health certificate endorsed by the appropriate government official (normally, the government vet in the Agriculture and Fisheries Department) is a must.

2. Import permits if required by the importing countries and vaccination records, especially the most recent ones, which usually includes all the important details of rabies inoculation and the multiple vaccinations such as SHLPP for dogs or FVRCP for cats.

Quarantine requirements vary from country to country, but in general all rabies-free countries require imported live animals from rabies-infected countries to be quarantined. However, some rabies-infected countries also require quarantine as well.

An Embassy of the country you are going to should be able to tell you the regulations for importing an animal, but be sure to tell the staff which country the animal will be relocating from, or where the animal's vaccination certificate/travel documents were issued from if different. Some countries have different rules depending on the origin of the animal; these variations are usually determined by whether the country is designated as rabies-free.

Once you know that it is possible to take your pet with you, you need to check what vaccinations are required and when they should be administered relative to the date of travel. Some vaccinations need to be done more than 30 days before travel and some need to be done within a few days of the date of departure.

If your pet is accompanying you overland you also need to ensure that your animal meets the entry requirements for all the countries you pass through on the way.

When sending your animal by air it can either go on its own as cargo, or travel with you on the same flight.

Some boarding kennels and veterinarians operate animal shipping services and can be a good source of advice on the best way for your animal to travel. Stacey Tucker of *Ferndale Kennels and Cattery* in Hong Kong advises, however, that all kennels do not necessarily help you to relocate animals.

Stacey says that pet relocation services should be able to do as much or as little as you want them to do. Below are some of the things that a pet relocation service should check on or be able to do for you:

1. Updating immigration regulations as these can tend to change without warning.
2. Advising you on the best way to ship your pet, either excess baggage or manifest cargo.
3. Booking the most direct flight.
4. Applying for import permits when necessary and preparing all the correct documentation.
5. Checking if vaccinations are correct.
6. Arranging veterinary health certificates.
7. Arranging transport for departure day.
8. Arranging agents/kennels if necessary.
9. Advising on kennel size to be used.

The *Independent Pet and Animal Transportation Association International, Inc.,* (IPATA, www.ipata.com) is an international trade association of animal handlers, pet moving providers, kennel operators, veterinarians and others who care for pets and small animals during transport locally, nation-wide and worldwide. Their members follow the rules laid out by the *US Dept. of Agriculture.*

If your accommodation is pre-arranged and will be ready and waiting for you to arrive, then taking your pet with you on the same flight may be more convenient. However, if you will live in a hotel while you find your own accommodation, it may be better to have your pet flown over later, unless you know there are good boarding kennels available, or your hotel accepts pets.

Small animals can often travel in the cabin of an aircraft with you, but larger animals will always have to travel in the hold. In almost all cases, the airline will require you to notify them in advance that you intend to bring an animal with you on the plane; in some cases they will also require you to book and pay for the cargo space in advance too. The earlier you can arrange the 'cabin carry' option of bringing your small pet the better. Many airlines only allow one animal in the cabin per journey.

For flights from the US, the *US Dept of Agriculture (USDA)* regulations, as quoted by *United Airlines* state that if the total weight of pet and kennel exceeds 100 pounds you must ship the animal as cargo (www.unitedairlines.com/au/travel/f_pets.html).

International Air Transport Association (IATA) rules mandate that certain sized animals must travel in certain sized containers that meet strength, ventilation and safety requirements; an escaped and angry dog, loose in the hold of an aircraft, would not be nice for the animal, or the cargo handlers.

The following information on shipping pets via air is taken directly from an IATA article *Introduction to Live Animals Transportation by Air* (www.iata.org/cargo/live.htm). However, despite the regulations IATA point out that ultimate responsibility for the shipment remains with the shipper (pet owner).

Container Requirements

IATA container requirements for animals are based on species needs and animal size. The IATA Live Animals Regulations describe minimum standards for container construction for all animal types ranging from insects to elephants. It is imperative for the safe and humane shipment of an animal that the proper container is used.

Preparation For Air Transport

Before animals commence their journey, it is important that advance arrangements be made and confirmed. The most suitable routing always needs to be selected, as many airports do not have adequate facilities at destination or possible transit stops. Consideration should be given to the day on which the consignment (or consignments) is dispatched and its date of arrival, because some customs authorities and other government agencies do not work during weekends or public holidays. Advance arrangements shall include confirmation that the consignee is aware of the shipping details and has made arrangements to take delivery of the consignment on arrival.

Before the consignment is delivered to the airline, the shipper or his agent must ensure that all import and export licenses, health certificates and permits have been obtained. When these documents are required to go forward with the consignment, they must be securely attached to the air waybill. The shipper is also required to provide the airline with two correctly completed copies of the Shipper's Certification for Live Animals. It is important to note that the Shipper's Certificate also contains a declaration in relation to endangered species. An air waybill must be completed on behalf of the shipper and must clearly show the number and species of animals in the consignment. Pets accompanied by their owners do not require an air waybill and the Shipper's Certificate.

Particular care and attention should be paid when selecting the type of aircraft used in the air transportation of animals, because aircraft specifications for holds and compartments vary considerably, and because some aircraft are not suitable for the carriage of animals. Care should be taken to ensure that animals are not stowed in the vicinity of other animals that may be natural enemies, or other commodities which may cause them harm.

To facilitate the movement of large bulk shipments of domestic farm animals, the airline industry has developed special aircraft pen systems which include additional ventilation. When a bulk-loaded system is used, specially designed walk-on ramps are required.

The ventilation requirements for full aircraft loads of animals must be considered during loading, off-loading or at a transit stop. People loading animals should be aware of the requirements and the action to take when problems arise.

The Captain must always be notified of the quantity, species and location of animals onboard the aircraft.

In the best interest of animal welfare, it is essential that all aspects of the IATA Live Animals Regulations be complied with. Since many countries have incorporated the IATA Regulations into their national legislation, non-compliance may result in possible destruction or confiscation of the animals or in legal action by the authorities.

Tips For Shipping Your Pet

The following is a list of frequently asked questions from pet owners. We hope the information is helpful and will assist you in asking more specific questions when you make reservations and transportation arrangements with the airlines.

Pets, in this instance, will mean dogs and cats. There are other requirements for exotic pets and birds.

Many airlines require a health certificate for any animal they are transporting whether in the cabin or as an unaccompanied shipment.

The questions you must answer before making travel arrangements are:

1. Is your pet going to travel domestically, within your own country, or will it be traveling internationally?
2. When do you want your pet to travel?
3. What is the size and weight of your pet?
4. How many animals will be traveling?
5. Is your pet to be accompanied?
6. Do you intend to break the journey, or stopover at an intermediate station?
7. What is the pet's final destination?
8. Do you have a suitable container for your pet?

Here are some answers to help you. Planning within a country is usually less involved than planning for international travels.

Where Are You Going?

Find the airlines that fly to your proposed destination, select one and contact them to check that they will accept your pet(s) on the day and flight that you prefer.

When Are You Going?

You must contact the airline at least 48 hours before departure, preferably longer, to be sure that there is space. Only small dogs and cats can go in the cabin, even so some airlines will not allow them to do so and they will be sent as special baggage in a heated and ventilated hold. Do not worry, cats and dogs actually travel better this way because it is quieter and they will rest in a darkened environment. Some airlines restrict the number of animals that they will carry on any one flight so the more advance notice you can give the better it is.

Find out how soon before the flight that you have to check in. Pets become stressed with all the crowds and bustle at an airport, so you want to keep this to a minimum. If you are allowed to have your pet in the cabin with you, check in as late as possible, so long as the airline knows that you are coming. If your pet is going in the hold, check in early so that it can go to the baggage area and be put somewhere quiet and dimly lit in order to relax. To prepare your pets for a journey reduce the quantity of food the day before but leave water available; take your dog(s) for a walk before leaving for the airport and again before checking in, allowing the animal to urinate and defecate. A light meal 2 hours before tendering the animal to the carrier will help to calm some animals and is a legal requirement in the United States. However, do not give a heavy bulky meal, as vomiting may occur or animals may soil their bedding.

If shipping your pet as air freight, check with the airline to ensure the air freight facility is open so your pet may be claimed by the consignee.

When Do You Want To Send Your Pet?

Make sure that there is no problem with proposed weekend or holiday shipment. Weekdays are preferable as all staff are working and liaison is easy all along the route. Transport of snub nose dogs, such as boxers, bulldogs and Pekinese, in hot season is not recommended. Dogs with snub noses have difficulty in maintaining a normal body temperature in hot weather. Check with the airlines for any special arrangements.

When Two or More Pets Travel Together

The *United States Department of Agriculture (USDA) Animal Welfare Act (AWA)* states that no more than two live puppies or kittens, 8 weeks to 6 months of age, that are of comparable size and weighing 20 lb. (9 kg) or less each, may be transported in the same primary enclosure via air carrier. This is a good practice to follow for all animal shipments, no matter what country they are traveling in.

Remember, animals may become stressed and aggressive when traveling by air and should not be placed in the same container unless they are young puppies or kittens. Animals which share the same household may become stressed and aggressive towards each other when traveling by air.

Some airlines restrict the maximum number of animals allowed in the cabin, check with your intended airline regarding their requirements if you are planning to carry your pet onboard.

When Pets Travel Unaccompanied

If your pet is flying unaccompanied, the preparation of the animal is the same but you will need a Health Certificate from your veterinarian to say that the animal is healthy and fit to fly. Check the documentation requirements and regulations for your country or the importing country if the pet is traveling internationally.

Minimum container requirements, as described in the Live Animals Regulations, are mandatory for transportation of animals by air. Food and water containers (troughs) accessible from outside the container are required. The carrier, or government agency, may require that additional food be provided in a pouch attached to the container with feeding instructions.

You can either find an animal shipper who can make all the necessary reservations and take full charge from collecting your pet, boarding it if need be, taking it to the airport and have it met at the other end and delivered to destination. In some countries, this may be the easiest and surest method and some airlines will not accept animals handled by anyone other than a shipper. The airlines can usually give you a list of shippers with whom they work. But it is possible that you can do all this yourself. Check with the airline for any special requirements for shipping your pet.

Shipping Your Pet As Cargo?

You must make a reservation with the cargo department of your selected airline who will give you the time and date of the flight and who will organise the routing. You should take the container and pet to the cargo department of the airline concerned as least 2 but no more than 4 hours before departure. Check on this when you make the reservation as it can vary from country to country. An air waybill has to be made with the description of the animal and the total weight and dimensions of the container with the animal inside. The cost of the shipment will then be calculated. The container must be correctly labeled with the standard IATA Live Animals Label, and the This Way Up labels on at least 3 sides of the container. (The official labels are not always available from the airline in which case you will need to contact a shipper for them).

The name and address of the owner, a 24 hour contact phone number and the consignee's name and address must also be clearly fixed to the top of the container.

Dried food must be supplied and attached to the container in case there is a delay and instructions for feeding and watering must be given in writing and also fixed to the container. Any medication that has/is being given must also be recorded with the name of the drug, the time and route of administration. Tranquilization is not recommended for air transport of animals.

Do not leave the airport until you know that the flight has been confirmed to leave. This helps everyone when there are unexpected problems and delays.

Make sure that there is someone to meet the shipment at the cargo department at the airport of destination, and who can contact when the flight leaves in order to give the expected time of arrival at your destination.

Don't Forget Health Requirements

Check that all vaccinations are up to date and that you have the vaccination and other required health certificates with you. Stressed animals (don't forget travel causes stress and dehydration to both humans and animals) are more prone to infections and if they are virus carriers their healthy status can break down causing sickness.

The Animal Transport Container

The container you are going to use can be a soft 'carry bag' for short trips when in-cabin flight is permitted. But for traveling in the hold, a rigid container that conforms to the IATA Live Animals Regulations must be used. The container must be big enough for the animal to stand normally, turn round and lie down. Air kennels with the correct amount of ventilation openings for good air circulation are required. The airline will be able to assist you in deciding how to select the right container size as they can check the IATA Live Animals Regulations when you make your reservation and advise you accordingly.

Buy the container ahead of time so that your pet can become accustomed to it. By placing a favorite bit of bedding and toys, and feeding the animal inside the container for a few days, the container can be 'personalized' to make the pet more comfortable in it when traveling.

Tranquillisation Can Harm Your Pet

Do **not** tranquilize your pet. It can be dangerous to their health. Drugs act differently at the pressure of 8000 ft above sea level, which is the approximate pressure in the cabin and cargo area during flight.

A Few Important Guidelines For Travelling With Your Pet Internationally

Travelling internationally with your pet is sometimes more complicated than domestic travel. While the basic requirements for containers, health certificates, and age remain the same, international travel usually requires additional documents as it does with passengers.

The first step in planning an international trip with a pet should be to contact the consulate of the destination country for their pet importation requirements. Some countries require a lengthy quarantine, others have more rigid standards than IATA's for container construction, while still others will only accept pets at certain airports. Once you determine which airport you will be flying into, check on national and local holidays during which customs may be closed.

A shipping agent, who specialises in animal shipments, can assist you in planning and arranging transportation for your pet. While you can make all of the arrangements yourself, nothing is worse than having your pet impounded or lost because of an oversight or lack of knowledge. Your airline or veterinarian should be able to provide information on shipping agents. They may also be found in the

Yellow Pages of local telephone directories.

Prior to shipping an animal internationally, you should have the answers to the following questions either from the consulate of the destination country, a shipping agent or the air carrier. Be specific as to the species of your pet, requirements may be different for dogs, cats, birds or other animals.

1. What documents are required to import a pet? Some countries require a health certificate signed by a veterinarian within a specific number of days prior to the shipment. Some countries require the veterinarian to be a government official while other countries will accept a health certificate signed by a registered veterinarian.
2. Are there any age restrictions (minimum and maximum) regarding importing a pet?
3. Are any special vaccinations or tests required for the pet?
4. Are there specific country restrictions regarding transportation of animals? (The U.S. has strict temperature restrictions which limit animal travel, especially in the summer and winter).
5. Some countries will only accept animals shipped as manifested freight, others will allow pets to travel as accompanied baggage.
6. Are there any country/local holidays during or around the time of your planned trip?
7. Is there any indication there may be a strike imminent, which may affect the timely transport of your pet?
8. Which airports have customs and health services available to clear your pet?
9. Are there any special quarantine requirements for a pet being exported or imported?
10. Are there any special container requirements, in excess of IATA standards, for transporting an animal into or within the desired country?
11. Are quarantine facilities available on the planned arrival date and station? Are quarantine facility reservations necessary?
12. Pregnant animals may not travel in late gestation.

In addition you should check with your desired air carrier and obtain the following information:

1. What are the carrier restrictions regarding the carriage of animals (quantity, container size - larger containers do not fit on all aircraft)?
2. Is a change of aircraft necessary to reach my final destination? Will the container fit on all aircraft types in the routing?
3. How long before departure and where should I drop off my pet?
4. Verify document requirements and other handling/shipping requirements with the airline. Some carriers are more restrictive than the country requirements. (For example some U.S. carriers have restrictions for pug nosed breeds of dogs and cats which are more stringent than the USDA rules. These restrictions vary from carrier to carrier).
5. What hours/days are customs and health facilities normally open to clear the animal?
6. Where and when can my pet be picked up?
7. Can pets be transported as baggage or must they travel as manifested freight?
8. Are there restrictions for unaccompanied pets (traveling as manifested freight) that are different than for pets traveling as baggage?
9. Are pets allowed in the passenger cabin? If so what are the limitations regarding size and quantity?

Separate food and water containers, refillable from the outside, must be secured in the container. Feeding and water instructions, as well as enough food for one meal, must be attached to the outside of the container. A duplicate copy of the feeding and watering instructions should be attached to the shipping documents. The food should be packaged in a strong plastic or cloth bag. Water or ice cubes should be provided to the animal to prevent dehydration.

Tranquilizing animals prior to or during air transport is not recommended. The conditions in an aircraft cargo hold in flight are quite different than conditions on the ground. Some medications which are very effective on the ground may prove to be unsafe or even fatal aboard an aircraft.

For more information on live animals transportation, please contact larper@iata.org.

Your veterinarian should also be able to advise you on the container requirements for your animal, but always check with the airline you will be using to confirm all the regulations specific to your animal and that airline.

Veterinarians also advise that direct flights are less traumatic for the animal, and should be used if at all possible. If direct flights are not possible, try to plan the route for the minimum number of plane changes, and for the changes to be at well-equipped airports. It is also important that aircraft changes and stopovers are in countries where the temperatures are not going to be a problem if the animal has to sit on the tarmac for a while. Shipping a Chow-Chow from China to Turkey via temperate Frankfurt, rather than desert Dubai, is going to be much better for the animal.

The Transition

What to Take with You on the Plane

Assuming you are shipping some of your belongings and not taking everything on the plane, what should you take in your suitcase?

Though your advance planning should reduce the likelihood of the following happening, it is always best to make contingency arrangements for:

1. The person who will be meeting you being delayed, or not turning up at all.
2. Losing your checked-in luggage.
3. Losing your carry-on luggage.
4. Losing your wallet and passport.
5. Not being able to find your accommodation, or it being unusable.
6. Getting lost soon after you arrive.
7. Your main shipment being delayed.

Always pack valuable, important and sentimental items in your carry-on luggage; luggage can be delayed or lost even by the best airlines. Before you leave your home country, find out what paperwork you will need within the first few days after you arrive and pack it in your carry-on luggage. Birth certificates, marriage certificates, driving licences and similar items of paperwork are difficult to replace quickly when you are in a foreign country; keep copies of important paperwork in a separate bag.

Margie Markram, a South African now living in the UK suggests that you:

...make sure you have copies (of very important papers) in your carry on baggage, and copies in your luggage or the moved shipment. I heard of a lady who was pick-pocketed on the tram the other day and ALL papers are gone and she has no copies! I always also pack my negatives for photos (not in my carry on but in the luggage). I love my photos and feel that if something should happen to the container at least I can make copies if I wanted to.

Alison Albon, a South African Foreign Service spouse with two children who has lived in Transkei, Israel, Switzerland and now Holland agrees with Margie.

I always have all my jewellery (not that there's a lot of it!) and my wedding photo negatives with me whenever we move country. We also make copies of all the documents (this includes wills and insurance things) and leave the originals in a safety deposit box at the bank at home, with a key and power of attorney with a trusted member of the family, in case we may need anything. I always find that we almost always lose one document in the move, this way it's always available to be forwarded to us.

Gillian Kerr, now residing in Australia has offered a very important piece of advice for people travelling with 'electronic visas', 'I have an electronic visa for Australia in my passport, which is read off a barcode. Some airports do not have the technology to read the visa barcode and require that you carry some form of hard copy documentation about your entry visa, before they let you board the plane. I've had a few difficulties in this regard'.

You should also make sure you include in your suitcase all the essential items you will need for the first few weeks of work, bureaucracy and settling in; before your shipment arrives, or you find the right shops to buy them.

Essential Items To Put In Your Carry-On Luggage

Item	Packed
Passport	
Valuable jewellery pieces	
Irreplaceable photo negatives	
Work visa & residence permit	
Address and directions, in the local language, for where you will be staying when you first arrive (even if transport has been arranged, because sometimes your contact is not able to meet you at the airport).	
Birth certificate, Marriage certificate, etc.	
Drivers licence & international drivers licence	
Medicine	
Local currency cash, plus international credit & cashpoint cards	
Copies of telephone, credit card and passport numbers	
Names, addresses and contact numbers of people you know at your destination	
Local guide book and map	
Phrase book	
Address of acceptable, alternative, emergency accommodation (hotel)	

Long-haul Travel with Children

When you are travelling on your own the travel part can be fun, exciting and adventurous, an escape from normality. As the saying goes, 'A change is a good as a rest'. But add a couple of kids and the likelihood of your being able to rest will diminish sharply, and the fun, excitement and adventure can become a logistical operation instead.

Kelli Lambe, who has travelled with her husband and three children on moves between Alaska, Oman and Amsterdam says:

We treat the plane ride like we do our schedule at home. We have meal-time, snack-time, reading-time, play-time, and on-your-own time. I try to keep things in order. Although sitting on a plane does not allow running and moving around a lot, you can play some easy game with them from their seats, Simon Says, Head, Shoulder Knees and Toes and I Spy.

Planes, airports and travel can be exciting for kids, but fourteen hours spent inside a metal tube, confined to a small area of seating and with nothing but clouds to look at can drag terribly for adults let alone children.

Kelli travels prepared to keep her children relaxed.

Between flights we try to get all cleaned up. The boys repack their backpacks and get washed up. If it has been a long flight we all change clothes and get refreshed. If the airport has shower facilities, we book a shower for all of us and get cleaned up. This not only helps our moods, but relaxes the kids as well.

If you have to change aircraft somewhere along your route, beware, some airports are definitely not children friendly. With a little planning of your own you can smooth most potential problems before they arise. Try to find out in advance what baby-changing facilities are available and where they are located. Also ask if there are any children's play areas located in the airport. If there are not, try to find a quiet corner where you can use your 'wet-wipes' to freshen-up faces, necks and arms of your children. Sometime a portable swab-down can work miracles for moods.

But it is not all bad news. Airlines and airports are increasingly providing parents and children with special facilities to help counteract the logistical problems of the parents and the problems of boredom for the children. Many airlines provide children's meals and activity kits for children.

Heathrow Airport has a great children's play area for transit passengers, Zurich Airport has excellent restaurants and Istanbul's new airport has snack kiosks spread all round the terminal that take most major currencies.

Gillian Kerr found, '

Sydney has renovated with kiddies in mind and not only has the usual soft play area for little ones, but also has the most interesting devices in the ladies toilets...each loo(toilet) cubicle has a fold-down seat with a five-point safety harness mounted on the wall for you to sit your baby in while you use the facility.

Apart from the actual travelling time there are meals, drinks, time differences, sleep patterns and jet lag to worry about; as much for you as the children.

Kelli Lambe also has other ideas for keeping her children in a routine:

We also pack a bag with all of their night-time things, blankets, tooth brushes, pyjamas and put them to bed at their biological clock bed-time. We keep to the same routine that we would at home. We take them to the bathroom and brush their teeth, change into pajamas, give them a little snack, read a book and make up their seat like a bed. This was the best advice my friend gave me. They sleep better, they act better and it helps keep them from getting over-tired. We even change them into clean clothes when they wake up.

Every parent has their own secrets for minimising the affects of international travel, Gillian explains here.

I travel often with my two little ones and find that keeping their routine definitely helps. I keep my watch set at their normal Sydney time for the trip and the first few days. My husband and I take it in shifts to mind them at night until they are into the time zone at their destination and stop wanting to play at 2 a.m. My two are presently two years and three and a half years.

Ask your travel agent which airlines offer special children's services and facilities and if you have to change planes along the way, try to make it at an airport that is child-friendly. Drawing kits, children's movie/cartoon channels, personal video games and assisted embarkation and disembarkation are offered by some airlines; ask your travel agent (or call the airline directly) to ensure they are available on your flight.

In a news release from June 27, 1996, *British Airways* (BA) announced that they were focussing more energy on the new breed of independent young travellers. According to the press information more and more children are flying these days, and of the hundreds of thousands that fly on BA, five percent of them fly alone. To accommodate these children, they have a special check in desk and an exclusive airport lounge at Heathrow's Terminals 1 and 4 and Gatwick for a scan of the morning's comics over a glass of orange juice.

BA say, 'The traditional children's meals have been replaced by trendy tuck boxes full of treats and nibbles as well as hot meals. This gives them the flexibility to nibble in front of the Rug Rats on the Kids Hour....'

Hamish Taylor of BA goes so far to say that, 'Entertainment is the key to a successful flight not only for the children and their parents but also for all our other passengers who want to travel in peace'.

The system seems to work. On the many occasions that Liam Callan has flown on *British Airways* between Asia and North America, or Europe and North America, he has enjoyed receiving the duffel bag full of 'freebies' that are given out on long-haul flights, which has made life easier for his parents.

Peter van Buren, on his website *(www.travelwithyourkids.com)*, suggests hanging a garbage bag on the back of the seat in front of you (use the hook that holds the meal tray in place). Kids on planes generate tons of trash and those little pockets with the in-flight service books only holds so much. When/if the bag gets full, then just give it to the flight attendant.

He also suggests that during the time between buckling up, setting up and waiting for takeoff, explain to the kids what to expect when the plane is getting ready to take off. If it is their first time flying, it is worth taking the time to explain why there are seatbelts, and how they work, what the table tray is and how it works, that there's a bathroom and video and when they come on. There are also the sounds your kids might hear as the plane is gearing up for take off (i.e. the air-conditioning and engine noise) and the fact that the lights often blink and there will be 'pings' as they do so.

There are many other aspects of flying that parents (adults) take for granted too, that children might become alarmed by. The wings shake; as the pilot moves the plane some pieces of the wing are supposed to move up and down, it is not breaking; ears pop with the change in pressure; etc. Either warning children in advance that it is supposed to happen, or be prepared to answer questions quickly and confidently will help stay calm during take-off.

Airplane toilets are also very different to standard ones. Making sure children know that the light only comes on when the door is locked, timing toilet-runs so that children do not have to stand in line just after mealtimes when they are desperate and explaining what happens when you use the suction flush system can allay many fears and reduce the number of times a parent has to accompany their child.

The following suggestions can help to reduce the stresses and stains of flying with kids, but always ask other parents for their advice too.

---

1. When travelling east to west, on a long-haul flight, keep your kids up late and take a late evening flight that arrives early in the morning, local time, at your destination. Hopefully, the children will sleep on the plane and allow you to rest for a few hours as well. Arriving at your destination airport early in the morning will give you time and daylight to reach your new accommodation and settle in.

2. If you are travelling east to west on a long-haul flight and cannot keep your kids up late enough to take a late evening flight (or there is no evening flight), leave home early in the morning. If you will arrive at your destination airport in the evening, you can go straight to an airport hotel, eat, sleep and hopefully avoid the worst of the jetlag.

3. For some reason, travelling west to east always seems to cause the worst jetlag. With long-haul trips in this direction, time-zone changes speed the clock forward, making journeys appear days long. Try to time your arrival for dusk so your body clock experiences the end of the day, hopefully then you will be able to think about sleeping and minimise the effects of the jet-lag.

4. Ask your travel agent which airlines are child-friendly. Some airlines (e.g. Virgin Airways, British Airways) provide children's packs of crayons, books and stickers as well as providing children's meals.

5. Alternatively, consider a long stopover halfway through the journey. Singapore is a great place to stop on the way from London to Australia or New Zealand. Hawaii or Japan can make a nice break when flying from New York to South East Asia. By relaxing en-route, you should have given yourself a chance to recover from the stresses of leaving one home and be ready to face the strains of moving into a new one.

6. Pay for a seat, even for small babies, and arrange for a child seat (like a car safety seat) to be available. Some airlines will provide them while some expect you to supply one. The seat will raise the child up closer to your level, hold the child more securely than a simple lap strap. It allows the child to sleep more comfortably and allows you more freedom during the flight.

7. Use backpacks instead of suitcases and carry-on bags. Backpacks leave your hands free to pick up toys, carry drinks and snacks and keep hold of your child in busy airports.

8. Encourage your child to pack and carry their own small bag with favourite books and quiet toys.

9. Bring along some new reading/picture books, colouring books and crayons as a surprise for when your child begins to get bored. Remember to make sure the colouring books are small enough to fit on airline sized tables.

10. Carry snacks of cheese, fruit or other favourite finger foods for your child (avoid chocolate and other sugary foods) in easy to reach pockets of your carry-on backpack. Add small drink cartons, with straws, to the snack box, as airline travel can be very dehydrating. Avoid drinks with high sugar content as this can add to the dehydrating effects of the plane and give your child unwanted energy boosts. Remember to bring diaper wipes to clean sticky fingers after snacks.

A New Home — To Rent or Buy

Most expats seem to live in rented accommodation, but long-term expats are increasingly looking to buy accommodation.

Renting accommodation will usually be attractive for those on short-term stays with little or no intention of returning to the country. It limits an expat's financial ties to a country and allows them to move easily once they learn the pros and cons of various parts of the city and the particular accommodation they are in.

Buying accommodation can be tempting for expats who are staying for an extended period of time, or who really like the country. Those who plan to stay for an extended period of time in one country may find it makes economic sense to invest in property, especially if it is likely to rise in value. Some expats made tens of thousands of pounds in Hong Kong by investing in property during the boom years prior to the handover to China.

When property is cheap and desirable, there may seem little reason to pay rent. Buying a home suitable for current needs that will become a holiday/retirement home in the future can also become a viable option.

Sometimes a company may want to buy accommodation for its expat personnel, especially if they plan to send a series of people to the country and the property can used by a number of people. This can also be helpful, logistically, when it can be more difficult to rent accommodation than to buy; Copenhagen in Denmark has a reputation for being like this.

Buying accommodation in some countries can be prohibitively expensive and even most locals rent. In others the opposite may be true. Websites such as www.expataccess.com/ offer advice on expat housing options, but so do many individual country specific websites that can be found through internet search engines by using the search string: +expat +(country name).

Buying property in a country you are unfamiliar with can be awkward due to a lack of understanding of local practices. Selecting which property to buy can also present difficulties, as you are unlikely to know if a large construction project is planned to begin nearby and whether the area is popular/unpopular and why, which can all affect your ability to sell the property again if you need to.

Unpacking

Once you have arrived at your destination you may still have paperwork to do before your shipment can be released by customs and delivered to your new home.

Make sure you have the contract, inventory, receipts and contact phone numbers of everyone involved with your shipment. Proof of your identity may also be necessary, so make sure you have some form of photo identification, other than your passport as your passport may be in the process of being registered with a government department, your employer or (worst case) you may have lost it.

The terms of the shipping insurance may stipulate that the shipper must unpack the boxes so that they can determine what has actually broken during transit. If you want to unpack yourself, consider asking the shipper to at least check specific boxes with items that are fragile, delicate or valuable. That way you will be able to make major claims if necessary.

Once you have unpacked, also consider keeping the boxes. In some countries finding boxes for your onward move may be a problem, or you may have to pay for them.

If you have had to pay a customs bond to import your possessions remember to keep all the items for the duration of your stay (even if they break), as in some cases you have to prove that you export them to secure the return of your bond.

Finally, keep all your paperwork, you never know when you might have to prove you own the items, correctly imported them, or paid the correct duties and fees.

Resources

Print Resources

Vacation Work *Live and Work* series: Australia & New Zealand; Belgium, Netherlands & Luxembourg; France; Germany; Italy; Japan; Russia & Eastern

Europe; Saudi & The Gulf; Scandinavia; Scotland; Spain & Portugal; USA & Canada.

How to Books series on *Living and Working Abroad.*

Online Resources

Avalon Overseas Movers: www.transeuro.com/av1.htm, for individual movers.

DHL Worldwide: www.dhl.com.

Direct Moving: www.directmoving.com has extensive lists of shippers, relocation consultants and other resources for international movers.

Electricity World Guide: http://kropla.com/electric.htm.

Federal Express (FedEx): www.fedex.com.

Household Goods Forwarders Association of America: www.hhgfaa.org, with links to state level organisations.

International Air Transport Association: www.iata.com.

International Federation of International Movers (FIDI): www.fidi.com, with an online directory of its members.

Independent Pet and Animal Transportation Association International Inc: www.ipata.com.

Latin American Caribbean Movers Association: www.lacmassoc.com, with an online directory of affiliated companies.

Overseas Moving Network International (OMNI): www.omnimoving.com, with an online directory of members around the world.

United Parcel Service (UPS): www.ups.com.

US Postal Service: www.usps.com.

Voltage Valet: www.voltagevalet.com.

www.airwebtravel.net/airports.html: a directory of airport maps worldwide.

www.smartship.com: Smartship, for package delivery services.

www.takeyourpet.com: a club for US resident pet owners who want to travel.

CULTURE SHOCK

What Is It?

Culture shock is commonly defined as, 'confusion, anxiety and stress experienced after arriving in a foreign country'. However, the symptoms of culture shock can appear even when you do not leave your own country. If you moved from rural Kentucky to urban New York, the transition may be as difficult to manage as if you moved from Zimbabwe to Australia, or Belgium to Chile.

Mark Bergman, a computer systems engineer, who moved from New York (US) to Ankara (Turkey) and then to Fredricksburg (US), says, 'Moving to Turkey was difficult and so was moving from there to Fredricksburg, but moving from New York straight to Fredricksburg would have been just as difficult'. It may be more accurate to simplify the description of culture shock to, 'stress caused by unfamiliar surroundings and significant lifestyle change'.

Reacting to the events of culture shock is not something to be ashamed of. When someone enters the different stages of culture shock it is important to press on, to find what they can gain from the experience of that immediate situation and for them to realise that everyone who moves abroad will suffer from it to some extent.

Barabara Schaetti, Principal of Transition Dynamics, has indicated that it is best to review culture shock simply as part of the 'going abroad' experience, and it is something that should be looked forward to because it is part and parcel of everything that comes with an international lifestyle. 'Culture shock is not something to be resisted or rushed. It is a gift to be engaged; its ambiguity, uncertainty, and emotional distress offer insight into the cultural self and the cultural other.'

Jeri Hurd remembers clearly when she realised she was in the throes of culture shock:

> I had been here (Turkey) for about four weeks and I was with these friends and we were sitting out on the balcony and we just had the best time talking. Just the night before I'd had a really bad night; I was playing a tape from home and just burst into tears. I was crying over this song and thinking 'God, you are such a sad person'. Then one of the people I was talking to, a very experienced expat, started talking about how the night before she started crying when she heard some song that made her think of home. I thought, hey, it even happens to them. This is cool, this is okay, this is what I'm supposed to be doing.

Culture shock is something you will experience every time you move to a new country, no matter how many times you move, or how many countries you move to. It is something that has to be faced up to not shied away from, but it should also be treated seriously. Culture shock should not be conceived of as a pariah to be beaten, hidden away from, or attacked. It should be welcomed as part of the experience of living abroad, and should be seen as a natural occurrence that is to be learned from.

Culture shock can be as much a physical experience as an emotional one. Climate, clothing, altitude, food and personal comfort are as much components of culture shock as language, traditions, attitudes, working practices, manners and religion.

One couple, despite their preparation for moving abroad, did not understand the extent to which culture shock would take them. Mike and Sarah van der Es were chosen by *Save the Children* to join the large field operation running at the time in Sudan in May 1985. In London, a doctor briefed them and their team on the need to drink at lest five litres a day on arrival to avoid dehydration when flying into a climate where it is over 27° centigrade day and night. As trained nurses they clearly understood. But on arrival in Sudan, Mike and Sarah were overcome by the thousands of sights and sounds of their first scorching, dusty, chaotic Arabic capital city. Like most of the nurses they drank only three litres a day and both suffered nausea and headaches in the first 48 hours. When travellers are overcome by hundreds of new impressions, rules of personal safety simply get overlooked. This is not unusual; it is typical of travellers everywhere visiting somewhere totally new to them, even the more experienced travellers. It is just one aspect of culture shock — the physical aspect.

Everyone experiences culture shock in a personal way. Your own personal background of culture, values and experiences will determine how you perceive and react to other cultures and societies. An American Christian moving to Muslim Jordan is going to view the culture very differently to how a French Muslim would. How you eat your food (knife and fork, chopsticks, or your right hand), how much personal space you need and social etiquette are as much a part of your culture as your religion, or lack of it.

Small Causes of Culture Shock

The small differences between cultures may not seem as important as the large variations and can be missed or ignored as causes of culture shock. But when many small niggling frustrations are with you all the time, it can be just as annoying as something much more obvious like the language barrier.

Jeri Hurd found that there are things she expected and gestures she knew, that are not the same as what she was used to. 'There are hidden rules and things that are different, and you don't factor those into the list of things you thought would be different, like going to the post office and expecting lines (queues) and there aren't any. Expecting pedestrians to have right-of-way; if you don't run they might not actually aim for you, but they won't try to miss either. It's all the little things you never think of because they are so taken for granted (in your home culture) and they don't hold true anymore when you go somewhere else.'

Quickly dealing with small things, learning to ignore them, or admitting they do really annoy you, may be more important than spending hours trying to escape from the big issues.

Small causes of big stresses

1. Not knowing why people are standing in a queue.
2. Not knowing which line to join.
3. Not understanding why people are shouting in the street.
4. Too much, or too little, personal space.
5. Always feeling different and under inspection.
6. Looking physically different from the local population and getting stared at.
7. Different attitudes to time and punctuality.
8. Different attitudes to cleanliness.
9. Different attitudes to tidiness.
10. Different attitudes to litter.
11. Different attitudes to noise.
12. Different attitudes to safety.
13. Different attitudes to traffic rules.
14. Different attitudes to animals.

15. Not being able to order home delivered meals.
16. The pace of life.
17. Segregation (or not) of the sexes.
18. Importance of gender.
19. Change in social status.
20. Superiority complex of the host nationals.
21. Racism from locals and expats.
22. Widespread poverty.
23. Conspicuous consumption (extravagant & flashy living) by wealthy locals and insensitive expatriates.

The attitude of someone towards an impending move and how rigidly they believe their way of life is the best is going to affect how they react after arrival. Being able to see that different things in life are normal for different people is a big help. Mike van der Es compares his perception of normality to that of an African friend: 'My friend, who was born and bred in a small village in Burkina, describes her first trip to England alone with laughter and horror. The escalator was as scary for her as loose buffalo are for us'.

Coleen McLeman, having prepared for four moves in ten years says:

I think attitude is key. Your attitude can colour any situation and when you are asked to uproot your life and move to a strange, far-off place, well, you are going to need that attitude to paint a rosy shade on the situation. Not to say that anyone should expect that everything is going to be rosy — but there is a need to be flexible, be open to whatever comes, expect that it will be difficult to adjust at times and appreciate the good things that come with the change.

Someone who does not want to move and is only relocating under duress is much more likely to have a difficult time coping with culture shock than someone who is looking forward to moving and cannot wait to investigate the differences and learning opportunities awaiting them.

Barbara Schaetti agrees, '

This is essentially the case, as with any life experience. Choosing the given experience makes it much easier to engage the challenges it may present, as well as the opportunities. Someone who doesn't want to move may have a more difficult time engaging culture shock as a learning opportunity.

Many people view culture shock as something to be faced head-on, trampled over and beaten, but in many cases this can actually make the stress worse, as is hiding away in your home, hoping everything will get better of its own accord.

Instead of trying to beat it, or hide from it, actively participating in it usually produces the best solutions. Coleen McLeman chose not to 'hide' from the hard parts because of the benefits she could gain from working through it. 'This whole experience may not lead me down the career path I had wanted to follow, but it is going to present opportunities that I would never otherwise have had. I realise that at times I will be unhappy with the situation, but on the whole I know that I can settle anywhere, and make the most of any situation.'

Learning to understand why, or how, a task is accomplished the way it is in the country you recently arrived in, can often be the most successful way to diffuse your frustrations. This is a primary aspect of benefiting from the experience of culture shock in both your every day life and your employment sphere. Trying to change local methods to match your ways, or ignoring them altogether, often serves to increase your frustrations. Once you know why people do the task the way they do, you will more readily accept the local practice, and may even understand why the method works best in that particular culture.

One expat on a first assignment in Japan recalls being absolutely frustrated with the rules governing the mailing of packages.

I went to the local post office with a Japanese speaking friend by my side to translate. I was asked, 'Is there a letter in this package?' There was, so I told them yes. The package itself was medium sized, and with the letter inside would cost about 3 times more than if the letter was not included. I was told that if I took the letter out and mailed the two things separately, it would cost much less. I argued. It didn't make sense that mailing two things should cost less than mailing one thing. My attempt to argue got me no where, especially when my translating friend did not want to be part of my argument. After all, he didn't see that there was a problem. It was the system. I just didn't know what the system was.

After I took the letter out (in front of them) and mailed it in a separate envelope (grumbling all the while) my friend tried to explain it to me on the way home. As written correspondence goes first class, and packages go second class, to include the tiny letter in the package would make the whole package 'correspondence'. Thus I would be charged for first class mailing of the package. Okay, so that was the system, and now, I understood. I couldn't see the logic to it still, but at least I understood the system. By recognising that there was a system and a reason for it, I was less frustrated with it.

Preparing For It

Learning the local language is another way of trying to take on the differences that arise as part of culture shock. Even moving from the US to the UK would be easier if you knew that some words and phrases mean totally different things in each country. In fact, there are certain English words and gestures that are commonplace or even complimentary in the US, but cause extreme annoyance if you use them the same way in the UK.

Karron Combs, an American independent expat in England, found standard phrases no longer had the meaning she was used to:

*The use of 'pardon me' or 'pardon' and 'excuse me' are not interchangeable in the UK. 'Pardon me', is used when you don't understand something a person has said. 'Excuse me' is used when you are trying to get around someone on the sidewalk (pavement), or bump into them by accident. It annoys them if you use them in the wrong way. One more thing, the gesture of holding up two fingers with the back of your hand toward the person to indicate two places or two people is **highly offensive**. It means the same thing as flipping them off with a one-fingered salute in the States. It is best if you simply say the word two, or use the thumb and forefinger to represent that number.*

Though not every Brit would agree with Karron's perception of the correct usage of 'pardon me,' 'pardon' and 'excuse me', it highlights the difficulty and perceived difficulty of moving to a foreign country, even if the host nationals nominally speak the same language as you.

By learning the language you can begin to understand the differences exhibited by your hosts. Often, this will help to explain why those differences make you uncomfortable. You may even learn that the person you thought was trying to stop you taking a short cut is actually trying to tell you that he wants to give a you lift in his car if you wait a few minutes.

Dell Harmsen, an expat spouse in Greece recalls:

It took a while to make some real friends, of course, but from the start my husband and I both focussed on the many positive aspects of our new country of residence. And, vitally, I learned Greek. Imperfect, simple Greek, but I can carry on conversations about weather, family, travel, history, destinations, holidays, food, etc. Many English speaking expats here say Greek is too hard and besides, it's not necessary. This is a mistake. Most other language speakers living in Greece — Germans, Filipinos, French, Albanians, Russians, everyone except English speakers — all learn Greek.

Work on learning some of the language before you relocate, so you can at least buy a drink in a restaurant when you arrive. If you can understand only a few words, you are not going to feel quite so isolated as if you have no idea what is being said around you.

Dell believes learning the language is a very important step towards making local friends.

If you really want direct access to local people you need to do your homework and learn basic communication in their language. 'Everyone speaks English' may be true at work, but not after work. If you want to make friends, there's no secret to it — you start speaking the language, laugh at your own mistakes, smile with a friendly attitude, and take a genuine interest in people.

Another good way engage your initial culture shock is to learn as much about your destination country as possible before you go. Read books, visit travel agents, watch movies and listen to international news programmes to gain as full a picture as you can.

Emanda Richards and John Toich a teacher and systems engineer respectively, tried this:

To help better prepare ourselves for our new life in Turkey, we collected much information. We wrote to the Turkish Embassy in Canada who sent us an abundance of tourist pamphlets full of pictures and general information. We bought a travel guide for the country, language dictionaries as well as a beginner language-learning cassette. We also watched a travel programme featuring Turkey. When we arrived we felt fairly well-prepared and not as shocked by language and other differences as we otherwise might have been.

Coleen McLeman, prior to a (later cancelled) move to Iran got busy learning too.

We are reading up on Iran, we have the Lonely Planet — which is good because they can be optimistic and up-beat about anything. I have also just started a history of Iran, which includes events up until the modern regime. I hate the idea of not knowing anything about the country or history or politics. I'm also looking at where I can take Farsi lessons here in Seattle. Besides books, talking to people is the most important resource. Before making the final decision on whether or not to accept the post, my husband and I spent an evening with an Iranian couple we know here in Seattle. We got their opinions, asked them questions and watched their home videos of the trip home just a few months before. This was very informative since we saw the streets, the roads, cars, houses — we saw how Iranians were living and that was very...comforting (?) to discover that they lead very ordinary lives. I also phoned the wife of a colleague of my husband and talked with her about what it was like to be a woman in a Muslim country.

Trawl the Internet for websites and chat groups where you can read about the country and ask questions of people already there. You can often find someone not only in the country you may be moving to, but someone in the same city. Many people ask questions about shipping agents, car hires, rental fees, local medical care and school options. Aside from the big questions, people also ask more personal questions about finding favourite foods, pet supplies or home decoration stores. Chat forums are a mine of valuable resources.

Use the advanced search option on search engines to find specific and applicable information (most search engines have simple guidelines to help you do this). By using combinations of keywords you can narrow your search to find the best information available, the more words the narrower the search. For example a search for Paris could look like:

1. +expat +living +Paris
2. +international +school +Paris
3. +expat +spouse +Paris

Though you need to prepare yourself for challenges, beware of expatriates and returned expatriates (repatriates) who do nothing but complain about a country; they may have their own personal an axe to grind, or never really tried to get past their culture shock. Learn why they disliked a country and then work to avoid the problems they came across. Always ask for a second opinion and never prejudge a country. Making your own mind up from first-hand experience after you arrive is much more fun.

Use the table below to help you organise your fact-finding mission about your prospective host country. The more you are able to fill in, the more information you will have under your belt to help you understand the cultural differences.

If you are already in your host country you might find some ideas you have not tried before, which can help if you are struggling, or improve an already enjoyable experience.

Information Sources

Guide books	1.	
2.		3.
History books	1.	
2.		3.
Holiday brochures	1.	
2.		3.
Movies/Travel Videos	1.	
2.		3.
Documentaries	1.	
2.		3.
Internet websites	1.	
2.		3.
Internet chat groups	1.	
2.		3.
Relocation consultants	1.	
2.		3.

If you are in the fortunate position of having the resources of a large, successful, or cash rich organisation, you might be able to persuade them to enlist the services of a relocation consultant. A good advisor can take you through the many aspects of moving internationally and help you find the resources that are best suited to helping you make the most of your time abroad. Barbara Schaetti goes further.

Individuals and families must also be provided basic information (by their employer) about the process of transition. Including their eventual re-entry, the intercultural dynamics they will encounter between themselves and the host nationals, about the potential impacts of an international sojourn on family dynamics and family members' cultural identities, specific strategies to mitigate the difficulties and maximise the possibilities. Individuals and families must be supported by their sponsoring organisations and by their expatriate communities in developing the capacities required. Capacities to self-reflect, to engage every experience consciously, to access personal well-springs of creativity, to intentionally construct meaning and purpose, to thrive in the midst of (and not merely tolerate) ambiguity.

Names and Adresses of Useful Organisations

Destination country Embassy/Consul
Foreign Ministry of your own country
Chambers of commerce 1. 2. 3.
Libraries 1. 2. 3.
Local universities 1. 2. 3.
Special interest travel agents 1. 2. 3.
Relocation Consultants 1. 2. 3.
Language schools 1. 2. 3.
Friendship Associations (e.g. Turco-British Association; Anglo-Chinese Association etc.) 1. 2. 3.

Though a consultant will be able to guide you through the steps and phases of relocation, over-reliance on a consultant can result in your not having the control and confidence to do things on your own. A good consultant will encourage you to take control and do as much as you can for yourself.

The table above is intended to give you extra ideas about which organisations might be able to help you in your search for information and keep yourself firmly in control of your experience. Some organisations may be in your home country and you can start your search before you leave. Some will be in your host country, and will help to provide you with a continuing source of information once you arrive. Contact as many of these places as possible because they will often offer different information about your host country.

Akiko Nishimura, from Japan, who expatriated to Hong Kong for five years with her family and then moved to Canada on her own, while her family has moved back to Japan without her, believes preparation is essential.

Transition from one place to another requires preparation, not just in a sense of packing everything you need but also in a sense of being prepared to encounter things that are completely new and sometimes even strange. Though you may pack your luggage with tons of instant noodles and your brain with tons of knowledge about the new place, you can never be too prepared.

The Cycle

No matter how much you prepare yourself you will still experience culture shock and this is not going to be a single event with a predetermined set of emotional and physical responses, though it does often follow a pattern. Three phases are common:

1. First weeks — exciting novelty.   2. First months — frustrating reality.
3. First year — adjustment & acceptance.

The actual length of these phases will vary from person to person, even within families. It varies even further for individuals who have lived in different countries. Culture shock never really goes away either, because the country you are currently living in will never be the same as your 'home' country and there will always be something new to discover. However, the effects of culture shock and how you work with it will get easier as you get used to the country.

First Weeks

The first few days after arrival are often a honeymoon period. Much of what you see is new and exciting, maybe even exotic and the joys of discovering new places, new foods and meeting new people and the mere fact that everything is different can be stimulating. The good aspects of international living will generally far outweigh the negatives at this time.

Coleen McLeman recalls the beginning of her posting to Vienna.

Initially, I seemed to have trouble comprehending that this was my new home and not just a brief holiday. Everything was new and I felt a little like a tourist. However, it was more exhilarating than a holiday because I had the added excitement of knowing that I was embarking on a brand new adventure and starting a brand new life. Many people long for the opportunity to start over again from scratch in an unknown place but never take the step — but for me this was real.

From the moment you arrive, and for the first weeks afterwards, you will almost certainly be busy too. Tasks including unpacking, setting up your new home, buying food, furniture and other necessities, as well as visiting the office will place great demands on your time and this too can reduce the negative impact of culture shock as you are achieving so much.

However, some people do experience the worst effects of culture shock really early, especially if they arrive unprepared for what they are getting into, or have heard a lot of negative comments about the country before the move. Though on occasions the simple fact that everything is different can be enough to overwhelm a new arrival.

Louisa Ledbetter, an elementary school music teacher, and her husband Steve, a composer and high school music teacher, moved from the US to Turkey and suffered severe culture shock from the moment they arrived. Their severe emotional culture shock then led on to physical illness. They, however, stayed in Turkey and are now in their third year abroad.

Culture shock is a mild term for what we experienced, although there were more issues than just the country itself which aided in causing stress for us.

We weren't really sure what to expect when we arrived and we did hear negative comments before we came, but we tried to ignore the negatives and think positively.

Having come from a very comfortable existence, I was rather shocked at the small size and bad condition of the apartment. We were fortunate to have REAL (a German owned hypermarket) so close, but products that I took for granted in the US, which made my life easier, were not available here. Therefore we adapted our diet.

So many factors contributed to our stress — not knowing the language, being unfamiliar with the city, having to rely on others to provide transportation (not having a car), changes in diet, and being out of contact with family and friends.

I will never forget the feeling I had the first night in Ankara. We had arrived on a non-stop flight from Chicago to Istanbul. I was already feeling overwhelmed by the heat and the disorganisation at Istanbul airport. After a three-hour layover in Istanbul we flew into Ankara, where we were faced with lines at customs and a long wait to retrieve all our luggage. We also had our cat with us.

The drive to the school was fine but we were exhausted. I remember not feeling too surprised about the Turkish terrain because it reminded me of the American South-West. When we arrived at the apartment things began to hit me. I was in shock over the size and condition of the apartment and remember thinking how can anyone live without screens on their windows. We had no phone so I couldn't easily call home. I began to get the feeling of suffocating and feeling trapped. We tried to get our cat settled though we couldn't even find a litter box here so we used one of the large plastic washing tubs. We decided to rest but I continued to awaken with feelings of panic because I felt trapped. I couldn't seem to find comfort in anything and it seemed as though our entire world had changed for the worse. There were none of the conveniences of home and we felt no connection with the outside world.

It was the stress of this first week that I feel lowered my immunities bringing on my tummy troubles since I was told it was viral. This stress probably also contributed to Steve's illness.

We learned to adjust over many weeks, but even to this day we are not completely at ease.

First Months

After the first few weeks of exciting novelty, the frustrating reality of the challenging differences can begin to catch up with you.

Bronwyn Davies, a New Zealander who has lived in Hong Kong for ten years says, 'At first it was a romantic, exciting notion — living overseas in such a foreign place was a challenge that I jumped at. But very quickly the reality bit.

Although still exciting, the day to day issues of living in another country diluted the romanticism — I just wish I had been better prepared'.

Everyday tasks such as trying to get a telephone connected, or having a new stove delivered, are not so easy in a foreign language. It will seem that tasks you found so easy at home and knew how to get done with one phone call now take all day to complete.

Jeri Hurd was surprised at what tasks she found difficult to complete on her first move abroad. 'When you arrive you can't talk to anybody; you go to the store and you don't know what you're looking at, it takes you an hour to figure out the damned washer. Everything took so much more time and you don't think about that, because that's the mundane everyday stuff.'

Even food shopping and cooking may not be simple anymore as Julia Ferguson Andreissen, an American in the Netherlands recalls:

I remember my first Thanksgiving abroad. I sent all my friends and family an e-mail asking for their favourite recipes. I received eight recipes and every single one had at least two ingredients that I couldn't get here. I remember explaining this to family back home in the US and they just couldn't understand how I couldn't get this or that. It's amazing what we take for granted and expect other people and other countries to have the same things.

There will be new systems to be learned, different bureaucracies to be finessed and different workmen to keep happy too, as Julia also found,

On various occasions I have had a utilities employee show up at my door around 8:30am and state he must enter my apartment to check something. Usually I have barely understood him. All I really understood was this person must enter my flat now and check something and so I let him in wondering 'who are you, what are you doing?' They always seem to have some official paper but here they don't warn you with a letter saying on such and such a day we will be by to check on this. They just show up and start walking about your home. Maybe this is one of the reasons the Dutch are known for being so clean and tidy within their house.

Working through these experiences will help you through the next stage of culture shock. It will take effort and a will to succeed; no one is going do it for you.

To help her settle into the new culture around her, Julia found she had to do more than she had originally thought.

Once I realised it was harder than I thought to acculturate in Holland, I worked diligently to find others who I could relate to and who could help me. I joined groups online, formed my own group for expats and joined an International Women's Contact. I realised it was up to me to develop the support system I needed if I was going to continue to stay in the Netherlands and like it. I would think a wrong way to try to get past your culture shock would be to put everything else into other people's hands and not take the time and effort to educate yourself on the country and culture, expecting things to just work out.

You will get used to the differences though, even aspects you might initially think you will never accept. Peter van Buren, author of the website *Traveling Internationally with your Kids* (www.travelwithyourkids.com) remembers:

I once paid almost $30 for a pizza in Taipei. Pizza shops being hard to find then and the usual ingredients not being a big part of traditional Chinese cooking, the price was a bit high. The cheese was clearly leftover from some failed genetics experiment and the moisture left that doughy crust long before I was toilet trained. It was about the best tasting thing I can remember eating.

By noting specific challenges about your new home and country, and analysing why (either by yourself or with a spouse or friend), you can begin to move past the difficult issues and look for positive reasons to enjoy your stay (and learn to enjoy strange pizza).

Causes of Your Culture Shock

The Cause of Culture Shock	What Actually Upsets You?	Why Does It Upset You?

In major cases of culture shock, resentment, anger, frustration and depression are common emotional symptoms. These can be exacerbated by the inevitable physical discomfort prompted by differences in the local fauna and flora in food and water, climate variations, altitude changes and the stresses of moving home, country and job. If this happens it may seem that there is nothing good about the country you have moved to, though there almost certainly are good points that have just been buried for a while.

To help you adjust and solve the challenges of culture shock (however severe the effects), try looking for positive aspects of the country you live in. Even in the most difficult situation you can usually find something positive. For every negative you write above, try to find at least one positive to put below.

Making the effort to find enjoyable things to do will give you a reason for working through your culture shock. Keeping active helps. Refer to *Going Alone* and *Equal Partners* for ideas of tasks and activities and places to meet new friends, so that you keep both busy and add pleasure to your day.

For children and accompanying partners, the first month can be especially difficult. The employed partner normally enjoys the structured security of a

Positive Aspects of Your Host Country

1	
2	
3	
4	
5	

Activities To Do & Places To Visit

1	
2	
3	
4	
5	

familiar work-setting, while the rest of the family has to learn new routines on their own and find its niche it an alien world. These first few months can be critical to the success of an international move as it greatly affect how well a new arrival will ultimately settle and adapt to the new surroundings.

The Accompanying Partner

An isolated and unhappy partner can be very detrimental to the professional life of the employed partner, and studies by various agencies are being conducted to evaluate the role of a partner's happiness in the success of an employee's contract fulfilment. Human Resource managers are now being hired by many corporations to attend to the requests and needs of partners who accompany their employees relocating abroad.

Without the traditional support network of work, family and friends it can be very easy for a partner to become unhappy, angry and depressed. These feelings can often be compounded because the employed partner is likely to be working longer hours than at the 'home' office. International employees are often expected to entertain clients and suppliers in the evenings, travel extensively and work late at the office to facilitate liaison with other offices in different time zones around the world.

An absent partner enjoying the new responsibilities and challenges of their international career can give an accompanying partner a suitable target of blame for their feelings of resentment and anger generated as the symptoms of culture shock. This can be especially true when the accompanying partner has left a career behind. One expat spouse in Europe recalls:

During the first year of being abroad I was constantly angry with my husband. It wasn't fair. He got to go to work every day and do something that was familiar to him. He got to talk to a number of colleagues about familiar things. He got to have a social life at his work place. He got to come home to a familiar face. I got to stay home and do the domestics. I got to go into town and try to figure out where to buy the things we needed. I got frustrated at figuring out how to pay the bills. I got to be alone a lot, with not so many people around to talk to. I didn't get to do anything familiar to me except cook and clean (and even that was different because of the food differences). I was very upset at the whole situation, and remember many times blowing up at my husband like it was his fault. I now know that I was experiencing culture shock, and that it was a stage of frustration that I was going through. Blaming it on my husband was just a way of coping.

A proactive partner who searches for solutions to the challenges of starting a new life in a foreign country is going to have a good chance of settling quickly in their new country. However, someone who stays at home, hiding away and waiting to be rescued, is going to find life much more difficult. Karron Combs living in the UK believes:

It is vital to the psychological health of the trailing expatriate spouse to find a way to interact with her new environment. The longer she puts it off, the harder it will become to find a new way to feel welcome among the community. It is up to the spouse to find her niche; the working expat is too busy trying to sort out his new job to worry about sorting out his spouse and her new life. Fear is the only thing that stops most of us from being and doing anything we wish. If the spouse faces her fear, she will be able to overcome it and move forward into new and great life changing adventures in her new country.

Though, if the partner can be well-supported by the working partner it helps greatly as Dell Harmsen has found:

You have to work together, function as a team. On a successful team each member contributes as best he can what's needed at the time, and each member's contribution is important and respected. Back home, where you have other support systems around, you can probably manage okay without teamwork. In a new country, it's a necessity.

The Children

The first few months can be difficult for expatriate kids. Children experience culture shock as much as adults, but they are also likely to mingle with more cultures at school than you would during your day, and can exhibit the symptoms in different ways. Children are very sensitive to the attitudes of their peers and the main place they are going meet them is at school or play group.

Adults with severe culture shock generally become depressed. Children may become depressed too, but they can also become one or more of the following:

1. Disruptive at school or at home.
2. Increasingly rebellious.
3. Increasingly conforming.
4. Under-achievers at school.
5. Workaholics on their schoolwork.
6. Excessive or obsessive in their leisure activities.

Most expatriate children attend schools established especially for them. These are predominantly 'International Schools', 'American Schools', 'British Schools', 'French Schools' etc., though they may take another format altogether (e.g. homeschool). Though the students at these schools may look like the students from a school in your home country, they are going to be different (by virtue of their cultural diversity and international life experiences) from the kind of student body your child would have been part of at home. It will take your child time to find their own way of feeling comfortable in their new social surroundings.

Brennen Young, a seasoned Third Culture Kid (see *Long-term Considerations* for an explanation of TCKs) who changed schools eight times, remembers trying to deal with the culture shock he met in school life.

I do remember, once school started, clinging to the first couple of kids who spoke to me in English, and the same thing happened for each of my brothers. Our friends for the first week or couple of weeks were completely different from the ones that we had for the rest of the year. It took a little more time before I could join the ranks of the basketball-playing group. In other words, when we were first there, each of us placed language as the top priority over similarity in choosing our friends. Once we were able to swear with the best of them, that changed.

Though the school may use English as the medium of instruction, the curriculum may be very different from what you and your children might be used to. There may be large numbers of children who speak various foreign languages in addition to the local language. As well as the language diversity, there will be children from diverse cultural, religious and social backgrounds. Americans and Britons can be as strange to each other as Spaniards would be to Iranians and Muslims to Buddhists.

Your child will need all the help and understanding that you would give them if they changed schools at home. Then add some more to help them adjust to the international differences too. The problem, as most parents anywhere would agree, is knowing when to step in and when to let your child get on with it.

Though it will be difficult to start with, as your child makes new friends they will learn from other children, who have made international moves themselves, how to adjust to the new environment. Because the other students are likely to have made such transitions themselves, they can be the best mentors to help your child adjust in the new country.

Andrew Kittell, US Dean of Enrolment Management at the *American Community Schools*, England has noted how students support each other.

International schools are among the world's most tolerant and supportive communities. Families whose children attend international schools tend to be impressive global citizens and culturally aware. Their families embrace diversity at home and the children from these households learn by example. As such, these children welcome new classmates with eager anticipation. They'll generally see to it that newcomers integrate quickly into school culture. At some international schools, these student self-help programmes are institutionalised and include formal transition-assistance programs. In most cases, however, it's a matter of new students being the norm rather than the exception. At most international schools, everyone's been the 'new kid'. This shared experience predisposes more-established students to reach out to their recently arrived peers.

The best way to successfully introduce children to something new is to make it exciting. Remember that a parent's attitude towards a move can greatly affect how children adjust.

Ideas To Prepare Children & Parents For An International Move

1	List, find and read age appropriate books on the country. 1. 2. 3.
2	List, find and watch videos on the country. 1. 2. 3.
3	List and visit travel agents to find brochures on the country. 1. 2. 3.
4	List restaurants and ethnic food from the country and then try them 1. 2. 3.
5	List and meet nationals of the country you can contact. 1. 2. 3.
6	List exciting and interesting activities to do after arrival. 1. 2. 3.

Once children have some knowledge of where they are going and are excited about a new experience they will be more open to accepting the novelty, and less worried about the great unknown. But it is always important to take your child's fears and concerns seriously, not try to brush them under the carpet.

One expatriate who moved his family to Tokyo, tried to impose reasons on why the move would be good for his teenager and had the opposite affect to what he intended. He reported that:

> *Because the point is to help them feel empowered, imposing reasons on the child as to why she will be fine can create the opposite reaction — being forced to accept a place's good points still means a loss of control. Being sensitive to how a child will respond to the way the issues are presented is as important as presenting them in the first place.*

The Employed Partner

In the first few months, the employed partner will have the structured normality of work to balance the new surroundings. They will meet people, be introduced to the country and culture on a professional basis, and have a much greater opportunity to learn the language and customs that allow them to relax and feel comfortable. But the image of normality can be deceiving. In addition to the social aspects of living abroad, there can be professional complications. Work practices and ethics vary widely around the world. Cultural taboos in one country are accepted practice in others. It can be hard for staff from some countries to understand why long hours in the office are more important than efficiency and a five-day week.

One expatriate lawyer in Japan remarks on ethical difficulties on the job.

> *Rampant practices in some countries, while being legal or nominally illegal locally, can subject foreign residents to substantial criminal liabilities in their home countries (e.g., the United States 'Foreign Corrupt Practices Act'). There are times when the expatriate would do well to know when it is a good idea to say, 'I realise this may be standard practice here, but I cannot do it'. Or at least, 'I don't know what you're all about to say, but I can't be here to listen to it', before leaving a conference room. It is also a good idea to know how governing bodies decided when and how to investigate and enforce common types of wrongdoing in your industry. On a more day-to-day level, however, I have also found differences very useful to know about while doing business negotiation; styles vary widely from country to country — even from region to region within a country (New York City is not Des Moines). Negotiators from some cultures are much more aggressive while others lose respect for a counter-party that uses too much emotion when making an argument. Deal structures change. Staff approaches to assignments from superiors also differ.*
>
> *In Tokyo, for example, I have struggled with the ability to obtain candid responses from recipients of my work assignments about whether they believe they can complete an assignment on a given timetable, though the work I have received has generally been done with a much greater amount of care to quality than what I received in Manhattan. It is very useful to have someone from your home culture help prep you on this sort of thing. Nevertheless, always remember that generalisations by definition do not cover specific situations. Stay flexible — you are bound to make misassumptions by the score!*

The First Year

Coming through the first few months and still wanting to be abroad is a good sign. The first months will be tiring; leaving one country and moving to another is bound to be hard work. But hopefully you will still be able to see the benefits of moving and working hard to make a success of it.

Victoria Lerma Simmons found this way to make her adjustment easier in the Philippines,

I can only advise people to find something outside yourself to expedite your adjustment. Volunteer, take courses you've always wanted to take, etc. My volunteering a year ago paid off recently when I landed a job with an agency which is headed by someone I met when I was a volunteer. Instant gratification is not the key for expats. However, be proactive and you will be adjusted in no time.

Having learnt the basics of the language in the first few weeks it becomes a slower process to learn enough to have a conversation, make local friends and learn why life is so different from what you are used to. But by giving up and deciding it is too hard to learn the language and understand your host culture, you risk missing out on some of the better aspects of a country and not moving forward in the process of culture chock.

Dell Harmsen worked through the process of culture shock and the key factor for her was language. 'I don't see any way around it. Here in Greece, an expat or the spouse, at least one member of the team, has to learn enough Greek to read the alphabet, travel, shop, and socialise in a variety of settings. Okay, lots of people here don't, but they miss the best of everything.'

Alternatively, if you start thinking there is no point in trying to make a home for yourself in your host country, you can become stuck in a circle of frustration and anger. By not taking on the challenges of culture shock that are offered to you, you could find yourself wallowing in self-pity. If this happens, it is likely that you will spend the rest of your posting counting the days until you leave the country. Not only would this be a big waste of your time, but it will also be detrimental to family members and friends around you.

However, if you keep trying and putting in the effort, one day you will find that you are relaxed and enjoying yourself. You will be able to understand the shopkeeper, the taxi driver will know where you want to go the first time you tell him, and as you walk down the street people you know will say hello to you and the waiter at your favourite restaurant will recognise you.

In an article Julia Ferguson Andreiseen wrote for the 'Crash Course' column of one expat website she said:

Feeling at home is more than having just the physical aspects of the move taken care of. Being recognised by the local butcher or baker is also a comforting feeling. Smile at everyone — it seems so obvious — but often when we are in a new environment and unsure of ourselves we tense up and forget to smile. Ask questions about cooking times or preparations and they will start to go out of their way to make you feel welcome and want to shop there.

Once you begin to relax into the pleasures of your host country you can start to enjoy the country to its fullest extent. With local friends and other expatriates, you can experience the joys of being invited to weddings, parties and people's homes where real people deal with life's crises, changes, customs and celebrations which you would only otherwise get a chance to see on television documentaries.

Dell has learned to enjoy her experiences to the fullest. 'I can't believe it's been nearly two years in Greece, and we have had quite a few wonderful opportunities to get involved with Greeks socially. Here, town, church and school festivals are a wonderful place to start, and they are easy to find out about through newspapers, posters and banners.'

Mike van der Es, agrees with this sentiment:

For many expatriates and their families, these will be their most meaningful and memorable experiences abroad. Participating in such visits will demonstrate the warmth and resilience of the local populations in the way few books, films or work experiences can. In addition, the more different your host country's culture is from your own, the more you are likely to be intrigued and fascinated when you are invited into such events.

Conversely an expatriate in Japan suggests:

It might be unfair, but I believe many of the expat children I've met here have missed opportunities just as their parents have by surrounding themselves in an English speaking world. It's ironic that many families take overseas postings to broaden their children's experience, only to make them bigger culture snobs as a result of sending them to the American school and of limiting their cultural exposure to special cultural events at the American club. I'm finding that many of the 'English bubble' expats take on a more colonial view of the world as a result of living abroad. I believe it's an insidious problem but I am certain that most of the offensive things I've heard said at the local expat club about the local culture or about members foreign childcare providers would never have come out of the person's mouth had they stayed at home.

Mike and Sarah van der Es, who spent time in Sudan, remember seeing six or seven young men whipping a fellow bridegroom to see if he had the grit and courage to take on a wife the next day and deal with the challenges and suffering that is entailed in marriage in a desert nomad's life. Different from a stag party! And in Nepal they went to the first rice-eating ceremony of their day guards' long awaited son; when it was nice to visit a mud hut where they all still slept on the floor and see a community that tourists miss.

The first year of living in a new country should be considered to be one long learning experience and settling-in period. Though the learning curve lessens, it will continue for your entire time abroad. This is born out by experienced international Human Resources managers who consider that due to both cultural and professional challenges, newly expatriated employees are unlikely to work to their full, professional potential until their second year in a country. Some experienced managers consider contracts of less than two years to be counterproductive and three or more years to be the optimum.

Though Tony Turton of *Arnett Associates*, an International Human Resources Consultancy (http://www.btinternet.com/~arnettassoc/), who was previously Personnel Director (International) of *Thames Water*, has found that shorter assignments can work well in certain special cases. He cites examples such as technically specialised work which do not need too much interaction with host nationals, or where an assignee can operate as part of an established team of fellow nationals which can shelter the short term expat from much of the culture shock. For any job where the employee needs to be effective within the new culture, though, a period of adaptation is unavoidable, and he supports the view that whenever possible, companies should think in terms of two year assignments being the minimum.

Recurrence

Beware, culture shock can be recurrent. Every now and then you can slip into a trough of 'First Months' frustration, as the foreignness of where you are becomes too much to cope with. Some people find it comes during certain seasons, others at particular festival times and many people find it occurs with illness, but it can come at any time.

Barbara Schaetti concurs,

Culture shock is a response to change, and any change, including the onset of a new season (e.g. a holiday) or an anniversary even — or the discovery that change isn't going to happen, that the sojourn is going to be longer than originally anticipated — can rekindle culture shock. My recommendation is again not to discount or seek to just get past it, but to engage it for all the value that it might have to offer.

If you are watching out for it you can catch it early and work with it; cook yourself that favourite dish from home, go out for dinner somewhere fancy, or meet up with friends. But do not give up, because it is almost always easier to work through a recurrence of culture shock than it was the first dose. Lori Mickle lives in France with her family and worked hard to keep moving forward.

*We need to know that the bad feelings will come but what we need to do is to explore how to overcome them and maybe even make them work for us. I now read a lot of Elisabeth Elliot's material. She is an ultra-conservative ex-missionary. One of the lessons is when you are so numb that you can't think straight, just focus on 'doing the next thing'. It is so simple but it really helped: when I find myself aimless, I ask myself, 'So, what is the next thing?', and then I do that one thing then ask the question again. Anyway, we can get all caught up in focussing on the negatives of loss of identity, or loneliness, or whatever. I am intrinsically a positive person so I find I **have** to concentrate on the positive things. I latch onto those so hard, especially when everything else seems to go wrong. Yes, I asked to be here. I thought it was the best decision for the entire family. Yes, there are some really tough days and some have been so bad that I've even sat crying in my car in parking lots, or actually broke down at the kids' school once. But overall, I think we all will come out so far ahead just in perspective alone, that I/we will stick it out **and** make the best of it that we can.*

The Implications of Culture Shock

Someone who does not adjust well through the phases of culture shock will affect those around them too. If the culture shock is left unchecked it can lead to an early return home and all the associated problems for employers, family and colleagues. Depression, anxiety and anger can have a devastating effect on an individual, destroy families, and ruin friendships. In the long term it can be better for that person and/or their family to go home than try to complete a contract at all costs.

For some people it is better that they do not move abroad in the first place, others try their hardest and still can not cope. It comes down to knowing what is right for you. No one can second-guess that; you have to figure it out for yourself.

Not every expatriate will enjoy every country and if you really want to live abroad and you are having serious difficulties living where you are now, another country may suit you better. But equally, there should be no shame associated with admitting that you really want to live 'at home'. Karron Combs has seen people return from unsuccessful postings.

Many people go home because they cannot live outside their normal lifestyle. That's wise of them if they determine they cannot cope. I do not see it as a failure to admit that you aren't cut out for the expat life. I see it as an honest and courageous thing to do. I admire the moxie (strength) they show in admitting this is not for them when they go home. It shows courage.

Though a return home may be necessary on occasions, it is better to work from the beginning to try and prevent a build-up of stress. The support of friends, family and colleagues is the key to successfully working through culture shock. Single people need to work harder than families to create a new support network (see *Going Alone*), but individual family members will each have new challenges to meet and need help to get through them and learn from them.

International living is not always easy. A certain level of culture shock is always to be expected, but there comes a point that some individuals will need professional psychological help. They should be encouraged to get it as soon as is practical in an environment that will be as secure and comfortable for them as possible.

Resources

Print Resources

The Art of Crossing Cultures, Craig Storti, Intercultural Press, ISBN: 0933662858.

Culture Shock Series, from Times Books International. Country specific books.

Figuring Foreigners Out: A Practical Guide, Craig Storti, Intercultural Press, ISBN: 1877864706.

First-Time Asia, Lucy Ridout and Lesley Reader, Rough Guides, ISBN 1-85828-332-9. Aimed at backpackers, but an excellent resource for expats to learn about the cultural and lifestyle differences they will encounter while living in East Asia (from Pakistan eastwards).

First Time Europe, Louis Casbianca, Rough Guides, ISBN: 1858285739.

Vacation Work *Live and Work* series: Australia & New Zealand; Belgium, Netherlands & Luxembourg; France; Germany; Italy; Japan; Russia & Eastern Europe; Saudi & The Gulf; Scandinavia, Scotland; Spain & Portugal; USA & Canada.

Online Resources

www.expatforum.com: hosts numerous online chat groups, both general expat issues and culture shock.

http://internationaled.about.com/education/internationaled/blcultureshock.htm: articles on culture shock from various expats and experts.

www.overseasdigest.com/teacher4.html: articles on living abroad from an American perspective.

www.petersons.com/stdyabrd/abroad4.html: Take the Shock Out of Culture Shock, an article for students.

www.thetimes.co.uk: keeping up to date with news back home can help tackle culture shock. This URL is for the regularly updated onlione version of *The Times*.

CHILDCARE OPTIONS

Outside the Home

When moving abroad with children who are not yet of formal schooling age, the prospect of finding acceptable childcare can be daunting. There can also be the issue of after school care for older children if both parents are working and for single parents. The options vary depending on the country you relocate to and the financial resources you have available. There are also the issues about whether or not one parent really wants to become a full-time carer.

Local custom is a major determining factor in what full-time childcare options are available to expatriates. The more developed a country is, especially one with a well established middle class, the more likely it is to have commercial day-care facilities, where groups of children are cared for by trained staff; though in some well-developed Asian countries, such as Hong Kong and Singapore, domestic helpers are still common.

In some countries it is common for only one parent to have paid employment and the other to care for the children and in others local residents use their own family members, or employed staff to look after their children only. In both these instances it is likely that expatriates will be able to employ local nationals to look after their children.

Foreign residents generally follow local practice, but the options are not necessarily cut and dried. Any new expatriate will have to investigate the available options and decide which childcare option they are comfortable with and which is most suitable for them and their child.

Parents can have problems finding the ideal solution to their childcare needs and the final choice is likely to involve some compromise of the parent's initial plans. Despite these possible hurdles, a child's early exposure to the local culture can be beneficial.

If children are cared for by host nationals, they can be exposed to a second language and new tastes, sights, smells, sounds and textures that they may never have experienced if the family had stayed in their home country.

If one parent decides to be the primary childcare provider, they can still create many opportunities to involve their child in the local atmosphere, language, and culture.

Jolynn Bellamy, who is currently living in the Netherlands, is expecting a child. She intends to raise her child multiculturally, having known international children herself and the benefits they received from being educated abroad.

I haven't had to worry yet about finding childcare here in Holland, but was watching the news the other night and found out that they need 16,000 workers in that field here. After my baby comes and gets a little age on him I am going to take Dutch classes and plan to open a bilingual day care centre to both our advantages.

I can remember in high school that we had a boy join us who had grown up in two other countries and he was so smart. He tutored everyone and he got the best grades in the foreign languages classes. I would like my child to have the same advantages as that boy did being brought up abroad.

Whether you intend finding external childcare support or not, if you have the opportunity to talk to parents already established in the community to which you are moving, you should take advantage of it. By contacting your employer or colleagues in your destination country you may be able to find out what types of resources there are and what the local custom regarding childcare is. Embassies, expatriate clubs and expatriate websites in the destination city (or country) might be able to supply you with information about organised playgroups (local or expatriate), day-care facilities or even information about hiring your own childcare provider.

By utilising the contact suggestions in the first two chapters, you can also build on the formal resources mentioned above.

Local Language Kindergarten/Crèche

Different nationalities use different names for childcare facilities. They can be called day-care, kindergarten or crèche, and they can come in a wide variety of formats and have varying standards.

Local language facilities can appear to offer the same structure and equipment as what you have seen in your home country. There may be bright pictures on the walls, toys, paints, crayons in their expected places and friendly staff. They may have a routine that is similar to those in facilities you have previously experienced. However, you need to remember that every country and culture has its own legal standards, as well as its own parental/staff expectations of behaviour, discipline, supervision and security for students. The best way to find out about these issues is of course to talk to other parents whose children are enrolled in the facility.

A local language childcare facility can be an excellent environment for your child to learn the language; this can be especially important if you are planning to stay in a country for a few years. A child who speaks the local language will have a wider variety of children to make friends with and is more likely to enjoy living in the country if they can communicate in everyday situations.

Fiona Nicholls' middle son, Cameron, was enrolled in a local Turkish crèche at the age of three, when Fiona accepted a part-time job. She and her husband, Paul, decided they did not want to hire a full-time nanny since they wanted Cameron to be in a child-oriented social setting. In sending him to the local crèche, Cameron was immersed in a wholly Turkish speaking environment, where he was able to learn socialisation skills and the local language. At such a young age, it was not difficult for Cameron to integrate himself into the crèche, and two years on, now in a bilingual kindergarten, Cameron continues to learn the local language which will allow him to progress to an elementary school that is taught half in English and half in Turkish.

> Many experts also believe that early exposure to a foreign language, even if it is later forgotten, enhances a person's ability to learn other languages later; a very useful skill to have in an increasing globalized world.

Bernadette van Houten, a professional in the field of children and language acquisition, has indicated that the earlier someone learns a language the more their skill to learn other languages develops. Many expatriate parents would like to see their children become bilingual in their new environment.

Bernadette however, cautiously defines bilingualism in children not as an ability to speak two languages fluently, but as being able to use two languages in their daily lives. For example, expatriates in non-English speaking countries will speak English in the home, yet while in school, or in their playgroup, children will hear and learn to speak the language that the local children use when playing. While they may not be able to speak fluently in the local language, they can interact socially in a language other than that used in their home environment.

Beyond the obvious benefits of being introduced to the local language, Fiona found significant differences in the way that the local system worked which simply had to be tolerated. As a vegetarian family, Fiona expressed to the childminders at the crèche that she did not want her son to be fed the meat portion of the hot meal that was provided. Fiona soon found out that the childminders did not believe that being vegetarian was appropriate for a child in their care, so they fed Cameron everything that appeared on the plate. Because of the attitude of the crèche staff, Fiona lost control over her son's midday diet.

Fiona also had difficulty with the local crèche's enforcement of afternoon napping. The children were expected to take a two-hour nap in the afternoons. Cameron had not been napping at all in the previous six months. The children at the crèche put on their pyjamas, crawled into bed and went to sleep for two hours every day. In the local crèches this was an accepted practice since so many parents were unable to pick up their children before 5:30 or 6:00 p.m., which resulted in a very long day for such young children. The napping in Turkey was not just expected, but approved of from the local parents' point of view, because it was common for the whole family to go out for evening meals. With the children well rested, they would be able to stay up much later in the evening and be able to partake in the evening events.

However, Fiona usually finished work much earlier and was able, on most days to pick up Cameron by 3:30 p.m. Having just woken from a two hour sleep, Cameron would be awake until late every night. Not being in the tradition of keeping children out until late hours for meals or gatherings, Fiona found this aspect difficult to deal with.

Fiona also found that the local crèche's rules governing parental visits were vastly different from what she expected. The parents were told that they were not allowed into the school (beyond the reception area) during the school day. Thus if you wished to pick up your child, you could not simply show up and collect your child. Nor could you visit the crèche during the day to see what activities the children were involved in. From Fiona's experience in England parents were often encouraged to visit the school so that they were aware of the ongoing activities in the facility. It seemed odd to her that the crèche would enforce this rule, though they said it was to the advantage of the small children staying there.

Yet regardless of these large issues, Fiona still believed that this was the best childcare solution for her son. He was safe, warm, fed, well looked after, and really enjoyed going to the crèche in the mornings. He was not ill nor bored, nor unhappy with the surroundings. Often, expatriate parents move to a new country and expect that things will be or should be the way they would be at home. This is not always the case and parents should be prepared, like Fiona was, to deal with the situation. She advises:

When looking at local crèches for your child do not expect them to be exactly as they would be in your home country. You should be conscious of the custom and system differences before you accept a position for your child in a local language facility. The way things are done there might not always match your preferences.

It is important too, for the parents to not only evaluate what they want for their child in a foreign childcare setting, but to be aware of what the child feels comfortable with, as Alison Albon found out when she moved to Switzerland.

In Geneva we took Matthew (then 2 or 2¹/₂) to a French speaking playschool. It was only for a couple of hours a day in the afternoons. The teachers were unable to speak any English to him and either because of this or the fact that he was just so used to being with me alone, he used to scream blue murder when we had to go. I did ascertain however that he did calm down after ten minutes and seemed to enjoy himself. He started learning the basics of French but not enough to be able to communicate with the teachers. When we heard we were moving to the Netherlands, I just kept him home with me. I didn't think there was much use in dragging (yes, almost literally) him to school every day, when he was obviously miserable.

On their subsequent move to the Netherlands the Albon family eased Matthew into a local Dutch playing class where Matthew coped well with the new surroundings. Alison suspects that it was largely due to the fact that the teachers were able to speak English and thus Matthew was able to communicate his needs, while at the same time reinforcing the local language that would help Matthew make friends in his new environment.

While bearing the child's needs and preferences in mind, a thorough investigation of both local norms and a specific facility's reputation are important when choosing a local language childcare facility. Though it would be helpful to investigate the options prior to arriving, often, a look-see at the facility is an important factor in deciding on the appropriateness. Be prepared with questions to ask the staff members.

A further aspect of childcare that parents can find troublesome is the varying attitudes towards discipline. The range of what is acceptable behaviour from the child and what form of discipline and punishment can be administered can cause much

Questions To Ask At A Local Language Kindergarten

How many non-local children have attended the school?	
How many non-local children still attend the school?	
How many of the teachers speak a language you understand?	
How many of the teachers speak a language your child understands?	
What activities are organised for the children?	
What toys, games and facilities do they have?	
Is the day structured, or do children have free choice of what to do?	
How many staff are on duty at any one time (especially at playtime)?	
Are the doors/gates locked when the children are inside?	
What happens if a child is hurt?	
What discipline is enforced?	
What training/qualifications do the staff members have?	
Are meals provided?	
Do the children sleep during the day?	

frustration and upset to expatriate parents and children. Corporal punishment may be acceptable in some countries, whereas in others children are rarely reprimanded.

Non-local Language Kindergarten/Crèche

In many countries, English language facilities are probably the most common medium after the local language. But where countries have close links with a country that speaks another language, or there are large communities of non-English speaking foreign nationals, there may also be facilities in other languages.

Local people or companies may establish these facilities, on a commercial or non-profit basis, to cater for both local children whose parents want them to learn a foreign language and the children of expatriates. Locally managed facilities may be run by either local staff, or expatriates, and their standards match local medium schools, or the country whose language is used.

In some countries where the government subsidises different social services, there may be further options for childcare facilities. In Australia, Gillian Kerr has sent her two children, Donald and Catherine, to a Council-run childcare centre. The municipality-run organisation is a tight operation she says with qualified teachers and childminders. Though the facility is close by and able to take her children, she has had a few problems because of her expatriate status.

As a non-resident of Australia, I pay the full fee to send my kids there. The Aussies get big social security funding so it only costs them a fraction of what I pay as a full fee paying member. Since it is so inexpensive for the locals, anyone can attend. As a result you get some really rough kids there with foul language and abusive behaviour, and they are not even five years old. In many of these cases, both parents are unemployed and have sent their kids to the childcare centre under the pretence that they are looking for work. My children were getting bitten, kicked, punched, called names etc.

My problem is that I can't afford to send them to a more upmarket daycare, as I would have to pay even more, and I can't afford it. So they are at another council-run centre, but hopefully that will change when I start work and can afford a better centre.

So even if facilities are available, the fees you are liable to pay if you have not achieved local residency status and the behaviour of other children attending may mean the facility is not viable. If the fees are acceptable there can also be the issue of whether the environment is acceptable/different to what your children are used to. It may be necessary to do a little extra preparation with your children so that they know that they are walking into an environment where acceptable behaviour is different to what they have been used to.

When expatriate children attend a local facility it is a good way for them to make local friends, though at the same time they may notice they are different from the local kids and initially find it difficult to cope with.

Apart from locally sponsored facilities, large international commercial companies and embassies may provide facilities for their employees and nationals. Sometimes these facilities allow other expatriates and local nationals to enrol if there are spaces available.

The management staff of sponsored facilities is often comprised of expatriates, with other staff employed locally. The quality and standards of these facilities are usually the same as, or better, than facilities in the home country of the sponsoring organisation.

The advantage of these facilities is that if you intend to return to your home country, or move again soon, your child will be in a familiar cultural and linguistic environment. Bronwyn Davies in Hong Kong, mother to Callum and Phoebe, preferred to send her children to day care facilities that are run by organisations set up by other expatriates of similar nationality. By doing so she knew her children would get the English language support that they required for the formal schooling system that they eventually attended. In addition, by sending her children to an internationally sponsored facility, she was able to communicate clearly with the instructors/child-minders. However, most importantly, Bronwyn understood and agreed with the methods of instruction, play, and discipline that were used in the facility.

While some parents are excited about the prospect of staying home themselves to look after the children while abroad, there are many expatriate partners that are not. Gillian Kerr is one such parent. She is not afraid to admit that she wants a life outside of the house, whether it be in her home country, or abroad.

I am not cut out to be a full-time mum. I went from a challenging career to nothing and thought it would be perfect to start a family and be home with my children until they went to school. I had my first child in our first year abroad. Two children later I was depressed and unchallenged at home, so I went back to full-time study to start my new career as a teacher. My children had to start day-care full-time (Donald was 3 and Catherine 18 months). I felt as guilty as all hell, still do sometimes, but the kids love the centre and even ask to go on weekends. They get to play outside all day with their friends. We have a rule that they are never there for more than eight hours a day, which means juggling our schedules a little at times when I have evening lectures or my husband has a late meeting. It is working well for us, even though it is expensive. The other families get financial assistance from the government if both partners are working, but because we are not Australian we have to pay the full rate, regardless of the fact that we pay taxes.

For some parents though, the decision to send a child to day-care when they are in a foreign country is not an immediate option. There are many parents who initially believe that it is not beneficial for a child to attend a day-care facility until they arrive in their new host country and have others around them discussing the benefits of such a situation. Cindy Rothacker in Belgium had not even imagined putting her child in day care at a young age, until she realised a break between mother and son would be a good thing for both of them.

To me, the use of day care facilities depends on the age of your children. In most European countries, starting at the age of three (and sometimes two and a half) your child can go to school for the day. I thought this idea absurd until I sent my three year old who was driving me insane from boredom (his, not mine). He absolutely loves school. He was going for half days at first (sometimes he still needs that afternoon nap) but they are doing great things with young kids in his kindergarten school.

Frances Brown, moving out of South Africa to the UK, carried much the same sentiment towards day-care with her during the move.

When I landed in the UK I had these great visions of being a stay-at-home-mom and doing things right, after all, my child was only 18 months old. Ha! After five months I was going mad. My daily highlight was Teletubbies at 10a.m. and going to the park after naptime. So I thought, best get a job and meet some people my own age. I secured a job and started visiting the nurseries in the area where I was going to be living and all the ones where I was going to work. Fortunately I was offered a four-day a week placement at the nursery of my choice, the one attached to the college where I work. It is very well run, and the kids learn a lot there.

Before you go out and investigate the different childcare facilities in your area it is a good idea to be equipped with information gathering questions.

Questions To Ask At A Non-Local Language Kindergarten

What is the medium of instruction?	
What is the mix of languages that the children speak?	
How much of the instruction is in another language because some children are not fluent in the primary language?	
What is the common language the children use when playing?	
How many of the teachers speak a language you understand?	
How many of the teachers speak a language your child understands?	
How many staff are on duty at any one time (especially at playtime)?	
What activities are organised?	
Are the doors/gates locked when the children are inside?	
What happens if a child is hurt?	
What discipline is enforced?	
What formal training/qualifications do the staff have?	
Are meals provided?	
Do the children sleep during the day?	

Childcare In the Home

Employed Staff

The nationality of staff employed directly by a family can vary immensely. Local nannies and low paid 'guest workers' are the most common employees outside of Europe and North America, where parents are more likely to use au pairs.

Local staff and guest workers are unlikely to be qualified nannies (with certification through a bona fide agency), though many will be parents themselves, or have worked as nannies/childminders for years. Filipino staff are well-known for being well-educated and midwives, psychologists and dentists work as guest workers in much of Asia because the wages are better than in the Philippines.

Depending on the country you are living in, local staff may, or may not speak a foreign language. Bilingual staff can be more expensive than monolingual staff, and you should be prepared to pay for the luxury of a nanny that speaks the same language as you do.

Guest workers are usually from developing countries, looking to work in a wealthier country, to send money home to their families. Filipinos are one of the more common nationalities of domestic guest workers throughout Asia and the Gulf States, but Indonesian, Indian, Pakistani, East Europeans and other nationalities often travel abroad to find domestic work as well.

The status of domestic staff can vary too. Depending on the country, staff may expect to be live-in, live-out, full-time or part-time. In some countries you may be expected to employ a husband and wife team for childcare, cleaning, shopping, gardening and security. You may even inherit staff when you move into company allocated accommodation.

Employing a domestic helper can make life easier and much more pleasant, especially when you find a competent and caring nanny. Hiring staff to work in your home allows the primary care-giving parent the enjoyable luxury of time to themselves to pursue work, hobbies, and a social life. Fiona Nicholls recently had a third child and though her first two sons are of school age, and therefore looked after during the day, she needed to find a minder for her little one so that she could continue to do the part-time work she so much enjoys. By finding home help to look after her son two days a week, Fiona was able to continue with a job that affords her mental stimulation and professional satisfaction that she would not otherwise have been be able to achieve.

Yet hiring someone to look after your children in your home is not always an easy decision to come to grips with. Many expatriates have a certain pride that drives them to resist the option of having either full-time or part-time domestic help. Judi Trudel found this to be true of her experience as a new expatriate. Judi struggled between not wanting any help at all and hiring a series of helpers when she found she was pregnant, twice, and unable to physically be there for her older boys. It was, and continues to be a very large personal issue with her.

When we came to Hong Kong I was adamant I would not cave in and hire a domestic helper to help with the children. I didn't work, so what if the place was a mess. Then in 1996 we moved to a very large flat with 'servant's quarters'. I was pregnant, we wondered what would happen to the boys when I went to the hospital so we hired our first full-time, live-in helper. She was great. When my daughter arrived, Rema, our helper, took the boys off to the playground and kept them entertained while the baby and I slept.

Since then we have had to find a new helper (our old helper was married and moved home). The new helper, Celia, wasn't so great at cleaning but she helped out a lot with the boys and the baby. When my first daughter, Xanthe, was one year old, I went back to work teaching English part-time so it was very handy having Celia to help out at home. However, I felt guilty and stopped working to be home more.

Our second helper moved back to the Philippines and I hired our third helper, Libby. Everyday I go through the pros and cons of not having someone to help, or having someone to help when I should be able to do it myself. I feel guilty for asking Libby to look after Xayla or Xanthe (my daughters) or even when she takes the boys out when I know I should be doing it. I know that when we leave Hong Kong I won't be able to have a helper, and I sometimes still wonder why I even need one now, but once you get used to something....

Aside from the obvious benefits in hiring child-minding help that has kept Judi employing replacement staff, expatriate parents should be aware of other drawbacks involved in employing domestic help. It can be difficult to accept someone else looking after the children when it first becomes necessary or possible. Many first-time expatriates are simply not used to the notion of hiring domestic help to look after the children and can feel pressured into doing so if they live in a country where it is the accepted norm (like Hong Kong).

Frances Brown, living in the UK, employed a child minder for the one day a week that her child, Jenna, was not in the nursery.

I did not mind leaving my child with a minder, but a minder I did not know — that was the hard part. The minder was not who I would have chosen as a primary care giver though, simply because she was not my cup of tea. But I was desperate at the time. And I feel I compromised my child's care just so I could go off to work. Childcare is so expensive here, and it does eat up most of my salary. But the sanity the job offers me offsets the guilt I feel at having someone look after Jenna.

Nannies of a different nationality than their employer may have different attitudes to discipline, diet, supervision and acceptable activities for children. Agreeing on standards acceptable to both parent and nanny can be difficult. If you find it difficult to agree on the diet provided for your child, consider what your own diet is and how the local nationals would consider yours. Potatoes are a basic staple in the UK, pasta in Italy and rice in much of Asia, even though local tastes differ, is one really better or worse than the other and will the local staple harm your child?

Questions To Ask Candidates

What experience/qualifications do they have for working with children?	
What experience do they have with expatriates and their children?	
What experience do they have with expatriates of your nationality?	
How sure are they that they can arrive on time, every day?	
How will they travel to work?	
Where will they be living?	
Would they be willing to undergo a health check, if necessary?	
If they have their own children at school, what will happen when those children are sick, or not at school.	
How do they want to be paid (hard currency/local currency)?	

Attitudes to fresh air can also vary enormously, Scandinavians and Canadians have a much different attitude to what is cold than someone from Greece or the Middle East. In some cultures it also a commonly held belief that fresh air causes illness and no matter how hard you try to encourage your childminder to take the children outside, they just will not do it when they think it is cold, because they believe it will harm your child.

Mike and Sarah van der Es have hired a number of child-minders in their many international moves. They both worked full-time and had to consider hiring a local helper. Because they frequently moved to third-world nations they were very concerned about the level of care that would be provided by local people. They found that some countries where they lived are more child/baby friendly than others and this made a difference in the kind of childcare provided by a child-minder. In selecting a home-based child-minder they found the following a useful basis to work from:

1. When you look for someone to help with your baby or toddler there will be many with ability, a likeable personality and relevant experience in developing countries. Still, follow the golden rule of not leaving children with anyone you do not trust. Many local girls/mothers have the care skills but lack the crisis management ability to deal with a life threatening situation like malaria or a rabid dog bite. They may panic and do nothing or the wrong thing. Where possible, leave them an emergency phone number and teach them to use the phone. And test them!

2. When living in a third-world country, we generally got the best results choosing and training a younger woman (19-20 years old) who spoke some English. They can learn quickly and are natural with children but will need training to deal with such things as electrical apparatus. Our first 16-year-old girl sucked water up in the vacuum cleaner.

3. Parents can also become jealous if a child seems to prefer the nanny to them. This is especially common if both parents work, or spend a lot of time away from the child. The common solution of sacking the nanny will not help either the parent or the child and is unfair to the nanny who probably believes she is only doing her job. What it may simply be indicative of is the child's comfort with the nanny. But it may also be indicative of the manner in which the nanny relates to the child; for example, referring to the child as my baby, or having the child call the nanny the foreign language equivalent of mother. Some parents in this instance may find a need to redefine the boundaries between the nanny and the child, as well as re-emphasising the fact that the nanny is an employee hired to look after the child, and not to act as a surrogate mother. This may be easier said than done and it will take a certain amount of will on the part of the parents to try to keep the relationship between their child and the nanny in check.

4. Learning how to manage domestic staff and find a balance between everyone's skills, responsibilities and needs can be difficult. It can be important to agree early on in any arrangement what everyone expects.

5. Employing staff that have a personal recommendation from another expatriate can make life easier. If your staff are used to working for foreigners with strange ideas (at least as far as your host country is concerned) life can be much easier.

6. Finally, when you are ready to move from your posting, you might find your child has a very difficult time with the loss of their nanny. Children can become very attached to their nanny, if both parents work or spend a lot of time away from the child; this can lead to a traumatic separation when you move away. Unless the child is very young, there is the possibility that when you leave your posting, and hence leave the hired help behind, your child will have to face a serious readjustment in the structure of their life. This might cause a lot of sadness and irritability for the first few weeks away. And the best way to combat their sadness is to be available to them as if you are taking over the nanny's job and provide them with all of the attention that you can muster. Keep your child busy and entertained and the missing nanny will not be so missed.

Employing staff who have worked for other expats can be a major plus as Michelyne Callan, one of the authors, found in Hong Kong when she was looking for someone to look after her new-born son.

Tessie, from the Philippines, came in to interview with us. I was concerned that she might not feel comfortable working with a Canadian family, and might not understand how we like things done. When we asked her about it she laughed and said there would be no problem since she had previous experience working with one American family and one Scottish family already and knew that 'you foreigners' did things differently. When it came down to cooking, for example, we asked her if she knew how to cook. She said 'Sure, I cooked for the Scottish family. I can boil anything.' Giggles put aside, we felt comfortable in hiring her knowing that she worked for foreign families, and had helped raise their children. She expected that we would want things done our way, not her way.

Parental Childcare

The opportunity for one spouse to stay at home and look after the children can be an important factor in some families accepting an international posting. Being able to afford for one partner not to work can be a great advantage of living abroad. Sometimes though, it is the cost of child minding facilities that makes the decision for a parent to stay at home.

Frances Brown, an expat in the UK has seen this frequently:

One can see why most moms stay at home. Childcare in the UK is just too expensive for the average family. Most of my salary goes to nursery fees and seeing as my daughter is starting formal school next year, I am registering as a childminder. I will be working from home in the near future, and I can be available to fetch and carry for her and a couple of other little ones.

The opportunity for a parent to look after their child(ren) while they are young can be an enjoyable and beneficial experience for many. Many parents see it as being good for the children and it can give the parent a chance for a career break, give them the chance to explore the host city/country, learn the language, or fulfil another long held dream.

Natascha Gaim-Marsoner is one parent who though she held a valid work permit decided to stay home with her kids, partly due to the expense of childcare costs in Germany where she relocated to, and partly due to her perception of the quality of the facilities available. Another important reason that Natashca opted to be a stay-at-home-mom was to help her children's adjustment into the new community.

But not working in a foreign country is not the same as it is in your home country. When you take the children to play in the park there may not be other parents you can talk to, or you may not consider the local park safe for your child to use. There may not be many parents at all, with similar age children, who speak your language and are within easy reach of where you live. It may also be difficult to travel around the town with a child due to inclement weather or dangerous roads and sidewalks.

Increasingly, men are becoming a sizeable portion of the accompanying partner group. Some of these men will take responsibility for childcare, but when considering this option it should remembered that being the only man in a traditionally female occupation can be difficult for both the man and the women. In some countries it can be so rare for men to look after the children that people will constantly ask where the mother is when a father is alone with the children. One expatriate father looking after two pre-school children started responding that, 'The children have no mother,' because he then received sympathy and help instead of the annoying assumption of people assuming he could not look after the children properly.

If you choose to keep childcare in the family, some preparation in advance can be helpful when both the childcarer and the child are trying to make friends. When you are looking after your children in your home country, virtually everyone you meet during the day, at the playpark, the shops or the bus stop, will speak your language; in a foreign country that can change dramatically. In some cities it is very possible that you will not meet anyone who speaks your language from the time your partner goes out to work until the time they return.

When co-author Huw Francis first started staying at home to look after his one-year-old son, there were no other parents and only one or two foreigners in the area that he could occasionally meet during the day.

Finding playmates for your children is important, but finding people for the parent to talk to is equally important; it is probably true to say that a happy parent produces happier children. Finding both playmates for your children and friends for you needs planning and effort. Children can be great icebreakers; so use every opportunity they give you to make friends.

If you hear someone speaking your language, say hello. Strike up a conversation if possible. If the conversation develops suggest going for a coffee. If the person has children, ask them if they can suggest good places for you to take yours to play. If you do not jump into a conversation, but decide to wait until next time you see the person, you may never actually meet them again. What do you have to lose, except the opportunity to make a friend? Someone has to make the first move, why not you?

One expat stay-at-home mother recalled a time when she bit the bullet and started talking to someone that looked like a foreigner as well. Being new in the area, she was looking for other playmates for her child to associate with. When she finally burst into friendly conversation, she learned that the family was also new to the area, and had just moved from France. The family had excellent English language abilities, and so after one more 'run-in' in the same location, they decided to make further arrangements for the children to get together. Not only did the kids benefit from the new friendship, but the expat moms really hit it off as well, and formed a very strong friendship for the duration of their stay in the country.

If you are trying to learn the language of the country you have moved to, meeting and talking to local parents in play parks can be free tuition. Most people will be really happy that you are trying to learn their language. You may even be able to arrange mutual lessons, you teach them your language and they teach you theirs. Your children will also be learning the local language while they play too.

Finding a playgroup, that uses your native language, can also be important in helping your children develop socially and linguistically. Most parents feel that it is important that their children are fluent in their mother tongue, even if it is an uncommon language. Ask your embassy if they can suggest such a playgroup, or if there is someway you can be put in touch with other parents from your country, or of countries that speak the same language.

If all else fails, try setting up your own informal playgroup, where you and other parents take turns supervising the children. This can be a great way to make friends, and also give you some free time to relax, shop, or do other jobs that having children around makes difficult. One group of expats who lived in a communal setting set up an informal playgroup session where two parents at a time would take care of the four boys while the other two parents would utilise this free time any way they wanted. Sometimes the parents who were on free time would go grocery shopping, while other times they would go for walks in the hills, just to have quiet time alone. For the four parents it was a wonderful break in their week, and for the children, it afforded them the opportunity to socialise and partake in structured play activities with parental supervision. It worked for all.

Questions To Ask Yourself

Will there be enough people around to support you?	
Will you be able to meet people and make friends?	
Do you have the patience to spend long days, alone, with your child(ren) if your partner works long hours and/or is away on business a lot?	
Will you have the patience to spend time with parents of a different nationality who may have different attitudes to childcare and discipline?	
Will there be the opportunity for you to have time without the child(ren) to do your own thing?	
Will it be practical to complete your daily tasks (shopping, banking, cleaning, etc.) with your child(ren) accompanying you?	
Will you be able to make contact with local people so your child(ren) has someone to play with?	
Do you need to have more freedom during the day than you would have if you looked after the child(ren) alone?	

An important issue for a stay-at-home-parent in a foreign country that arises from time to time is what to do when the primary childcarer is ill. With no supporting family nearby and because you are new in a community, you might not have many resources to call upon in a time of need. Finding a solution to this potential situation before it happens is very important and making friends and finding a support network of other parents as soon as you arrive can go a long way towards this.

Making the Decision

The environment in which you will be living will be an important factor in determining the best arrangements for childcare. You have to consider your family, your child and yourself when coming to a decision. What do you want your child to gain from a childcare situation? Can it be best achieved through one particular facility? Are those facilities available in your new host country? Do you want to be a stay-at-home parent? Do you think you have the stamina and interest required to do the job well? These are difficult questions that sometimes go unanswered until you are in the country and have already tested out the waters.

Investigating the formal day-care facility options in your host region will be important. Is there an international facility available where the majority of the children and the carers speak English? How does the standard of facility/childminder rank compared to what you would expect in your home country? Would you rather have your child in an environment where they are engaged in the local language? How important are the influences of the cultural differences that can be promulgated in a local language facility?

A local nanny can act as a language tutor for your child and introduce your child to local children, but their ideas of discipline, safety and diet may be very different from yours.

You will have to weigh the importance of these differences against the benefits of having a locally hired helper who will know where to take the child for outdoor activities, who can help you locate different items for your child that you might not have been able to find on your own, and someone who is able to find age appropriate friends for your child in the local community.

In some countries, guest workers form a large community of their own and meet during the day, with the children they look after, so your child would have the opportunity to meet children of their own age; your child may also learn the language of the nanny. Where large communities of guest workers exist, they form their own support network and will often be able to arrange cover for illness or holidays. But again, their ideas of discipline, safety and diet may be very different from yours.

It is important that you seriously weigh the benefits of the different options, looking at the implication of each on all those involved.

Finding safe and interesting activities for your pre-school child can be difficult in some countries. It can take imagination and persistence to discover opportunities, find friends and provide the experiences and lifestyle you want for your child; but it can usually be done. The more opportunities you allow your child, the more they can learn, though the opportunities may not be ones you would normally expect to take.

Resources

Print Resources

The Bilingual Family, Edith Harding and Philip Riley, Cambridge University Press, ISBN 0 521 31194 2.

Online Resources

www.expatexchange.com: an online community for expats, with associated experts to offer advice.

www.expatforum.com: host of numerous online chat groups for expats.

www.expat-moms.com: a forum for mothers to swap tips. There is also a bi-weekly newsletter.

EDUCATION: UNDERSTANDING THE OPTIONS

Their child's education is always of concern to parents. In their home country they probably know what is available and how to establish the quality of an individual school, but where do you start finding out about whether a school in a country you have never been to, or have only just arrived in, is suitable? If an expat child finishes school abroad, it also is likely that they will want to progress into Further or Higher Education in their home country, though many expat children stay in the country where their parents are, or move to a third country. Though progressing to Higher or Further education can be done almost as easily from a foreign country as when you are living at home, the processes and admissions policies of institutions can vary for international applicants.

The availability of suitable education for their children can often be one of the main determining factors on whether or not parents accept an international posting, and which country that posting is to.

For adults living abroad, there are also numerous opportunities for continuing their education, but the number of subject options and institutions offering courses can be bewildering. Continuing and adult education is addressed in the second part of this chapter.

Schooling for Expat Children

When deciding upon the best schooling option for expat children it is important to know and understand what schools and curricula are available. Not every system is suitable for every child, plus you must consider not only the immediate schooling needs of your child, but also how they will progress through the school system and beyond. Schooling options are wide and varied and though most are probably available in your home country, there are many you would not have seen the need to consider until you move abroad. The following schools and curricula may be available to you when you are living abroad:

1. International Schools
2. Local Schools
3. Home Schools
4. Boarding Schools (in home country, host country, or third country)

Each of these options, with the varying curricula they offer will be discussed individually throughout the chapter.

School Constitution

Schools can either be state run, or independent (private). Within the categories of private (non state run) schools, there are various ways they can be constituted:

1. An individual or private company may own a school and one person, or a very limited number of people, may be responsible for overseeing the running the school, with no external accountability.

2. A large company or a group of companies, with commercial or historical links to the area, may 'sponsor' the school. The extent to which the company is involved with the running of the school and how much financial backing it provides can vary greatly. Expatriate employees of the sponsoring company may be obliged to send their children to the school if they want school fees to be covered by their employer.

3. An Educational Foundation, or other philanthropic organisation, may fund the school and oversee its management through a board of governors. The governors may or may not be directly appointed by the sponsor.

4. A national government may sponsor a school in a foreign country. Such schools are often run as if they were a conventional state school in the sponsoring government's country.

5. A non-profit-making school is one where all revenues are kept in the school to cover salaries, consumables, expansion, maintenance, etc.

6. A profit making school is one that is run as a commercial enterprise.

Schools Available to Expatriates

International Schools

A true international school will have students from numerous countries and offer a curriculum suitable for these multi-national students. The programmes will generally lead to final awards or examinations that will allow students to easily apply to and study at leading universities around the world. The language of instruction will generally be English, though a school may also offer an education in Spanish, French, German or other language in tandem for non-native English speakers, students whose English language ability is poor, or to meet the legal requirements of the host country. There are also French and Spanish 'International' schools that offer the International Baccalaureate programme (see below) in those languages.

Not all schools that call themselves 'international' are of high quality or truly cater to 'international' students. They may offer an international curriculum, in English, but cater mostly to host nation students, or expatriate students from one particular country (i.e. Japan). Also, not all 'international' schools are accredited by outside agencies and some may not offer a recognised international curriculum, but an internationalised version of a national curriculum (i.e. Korea).

Mike Callan, an international school administrator from Canada, who has taught in Japan, Hong Kong and Turkey, has come across many schools that claim to be international.

Many schools call themselves 'international'. Many times however, the name is used to refer to its geographic location and may not reflect the philosophies and practices of the school. I believe that an international school is a school that clearly states its mission to teach internationally accepted ideas to its students; ideas such as cultural awareness, understanding and respect. I believe that an international school has a wider vision and therefore offers its students and staff an opportunity to experience something that they could not in their home educational systems. The degree of 'internationalism' international schools offer varies from school to school. Often the degree of internationalism in a school is determined by how much 'internationalism' the clientele want.

On what makes a good international school, Jim DiSebastian, a long-term American international educator who has taught in the US, England, Honduras, Spain and Israel, and who is now the Director of an international school in Turkey says:

What makes a good international school? Internationalism. And that may sound like a sarcastic answer, but there are international schools that aren't international in actuality. My idea of the best international school is one where no one nationality is in a large number at the school. However, reality is that that sometimes happens depending on the country and location of the school and also, the charter of the school. Some schools that are established with the help of, for instance, the US embassy, have to have at least 51% American students in the school all the time, and the same with the teachers. I really like working at schools where the students and the teachers are a mixture of nationalities. To me that's the most important thing because then everybody has to work together.

On the advantages of an international school education he says:

'...the advantages of sending a child to an international school outweigh the normal education that they would get at the best private school in their home countries, simply because it is international. As long as it is of some quality, the kids come out of it much better adults, and with a better worldview, I think, than those that stay in their home countries. Even university admissions go better for those students in a lot of countries who have lived overseas.

Harry Deelman, an experienced international teacher and administrator, who grew up in South Africa and England and has worked in Buenos Aires, Rome, Dubai and Bangkok, is now part of *Search Associates* (PO Box 168, Chiang Mai 50000, Thailand; deelman@loxinfo.co.th; www.search-associates.co.uk), an international teacher and school administrator placement agency. He believes that international schools are easier for expat children to settle into than other schools available to expats.

...one of the greatest assets of international schools is that there is no core of 'required behaviour' and peer-group knowledge and interests — except, perhaps, the cosmopolitan ease with the world which it does not take children long to absorb to some degree. Any 'local' school, even one with a bilingual or international curriculum, tends to have a way of doing things, and interests, knowledge, lifestyle, behaviour amongst its students, which automatically make a newly arrived 'outsider' very conscious of that label and that fact, for quite some time.

In contrast, almost every international school has an atmosphere of ready acceptance and welcome, no matter what the particular 'differences' the specific new arrival may have, because everyone is different already.

This even helps the very shy, or aggressive, or physically different child become accepted much more quickly than in most local-type schools, anywhere.

The key factor is the international mix and range amongst the children (not solely in their passports, but more in where they have previously lived, or frequently visit, to see family, etc.). Having an international teaching staff is not an important part of the above-outlined aspect of schools, though the range of nationalities of the teachers can affect the style of the school and the acceptance and tolerance of different previous academic habits and viewpoints which the child may have acquired.

There are disadvantages, which Jim DiSebastian's own children experienced:

Students can go through some pretty rough times. The child at school overseas has difficulties sometimes adjusting; doesn't want to go, or doesn't like the school, or doesn't like the country, or misses his or her friends. There seemed to be a period with one of our children especially, who after leaving the previous country, wanted to go back there, but the whole time they were there (in the previous country) they had complained about that country. But it was very difficult to make new friends; especially the older they got. It's harder the older the children get to make new relationships and to break into the cliques that exist at schools and things like that, especially if you're from a different country (to the majority of students).

Markus Ketola, a third culture kid from Finland found the shift from his home country's education system to that of an international school very severe, but it had many positive aspects too.

*I would say that the shift from my home country's schooling system to the international system was quite drastic. At the international school I was, in a way, dropped into the deep end of the pool, where I was expected to figure my way around the new system right away. Not knowing the language made it all that much harder, but it was all for the better. Not only the kind of education you get at an international school, but also the teachers and students had so much more to offer in terms of different perspectives, ideas etc. I became a more 'global' persona, and Finland was no longer at the centre of the universe, but rather some tiny meaningless place in the middle of nowhere, except when it came to hockey or the Formula 1 racing! The kind of education that's been offered at my international school in Turkey gave me so many new opportunities that I would not have dreamed possible in Finland. Instead of deciding on a university to go to I spent six months trying to decide which **country** I would like to go to, and only after that started looking at universities.*

The children of retired US army officer, Jim McDaniel, LTC, USA (ret.), were educated internationally and he found that:

Our education experience was generally positive but like anything else, there was an occasional glitch. The greatest gain was to the kids in the places they saw and visited; many of the places they see in the news are places they have been. They saw the ovens. They saw Brandenburg Tor, from both sides, when it still had a fence through it. The fall of the Berlin Wall probably had the greatest significance as they had been in the East before it fell and saw the armed soldiers of our military adversaries of the time. They still make direct comparisons to life on both sides of the wall. They are able to speak of history as well as current events to my grandchildren from a much broader perspective than they could had they remained 'colonists' all their lives.

When an English medium International School is not truly 'international', or has a large percentage of students whose native language is not English, the few English speaking students can find certain social aspects of the school difficult to cope with. As one English expat student found at an International School in Turkey, 'In my class it is difficult. As only one other girl and I do not speak Turkish, this means we are often left out of the conversation. However, I don't blame them I would prefer to speak in my mother tongue rather than in another language, though most of the time, if I am around my class mates will speak English so as not to exclude me'.

The *European Council of International Schools* — ECIS (www.ecis.org) and *International Schools Services* — ISS (www.iss.edu) maintain lists of the leading international schools (approximately 600) on their websites, though their lists do not contain all schools offering an international curriculum, nor can they be considered an exhaustive list of quality schools. The *International Schools K-12* organisation (www.intlschools-k12.com) has a more extensive directory listing over 850 schools and the *International Baccalaureate Organisation* (www.ibo.org) lists all its member schools on-line, though both these list a number of 'local' schools offering an international curriculum. Much of the information listed on these sites is aimed at teachers and administrators, but parents will be able to find contact details and links to the websites of the different schools. Other agencies list British and American schools in specific countries around the world and they are listed at the end of this chapter.

The accreditation agencies discussed and listed later in this chapter release varying amounts of information regarding the curriculum, student and staff numbers, nationalities of administration and teaching staff, the constitution and the accreditation status of schools registered with them. Much of the information is available on the agency websites.

Local Schools

Local schools are primarily for children of the host country. The majority of local schools will use the predominant language of the country, though some may use a minority indigenous language commonly used in the locality, e.g. Welsh in Wales, as their medium of instruction. A growing number of state-run schools, in non-English speaking countries are also instituting instruction in foreign languages. These foreign languages are commonly English, Spanish, French and German, though the language of a country with important trading, cultural or political links may also be used. For example, in Turkey, the *Anadolu Lisesi* accept students at age 13 for an intensive one-year English programme, after which teaching is mostly conducted in English for the subsequent four years.

State-run local schools, such as the Anadolu Lisesi, generally follow the country's national curriculum leading to local exams and local university admission requirements. Private institutions, however, sometimes opt to follow a different curriculum that allows students to sit for international examinations and/or enter foreign universities. These schools will often teach in a non-local language that is necessary for the curriculum offered. The most common foreign curricula and/or exams offered in these local schools are:

1. US curriculum aiming at the Scholastic Assessment Test (SAT),
2. US curriculum aiming at the Scholastic Assessment Test (SAT) and the Advanced Placement (AP) exams,
3. UK curriculum aiming at the General Certificate of Secondary Education (GCSE),
4. UK curriculum aiming at the International General Certificate of Secondary Education (IGCSE),
5. UK curriculum aiming at the Advanced Level (A Level)
6. Switzerland based International Baccalaureate Organisation (IBO) Primary Years Program (PYP), Middle Years Program (MYP) and Certificate/Diploma (IB Certificate/Diploma).

Cindy Rothacker and her engineer husband are American expats living in Belgium, where there are three official languages, who chose the local Dutch-language school for their children's education.

My husband is bilingual, so it was very important to us that our kids pick up the local language. We wanted to have local friends in our town and the only way to meet local people is through your kids since our language skills aren't the greatest and locals, for the most part, don't just meet you in the grocery store and invite you over. Finally, it was a financial consideration since the English speaking school is private and very expensive. The company would pay after they turn five, but what to do until then? It has been a wonderful experience all around and I highly recommend it when you are starting your kids at an early age. I think it is a bit harder and takes more work from the parents when the kids are older because they are more social and need friends and that is very hard when there is a language barrier. Markus started at three and there isn't a lot of verbal communication at that age so it went really well.

One couple from England who now live in Tokyo also decided to school their children in the local system.

My twins attend a local public kindergarten rather than an international school — we figure that the faster they learn Japanese the happier that they will be here (in part because we plan to stay more than a couple of years). The local vs. international school issue is a complicated one, however. For many expatriates, this is a non-issue because the international schools are too expensive, but for those who have a choice, I encourage all to give the local option at least a look before heading for the international school. We were advised by one expat family not to move because schooling for our children would not be paid for — that would have been such a mistake.

What works best for one's child is a complex mix of factors, including: the child's age, personality and maturity; the preparation made by the parents for the child's entry into the new environment; the length of time the family intends to stay in that locale; and the parents' ability to assist the child throughout the experience.

Nevertheless, I don't think I can understate the influence school and teacher have on the success of the experience (true both at home and abroad). While looking around, we found that one expensive, private kindergarten nearby had few foreign children (in spite of advertising to foreigners), no ability in-house to

Questions To Ask About Day Schooling In The Destination City

What types of school are available at your destination?	1. International 2. Foreign Curriculum 3. Local
Which ones seem to be suitable for your child?	1. 2. 3.
Will your child be eligible for admission?	1. 2. 3.
Are they accredited (see below for accreditation information)?	1. 2. 3.
What curriculum/exams do they offer?	1. 2. 3.
Do they offer suitable subjects within the curriculum?	1. 2. 3.
Does your child like them?	1. 2. 3.
Can you afford them?	1. 2. 3.

speak my children's language, and an institutional inability to accommodate my children's unique needs as they make the transition into the new environment. In contrast, we found that the local, public kindergarten had an English-speaking teacher (by far the best I've known), five of fourteen children with bilingual ability (one trilingual) and an excellent curriculum. The mothers of the other children have also been very supportive and that enthusiasm for my children has been communicated to their classmates. My children had only had limited Japanese training at home, but they have loved the experience. And it's cheap.

It might be unfair, but I believe many of the expat children I've met here have missed many opportunities just as their parents have by surrounding themselves in an English speaking world in Tokyo. It's ironic that many families take overseas postings to broaden their children's experience, only to make them bigger culture snobs as a result of sending them to the American school and of limiting their cultural exposure to special 'Japanese' events at the Tokyo American club.

Karron Combs moved from the US to the UK and has put her granddaughter Crystal in the local schooling system as well:

Crystal is in the British school. Why come all this way and spend tons of money for American school? Of course, if we had her in American school, we'd have to live where all the other American's live. Well, heck, I could have stayed home and lived with other Americans! Crystal loves the school, but she is only four, and the language is basically the same.

Home Schools

Home schools provide education away from the formal and traditional classroom environment. Many parents initiate home schooling for their children because they have very strong philosophical or religious beliefs that are not taught in the locally available schools. For parents who wish to instil their own family belief systems in their children in a strict manner, home schooling is a serious option. Some of the perceived benefits of home schooling include strengthening the bond of the family, reinforcement of the role of the family and the chance to provide child-specific learning styles suitable for children with special needs.

Debra James found a need to homeschool her children.

My younger son is 12 and severely dyslexic. I had to give up my job here in Ireland to home-educate him when he was stabbed in the eye with a pencil by a Down's Syndrome girl who he was forced to sit next to at the local primary school. (His reading glasses saved his eye from permanent damage.) The teachers at the local school just put all the kids with learning difficulties at a table at the back and let them get on with not learning anything.

In some instances, a need for homeschooling is born from the lack of other educational options. Sarah van der Es homeschooled her children in Burkina Faso and Nepal because there were no reasonable local schools. In both cases they withdrew their children from a local school. In Burkina, the better local school had classes of 80 students and students were often left in charge. Whilst the fee paying school in Nepal was better, the discipline in the classroom was not always what the headmaster claimed it was and could have been described as nineteenth century in style.

Not being prepared for homeschooling, Sarah found it difficult for three reasons:

1. She had no training as a teacher so she felt she was often not doing it well.
2. She had no other children to compare hers to and therefore often felt they were learning nothing, but could not reassure herself.
3. She had to be teacher and mother, so an argument in the house or in the classroom boiled over into the other area. It was difficult for the children to compartmentalise their lives and get away from a fight with their 'teacher'.

However, overall, Sarah found the experience satisfying for herself and for her children.

The learning programmes of home schools can be structured and scheduled according to the child's needs and academic performance whilst still covering the same curriculum/content that is studied at regular schools. For parents who do not work outside the home, home schooling can provide stimulation. Sarah says, '...it was a good way to spend time abroad given that in the rural areas of poor countries there would have been no work permit or alternative work possible'.

Home Schools can vary from one parent teaching all subjects to one child, with no physical assistance from other people, to a co-operative system of shared teaching by a number of parents to a group of children.

There are many support organisations for Home Schooling, that cover pre-Kindergarten to university entrance and some that provide booster programmes for special needs children. The organisations can supply curricula, textbooks, certificates, guidance and the many other needs of Home Schools. The organisations themselves may align their curricula towards particular religious, social or cultural beliefs.

Home schooling is not an easy option for the parents involved, but many who have followed this option say the advantages outweigh the hardships. The direct involvement of the parents gives them control over the content of the subjects taught as well as the moral guidance of their children, and they are able to provide the individual student attention that traditional schools can not always do.

Cathryn Hoard homeschooled both her children during their elementary years for philosophical reasons, before they entered an international school in the same country.

I wanted Christianity and Christian principles to be woven throughout our children's education. I wanted to be able to choose what I felt was the best curriculum for my children and move them along at an appropriate pace for them. I think in being able to homeschool them overseas in the morning, then send to Turkish school (primary) in the afternoon, we were able to capitalise on the best of both worlds. The children received the educational and religious foundation I preferred, but also learned the language like a native and felt extremely comfortable in this adopted culture. If, at this early stage, the children had simply gone to an English-speaking International school, I don't think they ever would have felt like they truly fit in Turkey.

Debra James has had to think about what education really is, especially in relation to her sons' abilities.

I have had to redefine what I consider an 'education' to be. I was a 'well-rounded', straight-A student, winning prizes for art and science, playing piano in recitals. I only discovered much later that I didn't know anything about the things that were really important in life. And that was not my fault; I went to a strict convent school. When not there I was kept in my room and not allowed to go out or interact with the world except for occasionally being taken to the ice-skating rink or a pony club...my son David cannot remember things very well, especially not the things like spelling. I have to teach him conceptually. What is 'conceptual' teaching? It is what I call the method I use to take David's own motivation to learn and channel it. I believe that motivation is the single most important factor in learning.

We watch documentaries on TV. All that we can find. About archaeology, about history, about nature, and we talk about them. David doesn't remember all the details, but the gist of it — the big concepts — he understands. So we don't use a curriculum. I do have workbooks that I buy in the school book shop for maths and science and environmental studies. But here we face the obstacle of his dyslexia.

Questions To Answer When Considering Homeschool Options

Do you have the time to devote to home schooling?	
Do you have the personality and patience to homeschool?	
What exams do you eventually want your child to sit and can you provide them with the education they need for them?	
Do you want to use a religiously or philosophically aligned curriculum?	
Is there a homeschool group in your area that your child could attend?	
Does the group use a curriculum suitable for you and your child?	
Is your child's personality suitable for home schooling?	

Traditional educators are mixed in their reactions to home schooling and its graduates. The most common concern being that limited resources and minimal social interaction can narrow the breadth of the children's education and make any transition and integration into traditional classroom education at school or university level difficult at a later date.

Jim DiSebastian points out some of the issues concerning homeschooling:

Quite often people choose home-schooling (when abroad) for one of two reasons.

1. Religious grounds, or
2. They feel that the school they have tried in their new country of residence is not up to standard and therefore they switch to home schooling.

I, personally, would say that home schooling is the absolute last resort. Not that I have anything against the various programmes that exist, but because it doesn't help the child to socialise at all. I've seen many students who were home-schooled for many years and then had a great difficulty adjusting into an actual school a few years later.

Jim DiSebastian also believes that the integration of students into the traditional schooling system is best done by the time a child is of middle school age, around 11, 12 or 13 years old.

When the van der Es children switched between homeschooling and classroom schooling, they noticed a difference. Their father found, 'In the second country when they were seven and nine, our children missed the traditional system because they had known what it is like to have school friends. But at the same time they liked it. It brought them closer to their mother and gave a lot of freedom'.

Despite the fact that Debra's dyslexic son, David, desperately wants to 'catch up' and go to what he calls 'big school', she is pleased with her efforts and is clear in what she wants to achieve. 'That's what homeschooling is all about, doing the best thing for each individual child. The best thing to set them up to face life. Real life — not the rarefied 'academic' trivial-pursuit vision of life.'

Home School programmes can lead students to the same examinations that their counterparts would take in traditional schools, but not always. You should check with the ministry of education for your country to see if the home schooling organisations you are considering offer programmes that are recognised/accredited, especially if you would like your children to continue into Further/Higher education. Once you find a home-schooling organisation that suits the curriculum/style you would like for your child, check with the organisation to see if there is already an existing home-school in your area and if there is a support group of parents you could join.

Resources on homeschooling options and the contact details of relevant organisations are at the end of this chapter.

Boarding Schools

Boarding Schools offer both educational and residential facilities for their students. A boarding school may be run as an 'International School,' a 'Local School,' or a combination of both. The curricula and examinations offered by boarding schools vary as much as they do in day schools.

For expatriate parents and children, a boarding school can offer a safe, secure and long-term education programme. There are many reasons that expatriate parents consider a boarding school for their children:
1. Some countries do not have suitable schools for expatriate children.
2. Suitable schools may be too far away from where you have to live to make daily commuting a viable option.
3. The country may not be safe, or suitable, for your children.
4. There may be no suitable accommodation available for families.
5. Frequent, or unpredictable, moves could mean a child changing schools halfway through a school year.
6. The series of countries you are likely to go to would make continuity of curricula and examination programmes difficult, or impossible.
7. Frequent moves would be too unsettling for the child, compared to the stable environment of a boarding school.

Some of the advantages of a boarding school education include:
1. Boarding schools frequently have smaller class sizes than day schools.
2. They offer a safe and controlled environment for their students.
3. Students can have similar lifestyles, interests, social and cultural background.
4. There are structured study hours throughout the day and into the evening.
5. There are opportunities for activities/sports on a more regular basis than at a day school.
6. Cultural education and sensitivity are developed when the boarding school is populated by students with a variety of nationalities, which allows them to become acquainted with students of different cultures. Students of different cultures are often embraced at boarding schools (as at international schools) which gives students the opportunity to learn to respect, understand and appreciate people from different cultures.

Sometimes the only viable option is to send a child to boarding school. Margo Rhinehart, an American who lived in Irian Jaya for five and a half years, sent her two children to boarding school because there was no high school near to where they lived. Even so, it was not an easy thing to do.

It was most difficult sending our oldest daughter off to boarding school, because we had to leave her behind in the United States as we packed our things and moved to Indonesia. Saying good-bye was very difficult and I began to question our decision to take the overseas assignment. Additionally, for this child it meant leaving her school at half term and starting all over at the new school. I would have probably felt some guilt even if it had been simply a transfer from one school district to another. By the second year, most of the guilt had disappeared, the communication glitches were worked out, and everyone seemed happy. There were many difficult moments when there would be some sort of crisis, such as the need for extra money for a field trip, when we would panic because it was difficult to communicate with a school that is open during the hours we are sleeping (there was a 14 hour time difference). All in all, it was a great experience for our daughter.

Our son is a different story. He had attended the International school in our town and was well prepared, as were all of his classmates, for the boarding school experience. Even so, we still located him close to relatives which I believe was the smartest thing we did. Any time there was a crisis, broken heart, needing money etc., his grandparents were there to help out.

Though the decision to send her children to boarding schools was the only viable decision in their circumstances, Margos' one regret was not being able to participate more in her children's extracurricular activities. Their daughter was a cheerleader but they never saw her perform, and their son was in the marching band but they saw him perform only once.

Edie Browne who works at the University of Hong Kong and her husband, a magistrate, sent their children to boarding school in England, even though there are a number of good schools in Hong Kong.

We sent the kids away to school because we didn't feel that there were schools in HK to meet their needs. They both suffer from a learning difficulty (not dyslexia but something akin to it) and whilst Hong Kong international schools are fine for academic kids, they don't serve the needs of kids like mine.

The advantages of boarding school for our boys are small classes, supportive staff and very good sporting facilities. Even if they don't get extra learning support, being in a small class means that their needs can be met.

They have both made good friends and the environment is more stable; both of them lost a succession of close friends as their families left Hong Kong.

One piece of advice I was given has proved very good — find a school with family support nearby if this is at all possible. In fact, the kids probably only need this for a while as after they settle in they tend to spend free weekends at their friends' homes.

Looking from a geographical point of view also means that you limit your choice of schools — this obviously has pluses and minuses, but essentially we ended up looking at only two schools which both would have been OK. To decide between them we spoke to parents who had children at both schools (i.e. one child at each of the two schools) and they were very helpful. You really do need to talk to other parents who are further down the road than you to find out about the realities rather than what is printed in the brochures. It also helps for the children to meet other kids at the same school.

Another factor in having family close by is that your children build up relationships with family members, which would not be possible otherwise — you can only see so many relatives on a vacation.

Neither Kevin nor I ever thought that we would be sending our kids away to school, but we had to for the reasons above, and quite honestly we haven't regretted the decision so far as Danny is concerned — not even for a minute. It is early days with Robert as he's only been away a term, but already he sounds much more positive and upbeat about school than he was in Hong Kong.

For the location of the boarding school parents have three choices.

1. Home country boarding schools have the benefit of assuring native language ability, a familiar curriculum and nearness to relatives who can provide support and a home during holidays.
2. Destination country boarding schools are closer to where the parents are, so that holiday and weekend visits with parents are easier to arrange and the parents are closer to provide any necessary support.
3. Third country boarding schools can provide alternative curriculum and foreign languages, or allow children to be much closer to their parents than they would if they were in the home country, but be in a more suitable country and environment than is available in the parents host country.

How to Choose a Boarding School

Boarding schools come in a variety of sizes and political, philosophical or religious leanings. They will also place differing emphasis on sports, extra curricular activities and academic excellence. Every boarding school has its own strengths

Questions To Answer When Considering Boarding School Options

Which country can/should you consider?	Destination country? Home country? A third country?
Which schools seem suitable?	1. 2. 3.
Will your child be eligible for admission?	1. 2. 3.
Are they accredited (see below for accreditation information)?	1. 2. 3.
What curriculum/exams do they offer?	1. 2. 3.
Do they offer suitable subjects within the curriculum?	1. 2. 3.
Do they have suitable after school activities?	1. 2. 3.
Does your child like the activities?	1. 2. 3.
Can you afford the fees?	1. 2. 3.

and to find the most suitable for your child you need to assess exactly what kind of education you want your child to have, as well as what kind of academic and social system your child will excel and be happy in. This decision making process can be more important for a boarding school than for a day school as your child will be 'at school' for months at a time.

Margo Rhinehart said that when they were choosing boarding schools:

...we considered many things including academics, extracurricular activities, facilities, and locations. We considered the personalities of our children as we eliminated some of the options. For example, one child was a self-starter and would do well in a very permissive environment; the other child needed more structure and guidance. All that said, the final decision was based more on location than anything else. We determined that it was more important to place our children near to a familiar support system, so that weekends and special events would not be so lonely. For our family, basing our decision on location seems to have paid off. I believe our children are now well-adjusted adults.

However, the Rhinehart's search for the right boarding schools for their children did not end with location and activities.

When looking at the academics of the various schools, we realised that we needed to look closely at the methods of teaching used by the various schools. For instance one of the schools we looked at in Australia used an integrated curriculum, but the schools in our hometown were more departmentalised. This could have been a big issue if in the middle of our child's high school career we suddenly found ourselves transferred back home.

When considering boarding schools it is important, as the Rhinehart's point out, to consider not just the school but how you and your child will find the style, environment and atmosphere. Visiting the schools and asking the same sorts of questions you would at any potential school are thus important steps in the decision making process.

Resources on boarding school associations and search services can be found at the end of this chapter.

Curricula and Exam Systems

The main English medium curricula that are offered in schools run primarily for expatriate children (predominantly international day and boarding schools) are based on the US and UK national systems, plus the programmes co-ordinated by the independent International Baccalaureate Organisation.

International Curricula

The International Baccalaureate Organisation (IBO)

Route des Morillons 15, 1218 Grand-Saconnex, Geneva, Switzerland, tel ++41 22-791 7740; fax: ++41 22-791 0277; e-mail IBHQ@ibo.org; www.ibo.org.

The International Baccalaureate Organisation (IBO) is a non-profit educational foundation, founded in 1968 and headquartered in Switzerland. It provides three related programmes:

Primary Years Programme: (PYP) for children aged 3-11.

Middle Years Programme: (MYP) for children aged 11-16.

IB Diploma: pre-university programme for children aged 16-18.

The Diploma Programme grew out of international schools' efforts to establish a common curriculum and university entry credential for geographically mobile students. International educators were motivated by practical considerations but also by an idealistic vision: they hoped that a shared academic experience emphasising critical thinking and exposure to a variety of viewpoints would foster tolerance and inter-cultural understanding among young people. The IBO has evolved from a service to the international community and now offers a full range of programmes to a varied group of schools, including a large number of state schools, around the world. Total number of schools offering all or some of the PYP, MYP and Diploma Programme is 1031.

Diploma level students must study six subjects (two languages, mathematics, experimental sciences, creative arts, humanities and a free choice), plus an interdisciplinary course called Theory of Knowledge, which challenges students to question the bases of knowledge. They must also complete a programme called CAS (Creativity, Action, Service), which involves participation in community service, and, for example, theatre production and sports. The final component of the Diploma is an extended essay of 4,000 words to acquaint students with the kind of independent research and writing skills expected of them at university.

Cambridge University Exam Board
University of Cambridge Local Examinations Syndicate and Cambridge International Examinations, Cambridge International Examinations, 1 Hills Road, Cambridge CB1 2EU, United Kingdom; tel ++44 1223-553553; fax ++44 1223-553558; e-mail international@ucles.org.uk; www.ucles.org.uk; www.cie.org.uk international examinations.
The Cambridge University Exam Board is based in the UK and administers the International General Certificate of Secondary Education for students aged fourteen to sixteen under the title Cambridge International Examinations (CIE).

Cambridge International Examinations, is a department of the University of Cambridge Local Examinations Syndicate (UCLES) whose examinations are taken in over 150 countries, by around two million students each year.

Cambridge International Examinations offers a range of Cambridge Awards and services including:
International GCE Ordinary Level ('O Level').
International GCE Advanced Level ('A Level').
International General Certificate of Secondary Education (IGCSE).
Advanced International Certificate of Education (AICE).
Cambridge Checkpoint.
Cambridge Skills Certificates.
Cambridge Career Awards.
Accreditation Services.
A wide range of subjects, including languages (over 30 of them), as well as science, mathematics, humanities, arts and work-related subjects such as information technology and business skills are offered. The examinations are based on a wide-ranging experience of educational assessment, both in the United Kingdom and throughout the world.

The qualifications are recognised by universities, colleges and employers worldwide. A key feature is that they are specifically designed for international use. Although many of them are based on the best features of the British qualifications system — and are equivalent to the examinations used in UK schools — Cambridge International Examinations aim to ensure that the examinations are equally suitable for students of any nationality and any cultural background. The examinations are designed to meet the needs of learners who are not necessarily native speakers of English, and careful consideration is given to this issue in setting and marking the examinations.

For the IGCSE's, students generally study eight or more subjects and sit formal examinations in English Literature, English Language and Mathematics and options from, but not limited to, Biology, Chemistry, Physics, General Science, History, Geography, Modern and Classical Languages, Art, Design and Computers/IT.

American Curricula

The American education system, within the US, is based on students acquiring course credits during the academic year from a curriculum that is often set by a State education board, but may be internally developed by an individual school.

An American school outside of the US may develop its own curriculum based on accepted American standards, or use a curriculum provided by an educational consultant such as *International Schools Services* (ISS — see below).

Students study similar courses to those required for the IGCSE above, but do not need to sit formal examinations administered by an external examination board to graduate from high school. A Grade Point Average (GPA) for each student is calculated by the school, based on the performance of the student during the year. Most GPAs are on a scale of 1 to 4, with 4 being the highest (though percentages and letter grades may be used), but universities require GPAs to be submitted using the standardised 1 to 4 scale.

However, many US universities require students to take external exams, such as the *Scholastic Assessment Test* (SAT) I & II, to gain admission. Universities in other countries may require students to have sat SAT and *Advanced Placement* (AP) exams too, especially if they have not taken other recognised exams such as the IB, CIE, or UK A Levels (see below).

Educational Testing Service — ETS

Corporate Headquarters, Rosedale Road, Princeton, NJ 08541, USA; tel ++1-609-921-9000; fax ++1-609-734-5410; etsinfo@ets.org; www.ets.org.

ETS is a private non-profit company that provides services to individuals, educational institutions and agencies, and governmental bodies in 181 countries. ETS develops and annually administers more than 11 million tests worldwide on behalf of clients in education, government and business. Among the many tests they administer are the SAT and AP test.

Scholastic Assessment Test (SAT) I

Currently 3500 schools, colleges or universities use or require the SAT as part of their admissions package. The SAT I is a three-hour test, run by ETS, that is primarily multiple-choice and measures verbal and mathematical reasoning abilities.

Scholastic Assessment Test (SAT) II

These are also run by ETS and are subject-specific tests used by universities to select students for specific courses and are supplementary to the SAT I. The SAT II exams are one-hour and mostly multiple-choice, they measure knowledge of particular subjects and the ability to apply that knowledge. Many colleges require or recommend one or more of these tests for admission or placement purposes.

Advanced Placement (AP)

Students can also opt to take the subject-specific Advanced Placement (AP) tests. Thousands of colleges will provide advanced college credits to people who have passed AP tests, but they do not always specifically require students to take and pass the exams.

The Advanced Placement programme (AP) is sponsored by the College Board (www.collegeboard.org), but is administered and operated by ETS. The AP programme gives high school students an opportunity to take college-level courses and exams, and earn credit, advanced placement, or both for college/university. Thirty-three courses in 19 subject areas are currently offered worldwide. In 1999, over 700,000 students took more than a million AP exams.

British National Curricula (English National Curricula)

The *Qualifications and Curriculum Authority*, (www.qca.org.uk) brings together the work of the *National Council for Vocational Qualifications* (NCVQ) and the *School Curriculum and Assessment Authority* (SCAA) with additional powers and duties. This gives it a unique overview of curriculum, assessment and qualifications across the whole of education and training.

The British National Curriculum varies in Wales, England and Northern Ireland to suit local cultural traditions. In Scotland there is a separate education system. Most British National Curriculum schools outside of the UK follow the standard English curriculum.

Two of the more well-known curricula and assessments of the British National Curriculum are the GCSE and the A Levels, which are offered in most British schools worldwide. The curriculum is broken down into Key Stages 1 to 4, where 4 is the GCSE. There are a number of exam awarding bodies in the UK, which must be approved by the *Department for Education and Employment* (DfEE).

General Certificate of Secondary Education (GCSE)

Most students will take GCSEs in English, mathematics and science at key stage 4 and up to a total of nine subjects overall.

For the science GCSE, students may take one of the following:
1. Separate exams in biology, chemistry and physics,
2. A double award exam (equal to two GCSEs) that covers all three sciences,
3. A single award exam (equal to one GCSE) that covers all three sciences less fully.

Design and technology, a modern foreign language and other subjects, such as information technology, geography, history and art are common.

General Certificate of Education Advanced Level (A & AS Level)

Advanced (A) Level examinations are usually taken by students wishing to follow an academic route to higher education or skilled employment and they are normally studied over two years. Students can choose between linear and modular A levels, each of which are assessed through written and/or oral examinations and for some, through coursework. Limits for coursework are set out in the A/AS Code of Practice and further information about the coursework for different A levels is available from the GCE awarding bodies.

Students taking linear A levels, sometimes called 'traditional' A levels, are examined at the end of the two years, whereas those who take modular A levels may be examined on individual modules throughout the course.

At A Level, the subjects listed below will have subject-specific criteria, (although 30% of the course is examined at the end of the two years). A student's work is given a letter grade, with pass grades of A-E.

Advanced Supplementary (AS) Level exams cover the first half of an A Level course, studied to the same depth as the full A Level, and can be taken after one or two years of study.

Subjects Available at A and AS Level (though not at all schools):		
Art	Biology	Business Studies
Chemistry	Classical Civilsation	Computing
Design & Technology	Economics	English Language
English Language & Literature	English Literature	Geography
Government & Politics	History	Latin and Classical Greek
Law	Mathematics	Modern Foreign Languages
Music	Physical Education	Physics
Psychology	Religious Studies	Welsh
Welsh Second Language		

Deciding on a School for Your Child

Harry Deelman, of Search Associates, an international teacher and administrator placement agency, advises that when expatriate parents are looking for a school for their child they should consider the following aspects.

Academically there must be doubts if a secondary/high school offers no external exams whatsoever — such as the IB diploma, GCE A Levels, Australian HSC, or other national school leaving exams, or American AP courses and tests. Note that in American-style schools just regular SAT-I tests are insufficient, let alone an internally assessed high school diploma without any such outside tests.

If external exams are entered, then the proportion of final-year students who take the exams and the success-rate of those students, are useful indicators. Most parents would need to check with teachers/educators experienced in the specific type of courses/exams to determine what constitute high quality. All schools are good at 'spin'! In many ways far more important than the narrow academic measures of a school's quality are the less measurable factors of student happiness, personal growth, development of interests and activities, concern for others (does the school have outreach and service elements? Schools offering the IB programme automatically do so) and thus the bottom line of, 'What kinds of young adults graduate from the school'?

Though there is usually less variety of answers and perhaps slightly less crucial an answer at elementary school level, even at kindergarten/playschool level, the same question can be adapted there too. Finding people who can give an honest and accurate answer to that question is not easy, but worth the effort.

For any particular child there is usually a particular slant to the questions, both academically and regarding the school's extra-curricular life. One child may need to know if calculus and highly advanced mathematics will be well taught, another how good the languages department is, etc.

Regarding the activities, a key focus may be sport, or music, or drama, or chess, or any other specific interest or combination of interests. Note the implication that the parents should genuinely know the child and his/her need and preferences. Sadly, so many do not, seeking only to fulfil their own parental ambitions (do many graduates go on to medical school?) rather than the true potential of each boy or girl.

Your own questions to the school on key issues (curriculum offered, range of activities, academic destinations of school-leavers, exam results if relevant, list of teachers with qualifications/previous experience) should elicit useful answers. Some schools will give names and contact details of current parents who are willing to communicate with prospective new parents, answering similar questions plus the all-important one of 'atmosphere' — will it suit your child(ren)?

If no suitable schools are available at your destination, you need to decide if you want to send your child to a boarding school or homeschool them.

Accreditation, Inspection, and Schools Support

Many countries have their own criteria for accreditation, or approval, of schools that are not always easy for non-nationals to ascertain or understand. Official accreditation or approval may be necessary before a school can accept students, or a school might need to demonstrate it can meet the necessary standards within a certain time period after accepting its first students. However, in some countries there may be no formal educational standards that a school must meet.

Some countries also have multiple levels, or options, for accreditation that vary across city, state and national level. For example, despite the introduction of the National Curriculum in the UK, Wales and Northern Ireland have exemptions and variations so that the Welsh language, Gaelic and regional history can be taught, while Scotland has an entirely separate system altogether. Privately owned, or other non-state, schools may have to meet the local standards of safety and curriculum content, or be able to run independently and choose to offer a foreign (non-local) curriculum that is approved/allowed by the local authorities.

Private schools open to non-nationals and private schools for local children may also seek accreditation, or registration, with international organisations outside of their country of operation. Schools do this to demonstrate their commitment to providing a quality education, raise their profile, attract more/better students, attract quality international teaching staff, raise their overall standards and justify higher fees. An individual school may seek accreditation and listing with one or more of the agencies and meet varying conditions to do so.

When a school is accredited it can show that education professionals have already asked many of the questions a parent would want to ask, and favourable answers have been received. Many accreditation agencies require follow-up inspections, or reviews, every few years after the original accreditation.

Accreditation, however, is no guarantee that a school is 'good', or that it is suitable for your child. Each child is different and parents have different expectations of what a school should provide.

Similarly, a lack of accreditation does not necessarily mean that a parent should keep their child out of a particular school. It does mean that a parent will have to ask more questions about whether the curriculum offered at that school will adequately prepare their child for entry into another school when they move, or for Further and Higher education if they will be staying in the country for some time. Harry Deelman points out:

Accredited schools have at least been checked (and have thoroughly checked their own thinking and actions), but very few are ever denied accreditation and the quality of accredited schools ranges widely. Not having been accredited in not necessarily a 'black mark' either. Although almost every American-system school must become accredited if its students and graduates are to be fully recognised by other schools, for schools of other backgrounds (notably the hundreds of British-system schools) accreditation is not seen as of much importance. Many of the best overseas schools are not accredited, and some amongst them have never formally sought an external inspection of any kind, yet they are very widely recognised as being of outstanding quality and performance.

Whether a school is accredited or not, it is therefore a good idea to ask the principal, staff and parents specific questions so you can ascertain how the school operates and sets its standards:

1. What external standards do they use to monitor their own standards?
2. How do they prepare the curriculum and what standards and benchmarks are used?
3. Do the students sit for any externally moderated examinations?
4. Is there any external assessment of the school, and if so, who are the assessments governed by?
5. Does the school have a mission statement?
6. Does the school have a clear focus on who they are, and what they want for their students?
7. If the school says it uses an international curriculum, find out which curriculum

> or curricula are used and which national benchmarks they strive to achieve. If the school does not have a clear focus on their mission or goals, then perhaps look to see if there are any other options in your new area of abode.

There are a number of international bodies who register and accredit International Schools' and they are spread across the following categories:

1. International accreditation organisations.
2. UK inspection organisations.
3. US accreditation organisations.
4. US support organisations.
5. Information Registries.

Information about some of the more common organisations is listed at the end of this chapter. However, readers should note that much of the information is provided directly from the organisations themselves.

Higher/Further Education

University Education for Expat Children

Traditionally, school students wishing to proceed to Further and/or Higher education have moved immediately (or within a year or two) on to college or university.

Many school students do still continue along this track and international schools have an outstanding record for placing their students on university level courses. It is not uncommon for International Schools to claim placement rates at over 90% of their graduating class; research in the US has shown that Third Culture Kids — TCK's (see *Long-term Considerations*) are four times more likely to gain a university degree than their domestically educated peers.

What Universities Look For From International Students

Applications from students who have been educated in more than one country are looked upon favourably by many of the top universities in the US, the UK and Europe, because of the diversity such international students bring to the universities. These students are unlikely to suffer in the admission process because they are applying from abroad, though their application may well be improved by their experience.

Sarah Robertson, International Admission Officer at *Queen's University* (www.queensu.ca) in Canada reports,

> *Canadian Students who have studied abroad are viewed in the same way as all students who apply to Queen's. We look primarily at academic performance to determine which students will receive an offer of admission. We also have a Personal Information component in the admissions process that gives students the opportunity to demonstrate their personal achievements (academic or non-academic). Canadians who have studied abroad often have very interesting experiences, and we encourage applicants to tell us about them. It could be that they speak another language, have travelled extensively, or have had amazing experience working and living in very different cultures. This kind of information can be beneficial to their application as Queen's strives to admit students who are not only academically qualified, but also well-balanced, interesting individuals who will enrich the Queen's community.*

Students who have studied for the International Baccalaureate diploma, A Levels, or SAT/APs are academically well placed to enter university in Europe or

North America. Universities recognise that the well rounded and demanding courses produce students who are eminently suitable to enter their degree level programmes.

Sarah Robertson says of the various exams international students offer,

The IB is considered an excellent preparation for University. We currently give students up to three first-year University credits for Higher Level subjects. A typical Queen's student would achieve 5 credits in the first year, so IB students are already ahead by more than half a year's worth of University credit.

The A level exams are widely respected and are also considered an excellent preparation for University. We are aware of the high standards and take this into account when considering students for admission. We know that the marking is strict, and recognise this when comparing A-level applicants to applicants with a basis of admission from a different system.

In the UK, Janet Laxon, Administrative Officer in the Academic Registry of *Cranfield University* (www.cranfield.ac.uk), says,

The International Baccalaureate is certainly a qualification we consider. The offer varies obviously from course to course but we expect them to achieve approximately 28 points including five each for Maths and Physics if studying for Engineering courses and suitable subjects for our Computing/Management Courses. We may consider high school graduates whose qualifications include a good performance in the Scholastic Assessment Test, usually not less than 500 in three subjects, or Advanced Placement Tests, in at least two, but preferably three or four subjects with marks of three and above. Again, this will vary with each course.

With regard to British expatriates who have attended International or American Schools outside the UK, we would look at each one on an individual basis, especially if they have attended a recognised school.

John Twiname, International Marketing Officer at the *University of Auckland* (www.auckland.ac.nz) has said that applicants from international students (including expatriated New Zealanders) who have studied the IB Diploma, the British A Levels or the American SAT/AP examinations are treated, '...as ordinary domestic applications. ROPAS, (Recognition of Previous Overseas Academic Study) will first assess the student's eligibility to enter the University based on study completed overseas.'

For the academic achievement levels necessary for application, John Twiname says,

1. For the IB a score between 25-31 is required and varies according to the proposed course of study.
2. For Canadian applicants a High School Graduation Diploma is required. Qualifications and grading systems vary from province to province. In general, a minimum overall average of 65% is required.
3. For applicants from the United Kingdom, passes with at least C grades in three GCE 'A' Levels (not including General Studies) or the equivalent number of combined 'A' and 'AS' Levels *or* award of the full five subject certificate with a minimum of 30 points overall in the Advanced International Certificate of Education.
4. For applicants from American schools, a high school diploma *plus* acceptable SAT 1 scores (varies according to proposed course of study, but a minimum of at least 1100 combined Math and Verbal) is required.

Kristen Morse the Assistant Dean of Admissions at *Union College* in the US reports, 'Here at Union College, we look very highly upon students who have been involved in an IB or A-Level curriculum. American students who have studied and lived in other countries are also looked at as bringing something very unique to the table'.

The Application Process

Applications to universities from students outside of the country are not only possible, but are also often encouraged. Many universities now employ full-time international admissions tutors (like those quoted above) to process international applications and visit schools around the world to recruit students.

For the UK

The British Council actively works with UK universities to promote UK educational institutions around the world and many British Council offices have an Education Counselling Service whose staff can provide personal and specific advice to students wishing to apply to UK institutions. Dr. Mirac Ozar, Education Counsellor at the British Council, Ankara, Turkey (www.britishcouncil.org.tr) says:

> *The Education Counselling Service (ECS) is at the heart of the British Council's international student recruitment promotion activity and is very well resourced. ECS provides face-to-face counselling service and answers enquiries on education in the UK in person, via telephone, letter, e-mail and fax. The work of ECS is directly concerned with the promotion of British education and training. Its purpose is to make British education the first choice for international students.*

> *The ECS mission is:*

> 1. *To work with member institutions and British Council directorates to recruit suitably qualified international students on to British education and training programmes,*
> 2. *To make ECS the world's leading national education and training marketing organisation.*

> *ECS provides up-to-date information and one-to-one interviews to prospective students or their parents about education opportunities and possibilities that exist in the UK. Students who would like to study in the UK for different degrees such as undergraduate, graduate, postgraduate, MBA, or various certificate and diploma programmes, are guided and helped by ECS staff. ECS maintains recent catalogues and prospectuses of universities in the UK.*

> *Anybody interested in studying in the UK is welcome and can be provided with professional help through ECS staff. A wide range of subjects/disciplines can be searched systematically with the help of ECS staff to meet individual needs. Students can also obtain application forms for undergraduate or graduate degrees from the British Council offices. The UK has a very effective 'one-stop-shop' undergraduate application service. This service, provided by* Universities and Colleges Admissions Service (UCAS), *co-ordinates applications to full-time, first degree, Higher National Diploma (HND) and Diploma of Higher Education courses offered by the universities and colleges. All UK universities (except the* Open University) *and most colleges of higher education are members of UCAS. Therefore, the majority of home and international students interested in studying for a full-time undergraduate qualification in the UK apply through UCAS. Up to six choices can be processed on a single UCAS application form. UCAS forms are available and can be provided by ECS.*

Information on specific entrance requirements can be obtained by consulting prospectuses or contacting institutions direct. Internet sites of ECS member institutions are also provided as part of ECS services. ECS is responsible for ensuring that students are provided easy access to the information they need to make informed choices within the British education and training sector. Students can also obtain some general information on the cost of living and visa issues from ECS staff.

More information on UK study opportunities can be found on the British Council websites: www.britcoun.org/eis/campus.htm or www.educationuk.org.

For North America

North American Universities have been much more active in recruiting international students, but they do not have a service comparable to the British Council. Instead they have tended to work through Alumni organisations, recruitment visits to schools and their reputation for providing high quality education. US and Canadian universities are also well served by education agents who represent universities in many countries around the world, education fairs and increasingly through websites such as the *American Universities Education Service* (www.aues.com) and *Study in Canada* (www.studyincanada.com).

Rest of the World

Australia, New Zealand and the European countries have tended to lag behind the UK and North Anerica in recruiting international students, but are becoming more active in providing information to students through their embassies and cultural organisations such as the *Alliance Francais* (France) and the *Goethe Institut* (Germany), that are located around the world.

Help Provided by International Schools

International schools often have a University Admissions Tutor, who will advise students and parents on the opportunities for Further and Higher education. In larger schools the duties may be split between a number of staff who specialise in different regions (e.g. Europe or North America).

Tuition fees

For UK and EU Universities

EU nationals living in the EU can apply to universities in any EU country and be enrolled as if they were a national of that country, which affects the fee rates. The rules for EU nationals living outside the EU can mean that 'overseas fees' may be charged, which are often much higher than the subsidised 'home student fees'. Advance planning is essential to assure the lower fee rates, even attendance at a UK boarding school is no guarantee that a university will accept a UK student on the 'home fee' rate if the family's permanent address is outside the EU. EU nationals normally have to reside in the EU for three years prior to university admission to qualify for 'home fee' status. Early contact with university admissions tutors is the best way to determine the basis on which each university will consider an application. Scholarships are becoming more widely available for UK university courses and information about them can be obtained from the British Council.

For US Universities

Fee rates at US universities are fixed for all nationalities, but scholarships are available for many courses and can significantly reduce the cost of degree level education. Scholarships are available for a wide range of students and can be awarded for sport, music, art and academic abilities. There are numerous books, websites and agencies that list scholarships and help students obtain funding, some of which are listed at the end of this chapter.

Kristen B. Morse , Assistant Dean of Admissions at *Union College* (www.union.edu) in the US says, 'The fees remain the same for students of all nationalities. However, scholarship money is limited for non-US citizens'.

For Canadian Universities

Many of the Canadian universities have a lower profile than those in the US (with the exception of a few large, well-established schools), but can be much cheaper, with no loss of quality. While international students will pay about 75% percent higher fees than domestic students, often the cost for the international student will be much less than US university admissions fees.

Universities in Other Countries

The cost of studying at universities in other countries varies greatly, as does their level of credibility around the world. European, Australian and New Zealand universities are well recognised, and some other countries do not lag far behind.

Regarding fees in New Zealand, John Twiname indicates that, '...international students (those that do not hold New Zealand or Australian permanent residence) pay about 75% more than a domestic student.'

Which Country?

No matter which country is being considered for university level education, it is important to consider long-term plans such as where the student wants to live in the future. Some degrees and qualifications such as Law, Medicine and Teaching are only recognised in limited numbers of countries, no matter where they are obtained.

Adult and Continuing Education

Apart from degree level courses there are many qualifications available that lead to specific employment opportunities. These courses are usually open to both recent school graduates as well as mature students. Technical and skills based courses are, however, often country specific and this needs to be considered when choosing a course. Information on full-time courses can often be obtained from the same, or similar, sources as for degree level education and the contact information listed for universities should be reviewed for these courses.

Distance Learning and Non-traditional Education

Full-time residential courses are now well supplemented by a growing number of institutions that offer correspondence and distance learning courses on both full-time and part-time basis; these courses can be at any level from High School to Doctoral level.

The advantages of enrolling in such courses can be:

1. Reduced costs (both fees and living costs),
2. Greater choice of courses, and
3. Access to courses in a country where you do not live.

These courses can be suitable not only for recent school graduates, but expatriate employees and their spouses looking to gain additional qualifications whilst they are living abroad. Many reputable universities and training organisations offer such courses and graduates gain a qualification equivalent to that gained by full-time residential students.

Distance learning programmes used to be known as correspondence courses, but increasing numbers of courses are now utilising the Internet to distribute course material, conduct seminars and discussions (using secure chat rooms) and for the submission of assignments. Depending on your computer skills and access to

Internet services it is important to determine whether courses of interest are:

1. 100% on-line.
2. Part correspondence, part on-line instruction.
3. 100% correspondence without a requirement for using Internet facilities.

Some courses also require students to attend summer school and/or attend an examination centre that may be in the country of the awarding institution.

For an expatriate employee who is likely to move part way through a course, they offer the chance to complete longer courses and for a spouse they are an ideal opportunity to improve their current qualifications, or study for a qualification to allow a career change.

Additionally, distance learning courses are available for recreational subjects. These can be an enjoyable way to expand knowledge on hobbies, gain coaching qualifications in sport, or learn a foreign language.

The Internet is an excellent source of information on distance learning courses, as are specialist print publications that cover the subject of interest. Refer to the end of this chapter for *Distance Learning Resources*.

Resources
Schools
Homeschooling resources

Christian Homeschoolers: thehowards@christianhomeschoolers.com; http://christianhomeschoolers.com/hssuport.html: lists many home-schooling organisations

Eclectic Homeschool Online: eclectic@eho.org; www.eho.org/world.htm: provides links to homeschooling organisations in Australia, Canada, France, Germany, Holland, Ireland, Japan, New Zealand, Puerto Rico, South Africa, Spain, Sweden and UK.

Education Otherwise: PO Box 7420, London N9 9SG, UK; enquiries@education-otherwise.org; www.education-otherwise.org. A homeschooling organisation with members in the UK and abroad. Its website has links to other homeschooling organisations in France, Belgium, Holland, Italy, Germany, Norway, Sweden and Switzerland.

Home School Central: dan@homeschoolcentral.com. http://homeschoolcentral.com: has regional resources for links to organisations in Australia, Belgium, Canada, Europe, France, Germany, Holland, Hong Kong, Ireland, Israel, Japan, New Zealand, Norway, South Africa, Sweden, Turkey, United Kingdom.

Home School Resource Guide: editor@homeschool.com; www.homeschool.com: offers information relating to the legalities and curriculum issues involved in home schooling.

Home School World: www.home-school.com: is a US based homeschooling organisation. It has branches existing in Australia, Canada, UK, Japan, Korean and New Zealand.

Jewish Homeschooling Friendship Circle: BHP@BnosHeyna.org; http://bnosheyna.org lists educational resources and Jewish homeschool pages.

Boarding School Resources

The Association of Boarding Schools (TABS): www.schools.com. Online directory (www.schools.com/tabs/index.html) has nearly 300 boarding school members in Canada, the US and other countries and has a searchable online directory for their member schools including 28 schools outside of the US. A free copy of their Boarding Schools Directory can be obtained by calling the Boarding Schools Answerline at 1-800-541-5908.

The Boarding Schools' Association (UK): www.boarding-association.org.uk. Comprises over 480 schools (fully boarding, weekly flexi boarding, or day schools with boarding provision; co-educational and single-sex; preparatory and secondary). The interactive UK Website allows users to move from BSA member sites to the individual school websites and lists the names and addresses for a number of international member schools.

Boarding Schools in the USA: www.studyusa.com/boarding/default.htm. Lists schools suitable for international students between 12 and 17 years of age. Schools focus on intensive English language learning and there are many schools listed in numerous US states.

The Catholic Boarding Schools Association (CBSA): www.cbsa.org. Has 33 college prep catholic boarding schools. The member schools are all located in the US and Canada but have an international student body. Various member schools offer boy/girl/co-educational school environments.

Accreditation Agencies and Education Support Organisations

International Accreditation

Most accreditation agencies that regularly work with international schools offer:

1. An internationally-based evaluation at elementary, middle school and secondary levels.
2. An evaluation instrument designed specifically for international schools.
3. A sympathetic but rigorous evaluation of the highest professional standard.
4. A cost-effective programme spread over an initial two-year period.
5. A seal of accreditation valid for a set number of years, that is subject to regular monitoring and renewal.

The agencies generally look for the general characteristics listed below when accrediting a school. Much of the information provided here has come directly from the agencies concerned.

1. The school is devoted to its mission and cares enough about what it does to seek validation by a recognised accreditation authority.
2. The school knows itself and has thought deeply about the services it offers to students, family and community.
3. The school keeps its promises and promises only what it can deliver.
4. The school is self-correcting and the school is constantly seeking to improve its performance.
5. The school is student-orientated and its philosophy of education encompasses the development of the whole individual.
6. The school plans for the future and is continually planning future development.
7. The school participates fully in the responsibilities of the academic profession.
8. Administrators and teachers participate in the self-renewing activity of evaluation and accreditation.

The standards of accreditation are usually concerned with:

1. Philosophy and objectives.
2. Organisation and administration.
3. School staff.
4. The separate issues of early childhood curriculum programme, elementary curriculum programme, middle school curriculum programme, secondary (high school) curriculum programme, special needs education.
5. Guidance services.

6. Health services and safety.
7. Student services.
8. Student life.
9. Library/media centre.
10. School facilities.
11. Finances and financial management.
12. Assessment of student learning and performance.

The accreditation process usually encompasses these three features:

1. A site visit, normally lasting two to three days, for the purposes of clarifying the evaluation process and procedure and ascertaining the school's readiness to undertake the self-study.
2. Self-study, where a school examines its philosophy and objectives, and its fundamental beliefs about education. Each area of operation is then examined with a view to determining how successfully the school's aims are being realised in practice, and what measures of self-improvement are indicated.
3. Follow-up visit when a school is visited by a team of administrators and teachers drawn from other schools. The team visits the school for several days — attending classes, examining instructional materials, inspecting the facilities, talking with staff, students and other representatives of the school.

Accreditation is the affirmation, by the specific agency, that they believe the school provides a quality of education that the community has a right to expect and the education world endorses (within the expectations of the country an agency is based in or has links with).

The chief purpose of the whole accreditation process is the improvement of education for youth by evaluating the degree to which a school has attained worthwhile outcomes set by its own staff and community. This is accomplished by periodically conducting a comprehensive self-evaluation of the total school. Through the accreditation process, the school seeks the validation of its self-evaluation by obtaining professional judgement from impartial outsiders on the effectiveness of the total school operation. The intent throughout the process is more than to focus on shortcomings; the chief goal is to seek remedies for inadequacies and to identify and nurture good practices.

Accreditation of a secondary school is on an institutional basis. It should be noted that the whole school, not just one programme such as the college preparatory courses, is usually covered by the accreditation.

The following are some of the many benefits of accreditation:

1. Greater clarity of purpose.
2. Stronger internal relationships.
3. Wider professional participation.
4. More effective methods of planning for school improvement.
5. Improved consistency between educational purpose and practice.

Questions often asked by accreditation agencies are:

1. What sort of school is it and what are the aims of the school?
2. How high are standards set by the school and are they achieved?
3. How well are pupils taught, both in terms of academic subjects and other learning opportunities?
4. How well does the school care for its pupils and how well does the school work in partnership with parents?
5. How well is the school led and managed by its administrators and board?
6. Is the school's own internal monitoring and evaluation acceptable?

International Accreditation Organisations

European Council of International Schools (ECIS): Executive Secretary, 21 Lavant Street, Petersfield, Hampshire GU32 3EL, UK (tel ++44-(0)1730-268244; fax ++44-(0)1730-267914; ecis@ecis.org; www.ecis.org). ECIS is UK based and was established in 1965 and the ECIS programme of *School Evaluation and Accreditation* (established in 1970) has become one of the best known for schools seeking international recognition. Over one hundred schools in fifty-six countries are now in the programme, which continues to develop on a worldwide basis.

There are a number of classes of membership and registration with ECIS and a listing in its directory does not mean that a school has been accredited. ECIS Accreditation is recognised in the United States, through the Recognition Program of the *National Association of Independent Schools (NAIS)*.

UK Inspection Agencies

Office for Standards in Education (OFSTED): Alexandra House, 33 Kingsway, London WC2B 6SE, UK (tel ++44-(0)20-7421 6800; www.ofsted.gov.uk). Officially the Office of Her Majesty's Chief Inspector of Schools in England, set up on 1 September 1992. It is a non-ministerial government department, independent from the *Department for Education & Employment (DfEE)*.

OFSTED's remit is to improve standards of achievement and quality of education through regular independent inspection, public reporting and informed independent advice. OFSTED's principal task is the management of the system of school inspection defined originally by the Education (Schools) Act 1992. This provides for the regular inspection of all 24,000 schools in England, which are wholly or mainly state-funded.

OFSTED also inspects service children's schools, outside the UK, for the Ministry of Defence. Such reports are available from their distribution centre by calling 0207-510 0180.

OFSTED trained inspectors also inspect non-UK schools under private arrangements between the school and a contractor. If an overseas school claims to have been 'inspected by OFSTED' there may not be a report at the distribution centre. This kind of inspection is not the same as 'accreditation' but is more a report produced in the style of an OFSTED report by an inspector who has usually worked for OFSTED. The school should be contacted directly for further details.

Independent Schools Council (ISC): c/o ISIS General Secretary, Grosvenor Gardens House, 35-37 Grosvenor Gardens, London SW1W 0BS, UK (tel ++44-(0)20-7798 1590; fax ++44-(0)20-7798-1591; www.isis.org.uk), and the **UK Independent Schools Inspectorate (ISI):** Northway House, 1379 High Road, Whetstone, London N20 9LP, UK (tel ++44-(0)20-8445 6262; fax +44-(0)20-8445 7272; www.isinspect.org.uk).

The Independent Schools Council provides a single, unified organisation to speak and act on behalf of the eight independent schools' associations that constitute it. The ISC promotes the schools' common interests at the political level by making representations to government ministers, politicians of all parties and civil servants. Its governing council includes representatives of the associations.

ISC has overall responsibility for the Independent Schools Inspectorate (ISI), which ensures high standards among ISC schools and which works under a framework agreed with OFSTED.

A school must pass an ISI accreditation inspection to qualify for membership of an association within ISC. Schools are evaluated in relation to criteria covering:

1. Aims.
2. Administration.
3. Organisation and management.

4. Curriculum.
5. Staffing.
6. Premises.
7. Resources.
8. Standards of achievement and quality of teaching and learning.
9. Assessment, recording and reporting.
10. Requirements for membership of an individual association.

ISC schools are now subject to rigorous inspection every six years, based on criteria approved by OFSTED and recognised by the UK Government. ISI also carries out statutory functions on behalf of central government to ensure standards required by law are met and enable schools to remain registered with the Department for Education & Employment.

British style private schools outside of the UK can ask to be inspected by ISI.

US Accreditation Agencies

The individual US accreditation agencies (listed below) are linked by the *Commission on International and Trans-Regional Accreditation (CITA)*, which is an accreditation agency created by the regional school accrediting commissions of *The International Council of School Accreditation Commissions (ICSAC), Inc.* This was established to align and co-ordinate US education standards, including those in International Schools. An individual school may be accredited by one of the agencies below.

Middle States Association of Colleges and Schools (MSA): Commission on Secondary Schools — Middle States Association, 3624 Market Street, Philadelphia, PA 19104-2680, USA (tel ++1 215-662-5603; fax ++1-215-662-0957; www.cssmsa.org). A voluntary, non-governmental, non-profit, peer administered organisation of diverse educational institutions in the Middle Atlantic States region of the United States, American territories in the Caribbean, and American and International educational institutions in Europe, Africa and the Middle East.

New England Association of Schools and Colleges (NEASC): 209 Burlington Road, Bedford, Massachusetts 01730-1433, USA (tel ++1-781-271-0022; fax ++1-781-271-0950; www.neasc.org). Founded in 1885, the NEASC is the oldest regional accrediting association in the USA.

NEASC serves some 1,800 public and independent schools, colleges and universities in the six states of Connecticut, Maine, Massachusetts, New Hampshire, Rhode Island and Vermont and approximately 80 American/International schools in 44 countries through the *Committee on American and International Schools Abroad (CAISA)*.

American and International schools located in foreign countries are eligible to seek regional accreditation through the *New England Association of Schools and College's* Committee on American and International Schools Abroad (CAISA). These schools must offer an educational programme at the pre-K through grade 12 level following an American-style or International programme of studies using English as the primary language of instruction.

Accreditation by NEASC, recognised by the *US Department of Education,* indicates that a school meets or exceeds established criteria within the profession for the assessment of institutional quality through a periodic process of self-study and peer review. An accredited school has the resources to achieve its stated purposes and provides evidence that its students are benefiting from the curricular and co-curricular programme offered at the school.

Northern Association of Schools and Colleges, Commission on Schools (NASC): 1910 University Drive, Boise, Idaho 83725-1060, USA (tel ++1 208-426-5727; fax ++1 208-334-3228; www2.idbsu.edu/nasc/). Accredits distance education, elementary, foreign nation, high, K-12, middle, post-secondary non-degree granting, special purpose, supplementary education, and trans-regional schools. The Commission on Schools accredits schools in some US States, as well as: Canada, China, Egypt, Jamaica, Macedonia, Mexico, Panama, Poland, Russia, Saudi Arabia, and Western Samoa.

North Central Association for Colleges and Schools (NCACS): Arizona St. University, PO Box 873011, Temple, Arizona 85287-3011, USA (tel ++1 480-965-8700; fax ++1 480-965-9423; www.sacs.org/pub/elem/cems.htm). This is a non-profit organisation, accrediting over 8000 schools divided up into 7 categories: Elementary, Middle, Secondary, College Preparatory, Vocational/Adult, Optional/Special Function, and Unit (K-12). Those 8000 schools are spread out over 19 states and also include the Department of Defense Dependents' Schools overseas. At its heart, NCA is an accreditation and evaluation organisation.

Southern Association of Colleges and Schools (SACS): 1866 Southern Lane, Decatur, GA 30033, USA (tel ++1 404-679-4500 Ext. 0; www.sacs.org/pub/elem/cems.htm). Accredits more than 12,000 public and private educational institutions, from pre-kindergarten through university level, in 11 states of southeastern US and in Latin America.

Western Association of Schools and Colleges (WASC): wascsr@wascsenior.org; www.wascweb.org. Covers institutions in California and Hawaii, the territories of Guam, American Samoa, Federated States of Micronesia, Republic of Palau, Commonwealth of the Northern Marianas Islands and the Pacific Basin and areas of the Pacific and East Asia where American/International schools or colleges may apply to it for service.

US Education Support Agencies

Christian Schools International (CSI): Dan Vander Ark — Executive Director, 3350 East Paris Ave., Grand Rapids, MI 49512, USA (tel ++1 616-957-1070 or ++1(800) 635-8288; fax ++1 616-957-5022; DanVArk@CSIOnline.org; www.ChristianSchoolsInt.org). A dynamic and growing organisation of Reformed Christian schools throughout North America and beyond. CSI serves over 475 schools, with a combined enrolment of over 100,000 students, and has been doing so since 1920.

CSI has its own accreditation programme called 'Vision to Action' which its schools use to both evaluate their accomplishment of standards and gain recognition in their communities.

Under their 'foreign' section, CSI lists Access Schools (P-12) as the schools they assist. CSI state, 'Access Schools are standard international pre-primary, primary, junior and senior high schools as well as a professional institute with dynamic broad-based and purposeful curricula. Our mission is to advance Christian education and to support schools in their task of teaching students to know God and his world and to glorify him through obedient service. We guide our schools with strong curricula and expert advice on governance, administration, and teaching'. CSI has a database of member schools on their website.

US Department of Defence Dependent (DoDD) Schools: 4040 North Fairfax Drive, Arlington, Virginia 22203-1635, USA (tel ++1 703-696-4235; fax ++1 703-696-8918; www.state.gove/www/about_state/schools; www.odedodea.edu/profiles/schoolinfo). Most of the children of military personnel attend schools established and operated by the US Department of Defense, and a number of civilian government agency and private-sector children also attend these schools on a space-available, tuition-paying basis. The DoDD schools number over 220 worldwide. They are divided into European and Pacific regions, and information on the schools and the city that they are located in can be found on the second website listed above.

US Department of State, Office of Overseas Schools: Director, US Department of State, A/OPR/OS Room H328, SA-1 Department of State, Washington, DC 20522-0132, USA (tel ++1 202-261-8200; fax ++1 202-261-8224; OverseasSchools@state.gov; www.state.gov/www/about_state/schools/wide.html). Assists over 180 schools in 130 countries provide a US-style education for American children living outside of the US.

Carol Sutherland of the Overseas Office for the State Department says, 'None of them (State Dept. assisted schools) are part of the Department of Defense system. They are all private and independent schools'.

This means that though some schools are often known as 'State Department Schools,' they are not operated or controlled by the US, but do provide a US-style education for American children living outside of the US.

The Overseas Office for the State Department says,

Ownership and policy control are typically in the hands of associations of parents of the children enrolled, who elect a school board to supervise the superintendent or chief administrator whom the boards choose to administer a school. In some countries the schools are closely associated with the US Embassy; in others, the local or international communities share direct concern for the school with the American community.

Most (US) civilian agency dependants abroad attend non-government, co-educational, independent schools of various kinds. Although these schools include those founded by US companies, church organisations, and individual proprietors, the majority are non-profit, non-denominational, independent schools established on a co-operative basis by American citizens residing in foreign communities. Many of the schools in this latter group have received assistance and support from the US government under a programme administered by the Office of Overseas Schools of the US Department of State.

No statement about the American-sponsored overseas schools would apply without exception or qualification to all schools. Variety is one of their basic characteristics. They range from tiny schools, such as the *American Embassy School* in Reykjavik, Iceland, with 10 students, to large overseas schools, such as the *Singapore American School* with 2,602 students. School facilities range from rented homes to multi-million dollar campuses, although increasing numbers of overseas schools now occupy purpose-built facilities. Very few schools have boarding facilities.

The instructional programmes provide a core curriculum that will prepare students to enter schools, colleges, and universities in the United States. However, depending on the proportion of the American student body and in accordance with the host country, certain schools must also fulfil host-country curriculum requirements.

Information Registries

Association for the Advancement of International Schools (AAIE): Dr Lewis Grell — Executive Director, Thompson House, Westminster College, New Wilmington, Pennsylvania 16172, USA (tel ++1 724-946-7192; fax ++1 724-946-7194; grellla@westminster.edu; www.aaie.org). Formed in 1966 to address the needs of the American/International schools and advance international and intercultural understanding. The AAIE is recognised as the pre-eminent organisation in the area of American/International education and the organisation in the United states that speak for American/International Schools. AAIE serves a network of over 200 American/International schools performing the function of the communications link and facilitator for relationships among those institutions.

190   *Education: Understanding the Options*

Association of American Schools in South America (AASSA): Jim Morris — Executive Director, c/o 14750 NW 77th Court, Suite 210, Miami Lakes, Florida 33016, USA (tel ++1-305-821-0345; fax ++1-305-821-4244; info@aassa.com; www.aassa.com). Established in 1961 as a non-profit membership association, currently serving forty-one American/International schools throughout South America and offshore islands. AASSA is administered by an executive director who employs a professional staff to assist with publications, in-service programmes, grant management, purchasing, shipping and accounting.

The association serves as a structure through which personnel in member schools can plan co-operatively to attain common goals and to solve mutual problems. AASSA seeks to broaden the dimensions of education and to enhance the quality of teaching and learning in member schools.

A major part of AASSA's efforts is devoted to annual in-service programmes for overseas school personnel. Once each year's in-service topics are decided by the membership, the association plans the locations and logistics of each workshop, and provides several expert consultants in the field. AASSA also supplements member schools for the costs of their attending teachers.

The Association of Christian Schools International (ACSI): Dr. David Wilcox, Executive Assistant for International Ministries, 731 Chapel Hills Drive, Colorado Spings, CO 80920, USA (tel ++1-719-528-906; david_wilcox@acsi.org; www.acsi. org). ACSI is a ministry with the goal of being an 'enabler' for the evangelical Christian community of pre-schools, elementary and secondary schools, and post-secondary schools. ACSI works to accomplish its mission by providing information, services, and products needed by more than 4,800 member schools in 95 countries. The combined student enrolment of these member schools now exceeds 1 million students.

Association of German International Schools (AGIS): Valerie Lark-Webler — Secretariate, Sigmaringer Strasse 257, 70597 Stuttgart, Germany (tel ++49-711-7696 0073; fax ++49-0711-7696 0012; weblerv@iss.s.bw.schule.de). AGIS currently has 13 schools. The service provides them with a professional support network in all matters relating to the successful management of international schools in Germany, in particular relations with the Federal Republic.

Association of International Schools in Africa (AISA): Miffie Greer — Director, c/o International School of Kenya, P.O. Box 14103 Nairobi, Kenya (tel ++254 2582-587; fax ++254 2580-596; aisa@isk.ac.ke). An organisation of 94 international schools in 36 countries throughout sub-Saharan Africa. AISA serves as a support organisation for these schools. In addition, AISA has 39 Associate Members, comprised of businesses, school-to-school partners, organisations, universities, and individuals from throughout the world.

British Schools in the Middle East (BSME): James Crawford — Chairman, c/o Al Ain English Speaking School, PO Box 17939, Al Ain, Abu Dhabi, UAE (tel ++971 3 767 8636; fax ++971 3 767 1973; aaess@emirates.net.ae; www.bsme.org.uk/main.htm). Members can be found in the countries of Bahrain, Cyprus, Egypt, Jordan, Kuwait, Syria, Oman, Qatar, Saudi Arabia, U.A.E. and Lebanon. By definition, a member School is an English Medium, essentially British Curriculum School, in which the Principal/Head Teacher, together with the majority of teachers (apart from those teaching local languages) have qualifications which are recognised by the Department of Education in the U.K.

The Central and Eastern European Schools Association (CEESA): David Cobb — Executive Director, c/o ul.Konstancinska 13, 02-942 Warsaw, Poland (tel ++48 22 40 9380; fax ++48 22 40 9380; office@ceesa.org; www.ceesacentral.org). Founded as a result of the growth of American and International schools in Central and Eastern Europe. In many cases, the schools were geographically isolated from each other and from the main stream of American and International Education. CEESA was formed to broaden the horizons of schools and to promote professional growth.

The primary goal of CEESA is to provide a forum for on-going communication, co-operation, and professional growth among member institutions. CEESA's objective is to promote intercultural understanding and international friendship, as well as exchanges between staff and students to foster professionalism, scholarship, and understanding.

CEESA has 44 schools that enjoy association via membership, associate membership and quality school level.

The Committee on American International Schools Abroad (CAISA): 209 Burlington Rd, Bedford, MA 01730-1433, USA (tel ++1 781-271-0022; fax ++1 781-271-0950; caisa@neasc.org; www.neasc.org/caisa/caisa.htm). CAISA monitors its overseas schools in relation to Standards for Accreditation designed specifically for American and International schools abroad and approved by the membership. It is part of the NEASC (see below).

Council of Independent British Schools in the European Community (COBISEC): Lucy's, Lucy's Hill, Hythe, Kent CT21 5ES, UK (tel/fax: ++44-(0)1303-260857; cobisec@compuserve.com; www.cobisec.org). Founded in 1981. It has 33 members in 12 European countries representing approximately 10,000 students. It is managed by an elected Executive Committee, which includes both Heads and Governors of Schools.

Membership of the organisation is by invitation only and is dependent on the quality of the individual school. All COBISEC schools follow a British curriculum, taught in English by appropriately qualified teachers. The age range of students admitted varies; some schools are primary only, some secondary and others cover the entire range from 3 to 18 years.

East Asia Regional Council of Overseas Schools (EARCOS): Executive Director, PO Box 82, Olongapo City Post Office, 2200 Philippines (tel ++63-47 252 1321/1322; fax ++63-47 252 1323; earcos@svisp.com; www.earcos.org). An organisation of 84 member schools in East Asia (54 associate members and 30 individual members). These schools have a total of approximately 50,000 Pre-K to 12th grade students.

The objectives and purpose of EARCOS is to broaden the dimensions of education of all schools involved in the Council in the interest of a total programme of education, advance the professional growth and welfare of individuals belonging to the educational staff of member schools, facilitate communication and co-operative action between and among all associated schools and to co-operate with other organisations and individuals pursuing the same objectives as this council.

Incorporated Association of Preparatory Schools (IAPS): John Morris — General Secretary, 11 Waterloo Place, Leamington Spa, Warwickshire CV32 5LA, UK (tel ++44-(0)1926 887833; fax ++44(0)-1926 888014; hq@iaps.org.uk; www.iaps.org.uk). IAPS is the national and international professional body which regulates preparatory schools. It covers more than 500 schools in England, Scotland, Ireland and Wales and some 40 schools overseas. Member schools must reach accreditation standards laid down by the Independent Schools Council (ISC), and must demonstrate this by means of inspection.

IAPS provides a wide range of services to its member schools, which help to create and maintain an excellent teaching quality and high levels of school management and administration. There is a first-class educational support service to schools, run by the Director of Education, giving advice on the curriculum, on teaching, and on classroom and school organisation. Regular national courses are organised for existing and potential Heads. Some of the activities run by the IAPS for their member schools include the annual IAPS National Symphony Orchestra and Band Concerts, a full programme of sports coaching and tournaments; a history prize competition; a chess congress; educational cruises; and skiing activities at home and abroad.

Independent Schools Information Services (ISIS): David Woodhead — Director, Grosvenor Gardens House, 35-37 Grosvenor Gardens, London SW1W 0BS, UK (tel ++44-(0)20-7798 1500; fax ++44-(0)20-7798 1501; national@isis.org.uk; www.isis.org.uk). ISIS maintains a registry and information about private and independent schools in the UK.

ISIS International retains a close professional relationship with ISIS member schools to find the most suitable schools for children who live outside the UK, or whose parents want them to attend school in the UK while they are abroad. ISIS International works to help families compete for places on the same terms as their British resident counterparts.

ISIS often visit and attend educational exhibitions and conferences overseas. At this time it is possible for parents to have a personal consultation with ISIS International advisors. ISIS International also has permanent ISIS representatives in Europe, the Far East and Middle East.

The International Council of School Accreditation Commissions (ICSAC): registry@epix.net; www.icsac.org. Formed in 1994, it maintains a comprehensive register of US-style schools, outside of the US, that are accredited by the (US) regional school commissions (see above) of the International Council on School Accreditation Commissions (ICSAC) and the Commission on International and Trans-regional Accreditation (CITA).

International Schools Services (ISS): 15 Roszel Road, PO Box 5910, Princeton, New Jersey, USA (tel ++1-609-452-0990; iss@iss.edu; www.iss.edu). A private, non-profit organisation founded in 1955 to serve American international schools overseas. The Princeton office of ISS is staffed by professionals experienced in the field of international education. ISS also employs teachers and administrators in the schools it operates worldwide. ISS services include establishing and operating international schools, recruiting and placing teachers and administrators, consulting, financial management, purchasing and shipping instructional materials, supplies, and equipment for schools, colleges, and universities, publishing, foundations management, and facility planning.

K-12 Islamic Schools (Islamicity): info@islamicity.com; http://islamicity.com/ Education/schools.htm. This is a commercial website, but it provides valuable links to Islamic Schools including 25 in the United States, 18 in Canada, three in the UK and one link to a European site. Links to Islamic virtual and home schools are also included.

London International Schools Association (LISA): Thomas J Lehman — Chair, c/o American Community School, Heywood, Portsmouth Road, Cobham KT11 1BL, UK (tel +44-(0)1932 867251; fax +44-(0)1932 869790; tlehman@acs-england.co.uk). LISA is made up of seventeen independent schools in the greater London area, and two outside of the London area. Generally, half of the students at these schools are American, while the remaining half come from over forty different countries.

The organisation is mainly concerned with professional development activities and providing opportunities for administrators to share their experiences and ideas with one another. They do not provide information or services to non-member agencies and organisations.

The organisation does not have a web site, although it publishes a directory of member schools which includes a description of school programmes, important administrators, and contact details for each school. A copy of this booklet can be obtained by mail from the address above.

The Mediterranean Association of International Schools (MAIS): Executive Secretary, c/o The American School of Madrid, Apartado 80, 28080 Madrid, Spain (tel ++34 1 357 2154; fax +34 1 357 2678; www.mais-web.org). This is a professional organisation that strives to improve the quality of education in its Member Schools through several venues. It promotes the professional development of Faculty, Administrators and School Board Members; effects communication and interchange; and creates international understanding. MAIS serves as a liaison between its 25 Member Schools, host country schools, Associate Member organisations and other regional, Professional, and In-Service Organisations.

MAIS is composed of schools in Spain, Portugal, Morocco, Tunisia, Egypt, Gaza and Italy. In addition, several Associate Members, such as schools outside the Mediterranean region, colleges, businesses, and interested individuals support MAIS endeavours and have joined the organisation.

National Association of British Schools in Spain (NABSS): c/o Hastings School, c/Azulinas 8, 28036 Madrid, Spain (tel ++34 91 3599913; fax ++34 91 3593521; www.nabss.org). NABSS was founded in 1978 to promote, uphold and defend British education in Spain.

One of its most important functions is to maintain contacts with the British Council, the cultural arm of the British Embassy, and with the Spanish Educational authorities in order to satisfy the requirements of Spanish legislation referring to foreign schools in Spain.

The NABSS provides information on each of its member schools, including, size, enrolment, curriculum, fees, contact information, and a fuller description of their ethos/facilities.

Those schools which are full members of the Association have been authorised to impart a British education in Spain. Those mentioned as affiliate members are not necessarily British, but have a particular interest in the British educational system.

Other NABSS services are the provision of professional training sessions for heads and teachers, the organisation of conferences and workshops on themes of interest to all members, exhibitions of textbooks and equipment and regular updating on changes and reforms within the British educational system. The Association also offers a legal advisory service to its members.

Near East South Asia Council of Overseas Schools (NESA): c/o American College of Greece, Gravias 6, Aghia Paraskevi,153 42 Athens, Greece (tel ++30 1-600-9821; fax ++30 1-600-9928; nesa@ath.forthnet.gr; www.nesacenter.org). NESA encompasses schools from Greece to Bangladesh, including the Saudi Arabian peninsula. Schools that qualified as 'American Sponsored Overseas Schools' were eligible for financial assistance from the US government. The requirements stipulated that the school be a non-profit, non-sectarian institution using American curricula and instructional materials and have a system of local controls and management.

Currently, NESA includes 41 Regular Members, 66 Associate Members, and 40 Supporting Members. It is an organisation encompassing over 30,000 students and over 2,000 professional educators.

Rome International Schools Association: c/o St. Francis & Clare International School, Via Massini 164, 00136 Rome, Italy (gideon@apexmail.com;

www.romeschools.com). Founded in 1974 by a number of headmasters and principals of schools in Rome desiring to share ideas for keeping up to date with the trends of education in their home countries, now has 14 member schools.

The schools are of varying sizes and offer different combinations of levels from pre-school through to secondary. The schools all share these common factors:

1. They are 'International' in the sense that they offer a curriculum either typical of a country outside Italy or one in which the culture and educational practice of two or more countries are represented.
2. They have students and sometimes teachers drawn from a number of nations.
3. Their sole or major language of instruction is English.

Swiss Group of International Schools (SGIS): Virginia Immergluck — Secretary, Stegstrasse 16, 8132 Egg, Switzerland (tel/fax +41 1 984 1662; timmergluck@access.ch; www.ecis.org.uk/sgis). SGIS has 32 primary and secondary schools using Swiss, French, American, British and other curriculum. The group offers opportunities for inter-school education, cultural and sports activities. It encourages members to exchange resources and promotes professional development for teachers and administrators. Among other activities, the SGIS sponsors educational research jointly with international institutes and organisations, and organises tournaments with member schools.

The Tri-Association: Mary V. Sanches — Executive Secretary, c/o US Embassy Quito, Unit #5372 — Box 004, APO AA 34039, USA (tel ++1-593-2477-534; fax ++1-593-2434-985; marysanc@uio.satnet.net; www.tri-association.org). The Tri-Association of American Schools of Central America, Columbia, Caribbean and Mexico, was established to jointly provide services and information to each of the three associations.

Distance Learning Resources

African Distance Learning Association (ADLA): gutaye@ncat.edu; http://unicorn.ncat.edu/~michael/adla/. The site is translatable into French, German, Italian, Portuguese and Spanish. The website of the association has a few links into online distance learning courses through African institutions.

Education Course Advisory Service Worldwide: www.edcasworldwide.com. A UK based independent educational advisory service offering impartial advice on programmes and courses across the tertiary education sector worldwide.

Edupoint.com: www.edupoint.com. An online marketplace for continuing education, providing centralised access to over 1.5 million learning opportunities, more than 3,000 education providers and a free online database with searchable tools for courses, subjects and locations.

Commonwealth Open University (COU): Palm Chambers, P.O.Box 119, Road Town, Tortola, British Virgin Islands (fax ++1 917-477-1321; commopu@box100.com; (international information centre: commopu@maptel.es). *College of Jewish Studies:* yeshiva@commonwealth.org; http://commonwealth. org; http://off-campus.org. Provides adult continuing education, it was developed to meet the needs of adults by offering non-resident degree and other programmes on an international basis.

The Consorzio per l'Università a Distanza (CUD): www.tvtecnologia.it. The website provides information about the CUD and its aims to set up a distance education consortium in Italy.

The Fern Universität (Gesamthochschule): Fern Universität, D-58084 Hagen.

Feithstr. 140, D-58097 Hagen, Germany. Admissions Office: Konkordiastr. 5, D-58095 Hagen, German. International Relations: Feithstr. 142, D-58097 Hagen; (international@fernuni-hagen.de; www.fernuni-hagen.de). The website is in German and English. The FernUniversität Gesamthochschule in Hagen ('University of Hagen') was founded in 1974 to provide distance higher education for students at home and abroad. The Fern Universität is the only distance teaching university in Germany and an integral part of the regular public higher education system.

Open Learning Australia (OLA): PO Box 18059, Collins St East, Melbourne, VIC 8003, Australia (tel ++61 3 9903 8900; fax ++61 3 9903 8966; advisers@ola.edu.au; www.ola.edu.au) has a searchable database for key words, levels of education and subject.

Open University-International Centre for Distance Learning (ICDL): www.icdl.open.ac.uk. Databases contain information on over 31,000 distance learning programmes and courses mostly in the (British) Commonwealth countries, at over 1,000 institutions teaching at a distance worldwide. It also offers over 11,000 abstracts of books, journal articles, research reports, conference papers, dissertations and other types of literature relating to all aspects of the theory and practice of distance education.

The Open University of Israel: tel ++972 36 40 40 40; infodesk@oumail.openu.ac.il; www.openu.ac.il. The website is maintained in Hebrew and English. The Open University of Israel is a distance education university designed to offer academic studies to students throughout Israel.

The Open University of the Netherlands: Mrs Lillian Janssen, Open University of the Netherlands, P.O. Box 2960, NL-6401 DL Heerlen, the Netherlands (tel ++31 45-5762222; lilian.janssen-grootenboer@ou.nl; www.ouh.nl/dhtml.htm). The Open University accepts students from all over the world, but most of the study material is in Dutch and only a few courses are in English. This means that the professional or academic titles (which are the equivalents of a Master's Degree) are out of reach for those who have no command of the Dutch language.

Peterson's Services: www.petersons.com links to the *Lifelong Learning* site (www.lifelonglearning.com) that has an online searchable database of distance learning courses.

University Continuing Education Association (UCEA): http://www.nucea.edu. UCEA is among the oldest college and university associations in the United States. The site lists programmes of independent study from accredited member universities, colleges and professional affiliates.

Print Resources

College & University Almanac: Peterson's Guides, ISBN 0768904269, also available through Vacation Work.

International Herald Tribune Guide to International Schools: Niki Chesworth, Kogan Page, ISBN: 0749433353.

The UCAS Handbook of UK Universities: UCAS, Rosehill, New Barn Lane, Cheltenham, Gloucestershire GL52 3LZ, UK (tel ++44 1242 222444; www.ucas.ac.uk; online directory www.ucas.ac.uk/direct/index.html).

MEDICAL SERVICES

Whether you are moving half way round the world to somewhere exotic, or to the country next door which is very similar to your own, looking after your health is important. The stresses and strains of life that are associated with being an expatriate, in a country that also has bacteria and viruses never before encountered, can make staying healthy much more difficult than when at home. Unfortunately, if you do get ill, it can also seem a lot worse when you are a long way from the comforts of home.

Preventative Healthcare

Before You Move

As soon as you know where you are moving to, it is important to investigate the health and safety issues of your destination country.

Some countries require visitors to have certain vaccinations before they enter the country, which has to be proven at the border, or they face mandatory vaccination at your point of entry in what can be less than sterile conditions. But even where this is not the case, there can be vaccinations that you may want to have anyway, and other healthcare issues you will be much safer for knowing about before you relocate.

Family practitioners based in one country will not always be familiar with the health issues of another, especially if the country is radically different in terms of environment and climate. Because of this, it is usually advisable to carry out your own research to learn about the health issues of your destination country and find a medical advisor who is knowledgeable, or can find out to your satisfaction, about the country you are going to.

In some countries there are medical clinics specialising in providing advice, assistance and medicines to people intending to travel abroad, which should be able to give the most up to date and practical advice possible.

Where these services are not available it may be necessary to visit your personal physician, a specialist/consultant physician, or your local hospital to discuss your destination and secure the necessary vaccinations and medicines you will need before you move. This, however, may not provide you with the most accurate picture, as one expat found before their move.

About to make a move to Hong Kong, one Canadian went to her family GP (general practitioner) for advice. By the end of the consultation she was so worried about all of the supposed health risks that she almost cancelled her plans. However, before doing so, she called a friend who had been living in Hong Kong for advice. Much to her surprise, and relief, she found that the family GP had been overly cautious. A local doctor in Hong Kong suggested that only two (as opposed to five) vaccinations were really necessary.

Mike van der Es and his wife Sarah, themselves expatriates in the health industry, believe that planning ahead and finding a professional qualified in international health issues is a necessary step towards safe health.

I think it is important to see your family doctor before you go, but expect good, up-to-date advice only from specialists in international health. Local family doctors do not have enough experience in the fast changing world of international health so their advice is frequently not very appropriate. At larger centres, their vaccines are purchased in bulk, so they are often cheaper too.

Researching basic health-related information about your destination country is essential for remaining healthy when abroad. The online Travel Medicine Consultants, *Travel Doctors* (www.thetraveldoctor.com), advise that problems can arise from unexpected sources and last much longer than anticipated.

(People) relaxing on sunny beaches can encounter parasites that penetrate the skin of bare feet and other exposed body areas. Some diseases, like hepatitis or malaria, may be resistant to a cure long after your return home. These diseases may be a permanent souvenir that may affect your health and lifespan.

Living in a foreign country is also going to raise issues different to those that would arise on a holiday. For example, the weather can vary hugely throughout the year, from extremely hot to extremely cold; Ankara, the capital of Turkey, has seen temperatures range from -20°C in winter to +42°C in summer during the authors' time there. Researching a country's climate (especially for the region where you will live) can go a long way towards preparing you for local health and hygiene issues.

Embassies and consulates can also provide up to date information regarding the latest health situation of their country and may issue advisory warnings of any new outbreaks or epidemics in the area you are moving to.

The Internet and specialist travel guides to the country or region you will be moving to can also be good sources of general information about health issues, though Internet based health resources are not always reliable and can never replace professional and personal advice from a qualified medical practitioner. A number of travel medicine clinics, in various countries, can be found by searching Yahoo! with the following search string: +travel +medicine. Online directories of Travel Medicine Providers can also be found at www.istm.org (*International Society of Travel Medicine*) and www.tripprep.com/providers_frame.html (*Travel Health Online*).

Health guides for backpackers and budget travellers are often better suited to expatriates than information provided for visitors on expensive package tours. This is because backpackers, like expatriates, generally spend more than a week or two in a country and are more likely to eat in local restaurants, use public transport and visit places off the beaten track than escorted package-tourists are. The *Lonely Planet Health Guides* listed at the end of this chapter provide excellent advice and information on illnesses and preventive health care for a number of countries.

The advice of expatriates who have recently lived in your destination city/country is also very useful, as they may know of restaurants, shops, or parts of the region that should be avoided or are strongly recommended.

If you will also be travelling to countries in the region other than the one you will be resident in, it is important to research the health and safety issues of those too. Though Singapore and Indonesia are very close to each other, their environment and levels of development are very different, as are the far-flung regions of Indonesia itself.

Basic Health and Hygiene Issues

In some countries the level of basic hygiene will be drastically different from what you are used to, but even where it is not, the water, the food and the indigenous bacteria and viruses are still highly likely to be different from what you have grown up with in your home country.

Bacteria in the water supply may not affect local residents, but foreigners may suffer severe intestinal upset (at least to start with). Sometimes expats can become used to these bacteria over time and are able to drink the tap water. Other times they are best off never drinking tap water and always buying bottled water or preparing their own safe drinking supply. Long-term expats are the best source of information on what is safe and what is not.

These differences are just as likely to make someone moving from your destination country to your home country as ill as when you move the other way.

If possible, the best thing to do is give your body time to adjust to the new environment and acquire its own immunity. However, care does need to be taken to ensure that you do not become seriously ill and a doctor should always be consulted if you are unsure about the severity of your illness, or the cause of your symptoms.

Attention to basic hygiene at home and in public places, and care over where and what you eat is hugely important.

Basic preventative action, especially the frequent washing of your hands and the drinking of bottled water, can be the two most important ways of staying healthy. For the first few weeks after you arrive it is a good idea to be extremely careful about what and where you eat. In high-risk areas some doctors advise soaking fresh produce in a diluted solution of bleach, followed by thorough rinsing in clean water, before eating. A tiny amount of bleach can mean the difference between enjoying a healthy meal or a night in hospital on a re-hydration drip.

In fancy restaurants it can be easy to forget about possible hygiene problems, but ice cubes are often made with local tap water and fruit and salads are often rinsed under the tap. In high-risk countries, unless other expats can vouch for a particular restaurant, exercise extreme care over where and what you eat.

Worms and other parasites can be transmitted from improperly cooked meat, so thorough cooking is recommended (no rare steaks or Steak Tartar). Even well-known fast food restaurants can be problematic. One expat asked for a special order, which was rushed through leaving the burger improperly cooked and containing parasites. This resulted in a couple of days in the hospital.

New expats should always turn to existing expatriates for advice on relief of basic stomach troubles. New arrivals usually become ill and old hands will often be able to give the best advice on whether to try to get through a few days of adjustment or see a recommended doctor immediately. Always visit a doctor if you are concerned about your health, no matter what anyone else advises.

As you become used to the local water and cuisine you will be able to expand your eating options, but do not do so indiscriminately. If you have two restaurants next door to each other and one is full and the other is empty, ask yourself why before going for the quiet option. Local residents will have their reasons for not eating somewhere, they may be valid ones that do not affect you, but equally a restaurant may have a reputation an expatriate is unlikely to hear directly.

Along with the health issues there are the safety issues too. A first aid kit from home can be a great help in the first few weeks before you have been able to stock up from a chemist or if you are in a remote area. Mike van der Es and his family know from experience the benefit of being fully prepared.

Take a first aid kit prepared with some thought and be prepared to use it if going off the beaten track. We took steri-strips and used them twice when the children gave themselves deep cuts during a period living in an isolated setting. That way, you can deal effectively with a cut that would otherwise need a long trip to a doctor for a couple of stitches. Another must for any first aid kit is something to counteract diarrhoea.

Post-arrival Care

Climate and other environmental changes can produce unexpected effects. Apart from the well-known ones listed below, expats should be aware that they can develop illnesses and/or allergies that they have never previously suffered from. *Special Needs* discusses these in greater detail.

One of the authors, Michelyne Callan, began to experience bouts of breathing difficulty at certain times of the year after she moved to Turkey, where it is extremely arid throughout the year. A specialist advised her she was exhibiting signs of asthma, most likely related to the change in environmental conditions (it had been extremely humid in Hong Kong where she had previously lived) and prescribed asthma medication, that relieved her symptoms.

Altitude Changes

If you are moving to a destination at a markedly higher altitude from where you are currently living, be prepared to spend time acclimatising. Even relatively small changes of a 1000 metres can affect people, especially if there is also a change in climate.

Children, elderly people and those with health problems are likely to suffer the most, especially asthmatics and those with heart problems, but healthy people can suffer symptoms too.

Lethargy, tiredness, breathlessness, headaches, dizziness and dehydration are the most common reactions to an increase in altitude. Acclimatisation takes patience. Strenuous exercise should be avoided for the first few days, and non-alcoholic, non-caffeinated fluid drunk regularly.

Coping With Heat

Hot weather and lots of sun can be great on holiday, but living and working in them can be very different. Carrying the shopping home, walking around the streets or playing sports can be enervating. Add high, or low, humidity into the equation and the effects are enhanced.

Avoiding heat stroke, sunburn and dehydration are important, especially for children who can be more susceptible than adults. Acclimatisation takes time, but can be quickened by judicial use of air-conditioning, fans and an increased intake of fluid and salts. The heat is usually greatest during the middle of the day when it can be a good idea to avoid strenuous activity and spending long periods in direct sunlight. When this is not possible, use of high-factor sun cream, the wearing of a hat and cool clothes that cover your arms and legs, and the drinking of plenty of fluid can mitigate the effects of sun and heat. It can also be a good idea to keep a supply of rehydration salts in case you do become overheated and/or dehydrated.

Extreme Cold

Cold weather can seem to be easier to deal with; just add more clothes. Lightweight wind and water-resistant coats over various other lightweight, warm layers can be better than a few thick layers of clothing. Gloves, warm socks, lined boots and a warm hat are also important. If you do become too cold and hypothermic, warming yourself gently and slowly is the recommended procedure. Frostbite should always be treated professionally.

Dry, cold air can also exacerbate asthma and increase the likelihood of suffering from bronchitis and other chest-related problems. Those susceptible to these illnesses should be careful not to overexert themselves and should always carry their medication.

Sickness and Diarrhoea

For mild cases of sickness and diarrhoea avoiding dehydration is the major concern. Increased fluid intake and the use if rehydration salts will help reduce the likelihood of this. However, sickness and diarrhoea can be very serious and develop rapidly. If you are at all concerned about the severity of an attack you should seek medical help promptly.

Childbirth

Giving birth is a major undertaking and good medical supervision is essential. However, good medical care during the birth is not the only consideration of expatriate parents-to-be when a baby is due. Whether you choose to give birth in your host country, or return home, can depend on many factors.

Ante and Post Natal Care

Establishing the quality of the medical care available to you should be a primary concern and asking the advice of other expatriates in your host country, as well as your embassy, is essential. Babies are born every day in just about every country in the world, but local medical practices vary greatly.

Locally trained doctors in Asian countries can be as good as doctors in the US or the UK, after all they may deliver many babies every day; in one hospital in Hong Kong it is not uncommon for over 200 babies to be born each day. However, in many countries there will be doctors and midwives who have trained both locally and in countries such as the UK and the US. This will mean that they have experience in the latest techniques and are likely to be as well qualified as a doctor in those countries. Expatriates will often visit these internationally trained medical personnel because they are comfortable with their bedside manner and have little trouble communicating with them in English. In developing countries with close historical and economic links to developed nations there will also be doctors who trained in the developed country and speak a language other than English.

Kelli Lambe became pregnant in Oman and found acceptable international services there. She recalls:

I got pregnant with my third son in Oman. We had a camp clinic, and while it was good, it was run by a group of doctors made up from around the world — Dutch, Indian, British. I always went to the British doctor. She was more like the American style (gave out antibiotics) the Dutch and Indian doctors were less likely to help, it seemed.

Seonaid Francis gave birth in a government hospital in Hong Kong in a communal birthing room, while another woman gave birth on the next bed. This thought might not be acceptable for all mothers, but Seonaid Francis did not actually realise there was another woman behind the curtain and only found out two years later when her husband, co-author Huw Francis, was telling friends about the birth. As she said, 'They could have paraded a circus through the room and I wouldn't have noticed a thing'.

Apart from the quality of the medical care, the quality and style of the hospital facilities are also important. An Intensive Care Baby Unit is not something parents necessarily want to use, but its availability in case of need can be reassuring. The arrangement of birthing facilities can also vary greatly as can the amount of control the mother is allowed in deciding where and how to give birth. The acceptability, commonality and availability of birthing pools, private rooms, medical intervention, epidurals and paternal involvement vary greatly from country to country, doctor to doctor and hospital to hospital.

Anne Jordan, an American teacher, has given birth in Norway and plans to do so in Turkey.

The facilities and philosophies of course will vary greatly from country to country. A tour of the hospitals is vital, if they will allow for it. Talking to your doctor about your desires is key, but for me it has been more informative to talk with the expat community as well as Turkish women about the birthing experience here. My little chats with women from all walks of life have been very interesting, especially the Turks. I feel like I am prepared in that I know how the Turks do it. Unfortunately I don't agree, but when in Rome...

Though the facilities and quality of medical staff may be excellent, the local culture can still impinge on the experience of the expat mother-to-be, as Kelli Lambe found in Oman.

I had an ambulance driver who knew how the ambulance worked, but he didn't know where the hospital was. The Omani nurse who rode with me was fabulous and told the very new ambulance driver where to go.

I had a doctor who gave me an antenatal scan and left very quickly, without saying a word, and then didn't come back. My husband went to find the doctor and after 20 minutes of waiting the doctor said, You are having a boy, what else do you need to know?

In retrospect Kelli says, 'While it wasn't funny at the time, now that I have a healthy baby we look back at it all and laugh. I guess the bottom line is to trust your instinct, and hope that you have prepared yourself enough to do things yourself if you need to'.

Post Delivery Support

Once the baby is born and the mother and child go home from hospital, will the family need outside support? In your home country friends and family are often on hand to help out, but as an expatriate this is not always the case.

Alison Albon returned to South Africa from the Netherlands for the birth of her son, and was relieved to have the help when needed:

When I had Matthew in South Africa it was nice to have my family around when we got home. There was always someone to call when we didn't know what to do, or someone to come over when all I could do was cry because I was so tired. I had a severe case of 'the trots' that lasted a week. I hadn't been able to take anything because I was breast-feeding and it hadn't gone away on it's own. So after a week of jumping up every so often to go to the loo, and having to get up whenever Matthew cried — which was usually just as I had gone back to sleep after getting up to go to the loo — my mom came and spent a whole day, while I slept. It also makes a difference being in your home country where you know the language and 'medicinal culture'. You can go into a pharmacy and talk to the pharmacist and they'll suggest something that will relieve baby's cramps etc.

If you have a good circle of friends (found by following the suggestions in the second and third chapters) in your host country, you may be confident of receiving support when you need it. But for expats who have newly arrived, or who live in remote areas, it is important to decide, prior to the birth, whether the mother will be able to cope with a new baby, running the household and looking after other children (unless the father is a trailing male and will be at home too).

This can be a major concern for expatriates, especially if the spouse travels extensively, works long hours, the birth was difficult or a caesarean section was necessary.

For first-time parents, the first few weeks can be stressful as they get used to having a baby and being able to ask for advice (when wanted) can make life much easier. As an expat, having friends nearby to ask for help can save a lot of money on phone calls home.

Some expatriates, whether or not they have friends nearby to help, ask grandparents, siblings or friends to stay with them for a while to help out soon after the birth. This arrangement is best planned in advance and can serve two purposes;

it makes the first few weeks easier for the new parents and, it gives friends/relatives the chance to see the new baby (which they may not have until next time you visit your home country).

Though Alison had returned to South Africa for the birth of her son and knew the benefits of having a baby at home with a built-in support system, she chose to give birth to her daughter, Meg, in her host country, Switzerland.

The prenatal care was on par with South Africa's, and my hospital stay was just fine, but the language barrier did cause some problems. Luckily, my parents came to Geneva for the birth. I was due on the 27th of July, so we arranged for them to fly in on the 22nd. They had a week planned with us then a trip to Italy for a week, then back to us for a follow-up week. It worked out perfectly.

I had Meg on the 24th and my mom was able to stay with Matthew while Mark (my husband) stayed with Meg and me. I stayed in the clinic for two days and had a bit of trouble with the nurses speaking French and therefore had very little help, then went home. We had my parents around for two days, with mom helping out with the cooking, and calming me down when a minor complication set in, and then they left and gave the four of us time to bond as a family.

They were away for a week, then came back to us, and by then we had settled into a kind of routine, and it was nice to have them back to help out with the extra chores. I would definitely recommend having a close family member or friend around at that time. My husband is super helpful and understanding, but there are some things that just need one's mum, you know.

Having grandparents to stay around the time of the birth is not always so successful, as Gillian Kerr found.

When Don was born my mum came to Scotland to help out and it was fantastic. When Catherine was born in Australia, my mother-in-law and her mother both came out and it was a disaster. I only spent one night in hospital because I didn't trust her to look after my then 18 month old Donald. The next day I was expected to be tour guide again. The ultimate was when I had Catherine breast feeding, Donald having a jealous tantrum, and the two in-laws on the sofa watching TV had the audacity to say, 'So what's for dinner?'.

Cost of Childbirth

Childbirth is expensive in some countries and free in others. Investigating your options can save you a lot of money.

Check the cost of giving birth in a local state hospital, local private hospital, your home country, or even a third country. If you have medical insurance you may be covered for all or part of the cost of a private delivery, though beware of upper financial limits and qualification periods for the maternity cover to become active. Your insurance policy may cover all the cost of a private birth in your host country, but only a percentage of the cost in your home country if there is a maximum amount you can claim. Some insurance policies exclude pregnancy altogether, or exclude pregnancies that begin within the first six months of the policy start date.

Gillian Kerr moved from Britain to Australia. She was fortunate that some of her financial costs of the birth of her daughter would be covered.

Australia is much like Britain. They have Medicare instead of the NHS. Unlike the UK though, you can go to any doctor you want; you don't have to go to one in your area. I had Catherine (my daughter) here in a public hospital which was of an incredibly high standard. I was very impressed. I did however pay extra and had my own obstetrician for antenatal visits and to deliver Catherine. I could not get private health insurance (to cover my hospital stay or use of private obstetrician), as I was already pregnant when I arrived.

If you will receive no financial aid you may have to consider giving birth in a host country government hospital, or returning home where you may qualify for cheaper or free health care under your country's national healthcare scheme. Some UK nationals return home to give birth solely because it is free for them in the NHS hospitals.

One expat, without pregnancy insurance cover, gave birth in a government hospital in Hong Kong, primarily because of cost considerations. Giving birth in a private hospital would have cost well over £5,000, but the bill from the Government hospital was only £15.00. The facilities in the government hospital were, however, excellent if not better, because some emergencies that occur during childbirth would have necessitated a transfer from the private hospital to the government hospital anyway.

Nationality Issues of an Overseas Birth

Giving birth in a foreign country can have advantages and disadvantages as far as nationality is concerned. The baby may be eligible for the nationality and a passport of the country of birth (often the case in the US), if you are a legal resident. Alternatively, the baby may be discounted from obtaining the same passport as their parents (e.g. a child born outside the UK to a UK passport holder who was also born outside the UK may not be eligible for a UK passport). It is important to seek advice on nationality issues directly from a qualified reputable source, your embassy, or the applicable government department of your own country and your host country.

Medical Facilities at Your Destination

The general level of healthcare provided to the residents of any country by its government can vary from non-existent to excellent. No matter what the level of state provided healthcare, most countries seem to have at least one private healthcare provider that is of international standard, and this provider is likely to be located near to any concentration of expats.

Expatriates are not generally eligible to receive free healthcare under their host country's social security system (unless they are EU citizens resident in the EU or there is a reciprocal agreement between individual countries).

When an expat moves from a developed country to a less developed country and can utilise local government health centres, they may not want to anyway. Even in places that may seem to be well developed, the government healthcare system may not be what an expat would expect. Reasons for this can be lack of hygiene, lack of clean blood supplies, lack of privacy, or massive overcrowding resulting in unacceptable waiting times. Medical insurance is therefore essential if you want to receive international standard care from a private healthcare provider (unless you have extensive private means to cover any expenses incurred).

One expat in Hong Kong, without medical insurance, ended up in a government hospital there with appendicitis. Placed in the general ward, both pre- and post-operative, he was surrounded by opium addicts and other seriously ill patients. The ward was so overcrowded that the beds were only inches apart and other patients were on camp beds in the aisle. Patients were treated and died without any privacy at all. Though food was provided, little else was and the nursing staff only fulfilled medical tasks and did not change bed sheets or clean patients.

When moving to a developed country, with a well-developed government healthcare system, medical insurance may not seem so important as South African expat, Frances Brown, found in the UK.

In South Africa, we had private medical aid so had the choice of doctors, hospitals and so forth, as did most of the employed population. Only if you were down and out did you use the state facilities, which were dreadful to say the least. Here in the UK, I have found that although we are on the NHS the level of care is amazing. We have our own doctor, who does house calls in emergencies, who does preventative medicine. They are also interested in the medical case, and are not just trying to push patients through the surgery. One thing which is very much in the favour of the NHS is the free treatment of children and also the once-off fee per prescription so everyone can afford to buy their medicines. Also the cost of over the counter medicines is far lower than that in South Africa.

The extensive state management of the healthcare system did raise some problems too. 'But as with everything, there is a downside. They are so cautious here about selling you things like cough remedies and usual things which we could quite happily buy over the counter in South Africa, so you end up going to the doctor for minor primary health issues that just need a bit of medicine to cure.'

Once you arrive at your destination it can also be a good idea to find and visit a primary care physician and emergency medical facility before you need them, so you do not have to search for them in time of need.

If you are moving to a major city it can be possible to learn the names and addresses of doctors and major hospitals before you go. Some backpacker guidebooks (*Lonely Planet, Rough Guides*, etc.) list the main hospitals in big cities and your embassy in the destination country may be able to provide you with a list of local doctors, dentists and specialists who speak your language. Your employer may also be able to provide such information. Large cities may also have a local newspaper, what's-on guide, or locally produced handbook of facilities and services. Obtaining copies of these publications will give you a head start in your research. The embassy of the country you are going to may be able to supply you with back copies, or the address of the publishers of such guides. Some websites, such as *www.directmoving.com* and others listed at the end of this chapter, also list medical service providers in major cities around the world.

If you are moving to a smaller town, or a rural area, finding the information prior to your departure may be more difficult. If this is so then you may need to rely on your employer for the information, or turn to the contacts you hopefully made by following the suggestions earlier in this book.

A good way to determine the quality of the medical care at your destination is to look at the job adverts of other organisations (especially well-known/reputable ones) that employ expatriates there. The packages offered to their employees can be an indication of how they perceive the local services. If most of the organisations offer only basic medical insurance the local services are probably fine. But if some are offering extras such as emergency casualty evacuation or emergency blood supply services (where screened blood and other intravenous fluids are couriered to the destination from a safe source), then you may want to consider asking your employer for similar coverage, or buying your own top-up insurance separately.

Finding a local health care practitioner that speaks your language should not be your only concern. Dr. Arseven, a Turkish doctor who has trained or practised in Turkey, the US, the UK and Germany and is official doctor to fifteen embassies in the Turkish capital, Ankara, has found that the requirements and expectations of patients from different countries vary enormously. As expats are usually affected in different ways to local residents by local bacteria and viruses, Dr. Arseven also emphasises that it is important for expatriates to find a primary healthcare physician who understands the needs and the medical problems faced specifically by expats.

In a country where there is severe risk of being exposed to non-sterile medical equipment during emergencies, it can be well worth carrying a personal sterile medical pack containing disposable needles, syringes and sutures. These kits are now widely available from specialist travel medicine providers and many pharmacists.

Pharmacies

The role of pharmacies in the provision of healthcare can also vary around the world.

Rather than being purely dispensers of medicines, pharmacists in some countries may be willing to make diagnosis for minor illnesses and in others can even act almost as doctors, especially in rural areas and where medical facilities are poor or financially out of reach for most local residents.

As far as the drugs dispensed are concerned, the rules vary enormously too. In some countries just about every drug is available over the counter without a prescription, whilst in others many drugs are restricted and require a prescription from a recognised doctor before they can be dispensed.

Even in countries where drugs are freely available over the counter, the range of drugs might be limited. This can be for cultural and legal reasons (e.g. contraceptive pills and the morning after pill), or purely due to lack of demand by local customers or distribution by the manufacturer.

The validity of the drugs provided also needs to be checked as far as possible too. The sale of date-expired drugs is common in some countries and is done in three ways:

1. By blatantly selling the out-of-date drug and hoping nobody will notice (how often do you check the date?).
2. By covering the original label in a local language version with a new expiry date (so beware of second labels on medicine bottles and try to find an unaltered bottle/label).
3. Re-labelling the bottles with a new label, having first removed the old label, or changed the bottle (which leaves you none the wiser).

If you require ongoing medication while you are abroad, always learn the generic name of the drug, or the active ingredient. Medicine is likely to be labelled in the local language, especially around Europe, and local drug companies may dominate the market with their own brand of a drug that you are not familiar with. Most doctors and pharmacists have a directory of drugs that list alternative brands of the generic drug that are available in that country.

Knowing the dosage you require is also important, as alternative brands may come in different sizes to what you are used to, so you can not just take one pill and expect the same result.

Dental Care

Dental care is usually treated as a separate service by expatriate employers and is not always included in the medical insurance cover. If dental care is not specifically mentioned in your contract, ask about it.

The quality of dental services available is generally of a similar standard to the local medical care. In countries where healthcare provision is limited, private hospitals often provide dental facilities too (though they may not be covered by your medical insurance).

Resources

Print Resources

ABC of Healthy Travel, E. Walker, G. Williams & F. Raeside, published by BMJ.
The Back Packers Handbook, Chris Townsend, published by Oxford Illustrated

Health.

Health Advice for Travellers is a booklet published by the UK Department of Health that outlines many of the basic preventative measures that travellers can take to stay healthy. The booklet is available from UK post offices and travel agents and multiple copies can be ordered from the Department of Health (PO Box 410, Wetherby, LS23 7LN, UK or individually in the UK from tel 0800 555 777).

Staying Healthy in Asia, Africa, and Latin America, Dirk G. Schroeder ScD MPH, Published by Moon Handbooks, ISBN: 1-56691-026-9.

Travellers Health, Richard Darwood, published by Oxford University Press

The Tropical Traveller, John Hatt, published by Penguin.

Lonely Planet pocket series of comprehensive and informative health guides that are primarily aimed at backpackers but equally applicable to expats.

Healthy Travel — Asia & India, by Isabelle Young, published by Lonely Planet, ISBN 1-86450-051-4.

Healthy Travel — Central & South America, by Isabelle Young, published by Lonely Planet, ISBN 1-86450-053-0.

Healthy Travel —Africa, by Isabelle Young, published by Lonely Planet, ISBN 1-86450-050-6.

Healthy Travel — Australia, NZ & the Pacific, by Isabelle Young, published by Lonely Planet, ISBN 1-86450-052-2.

Online Resources

The Blood Care Foundation: PO Box 7, Sevenoaks Kent TN13 2SZ, UK (tel ++44(0)1293-425485; fax: +44 1293 425488; email BCFgb@compuserve.com; www.bloodcare.org.uk). Offers safe blood supply services. *British Airways Travel Clinics* (www.british-airways.com/travelqa/fyi/health/docs/clinfone.shtml) in the UK and South Africa, and other travel medicine service providers throughout the UK and around the world offer BCF services directly.

Centers for Disease Control (CDC): www.cdc.gov/travel/bluesheet.htm. Has a travellers' health page containing up-to-date information on specific destinations, travelling with children, epidemic outbreak notices, food & water, vaccinations etc.

The Medical Advisory Service for Travellers Abroad (MASTA) maintains a website of information www.masta.org.

Travel Health Online: www.tripprep.com.

World Health Organization (WHO): www.who.int/ith/english/index.htm. International travel and health website designed to offer help to national health administrators, various travel related health concerns and health hazards of international travel. The site has a separate links to various regional offices worldwide including Africa, Pan America, East Mediterranean, Europe, South East Asia and Western Pacific at: www.who.int/regions.

www.hc-sc.gc.ca/hpb/lcdc/osh/tmp_e.html Canadian Government sponsored travel information site.

www.highwaytohealth.com Travel Health Insurance site that lists hospitals and medical service providers in major cities worldwide.

SPECIAL NEEDS

A special need, be it physical, educational, dietary or allergy related, does not have to signal the end of your dreams for living abroad. It may be true that not all countries have a multitude of resources to handle specific special needs, but some countries are definitely better than others are and there are often creative ways to get around the difficulties that do exist. When you are in the process of considering a move abroad, there are a number of places you can search to identify the resources, facilities and allergen-sources present in a country. There are also resources to help you become self-sufficient in managing some special needs, wherever you are in the world.

Allergies and Intolerances

Determining what allergens, facilities and resources are present in any particular country will help you decide whether a destination is a suitable place to make a new home. You may even find that relocating abroad improves the quality of life of the person with the special need.

Food Allergies and Intolerances

Many expats have special dietary needs, that require them to monitor their food intake in much the same way as if they had stayed at home.

For people with allergies and intolerances that cause minor irritations and non-serious illness, good local language skills can often mitigate the effects by allowing packaging labels to be read and food to be ordered in restaurants, without the problematic ingredient. Even if the ingredient is commonly used it is often possible (though persistence may be required) to ask for special orders of food without the item.

Anne Jordan, an American expatriate teacher who has lived and worked in the Philippines, Norway and Turkey has an acute intolerance to pepper.

My best weapon when living overseas is to first learn how to say/read pepper in the native language and then how to clearly state that I cannot eat it when dining out. I think that was the first thing I leaned how to say in Turkish.

*In addition to the basic: 'I can't eat or don't eat peppers of any type', I also learned different ways that the locals refer to peppers. However, I have not always had success in getting pepperless foods (in stores or restaurants). I really believe it was their fault and not mine since the usual response from a restaurant would be, 'Oh, but it's not hot', or 'Oh, it's just a small amount', even though I had clearly expressed that I wanted **none**. I would always have to send the meal back or have Bill (my husband) eat it. That is, I guess, the only way to deal with it especially when I feel my communication is very clear.*

If the troublesome ingredient is not commonly used in the host country the risk of exposure is considerably reduced. One expatriate has an allergy to Prickly Pear, which is rare in her host country, but North Africa, where this particular allergen thrives, might not be such a good place for her to live.

Apart from doing her best to avoid dairy produce, Elizabeth Lanphier carries medication to counter her lactose intolerance and has lived in Hong Kong, Malta and Japan, where dairy products are rarely used in the local cuisine.

I have enough medication to counter the effects of an ill-timed encounter with dairy products to last me until the next time I can get home and obtain a refill. I have to be careful when I am on vacation travelling around since having a bout of illness would not only mean pain and discomfort, but could mean the difference between my making a travel connection or not. Being holed up in a hotel because I had a hunk of cheese without preparing myself medically, and missing my connecting train to wherever, is not my idea of fun.

For serious (including life-threatening) allergies and intolerances, the impact will be greatest where the item is commonly used in the diet of the host country.

For example, China would be a difficult country for people with a fatal peanut allergy to live in, as most food is cooked in peanut oil. Many other dishes contain peanuts and they are frequently eaten as a snack like crisps (chips) are in the UK.

Though Hilary Roy's son, Wheaton, has a fatal allergy to peanuts, the Canadian family lived in Malaysia for two years (where nuts are as common as they are in China) and now lives in Taiwan. Hilary says of the experience, 'It's hard, but not impossible for a child with the peanut allergy to live in Kuala Lumpur. Basically, he doesn't eat anything that isn't made in my kitchen, on our plates and pots etc. The risk of cross contamination is way too high.'

Because of Wheatons' allergy, the Roy family does not travel much from their international base, but when they do their experiences have been mixed.

We have not done a lot of travelling, as I need a kitchen and my own dishes. But we have stayed at some resorts, like the Sheraton, where the kitchen staff set up his own refrigerator and used my pots and pans to cook his food in (after he had a very bad reaction to the first meal). I would love to say it's a normal life, but it can never be, especially over here, for a child with allergies to peanut, tree nut and shellfish.

However, the vast differences in culinary tastes around the world means that specific food items (allergens) are not common everywhere. Add to this the staff of local restaurants who can be very helpful in assuring customers that their food contains no trace of the specific allergen and the quality of life can improve dramatically for someone with an allergy.

A major reason Michelyne Callan, one of the authors, and her family moved to Turkey from Hong Kong was because her son, Liam, was diagnosed as having a fatal allergy to peanuts, which are much less common in Turkey. Turkish restaurateurs have been very helpful in assuring the family that their restaurants are safe for Liam, and even allow the family into their kitchens to check for themselves. The manager at the local *Burger King* even pulled out a packet of every food item they used, to show them the labels.

However, just because a chain restaurant in one country is nut (or other allergen) free, its counterpart in another country might not be and each restaurant should be checked individually. When the Callan family returned to their native Canada for a summer visit they found that the Burger King restaurants were not nut-free.

Apart from living abroad, travelling to the country is a consideration too. For those with severe (life-threatening) allergies it is always essential to check with an airline that the in-flight meals and snacks are allergen free. If they are not, care must be taken to avoid coming into contact with the allergen during the flight, or if this is not possible, then the trip is probably best made with another airline.

Non-Food Allergies

The impact of non-food allergies, such as those to insects, pollen or pollution, will greatly depend on how common the allergen is in a particular country and how readily available appropriate allergy medication is.

For people with an allergies to bee/wasp stings, the availability of Epipens (automated injection needle containing pure epinephrine) may be enough to make a country no more dangerous than their home country. In some countries and big cities wasps and bees are rarely seen, while the strain of wasp/bee in others may mean that the affect of a sting is less severe (though it may also be worse). Other insects are also indigenous to specific countries so moving abroad may ease the problem for allergy sufferers.

Troy Puddington, a young Canadian expat, found that living in Turkey with a life threatening bee/wasp allergy was more difficult than living in Canada.

I find Turkey to be more dangerous because of the great number of wasps and bees that are around. There are many more here than in Canada. I have seen many different sorts of bees, which have varied in size considerably, and because it is hotter for a longer period of time here throughout the year compared to Canada, bees and other insect infestations last longer.

Though the risk of being stung is higher in Turkey than in Canada, Troy feels confident that he can deal with the situation.

I do think there are a great deal of bees where I live and where I go to school, but I am not too disturbed by them because I feel that I am well prepared if something happens. I always carry with me, in my bag, a little kit that my dad and I put together which contains instructions of the procedure to take when I am stung in case I fall unconscious after being stung. It also contains two types of antihistamine, pills and liquid, which reduce the swelling and itch due to allergic reactions, as well as containing an Epipen, which injects a massive heart stimulant that I would use in extreme situations.

Moreover, all my friends and teachers are aware of my allergy and most of them have a basic idea of what to do in case I am stung. I'm always with my friends or a large group of people so someone can go tell a teacher if I have been stung and I just stay away from bee-infested areas like flowerbeds and shrubs. If I am out in the city, I am usually with someone who is aware of my allergy and knows what to do, but just in case, I carry a card in my wallet which tells my name, that I have an allergy, who to notify and what to do.

Tony Soave, who emigrated from Belgium to the US and later relocated to Turkey as a teacher, has fatal allergies to bees and peanuts, but decided they were not going to stop her living abroad.

There's no way I'm going to let my life be dictated by my allergies, no matter how bad they are. I am as capable of dealing with them in foreign locations as I am at home. Since I have moved to Turkey, I have travelled to Malaysia, Bulgaria, Egypt, Tunisia, Greece and Cyprus and only once did I feel I lost control of the situation such that my life was at risk, and that was my fault for believing someone understood my allergy as much as I did. I won't make that mistake again.

Life-threatening allergies are not always treated seriously because in some countries people are unaware of them. Tony Soave has found that, 'Allergies are not always believed to be real in some countries. In the many countries I have been in recently, I have been giggled at when describing the severity of my allergies'.

As well as avoiding the allergen, a ready supply of medication to be used in the event of exposure is important too. Allergy sufferers advise carrying enough medicine to cover at least a one-year supply when first travelling abroad. Though finding a local supply of the medicine must be a high priority after arrival in the host country, so supplies can be replenished as necessary.

Medical Needs

Diabetes

For people with illnesses such as diabetes there are not only the dietary requirements to consider, but also any ongoing medication. The local availability and quality of the medication and its cost are the two prime issues. Many expatriate health insurance policies do not cover ongoing treatment, or treatment of a pre-existing condition.

Contacting a local doctor before you relocate is one way to ascertain if the necessary medication and medical support is available in the destination country and will allow you to make an informed choice as to whether or not to relocate. Your embassy (or one representing your country's interests) in the host country should be able to provide you with the necessary information.

Yasemin Olcay is diabetic and the daughter of a Turkish diplomat posted to Sweden. Her mother, Petek, recounts what she does whenever they move somewhere new.

Of course, the first thing we have to do when we move is find a doctor and a good hospital. In all schools they have nurses and/or doctors. You have to notify the school of the child's condition and get an appointment with the nurse/doctor. They will give you the name of a good hospital. Needless to say, I always ask for the best hospital. After that I call them up and get an appointment from a doctor in the special unit. They will give you an appointment with any doctor and if you are not satisfied you can always switch to another one. It's important to get an appointment ASAP, because they usually can't give you an appointment for any time in the near future.

So it's better to be safe. There might be an emergency and it would be scary if you didn't know where to go or whom to contact. Also, it is important to locate the hospital closest to you as soon as you arrive.

Another thing that's important is as soon as we arrive I find the emergency phone numbers of that country, ambulance, fire, police etc. In addition, in most countries you cannot get medication without prescription. So finding a doctor should be on top of your list.

I have to go back a step and talk about airplanes. If you need special food you need to let the airlines know a couple of days in advance, but no less than 24 hours. For example, diet food is needed in Yasemin's case. It's always good to check with the airlines one more time before departure. In fact I always have her snack or food with me just in case there is a problem. We might not need it but it's better to have it with you. I always have a special carry-on bag with only Yasemin's medication. It's a good idea to keep all of it with you on the plane just in case luggage is lost. If you need to keep anything in the refrigerator during the flight the flight attendants are usually very helpful.

Letting the new school know of the condition is very important. I have a copy of information on Yasemin's diabetes that I wrote a long time ago on my computer. What I do is, after we have found an apartment, get a phone number, find a hospital and a doctor I change all the information accordingly. It's about four pages long and gives information on diabetes, Yasemin, her doctors' and hospitals' phone numbers and our phone numbers (work and home) and what to do or what not to do during an emergency. Yasemin will give a copy to each one of her teachers.

Asthma and Respiratory Ailments

Expatriate asthma and hay fever sufferers report that the pollens and pollution levels of different countries and cities produce different levels of reaction. Expats have variously reported developing allergies they never suffered from before relocating, and losing allergies they previously suffered from. So while moving abroad may be a problem for some, it may be a healthy move for others.

The availability of antihistamines for relief of hay fever symptoms and asthma medication also varies between countries and this can also effect how well you are able to cope with the way the new environment affects your health.

Certain cities suffer from high levels of pollution, which can cause, or exacerbate, asthma and other respiratory illnesses. Older people and children, especially, seem to suffer more from pollution than healthy adults; pollution indexes for some cities are listed in their local newspaper (especially if they have a pollution problem) and may also be on the city's website. Other sources of air pollution indexes are websites such as www.weather.com/health/airquality/, which lists pollution levels for US cities.

Information Resources

Information relevant to those with allergies and other long-term health issues can often be found through expats already at the destination, or by contacting medical professionals in the destination country, that expats have recommended. Cookery, lifestyle and travel guides will also provide information on the food and culinary tastes of the country too. In addition, if you can contact your embassy or consulate in advance of arrival, they may be able to not only locate the closest emergency hospital to where you are likely to live or work, but they can also help to locate the kind of allergist you require.

Before Mike Callan made the decision to accept his teaching job in Turkey, Michelyne Callan, his wife and one of the authors, researched the country extensively.

I immediately sought out Turkish cookery books to see if there was any mention of the use of peanuts in any of the traditional foods. I contacted people who were already living there to see if they noticed the prevalence of peanuts in the grocery stores, or if they could easily find things like nut flour and nut oils. They were also so helpful as to assure me about the closeness of a very good hospital with excellent emergency facilities. I searched the Internet for resources on Turkey to see if peanuts were regularly farmed there. After I gathered all that information, my husband and I felt so much more at ease with the idea of moving to Turkey.

Physical Needs

Before making a move abroad with a physical impairment, there are two important aspects to consider:

1. What facilities are there to make life easier for physically impaired people?
2. How do local people react to the physical impairment?

In some countries there are anti-discrimination laws, in others there are not. Some cities are very flat and have wide pavements, whilst others are not and make life difficult for people in wheelchairs. In some cities there are lifts, elevators and access ramps everywhere, but in others stairs are the only means of access to many places. Public telephones in some countries, though by no means all, are adapted for use by people with hearing aids. And some countries assist the blind to cross roads with audible warnings to supplement the green man at traffic lights, and textured crosswalks that can be followed by touch (of the foot). Moving abroad can actually be better for some disabled people.

For children, the availability of a school with provision for their specific physical disability is important. Some, though not all, International Schools have extensive special needs facilities. However, it will still be necessary for parents to check that a specific school is set-up for the particular needs of any child as will the availability of special facilities outside of school.

Karin Bisschoff is a South African who has been investigating the services that would be available to her son, Niel in the UK. Karin is specifically looking to move abroad to find the best care possible for their son, which is not available in South Africa. When Niel was 14 months old, he fell into an icy pool and was found face down, having drowned. He was resuscitated, but was brain damaged and now requires specialised treatment.

As we all know, many professionals are leaving South Africa and the doctors are leaving in packs. The school system is crumbling too. So, it's not a choice, it's necessary that we get out. We made the decision to go to Britain because I am familiar with St. Braivels and what they can offer Niel. I have contacted St. Braivels College extensively, and have made the decision it is the best place for Niel to recuperate at his optimal level. That is why we are leaving our home. We need more for Niel. We still have to find jobs and secure work visas, but that is just a technical issue. We need to move to obtain the best care we can find.

Apart from the physical facilities of a country for people with physical special needs, the reaction of local residents to a disabled person also needs to be considered. In some countries disabled people are hidden away and local people will commonly stare and even laugh at a disabled person in public. In many countries, though, this will not be a problem and local people will supportive of a disabled person.

Expats already at the destination will be the best source of information on the suitability of a country to provide the necessary services, the essential supplies as well as the local attitude towards various disabilities.

Educational Special Needs

The educational special needs of children can often cause great concern to their parents. The level of support a school can and is willing to offer special needs children varies greatly from school to school as much as it does from country to country. One expat parent, who works in the education field, reports:

I can only speak for Hong Kong and I think a big issue with countries whose first language is not English is the fact that often there is often no obligation by the Government to educate any child in English, let alone provide them a special education. Even in Hong Kong, with the English Schools Foundation, technically if there are no places available at the time of application then there is no obligation to do anything about it. There is certainly a huge shortage of places in the special needs system and for some children the English Schools Foundation admit they have no appropriate places at all.

Special needs, in the school context, can cover dyslexia and other reading/writing difficulties, general learning disabilities, ADD/ADHD (Attention Deficit Disorder/Attention Deficit Hyperactivity Disorder), or any of physical, psychological, or mental disabilities.

An educational special need is often perceived as an impairment and some schools may be unwilling to accept highly able and/or gifted students as special needs children, despite the well known (to the parents of gifted children and experts in the field) emotional impact on the children.

Close liaison with a school and parents of other special needs children attending the school, before admission of the child, is strongly recommended. One special needs teacher reported that though the school where he worked claimed to have a special needs programme, they really only paid lip-service to it so as to gain accreditation and attract more students.

Some schools do have extensive special needs programmes and even a separate department to work with special needs children. There are also a number of schools that specialise in providing education for special needs children, some of which offer boarding facilities (e.g. *Gstaad International School:* 3780 Gstaad, Switzerland; tel ++33 744-23-73; fax ++33 744-35-78; www.gstaadschool.ch).

Bridget Nisbet is the Co-ordinator the *Support Group for Parents of Autistic*

Children — English Speaking (SPACE), in Hong Kong. The group was established for parents to share experiences and information and to support each other, both new parents and those with older children alike. The vast majority of members are expatriate as they want to share the more up to date information that is available from abroad, and often feel more at a loss at the first stages of diagnosis (which often comes when the child is a toddler).

During her time in Hong Kong Bridget has gained much knowledge about the facilities available for autistic children.

Autism is a very difficult disability for the general public to cope with generally and even more so in less developed countries. I'm not sure it would be fair to have any higher expectations abroad. Because each child is so different, and the resources even more scarce in a non-English speaking country, the likelihood of getting into a programme that is right for your child is quite remote. I don't think Hong Kong is unique in expecting the children to be in the country before they can go on a waiting list for a facility so that also makes forward planning difficult. However, in a country like Hong Kong, which is a 'small pond', it is easier to become a 'big fish' and, with the help of others, get involved and set things up to suit your child's needs. Of course that doesn't always happen and, if your company won't pay the difference, this can get expensive. Following discussions with professionals in the UK that assess James they do not believe there would be a better facility in the UK than Springboard (see below) is for James in Hong Kong.

For more severe cases there is not a specialist school to meet their needs. A group of parents got together to try and address this, but no class has yet opened.

The other issue of course is medical coverage. None of the common therapies for autism are covered by usual policies, so all speech, occupational, behavioural therapy etc. is usually paid for out of the parents' pockets. For those on intensive ABA (Applied Behavioural Analysis) programmes this can cost around HK$25,000 per month (£2000). Ironically, because it is front-edge approach, most will cover for medical investigations and treatments for food allergies and intolerances, though there is no chance of having gluten-free products prescribed. It would definitely be worth seeing if proper cover could be negotiated as part of a package in advance. Also check to see that the extra costs of special education might be covered if the package includes general schooling costs.

I'm not sure that being in a different country per se is especially more difficult for an autistic child than just moving in the UK might be. One slight advantage is that the majority of the other children (including in ESF schools now) do not have English as a first language. Therefore, if you have a high functioning child whose language is a bit eccentric this may not be noticed by the other children and there is much less chance of bullying because of it. Also, the preferred style of teaching for the locals is for a quite rigid structure and less free expression — again something that would suit an autist. Not to mention the fact that if they are Caucasian they stand out from the crowd and therefore you are much less likely to lose them in a crowd if they are 'runners'. Even just watching them in a playground is easier.

The older the special needs person gets the more in the minority they become and so the fewer the facilities there are. There is a Hong Kong Vocational Centre to provide some training for young adults with disabilities, but they again were set up by parents and still have very limited resources which limits the number of students they can help.

Springboard is a charity set up to address gaps in the English Schools Foundation in Hong Kong. Springboard launched a special needs programme within the *Korean International School* (International Section, 55 Lei King Road,

Sai Wan Ho, Hong Kong; tel ++852 2569 5500; fax ++852 2560 5699 or 2886 2545; email kisengs@netvigator.com; http://home.netvigator.com/~kisengs) to provide the sort of education the parents wanted for their children (about half of whom are autistic). This is an English-speaking programme because it was parents of English speaking children for whom there was no provision.

On a more positive note Bridget reflects:

*Reading this, it all sounds very negative. Having said that, because we now know the system and the personalities within it, we are very comfortable. In fact, I would be more nervous about moving back to the UK and facing battles with LEAs (Local Education Authority) for statementing and always feeling I was fighting for every resource with other parents in the same situation. James is **very** happy here and this is home for him. This is the same for most of the families because they are happy here too. The big uncertainties are faced in the first days of diagnosis and then on the education options. There are lots of very friendly people here and lots of places for the children to visit and enjoy.*

*Being here does not mean you have to lose touch anyway. There are several discussion lists run through the e-mail from the UK and the US. There are now several professionals who have a lot of experience as the number of autistic children is rising here as it is everywhere. The other big advantage of living is Asia is having help in the home, which is a **great** respite. If you can find a helper who can understand the condition this can really help take the strain off having to cope with all of the problems yourself and give you the chance for time out when you need it. I imagine this is especially attractive for those whose children do not sleep much — at least it would enable them to catch up during the day if necessary.*

Our son is eight and, given that we aren't going to retire here, we certainly have to think about being back in the UK by the time he is 15-16, to ensure that he is sufficiently comfortable with the way of life there to fit into a community and be as independent as possible. If there is no obligation by the Hong Kong government to educate a special needs child there is even less obligation to employ one. No form of learning disability is readily accepted here so autism is not singled out here.

Exhaustive research through prospective schools and expat parents of special needs children is strongly recommended to ascertain the suitability of a country and school for a special needs child, before making a move.

Jeremy Daynes has been Head of Learning Support at the *British School of Paris* (38 Quai de l'Ecluse, 78290 Croissy-sur-Seine, France; tel ++33 1 34 80 45 90; fax ++33 1 39 76 12 69; e-mail bsp@calva.net; http://atschool.eduweb.co.uk/paris/) since 1994 and previously worked in two UK special needs schools for eight years. The British School of Paris has extensive provision for special needs education and is currently developing a specific programme for the academically gifted. The information and questions opposite have been provided by Jeremy Daynes, to help parents select a suitable school for their special needs children, and is based on his qualifications and classroom experience in special needs education:

1. Unless a school has specific provision for special needs children (either a department or a teacher qualified in the area of special needs education) it cannot adequately provide the support they require. And even if a school does have special needs teachers it is important that mainstream staff have the expertise to help deliver a curriculum relevant to the children.
2. A dyslexic child in mainstream education for most of his/her curriculum requires, ideally, one-to-one assistance for the periods that they attend the special needs department.
3. The 'less able' child can usually be supported in a small group situation of three

General

Can the school meet the specific special needs of my child?	
How?	
Does the school have specific resources for pupils with special needs?	
Can parents meet the special needs teachers and visit the department?	
Will my child be thoroughly integrated into the mainstream school?	

Regarding Dyslexia

What special arrangements do you make for the dyslexic child?	
Do you have anyone on the staff who has had experience of/is qualified to work with dyslexic pupils?	
What specialist resources does the school have for the dyslexic child?	
Will my child be doing a normal timetable? If not, how will it be modified?	
Does the school organise the examining board certification to enable my child to have extra time in the exams?	
Is my child allowed to use a computer to do most of his written work?	
Will my child be allowed to use a computer to write his exams?	
Will my child be allowed to do exams orally?	

Regarding Attention Deficit Disorder
and Attention Deficit Hyperactivity Disorder (ADD/ADHD)

See questions above for dyslexia and substitute ADD/ADHD as appropriate.	
How familiar is the teaching staff with pupils with ADD/ADHD?	
How much allowance is made for the challenging behaviour that is often associated with ADHD?	

Regarding Allergies or Other Health Issues

Does the school have a full-time nurse?	
How are staff members kept informed about a pupil's medical conditions?	
Does the school look after medication for pupils while they are at school?	
What sort of system does the school have in place if there is a medical emergency?	

Regarding Physical Disabilities

Is the school able to accommodate pupils in wheelchairs?	
Are there ramps, lifts etc. to enable wheelchair access to all parts of the school?	
What provision does the school make for pupils with specific physical disabilities?	
Is the school prepared to modify its existing arrangements to accommodate a pupil with a physical disability? If so, how?	

> to five pupils, though the staff/pupil ratio should be adjusted according to the severity of the pupils needs. However, this also depends on the subject being studied, the disparity or homogeneity of the group and the amount of help available.
> 4. Academic qualifications of special needs staff should include at least some sort of specific training in the field of special needs. Personal qualifications would include those for a good teacher, plus a lot of patience and a sense of humour.
> 5. Special needs support teachers generally cover: dyslexia, the academically disadvantaged and gifted, ADD/ADHD, emotional and physical problems.
> 6. The needs of gifted children and those with medical related problems and syndromes are often not covered in general special needs programmes.
> 7. Gifted programmes often come under the umbrella of special needs, but are probably better handled by a whole school policy driven by a teacher with special responsibility.

Parents should also bear in mind that although a school may have the facilities to accept and educate special needs children, there may not be extensive testing, psychological services, and specialist medical personnel available in the local community to diagnose specific special needs and provide any necessary medication.

Resources

General

American Diabetes Association: Attn: Customer Service, 1701 North Beauregard Street, Alexandria, VA 22311, USA (tel ++1-800-DIABETES (1-800-342-2383); www.diabetes.org).

Diabetes UK: Central Office, 10 Queen Anne Street, London W1G 9LH, England (tel ++44 (0)20-7323 1531; fax ++44 (0)20-7637 3644; info@diabetes.org.uk; www.diabetes.org.uk). Diabetes UK (formerly the British Diabetic Association) produces a booklet aimed at the diabetic traveller. Copies can be obtained from the BDA Careline, tel: 020-7636 6112 (for a small fee).

Disabililty Information Resources: www.dinf.org. A New Jersey non-profit corporation that collects information on disabilities and disabilities related subjects and makes it available through the World Wide Web. Offers a section on international organisations who aid disabled individuals in travelling worldwide.

Disabled People's Association of Singapore (DPA): 150A Pandan Gardens, #02-00 Day Care Centre, Singapore 609342 (tel ++65 899 1220; fax ++65 899 1232; dpaadmin@dpa.org.sg; www.dpa.org.sg). Welcomes expatriates into their association on a regular membership.

Disabled People's Association — International: (run under the auspices of DPA Singapore listed above) maintain a link for international resources with disabled-friendly travel services, hotels and similar organisations on the website: www.dpa.org.sg/DPA/travel/travel.htm.

Emerging Horizons: http://emerginghorizons.com. A newsletter for travellers with mobility disabilties.

The European Federation of Asthma and Allergy Associations (EFA): An alliance of 27 organisations in 14 different countries across Europe and a list of members can be found on their website: www.efanet.org.

Food Allergy Network (FAN): 10400 Eaton Place, Suite 107, Fairfax, Virginia 22030-2208, USA (www.foodallergy.org). Currently the largest organisation catering to the needs of food allergy sufferers. They provide a monthly newsletter for a small subscription. The website provides food product alerts, coping strategies, etc.

Food Anaphylactic Children Training and Support Association (FACTS): 16 Lumeah Avenue, Elanora Heights, NSW 2101, Australia (tel/fax ++61 (0)2 9913 7793; coordinator@allergyfacts.org.au; www.allergyfacts.org.au). Exists to allow its members to share their skills, time and energy on a voluntary basis to help families with food anaphylactic children.

Royal National Institute for the Blind: www.rnib.org.uk. Provides a free access database of over 2000 international agencies for blind and partially sighted people throughout the world (http://info.rnib.org.uk/Agencies/allagencies.htm). RNIB information, support and advice for anyone with a serious sight problem, Monday to Friday 9am to 5pm, tel 0845-766 99 99 (UK Helpline callers only), tel ++44 (0)20-7388 1266 (switchboard/overseas callers); fax. ++44 (0)20-7388 2034; textphone users call via Typetalk 0800-51 51 52; helpline@rnib.org.uk.

Education-related Resources

ADD/ADHD Europe: www.pavilion.co.uk/add/. A developing site that provides links to country specific ADD/ADHD sites in Europe.

ADDNet UK: www.btinternet.com/~black.ice/addnet/. Provides links and infoormation regarding support groups and specialists in the UK.

Autism Society of America: 7910 Woodmont Avenue, Suite 300, Bethesda, MD 20814-3015, USA (tel (800)-3AUTISM, extension 150, or ++1 (301) 657-0881; fax ++1 (301) 657-0869; www.autism-society.org).

The International Dyslexia Association: International Office, 8600 LaSalle Road, Chester Building, Suite 382, Baltimore, MD 21286-2044, USA (messages +800 ABCD123, tel ++1 410 296-0232; fax ++1 410 321-5069). Maintains a website of information at www.interdys.org. It is an international, non-profit organisation dedicated to the study and treatment of dyslexia. The organisation has 45 branches (43 in the US, 1 in Canada, 1 in Israel) as well as 36 international members. For a small fee, membership will provide access to an international network of teachers, tutors, physicians, psychologists etc as well as affiliation with a branch that will be able to assist you with the local school systems, tutors, private schools, and other resources you may require.

National Association of Gifted Children — UK: Elder House, Milton Keynes, MK9 1LR, UK (amazingchildren@nagcbritain.org.uk; www.rmplc.co.uk/orgs/nagc/index.html).

National Association of Gifted Children —US: 1707 L Streeet NW, Suite 550, Washington DC 20036, USA (tel ++1 202-785-4268; request@nagc.org; www.nagc.org).

National Attention Deficit Disorder Association: 1788 Second Street, Suite 200, Highland Park, IL 60035, USA (fax ++1 (847) 432-5874; mail@add.org; www.add.org).

National Autistic Society — UK: 393 City Road, London, EC1V 1NG, UK (tel +44 (0)20-7833 2299; fax ++44 (0)20-7833 9666; nas@nas.org.uk; www.oneworld.org/autism_uk/). The site includes information on Asperbers Syndrome.

Special Needs Education Project: sne@canada.com; www.schoolnet.ca/sne/e/intallsites.html. A Canadian organisation that is run under the auspices of SchoolNet. It is a co-operative initiative of Canada's provincial, territorial, and federal governments in consultation with educators, universities, colleges and industry which has a list of resources located internationally to help people find a variety of special needs organisations and schools outside of Canada. Links cover blindness, deafness, developmental disabilities, disability Studies & Research, general resources (disabilities), general resources (special education), inclusion and integration, learning disabilities, attention deficit & related Issues, organisations (disabilities), organisations (special education), schools.

Support Group for Parents of Autistic Children (English Speaking) 'SPACE'in Hong Kong and *Springboard Education for Special Needs Children in Hong Kong:* Bridget Nisbet (tel ++852 2872-8741, or ++852 2791-7099), or the *Matilda Hospital Child Development Centre* (tel ++852 2849-6138).

LONG-TERM CONSIDERATIONS

The experience of living in a foreign culture for an extended period of time can have profound long-term effects on families and individuals, especially children. If you live abroad for a short period of time, the effects will probably be less pervasive, but nevertheless, as with any move, the effects can still be considerable.

In the short-term, exposure to alternate life-styles, different cultures and religions as well as different family values can affect family dynamics. Expatriates who have lived abroad for an extended period will, however, absorb many more of the influences that affect their personal and professional outlook.

Barbara Schaetti, of Transition Dynamics, defines people who spend a significant part of their life abroad as **Global Nomads** and has adapted the definitions of David Pollock (Director, *Interaction Inc.*) and Norma McCaig (Founder, *Global Nomads International*) of **Third Culture Kids** and Global Nomads (see the section on children below) to include everyone who has spent a significant part of their life abroad.

Global Nomads are individuals of any age or nationality who have spent a significant part of their developmental years living in one or more countries outside their passport country(ies) because of a parent's occupation.

Global nomads are members of a world-wide community of personas who share a unique cultural heritage. Developing some sense of belonging to both their host culture(s) and passport culture(s), they may not have a sense of ownership in all. Elements from each culture and from the experience of international-mobility are blended, creating a commonality with others of similar experience.

Global nomads of all ages and nationalities typically share similar responses to the benefits and challenges of a childhood abroad. (The Global Nomad Profile: Women on the Move Conference, March 1998 Paris).

The most obvious short-term effects of living abroad are the reactions caused by culture shock. As you work through culture shock and learn how to function professionally and socially in the new environment, you will absorb knowledge about many aspects of the new culture. This knowledge includes the social behaviour of adults and children and how they interact, the local religions, local philosophies, the local professional ethics and work ethos as well as the political and historical background of the country and its people.

Adults who grew up predominantly in their home country will have a profound sense of that culture that will limit the amount, and the way, that their new knowledge will affect their outlook on life. With a move to a foreign country, these *Modern Nomads'* perspectives will usually be broadened by their experience, not formed by them.

In contrast, a child who spends a significant amount of time in a 'foreign' country and who does not have the same solid basis of cultural preconceptions as an adult will be affected in a more formative way. If a child spends a significant amount of time in a number of 'foreign' countries the effects are enhanced and they can gain a variety of cultural perspectives.

Long-term Effects on Adults

All the issues discussed in the previous chapters of this book will have an effect on the people who go through them. From the time you decide to move abroad and begin the process of planning the move, executing the plan and arriving in a new country where you need to establish yourself (and your family) in a new social and professional environment you will be on a learning curve.

Modern Nomads who make the transition to living abroad find themselves with a whole new set of issues, problems and situations that they have never been presented with before. Think of this as an opportunity for active learning, where you are being educated in a way that classroom teaching can never rival.

It does not matter how long you stay abroad, or even if you never return home. You will learn things about yourself and others around you, that you were never aware of.

Everything you learn affects you and how you behave, whether you learn it in your home country, or in a foreign country. As an adult living in your home country you may not notice many changes in yourself, except after a rare, major event. This is most probably because you have been exposed, in some way, to the majority of experiences your country has to offer and your personality has been well shaped by those experiences already.

When you spend an extended period of time in a foreign country, much of what you will experience could be classed as a major event, because it is likely to be far removed from your traditional, home-country life.

How Others Perceive You

To live successfully in any country you have to be willing to understand the ways of that country, at least to a certain extent. You do not actually have to adopt these ways, but you should be willing to learn about them and attempt to understand why they are important within that social context. Sometimes however, it is better to try and adopt a few of the 'foreign' cultural attitudes to minimise the chances that you will land yourself in a difficult situation.

In Saudi Arabia, for example, dressing according to local tradition can go a long way towards making your stay in the country more comfortable. One North American, expatriate woman, having lived and worked in Africa and Asia moved to the Middle East. She learned quickly that to go against the local ways in the respect of clothing not only complicated things for her, but would also be problematic for her husband.

There are laws in certain areas of the Middle East where the women cannot show any skin. Even having your face and hair exposed is sometimes a problem. It's not as bad a problem for me as it is for my husband though. He can get into trouble from the mutawa (religious police) that constantly monitor people on the street. On a few occasions when I have not used a headscarf, my husband has been pulled aside by the mutawa and told that he is disgraceful for allowing me to present myself in such a way. If I were to step out of the compound without my abaya (traditional cloak worn by Arab women) on at all, my husband could be fined, brought to court, or thrown in jail. As a guest in their country, and because I choose to be a Modern Nomad, I do not feel I have the right to go against traditional rules established for the people of that particular land.

The obvious outward manifestations of a country's culture are, however, not the only aspects you may want to adopt. The way you walk around the streets of Bogota, Colombia, is going to be different from how you walk through a rural Scottish village, as is the way you would react when a local you have never met before stops to talk to you. Learning the implicit, as well as the explicit, rules of a country is important in helping to adjust smoothly and without unnecessary incident.

In Japan, blowing your nose in public is a sure way to offend local people, though it is not quite as serious an offence as a woman going about uncovered in Saudi. Whether you are in a predominantly locally staffed office, or walking in public, blowing your nose in Japan can get you unwanted, negative attention (sneering, jeering and staring).

You can become very used to the hustle and bustle of Hong Kong and not think twice about pushing someone out of the way who has stepped in front of you as you try to get on the MTR (underground railway) during rush hour. Yet similar behaviour in the US would probably not be wise, as one US expatriate struggling through rush hour in Hong Kong often used to comment, 'I would have been shot if I'd done that in LA'.

However, living with certain behaviour patterns for years can leave them so ingrained that they are hard to drop when you are away from the place where they are accepted as normal. Depending on how frequently you change countries the ease of adjustment will vary and you will have to take stock of the habits you have acquired from living in each country, and then be sensitive to the behavioural expectations of your new country of residence.

Apart from the way you behave physically, it is also important to consider the way you talk to people. In some countries a class-system is very much ingrained and there are specific ways of talking to people to get them to do the job you want them to while retaining your professional position. For example, one American administrator in Turkey found that in order to have anything accomplished, he needed to scream.

I have tried the nice approach. I have tried the courteous approach. I have tried the buddy approach. I have tried the please and thank you approach. I have even tried the 'repeat twelve times approach', and still the work doesn't get done. The day I learned how to ask is the day I screamed at my staff to get the job done. They simply don't respond to a kind request here, they need a threat to get them to do their daily tasks. It is not nice for me, and it's a bad habit I am growing now since I need to do it every day. I hope it is a habit I will be able to shrug when I move from here.

Though this kind of communication will not be considered rude in that country, you only need to talk like that once when you are somewhere else in the world to end up a pariah, or in hot water at the office.

Learning the subtleties of something as simple as how to accept a gift can be difficult too, and getting it wrong can either be construed as a simple faux pas, or a gross breach of social protocol, depending on the country you are in.

In some countries (notably the Middle East) it can be considered rude to accept something the first time it is offered, because if the person is making a serious offer they will repeat it a few times. By your first refusal and the offer not being renewed, nobody will lose 'face' by appearing to be greedy or stingy. If on the other hand the offer is repeated and then accepted, both parties have shown the correct sincerity in the arrangement.

Either way, everyone is comfortable in that country that the correct ritual of offer and acceptance has been performed. However, if you are in a country that does not operate with this particular ritual and you refuse the offer from the outset, you may lose the opportunity to have the item presented to you again because a present will only be offered once (take it or leave it). Depending on the nature of the gift, your lesson could be costly, or a simple annoyance.

How You Perceive Others

The above effects of living abroad usually fade and can be mitigated through careful review of your actions once you move to another country or return home.

There are, however, other long-term effects that may not be so easily divested, even if you wanted to.

Living abroad is, by its very nature, an international experience that provides an opportunity to meet people of diverse backgrounds and observe cultures from within. Not only will you have the opportunity to meet nationals of the country you are moving to, but you will also have a greater opportunity to meet other expatriates from various countries, who are enjoying the same kind of experience as you.

As a *Modern Nomad*, you may perceive yourself to be markedly different from the vast majority of people around you (except in expatriate compounds or countries where there are few economic and cultural differences between you and the local population). Getting used to being different takes time and expats can find it an ongoing cause of stress to be stared at and talked down to purely because they are different. Donna Young remembers being stared at in Hong Kong, and still notices it in the UAE, though she has lived there for six years.

Every time I walked out of the house in Hong Kong I felt that we not only looked different, but that everyone noticed we were different. We lived in a very local area, with only a handful of foreigners around. In the Emirates, though there are expatriates in abundance, they are usually Pakistani or Sri Lankan male workers. Not very many foreign women walk along the back streets of the souks where I like to shop. I don't think, I know, that I get looked at. I am used to it, but I still feel it, and I don't get angry any more. It's just not worth it. I just get on with my day.

Apart from feeling uncomfortable from always being watched, expats often react by becoming more strident in their own sense of national pride (for their home country). After three years abroad, and having a few friends visit, Jeri Hurd found herself scolding one of her friends who was making derogatory comments about their home country, because it now offended her.

Beatrice Nesme, a French national who was posted for three years to Turkey and is now on a short-term posting in Bucharest, Romania with her husband and two daughters expands on this idea:

.. living in a foreign country is opening our eyes significantly. You know, for me, France is the most beautiful country in the world. Landscapes, mountains, countryside, coast, sea, food, monuments etc., but I am certain that the majority of French people don't know that. But if I think this about France, it is because I travelled and I saw other realities. Especially living here in Romania. It is in Europe, but it is another world. It is dirty, run down, people are so poor. It makes me realise what a wonderful country I come from, but also makes me want to share this learning experience and my pride in France with my children.

However, being different does have the immediate benefit of being able to get away with idiosyncrasies purely on that basis. Most expatriates have the feeling that local nationals often think, 'They are a weird foreigner, so they're bound to do strange things'.

This lack of constraint on the social and professional behaviour of an expatriate can be liberating and hugely enjoyable. It allows expats to explore hobbies, lifestyles and work-related projects without running into comments like, 'We don't do that here, so you can't do it either'.

This freedom can be positive or negative, either allowing people to find their true vocation in life, or behave in totally inappropriate ways. Either way it can have a major affect on the way their life develops as an adult.

The international aspect of the expatriate lifestyle can also expand the expatriate's awareness of issues affecting people in places they have never previously considered. A European and an Indian in Hong Kong can become great friends and in discussing their enormously different cultures they can become very fond of both their host country and the joys and problems of their friend's country. If the Indian and European expatriate then return to their home countries, their friends and relatives can seem very parochial by comparison because of their lack of knowledge and interest of much that is happening outside their home country.

Many expatriates report that it is difficult to translate their experiences and newly found knowledge to their old friends and family who have remained at home. One woman who left her home country and previous lifestyle to try the *Modern Nomad* lifestyle almost ten years ago reports:

> *I want to share my adventures with people, family and friends when I go home to visit. But when I get there and they ask me, 'So, how is Asia?' all they want to hear is that it's fine, and I'm fine. They aren't really interested in pictures, or in the important world event I was just witness to. Many of them aren't even sure where I have been living for the past several years. And they're related to me! They are more interested in filling me in on what has been happening around them, in relation to the people that I know there. It seems like we aren't meeting in the middle when I visit, and it frustrates me that they have such a small world view.*

This widening of perspective is probably one of the most profound effects that living abroad has on an expatriate. At the 1998 *Women on the Move* conference in Paris a panel of participants was asked what the most obvious benefits were for adults that made an international transition, the majority indicated that it was their acquisition of world knowledge from an experiential point of view.

While expats can view this effect as positive whilst they are living abroad it can make them restless and feel culturally claustrophobic when they return home (even for vacations) — see *Returning to the Country You Used to Call Home*. This acquisition of world perspective convinces some expatriates to stay abroad on a long-term basis, so that they can continue to enjoy the wider social and cultural spectra that they feel is not available in their home country.

While some expats repatriate to their home country after living abroad and resettle successfully, many *Modern Nomads* find themselves searching for ways to make another international move soon after returning home.

Beatrice Nesme intends to stay abroad as long as possible. Though she is partial to her native France where she lived until she was 27, she has developed a keen interest in global matters:

> *I would like, very much, my daughters to grow up knowing that there are other things in life that they can learn and the world does not revolve around France. In living abroad, I have learned much more about other parts of the world that seem so important to me now. More important than they would have been had I not moved from France.*

For a *Modern Nomad* who has left extended family, friends, and perhaps even a profession behind, it can be traumatic having reinvented their social and intellectual interests, to try and remain close to those at home. Doing so draws on some of the primary skills of a successful *Modern Nomad*, flexibility, adaptability and tolerance.

Effects On Professional Life

Whether you are single or part of a family, the effect on your professional life can also be marked. Having worked with people from different cultures you will probably have encountered alternative attitudes towards work ethics, job responsibility and work processes. Sometimes you might come across aspects that

ʹou will want integrate into your work environment when you have returned home ɔr moved elsewhere, because you believe they are beneficial. Though you have ᴇarnt knew techniques and skills that benefit you in your career, trying to ᴨtroduce these ideas to colleagues in another culture may raise resistance, or even ʜostility, from colleagues and subordinates.

Tony Turton of *Arnett Associates* (www.btinternet.com/~arnettassoc), an ᴨternational Human Resources consultancy, has found that work attitudes vary ιcross cultures and trying to import ideas from one culture to another is not easy.

For Western Europeans or North Americans, coming to terms with the way business is done in many other parts of the world can challenge their ideas of ethical practices, and force them to re-assess where to draw the line between what is and is not acceptable.

But even attitudes to less challenging processes, like training, can be difficult to import to a new culture. Broadly speaking, people from Western business cultures are used to being involved, working in task forces, focus groups, and the like. They are happy to participate, to share their thoughts and ideas. There are other cultures where people are more reticent and defer more to authority. They expect their managers to tell them the answers to problems, not ask them to find the solution. A manager who tries to set up a Western-style participative training programme in such a culture is heading for disappointment and frustration.

Even though you may have difficulty introducing what you have learnt to other ᴨeople, the professional knowledge you acquire can be of great benefit to you in ᴛhe future, whether you continue to work abroad or return home.

As European businessmen who have spent a few years in Hong Kong ᴨegotiating with the notoriously driven and competitive businessmen there have ɔund, returning to negotiations with European executives can seem dramatically ᴇasier.

For expat spouses, facing the changes that they meet and actively adapting to ᴛhe situation can lead to greatly expanded options in their careers. One expat ᴄpouse reports,

I am more flexible than any of my adult friends back home simply because I have had to reinvent my professional self five times in the last ten years. I have been an EFL teacher, a university employee, a stay-at-home-mom, a researcher and am now a high school teacher. I know that I could move anywhere and find a profession for myself because I am flexible and I can think creatively to satisfy my professional needs.

Long-term Effects on Children

Defining the Terms

Children who spend the majority of their childhood abroad are often referred to as *Third Culture Kids* (TCKs). The origin of this term can be traced back to Dr John Jseem and Dr Ruth Hill Useem who, in the 1950s, began investigating ᴨternationally mobile missionary families and the effects that such a lifestyle had ɔn their children.

In summarising that which we had observed in our cross-cultural encounters we began to use the term 'third culture' as a generic term to cover the styles of life created, shared, and learned by persons who are in the process of relating their societies, or sections thereof, to each other. The term 'Third Culture Kids' or TCKs was coined to refer to the children who accompany their parents into another society. (Newslinks, Third Culture kids: Focus of Major Study — TCK 'Mother Pens History of Field'; www.iss.edu/pages/kids.html).

The doctors Useem initiated a study involving approximately 680 TCK participants between the ages of 25 and 84 who had spent at least one year outside of the US, because of their parents' career, and who were now residing in the US. These TCKs were adults at the time of the study and became known as ATCKs (Adult Third Culture Kids). This term generally refers to people who have now settled in the 'home' country.

Enlisting the sociological expertise of Dr Ann Baker Cottrell, and counselling/guidance expertise of Dr Kathleen A. Finn Jordan, a series of five articles were completed identifying the key features of children who are now referred to as TCKs. The five articles are reprinted in *Newslinks*, at the web address mentioned above.

Norma McCaig is credited with coining the term *Global Nomad*. In 1986 she founded a non-profit organisation called *Global Nomads International* (www.globalnomads.association.com) to provide an opportunity for global nomads to discuss and share their experiences as expatriate children. It offers a forum for these children to learn that they are not alone in their experiences abroad, and that they are part of an ever-expanding community of similar individuals.

Many experts do not differentiate between the term TCK and Global Nomad. David Pollock, Director of *Global Associates* (www.global-assoc.com) and *Interaction International* (www.tckinteract.net), has many years of experience in training and consulting internationally mobile employees and their families. He clarifies TCK as:

> *Third-Culture Kid (TCK, also known as Trans-Culture Kid) is an individual who, having spent a significant part of the developmental years in a culture other than the parents' culture, develops a sense of relationship to all of the cultures while not having full ownership in any. Elements from each culture are incorporated into the life experience, but the sense of belonging is in relationship to others of similar experience.*

Barbara Schaetti believes that regardless of how long or when a child lives abroad, the experience is enough to denote a change in their lives that will make a mark on who they become as adults.

> *Somebody who grows up internationally, may as an adult settle in one country, perhaps the country of nationality or not ... (and) may never move again. If that person was internationally mobile as a child, he or she is still a Global Nomad. Once a Global Nomad, always a Global Nomad. (The Global Nomad Profile:* Women on the Move Conference, Paris, March 1998.)

While all TCKs or Global Nomads are not carbon copies of each other, they do tend to exhibit similar characteristics when they are ATCKs. However, the degree to which they might be affected will depend on various factors such as:

1. Why the family moved abroad in the first place (i.e. the parent is employed by a large supporting corporation or the parent is self-sponsored and has no immediate support from any corporation).
2. The actual length of time spent in any one country.
3. The similarity of the host country to the passport country.
4. The age at which they entered or left the country.
5. The attitudes of the parents towards the move.
6. The lifestyle the family had in the host country.
7. The frequency of moves.
8. The innate personality of the child.

Though the TCKs surveyed by the Useems were American children raised abroad, many generalisations of TCKs or Global Nomads can be applied whatever their nationality.

The life experiences and upbringing of every child, whether they live in their home country or abroad, will affect how they grow and mature into adulthood. TCKs are not unique in the fact that they are shaped by the country and culture they grow up in. Their uniqueness manifests itself when TCKs make a transition to their 'home' (passport) country and they find that their upbringing has had a significant impact on how they matured, relative to their home-based peers. When TCKs are living abroad, they will be similar to the other children around them, because they are all TCKs.

Observed Benefits of a TCK Mobile Life

TCKs report that they feel different from their non-mobile counterparts. They feel different because they are. Having lived in a foreign country, where their peers have never been, the culture of that country has impinged on their life and their attitudes. Generally, Global Nomads and ATCKs exhibit combinations of the following positive benefits:

1. They are more mature and self-disciplined.
2. They are more able academically.
3. They are more at ease dealing with people of any age.
4. They have very strong nuclear family (parents and children) ties.
5. They are more able to adapt to a new culture, and are more culturally sensitive when in a new group or social setting.
6. They look at events from a global perspective and are able to interpret events more broad-mindedly.
7. They have more facility and ability to learn foreign languages.
8. They are often exasperated by the narrow attitudes of non-internationally aware people.
9. They feel at home in many different places, while feeling completely at home in none.
10. They are more likely to get a post secondary education than their home country counterparts.

Educational Achievement

Regarding education and academic ability, the second article of the ATCK survey pointed out that, 'One characteristic of these adult TCKs which stands out is that the overwhelming majority of them are committed to continuing their education beyond high school graduation'. For many expatriate parents it is a great selling point of their lifestyle that their children are likely to benefit educationally. The study reports:

Only 21 percent of the American population have graduated from a four-year college. In sharp contrast, 81 percent of the adult TCKs have earned at least a bachelor's degree. Half of this number have gone on to earn master's degrees and doctorates.

Many ATCKs have indicated that they believe that their unique life abroad was probably a decisive factor in the success of university entrance. One ATCK who was educated in five different countries said, 'Being educated internationally definitely helped my (university) admission. American universities often want an incoming student with a special quality. I felt my life was my special quality and I guess my college did also'.

Further, because the ATCKs have a more dedicated view towards education, and a more refined ability to be creative with their skills, their career achievements often reflect their high levels of education. In the fifth article in the ATCK survey, Dr Cottrell says of the respondents that:

The majority (over 80 percent) are professionals, semi-professionals, executives, or managers/officials. Only six percent, half students, half homemakers, report no job beyond part time/summer work in college. Fully one quarter work in educational institutions as teachers, professors or administrators. The next largest number (17 percent) are in professional settings, such as medical or legal fields. An equal proportion are self-employed, one-third of these as presidents of their own companies. The self-employed , in particular, reflect the creative and risk-taking streak found in so many TCKs.

Adaptability and Creativity

Whether or not an ATCK is more 'refined' than peers from their passport country is a subjective observation. But the ATCK survey showed that, 'Two thirds (of the sample) feel they have more transitional knowledge and skills than they have opportunity to use in their domestic lives'.

For many ATCKs this could very well translate into an air of confidence when contrasted to their national peers. They may feel that their international education and lifestyle has put them ahead of their peers. Andrea DiSebastian, who moved from the US to England, Spain, Honduras and Israel as a child before returning the US to enter university, firmly believes this.

I think being a TCK has made me a more mature individual. It has allowed me to have a better understanding of all people and has helped me to deal with people in an open-minded way. I had the opportunity to see a large chunk of the world, whereas many people don't leave the country they were brought up in. I do feel very lucky and blessed to have had the life that I did.

The Useems ATCK survey also describes, in the second article, that along with feeling a certain sense of ability, most ATCKs have a unique talent to be creative in finding a niche for themselves when they settle. They do not simply adjust to the new culture.

They adapt, they find niches, they take risks, they fail and pick themselves up again. They succeed in jobs they have created to fit their particular talents. They locate friends with whom they can share some of their interests, but they resist being encapsulated. Their camouflaged exteriors and understated ways of presenting themselves hide the rich inner lives, remarkable talents, and often strongly held contradictory opinions on the world at large and the world at hand.

Another ATCK is sure that her internationally mobile life contributed to her ability to obtain a good job.

I think it has helped my ability to join the workforce. The school that I am working at is very international (even though it is in the US). I believe that my background was one of the reasons I was hired. In general, I believe most countries in the world are looking for people to hire that have knowledge about the whole world, not just their own country. I think we are all working towards an acceptance of each other and focussing on multiculturalism.

Internationalism and Understanding

Many parents of children raised abroad have reported that their children develop a sense of internationalism and an understanding of the use of being bilingual. They are also perceived as having a sense of fairness and justice that might not otherwise have been introduced into their lives had they remained resident in one country.

Brennen Young, who moved a number of times as a child, feels that he has gained a sense of global knowledge that his friends who have always remained at home do not have, though he does find it exasperating at times.

It really annoys me sometimes when I see that a lot of people at home are really ignorant about anything that goes on anywhere else in the world. It really annoys me sometimes when I think about how domestically centred most people here are. I am very thankful that I've been able to see a little more of the world than the average Joe. For example, you can learn a lot from other cultures just in how they do things, and how some ways might be better than the way you know. I also think that having a nomadic lifestyle has made me more tolerant, and I have more things to base my opinions of life in general on. I'm not closed minded and stuck in one culture, one view.

Many other Global Nomads, when they visit their passport countries or when they reintegrate into their passport society, often find that the local outlook on life is very parochial. One Global Nomad reports:

I think that a lot of the people in my home country are really ignorant about anything that goes on anywhere else in the world. The first summer I left Hong Kong and went home for a visit, I was always being asked if I could speak Japanese. The newspapers here are atrocious; pages and pages of editorials about Clinton's sex scandals, but only an article smaller than a mouse about the earthquake that happened in Afghanistan a few months ago, where 4000 people were killed.

Dr Ann Baker Cottrell's fourth article in the TCK series also points out that ATCKs are frequently more proud of their passport country than are their counterparts at home. ATCKs international experiences make them appreciate much in the US that Americans take for granted, and most feel the US, at the time of the survey, is the best place for them to be living.

So, like the *Modern Nomads* that make an international move later in life, the children of those expatriates also tend to develop a sense of pride in the nation of their heritage. While there might be tendencies to feel lonely at times, or out of synch in the US when they settle, they are outweighed by the feeling that it is the right place to be, for them, and that they have made a good decision in the long run.

Marriage and Family

When it comes to family and community considerations, the majority of TCKs, though having feelings of unease when it comes to commitment, still get married and settle into a community. The divorce rate of ATCKs is lower than the national (American) average and two out of three who get married only get married once.

Many of the ATCKs married other ATCKs. While this in itself is not an inherent benefit, it highlights the need of ATCKs to have people of similar background around them, someone who is able to appreciate the complicated feelings and experiences that formed a third culture adult.

Observed Challenges of a TCK Mobile Life

When a family lives in its home country, the parents will usually have a general idea of how their lifestyle will affect their children. However, many first time expats know little about how their international lifestyle will affect their children. Expat children are often exposed to experiences that their home based peers will never meet, in addition to what they would encounter if they lived at home, which often means that when they grow into adulthood they feel different from their non-travelled peers.

Being Different

To counter this feeling of difference many ATCKs find that they seek out other ATCKS. When she returned to the US after spending much of her childhood abroad, Andrea DiSebastian found that most of the friends she made were TCKs themselves.

In the third article of the TCK survey Dr Cottrell states,

...three-fourths of the respondent ATCKs feel different from others who have not lived abroad as children, and especially from those who have had no international experience. Only one out of every ten of our nearly 700 adult TCKs, who range in age from 25 to 80, say that they feel completely attuned to everyday life in the US. The other 90 percent say they are more or less 'out of synch' with their age group throughout their lifetimes.

Brennen Young, who lived in Canada, Belgium, Hong Kong and the UAE before returning to Canada, his *home* country, says, 'Up until last year I still felt weird about not having had the *normal* life'.

This feeling of difference can be difficult for ATCKs to deal with and they can find it hard to interact with other people once they return home. After her return home Andrea said, 'I have mixed feelings about being back. I love the US, but sometimes feel misunderstood by friends here and long to find someone else who truly understands my life'.

Much of the feeling of being different often stems from the frequently asked question, 'Where are you from?'. Many TCKs who have lived in more than two countries not only shy away from this question but go so far as to feel reticent to even attempt an answer. While many people would like to coin the label 'world citizen', some TCKs feel that it is a cheesy cliché and that 'a citizen of nowhere in particular' is more accurate.

Brennen Young has struggled with this issue not only as a new kid in a new school, but as a young adult when he repatriated to his passport country. The year he left the Middle East and went to an international boarding school in his native Canada, he felt like he wanted to fit in so many different ways, but was unable to do so in a complete fashion:

Every now and then I'll break down into an identity crisis because I figure I don't belong anywhere. People call me the most Albertan person on campus, but nobody sees me as a Canadian. The Albertans enjoy calling me an Arab, and the Arabs just think that the fact that I can swear in Arabic is pretty cool for a Westerner. There's a few people here who aren't viewed as properly presenting their countries, and we all find it pretty annoying, because I did spend 12 years in Calgary, and they did live in Zimbabwe or Bermuda even though they may act British.

It was just at the end of the evening, after the traditional concert that gets put on at school, and the Middle Easterners and Subcontinentals all got called down onto stage to show who represented which country at the college. However, the Emirates, whom I felt I represented because I had lived there for a few years, were never called. It sounds trivial, but it just underlies the nowhereness that people think I am from.

Rachel Lane, who is nominally English, but has spent only three out of seventeen years of her life there (the rest were spent in Germany, Nigeria and Turkey) condenses this sentiment further and says she has missed out on, 'A real sense of 'home', as in a place where I go back to every once in a while, where I know the people there and my way around'.

Barbara Schaetti considers this a sense of 'cultural marginality', but indicates that it is an experience that should be viewed as neither good, nor bad, it just is (Schaetti, B. *The Global Nomad Profile:* Women on the Move Conference, Paris,

March 1998). TCKS, though, can feel trapped by this sense of separation.

Many Global Nomads have an alternate sense of belonging, which is tied to the history of where they have lived around the world. One expatriated teenager viewed his community inclusion this way.

Another thing that I often catch myself doing is referring to people in the countries I have live in as 'We'. 'We' are near this other country, 'We have the densest population of any other city in the world', for example. I am one person in many groups and cannot separate them. When I refer to myself in those contexts, they are not foreign to me, so I consider it a 'We' scenario.

This is the reverse side of Schaetti's 'cultural marginality', the more positive 'constructive marginality'; the feeling of being at home anywhere. Like Brennen feeling comfortable representing the UAE, though he did not carry its passport.

Many Global Nomads balance these two feelings by feeling different, but not feeling trapped by the difference. The difference defines who they are and where they have been. It does not necessarily weigh them down. Though TCKs can feel different on their return home, they usually do not feel totally isolated and the vast majority settle comfortably into the home country, and though they would find it painful to actually leave their friends and community, they could, '...easily move and would enjoy meeting new people and new challenges'. (Schaetti, B. *The Global Nomad Profile:* Women on the Move Conference, Paris, 1998.)

Language Acquisition

Whilst a TCK is abroad there are the obvious challenges of learning the language. For younger children, who operate at a much less academic and more 'play' oriented level, learning and playing in languages does not appear to be as challenging as it is for the teen TCK. Parents need to recognise that for some TCKs who are attending school in a bilingual atmosphere, working in two languages is extremely draining. Yet it should not be looked at as a negative challenge.

There are easy ways of meeting the language challenge and there are difficult ways to do it. The attitude presented by the parents to their children can make it either a negative or a positive factor. When trying to achieve the positive, one expat parent who encouraged his children to live in the local language had the following approach in mind:

...the single best thing you can do with this is to help him or her feel like the language barrier is a fun code to be cracked and that making mistakes can be entertaining. I have watched children and adults here have widely varying degrees of success, and those people that make the quickest adjustments are those that expect to slaughter the language and laugh when they do. They're the ones best prepared to celebrate their little successes and that reinforces confidence. On the other hand, people worried about sounding stupid or being laughed at get slowed up considerably because they deny themselves the chance to have small victories. Even if it is only getting him to feel excited that he was able to order his own fries at McDonalds, he'll be able to leave Germany with positive feelings about overseas living, and because he's living there for only a short time, that should be your primary goal.

Bernadett van Houten, of *Consultants Interculturale Communicatie*, having worked with innumerable families on the issue of learning languages whilst abroad, points out that it is the parents' responsibility to encourage language reinforcement. Consider that some TCKs are educated in a language other than the language that is used at home. If there is not enough opportunity for the children to rehearse their home language outside of the home then the parents must be proactive in attempting to help their children with this particular challenge. She

suggests that, 'If you are afraid of your children losing their home language, m
recommendation is that you send them to a sports camp or something in th
country you consider home'. (*Raising Children in a Multilingual Environment*
Women on the Move Conference, Paris, 1998).

Language ability is probably one of the most important aspects of thi
background knowledge. Though it can be difficult to encourage children to spea
their native language, especially if they spend a long time in one country where n
one else speaks that language, it can greatly help them foster their sense of cultura
identity and maintain links with relatives who remain at home.

There are many ways to work through language issues, whether you want ther
to learn a new language, or whether you want them to retain the home language.
is ultimately a challenge that the TCK will require assistance from the parents i
order to work through without meeting with failure.

Maturity

From the ATCK study, it would appear that TCKs mature later than their peers dc
The third article in the TCK study refers to this phenomenon as prolonged o
delayed adolescence.

While their adolescence may last longer, this extension often means the
eventually become well-functioning adults in the longer term. (A)TCKs may dela
making decisions about their university education, their careers and where the
want to live, but when they do decide, they make decisions they are happy witl
Others appear to settle down quickly, but then make major alterations in thei
lifestyle later in life and go back to college, change their career, or move overseas.

Whereas most people are educated and remain in one location their entire lives
ATCKs have had mobile lives and therefore, reveals the ATCK study, need t
spend time trying to bring a sense of order to the chaotic nature of their childhoo
This may be the reason that they delay their maturation process as they deal wit
the cumulative effects of the many transitions and changes throughout their lives.

One of the challenges that TCKs frequently meet when they relocate to thei
passport countries are the views which their home peers have of them. It can b
difficult for a TCK not to talk about where they have been, what they have seer
what they have learned from first hand experience. Frequently, the way in whic
they communicate their experiences to non-TCKs can leave them looking like the
are 'better' than others, or just arrogant. Dr Cottrell and Dr Hill Useem noted how
others tend to perceive young adult TCKs.

*Some young adult TCKs strike their close peers, parents, and counselors as
being self-centered adolescents, as having champagne tastes on beer incomes
(or no incomes), as not being able to make up their minds about what they want
to do with their lives, where they want to live, and whether or not they want to
'settle down, get married, and have children'.*

All of these views can translate into a new challenge of having to fit into ye
another society. The difference is that those who are in this society do not expect t
find, let alone understand, the different lifestyle of those ATCKs who hav
reintegrated into their society.

ATCKs can also be left with a migratory instinct. If a child makes a number c
moves, on a regular basis, or if people continually come in and out of their lives, a
ATCKs they can become addicted to the need for change.

Some ATCKs go so far as to create change for themselves. They do not know
what to do when things stagnate, they do not feel comfortable, so they seek ou
whatever change they can orchestrate — anything from changing jobs, to movin
to a new house, to changing relationships with people around them. These are ne
necessarily good things to do, but they are part of how ATCKs feel about th

constriction of stability. They are flexible and pride themselves in the ability to change, and the need to move with changes, even if they are forced, or they create the change themselves.

Perhaps linked to both the issue of maturity and the issue of a constant need for change is the slow and disjointed way in which some ATCKs gain their post secondary educational qualifications. In the second report of the TCK study it was discovered that:

> *A considerable proportion of the young adult TCKs change colleges and/or majors two or three times. Others drop out, as they put it, to 'take advantage of opportunities' that happen to come up.*
>
> *Such detours on their road to obtaining a degree can include:*
> *1. Taking a semester off to 'bum around Africa; a place I haven't seen'.*
> *2. Doing full-time translating for a professor outside of their major.*
> *3. Dropping out to get married and start a family before returning.*
>
> *These detours may add a year, or more, to the time required for 'getting through'.*
>
> *Occasionally ATCKs drop out because a course of study is beyond their capacity, but more often they feel their overseas schooling and experience put them ahead of their peers (and even their teachers). Thus they are often 'out of synch' with their all-American-reared peers.*

Relationships

Life as a TCK, (like life in general) is not all roses and Andrea DiSebastian found leaving her friends when she moved one of the hardest things to do. 'It's the worst feeling in the world to never know if you are going to see, or talk to, or hear someone again. It still makes me upset to think about all of the ended friendships that I have because of losing contact with one another.'

This fear of losing friends can lead to a more abrupt manner of making friendships and severing ties. David Pollock of *Interaction Inc.*, a TCK centred organisation, utilises a scale (adapted from *Why Am I Afraid To Tell You Who I Am?*, John Powell, Tabor Publising, reprint 1995) on which he believes internationally mobile people develop relationships. It is a survival skill to be able to build relationships quickly, yet at the same time to abandon them when they are no longer required.

> *1. At the top level there is the cliché, or non-sharing conversations, that talk about weather, sports, music, etc., just simply to allow the other human being know that we are alive and well.*
> *2. Next level, at a deeper point, is fact. Where we share what we know.*
> *3. Lower is opinion sharing, what we think.*
> *4. Next is emotion, sharing what we feel.*
> *5. And transparency is at the bottom, the most intimate level, where we share who we are, which is a composite of the above.*

While this kind of relationship building is not true of every single Global Nomad, those who live abroad in a variety of countries for short periods of time (as opposed to expats who live abroad in one or two countries for extended periods) often find that the late-in, early-out version of the scale applies. Many people have indicated that they are unable, or almost unwilling to form a close friendship with people that they know are leaving, they may also back away from friendships when the directive to leave a country has come down from the head office.

Home Culture

Though TCKs gain different and additional experiences whilst abroad, many expat parents believe it is important for their children to learn and experience as much of their own culture as possible too.

By celebrating traditional festivals, telling fairy stories from home, watching videos and reading books together, expat parents can educate their children about the culture they come from. This background cultural training prepares the TCK for when they do visit, or return to live in, their home country, which many TCKs do when they are adults, even if they have never lived there as a child.

TCKs often want to return to their home country for a while, to attend college or to work, to develop their sense of cultural identity and establish a sense of belonging, especially if they have moved a number of times while they lived abroad. This development will be easier and less painful if they already have a theoretical knowledge of their cultural heritage and some practical sense of the importance of the religion, festivals and traditions in life at home.

The Outcome

When expatriate parents and ATCKs get together to assess the pros and cons of being a TCK, the majority agree that it is something they would choose to do again, rather than the alternative of going to the same school, living in the same town, having the same friends, and doing the same things as everyone else. In effect, they believe they have gained rather than lost by growing up abroad.

When reflecting on their lives, most ATCKs will tell you that if they had to do it all over again, they would not change a thing. But even more telling, is the general consensus that they would like their children to enjoy the same lifestyle and challenges that they had.

One important feature reported in the fourth article of the series is that generally, the respondents agreed that they are happy and satisfied with the way their life has gone, and that their experiences as TCKs do not pose significant difficulties in the long-run.

In contrast to the re-entry period, ATCKs generally credit their third culture background with positively influencing their adult lives.

The study concluded that the perceived negative aspects of being a TCK are not due to the internationally mobile lives these children have had. Rather, they see that it is more of a result of the fact that they go about constructing answers and living their lives in a distinctly non-American way; the problems they face are more related to the 'American scene'.

Long-term Effects on Families

Living abroad can be stressful, even when it is fun. The constant challenges that have to be faced when living in a foreign country can leave whole families tired and stressed. The different social attitudes to marriage, relationships and 'correct' behaviour of the cultures and people that an expat encounters can lead to relationship problems within expatriate families. It is, unfortunately, sometimes the straw that breaks the camel's back.

As Phyllis Adler comments in her article for *Woman Abroad,* 'Moving can often highlight imperfections.'

Helena Snedden remembers thinking that her relationship with her husband would have a chance to heal when they moved abroad. 'When I first came over to Scotland my husband was with me, and I was hoping the move would make us closer and resolve some of our problems. They actually worsened to the extent that we are getting divorced and he has moved back to South Africa.'

Expatriate families repeatedly comment that if you are not good friends with your spouse and children before you leave home, the relationships usually get worse. Yet when you are already a family unit that knows the value of trust and support, becoming expatriates in challenging circumstances can lead to growth in your ability to rely on each other which is necessary during times of frustration and culture shock.

Though Helena's relationship with her husband did not benefit by their international move, her relationship with her daughter grew and they have become much closer in the time of transition.

Frances Brown, an expatriate from South Africa who moved to the UK says,

...if the two people in a marriage are not happy before they trek halfway across the world, nothing is going to strengthen the bond. You have to start off with a good relationship with one another and then things improve from there. But the partner is the only friend you have initially and the only adult you can really converse with for a long time, locals are friendly but do not give a damn about your situation. It is self-inflicted most times, so you tend to get on with things with only your spouse to agree or disagree with your choices. Family back home, sure as anything, do not grasp the enormity of the first year away, so no amount of bouncing ideas off them is any good.

As was previously discussed in *Equal Partners*, it is important for couples to take an inventory of their relationship so that they know there will be support there when they land in their host country and need it most.

Though difficulties can become worse when they already exist, many expatriates acknowledge that being Modern Nomads has strengthened the bonds of their nuclear family. These family relationships, while strained when under the stress of making a move, offer the support and comfort that is required to help meet the challenges that starting a new life can create.

Barbara Schaetti states:

It's you and your family alone in a way that not even those who coined the term 'nuclear family' could envision. Consider for a moment a typical nuclear family: wife, husband, child. Consider now the context within which that family system functions when it has lived in one place for an extended period of time. Ongoing relationships have been cultivated: friends, colleagues, neighbours, doctors, teachers, religious leaders, shopkeepers...The geographically-stable nuclear family is part of a larger relationship system that nurtures and supports the family as a whole and is available to help its individual members.

Consider now a typical internationally-mobile family: wife, husband, child. No relatives nearby. No web of ongoing relationships — except those renewed on home leave, those cultivated at a distance via annual holiday greetings, or for the multimover, those expatriate friends from prior postings encountered again in the new location. The larger support system available to the internationally-mobile family consists of the wage-earners' employing organisation, the school(s) the children attend, and the expatriate community itself. This support system, however, has some fundamental limitations. (Schaetti, B. (1995). *Families on the Move: Working Together to Meet the Challenge*. Inter-Ed. 23(75))

Barbara goes on to point out that there are obvious aspects of support that these technical organisations cannot help with, including consistency. Children's educational institutions offer what support they can during school hours, but often they cannot help with the stress in a household. While the assitance of expatriate communities can be perceived as superficial support (where to find things and how to get around), real emotional support cannot always be garnered from these kinds of institutions.

For these reasons, Barbara concludes that:

...the internationally-mobile family is the ultimate of nuclear families. Members must rely foremost on one another: spouse on spouse, sibling on sibling, child on parent and even parent on child. In the final analysis, an internationally-mobile family must sink or swim on its own. To what degree it does either, depends on how well family members work together. (Schaetti, B. (1995). *Families on the Move: Working Together to Meet the Challenge.* Inter-Ed. 23(75)).

When the employed partner spends long hours at work, the non-employee partner and children can become resentful and feel left out. Communication can break down through lack of opportunity for family quality time.

Making time to spend with the family can be difficult, but it is important for maintaining a happy home. Marriages and families of expatriates can break up due to the increased conflict between work and home that leaves a non-employee partner feeling they are taking second place to the office. Working expatriates need to remember the maxim of 'work to live, not live to work' if they want to retain their family.

Effects on Partners

Life as an expatriate spouse is not always easy and exciting and full of coffee mornings, shopping and happy days at the club. It can be a life of loneliness, boredom and waiting up late for a partner to come home from work while the children are misbehaving until they are spoiled and pampered by a guilty parent who only spends an hour a day at home, awake.

Divorce among expatriates seems to be rare, but reportedly it is common once a family returns home and a build up of problems are resolved by a sudden separation. The timing of the separation is often put down to the fact that an expa spouse, with no job, income, or legal back-up, waits until the family returns home to announce their decision. The working spouse may have no intimation of the extent of the problems of their spouse — because they were rarely at home when they were not tired and stressed about work.

Non-working partners also need to work hard at maintaining a home environment that their partner likes to come home to. When a non-working partner works hard to make their life interesting and active, primarily for their own benefit they can also improve the time they get to spend with the employee. By losing their identity and personality in boredom and passivity a non-working partner can become a faded and jaded shadow of the person they used to be, with a disastrous effect on a marriage.

Effects on Extended Family

Grandparents can feel resentful at being so far away from their children and grandchildren. Grandchildren can also miss the experience of spending weekends and holidays with their grandparents when they hear stories and acquire some parts of their sense of identity, family and history. Cousins, aunts, uncles and other relatives also add much to the sense of belonging that children have to an extended family. It can be important to maintain good communications, through e-mails, faxes, letters and telephone calls, but photos, videos and personal websites (with photos) also add intimacy to the relationships.

If possible, it can be a good idea to arrange for grandparents (and other family members) to visit you in your host country, so they can better understand the experiences that are shaping their grandchildren, nieces, nephews and cousins.

Expatriates who have been abroad for more than two years have found that by bringing their parents to their host country, many of the fears that the parents have of where they are living are put to rest. While young *Modern Nomads* are frequently excited about setting up home in a foreign country, their anxious parents, who have never lived abroad, or even travelled much, often worry about their children's quality and standard of living and the safety of (future) grandchildren.

Even when expatriates have lived abroad for a number of years, a further international move can make extended family members anxious again. Kelli Lambe, who moved three times in two years, was nervous about telling her family about an impending move to Saudi. She decided that she would just tell them she was moving, and hopefully, with her positive attitude she would reduce their concerns. 'My family is not very happy with us moving to Saudi. I just told my dad this morning and for the first time in our relationship, he seemed a bit worried. I think when we are home for the interlude between here and there, it will help to sit with him and discuss it.'

For expatriates, clear and open discussion of fears, concerns and problems is necessary to maintain successful relationships with their family, who for the most part are their only consistent support mechanism. The closer the family members the more important this communication is, so that all members of the family feel they are an integral part of the unit and are not left to face the many issues of international living on their own — until they feel ready to do so.

Further discussion on maintaining close relationships with extended family members can be found in the next chapter *How Long Will You Really Stay Abroad?*.

Resources

Print Resources

Hidden Immigrants: Legacies of Growing Up Abroad, by Linda G. Bell, Cross-cultural publications, ISBN 0-940121-35-2.

Notes From a Travelling Childhood, Foreign Service Youth Foundation, Karen McClusky (Editor), available from Foreign Service Youth Foundation, PO Box 39185, Washington DC, 20016, USA.

Raising Resilient MKs, Joyce M. Bowers, Ed., Association of Christian Schools International, PO Box 35097, Colorado Springs, CO 80935, USA.

The Third Culture Kid Experience: Growing Up Among Worlds, David C. Pollock and Ruth E. Van Reken, Intercultural Press, ISBN 1 877864 722.

Why Am I Afraid To Tell You Who I Am?, John Powell, Tabor Publishing, 1995, ISBN 0 883473 232.

Online resources

Global Nomads: http://globalnomads.association.com, a resource site for TCKs and their families.

Global Nomad Virtual Village: www.gnvv.org, an internet-based, non-profit organisation providing global nomads and TCKs a place to keep in touch.

Military Brats Online: www.lynxu.com, providing a forum for US military kids to keep in touch with their friends through a members list and alumni organisations.

Overseas Brats Homepage: http://users.capu.net/~mcl/osb/osbmain.htm, not just for military kids, but for all global nomads. Has resources for 'Brat', 'Teacher', 'Spouse' and 'Parent'.

Shijo-Tsushin; www.roots-int.com/S-T/extra/index-e.html, an online version (in English) of a Japanese language magazine from three Japanese Global Nomads.

TCK World: www.tckworld.com, a resource site for TCKs and their families.

HOW LONG WILL YOU REALLY STAY ABROAD?

Understanding the Variables

As you are planning your first move abroad the one question that just about everyone will ask you is, 'When are you coming home again?' Most people will just be curious, your extended family and friends will probably only expect a best estimate, but grandparents and children are likely to want the answer to be absolute.

Even when you have been living abroad for some time, and have made it clear you are happy and hope to stay for longer, you are still going to be asked the same question. Kelli Lambe is preparing for her third international move in two and a half years and says:

...the big question everyone keeps asking is: 'When will you be back for good?' My answer is always the same, 'When we are ready'. No one really likes that answer, but then again, I don't always like the way they ask the question, so we are even. Most of the time my family is okay with it, but it's because we live in Holland now. Saudi (our next move) is not going over well at all.

If you believe you are going abroad for a pre-determined time and plan on returning to your current home in a few years, or expect your ongoing contract to be open-ended, think twice about saying so, or banking on that fact. The reality is that the length of time that many expatriates spend abroad turns out to be different from their original expectation. Some people go abroad for a year and end up staying for many more; on the other hand, postings can suddenly and unexpectedly come to an abrupt halt, through no fault of your own or your employer (as many expats found in Kuwait in 1990 and Indonesia in 1998).

Many of the reasons for these changes in the time spent abroad have been mentioned in the various chapters of this book, but they are listed again below.

1. Early return due to personal reasons (unhappiness of expatriates, family responsibilities at home, family health, etc.).
2. Early return due to regional conflict, or political or financial collapse.
3. Early completion of the business reason for being abroad (project completed quicker than expected, lapse of an expected project, etc.).
4. Early return due to a change in focus of employer's business.
5. Late return due to project delays.
6. Late return due to contract extension owing to the growth of the business and the employer wanting current personnel to stay on.
7. Late return due to contract extension owing to a lack of replacement personnel.
8. Continued stay due to partner's acquired employment.
9. Continued stay because the expatriate (and family) enjoy living abroad more than they expected and want to stay (either with same employer or a new one).
10. Continued stay because primary employee lacks a job to return to at home.

The effect of any change in the expected length of your time abroad will vary on the many people affected. Not only the expatriate employee, but their partner, children, parents, other family members, their friends, colleagues and employer will all be affected in different ways.

Friends and family may want you to return home because they miss you, or may want you to stay longer because they enjoy visiting you so much where you live. One expat couple, who have been living abroad for ten years have found that many of their friends tell them to stay away, and to go somewhere interesting, so that they can visit.

Colleagues and superiors may want you to stay longer because you do such a good job, or alternatively, and more selfishly, might be glad to have you a long way from the home office and out of the promotion ladder or the office politics.

You may also be approached by another company whilst you are abroad that wants to gain your expertise. One expatriate administrator in Asia was headhunted by a competing organisation within the same city. They approached him with a bigger salary package; his current employer countered with an even better one. When the administrator admitted to his current employer that he wanted to change jobs and work the job with the competing organisation, his current employer tried hard to convince him to sign an extended contract. However, the administrator finally decided a change was necessary and changed employers.

If you return home early your employer may feel that they wasted the large amount of money they spent establishing you as an expatriate, because they have not seen a full return on their investment. This can mean that your future career prospects with the firm are harmed.

Your partner and children may love, or hate, the host country so much that a change in the length of stay (longer or shorter) will cause resentment. The partner of one expatriate who renewed his contracts yearly repeatedly hinted that she wanted to leave at the end of every year. When he renewed for the fifth year because the job was good, the pay decent and he had no other job to go to, his partner became so upset that after six months she headed off to a more 'suitable' destination, and left him to finish his contract alone.

The employed partner will have his or her own feelings about the posting too. They may be enjoying the job and not want to return to their old position (or there may be no old position to return to). On the other hand, they may dislike their job so much they want to return home or move to another position abroad.

Even when a contract is nominally fixed before a move (by the employee or the employer), the situation that determined that decision can dramatically change during the time of the posting. The ideas and attitude of the employer, employee, the employee's partner, their children and their immediate family towards the international posting can all change once a move is made.

If these possible changes are not considered from the outset, then dealing with them once they arise can be much more complicated. Unexpected changes can be unsettling and stressful, especially so when they are not wanted, or the different people affected have competing ideas and concerns about the changes.

Deciding which of the people involved have the most important concerns and how everyone's concerns can be taken into consideration will be difficult. Addressing each of the concerns individually can help resolve as many of them as possible.

Children

For school age children, a change in the length of an international posting is most likely to affect their schooling and social life.

If both the children and parents are happy with the children's school and the proposed change is a lengthening of the time abroad, then any concerns will be less than if either the parents or children are unhappy.

If the posting is being extended and the parents believe the child's current school is unsuitable, then alternatives can be investigated (refer to *Education: Understanding the Options*) and the employer approached about supporting a change of schooling.

If there are no feasible alternative schooling options then a decision will have to be made as to whether the current school is acceptable despite its problems, or a move is necessary for the benefit of the children. A move might not involve a return home or a change of employer; some companies will consider a move to another country or the relocation of an office to another city within the same country to retain their employees.

If the children say they are just unhappy being abroad, then the parents need to determine the level of the unhappiness and whether this situation can be improved by a change of school, location (in-country or a new country), or a return home. Depending on the employment prospects of the parents it might be necessary to remain despite a child's objections.

If the posting comes to a sudden end during the middle of a school year, the children will probably have to join a new school, or return to their old one part way through the academic year. This abrupt change can be traumatic for the child(ren). If there is any possibility that an abrupt departure may occur, parents should prepare the children for the eventuality, because, like the initial move away from home, an unannounced move is much more traumatic than an expected one.

Many expatriate children have said they found it easier to cope with changes to planned lengths of stay if they knew there was the possibility of change from the outset, or at least as soon as their parents did.

Making friends in a new school can often be difficult, but having to do so when most other children have already established their social groups makes it even more difficult. Close liaison with the new school (as discussed in *Education: Understanding the Options*) and careful selection of that school can go a long way towards helping your child settle quickly. If your child has been attending an International School whilst abroad, it might also help them settle if they attend one upon returning home, or in a new country.

Partner

Stories of expatriate partners miserably counting the days until they go home are common. Some of these have begun counting from the day they arrived, which, if you have been able to read and act on the ideas discussed earlier in this book, should hopefully not be you. Others have, despite their best efforts, not been happy in their host country and are desperate to return home or move elsewhere.

Even if a partner is happy living abroad, a sudden change in the length of that stay can be very upsetting. A partner who has happily agreed to take a career break of a specific length, and is looking forward to returning to employment, can find himself or herself devastated at the thought that the break may become indefinite.

Other partners enjoy the lifestyle, being a full-time parent, or having the time to study without the financial worries that they had at home. A forced return home where work would be financially necessary could have a similar negative effect. When Dell Harmsen learned that her husband's position in Greece was likely to be shortened, she was very upset. 'I can't believe it's almost over, and I'm just getting started. My husband is going to try to get the posting extended. I am not ready to leave.'

If a partner knows there may be a change in the length of stay from the outset they can at least mentally prepare for that scenario. However, if they have come to the conclusion over a long time that they cannot face an extension to the length of stay, then a move might have to be made for their mental wellbeing and the health of the relationship.

A move does not have to be a return home, it might be to another country that allows the partner to return to work, or continue in the lifestyle they are enjoying so much. A current employer might consider a second international posting, or a change of employer might be necessary to continue living abroad.

Sometimes a move can actually be very beneficial, as not every expat will like every country; an unhappy expat in one country can be a happy one elsewhere.

Extended Family and Friends

Grandparents, especially, can find that having their grandchildren live abroad is hard. They miss seeing them grow up and look forward to visits and an eventual return home. If a stay abroad is lengthened unexpectedly they can feel betrayed and hugely disappointed and go so far as to make life difficult for the expat parents.

Kelli Lambe's parents, though understanding of her international lifestyle, miss their grandchildren greatly. Prior to a new move to Saudi Arabia, Kelli planned a surprise visit to them, to help soften the blow of their grandchildren spending more years abroad.

Since no one at home knows we are going back to Alaska for Christmas, emotions are all on a shoe string with my parents. I think that our trip home will be a bit of a bandage; it won't make the sore go away, but will delay the pain until we have moved. It is difficult for them. The last time we lived in the Middle East, our families were always faxing stories from the newspaper about what was happening in the Middle East. They were the cause of a lot of my stress about living there, and I am going to have to ask them not to do this to us again.

Before a first international move it can be a good idea to tell your family that although the length of the move is nominally set, it may well be lengthened for a variety of reasons, some of which are out of your hands. In the long run, this can be easier for them to cope with and make home visits and their holidays with you easier and more enjoyable if they are not continually asking when you are coming home.

However, some expats bend the truth to soften the impact of their move on the family members who remain at home.

When I did get around to telling mom and dad about my decision to accept the job, I was faced with the problem of telling them how long I was going away for. I kept telling them that it was just a two year contract, and that I could go for one year and if it was bad, if I didn't like it, if it wasn't a safe place to live, that I would break my contract and leave. However, I had no intention of breaking my contract, I'm not that kind of person. I just told them that to make them feel better about the whole thing, so that they would not lose all hope of us returning. I just felt better delivering it that way.

How to tell family members of your intention to move can also be a difficult decision to make if there is any concern that they will not be supportive. Palma Pisciella recalls delivering her news gently.

We didn't tell our families that we were considering this seriously until the very last minute. We did not involve them in our discussions of whether or not we wanted to move. Until we knew that this was something that we were definitely going for, there was no point in saying anything to them. So when we decided to start the whole process of finding work overseas, we slowly worked them up to the idea that we were going. We had to be careful. My then boyfriend still lived at home. His mother couldn't take it when he lived an hour's drive away when he was in university. I knew my own parents wouldn't disown me, but I thought I would break their hearts. I knew they wouldn't think that we were doing this as a slight to them, but I'd be hurting their feelings. To see them like that would have killed me.

However, Frances Brown used a very direct approach.

We were so brutally honest with our families and friends, we told them that we had no plans to come back to South Africa, ever, except on holiday. If we did not like the climate in the UK we would move to Australia, so they had no false hope to cling to. My dad's last words at the airport were very understanding, 'If anything, anything goes wrong, you always have a home with us, okay?' So I suppose they still, in their hearts, wanted us to get over the nomadic thing and come home eventually. My dad has recently been for a visit and so enjoyed himself that he kept saying, 'I can see how happy you are here, I also would not want to leave here, you have made the right choices'.

Once they are abroad, some expatriates pay for their immediate family members to fly out for visits, which can go a long way to smoothing the ruffled feathers of grandparents. Bronwyn Davies helps her parents come to Hong Kong every year from New Zealand which means Bronwyn's children have got to know their grandparents intimately. She found another way of keeping in contact too.

I bought a fax machine to send pictures and letters back and forth, we have e-mail to communicate with each other daily if we want to, but there is nothing quite like an 'in person' visit from the grandparents. My kids know their grandparents as well now as if we lived in New Zealand in a neighbouring city. Our travels there once a year, combined with my parents visits here in Hong Kong, have enabled our extended family to feel like a close family.

Explaining an international move to close friends can also be difficult, especially when they have no intention of ever moving abroad. For those friends who may not accept the honest truth about your intention to live abroad for as long as you enjoy the experience, or need to for career reasons, a gentle explanation similar to that Palma Pisciella used for her family may be the way to go.

Employer

If you decide that you want to vary the length of your stay abroad your employer may not agree with your reasoning or may not be able to honour your request for a variety of reasons.

It is expensive to establish an expatriate and it can take years to recoup the cost of doing so. Not only are there the direct costs of salary, training, bonuses, allowances and airfares, there are also the indirect and invisible investment of developing the company's status in the host country.

If you decide you want to return home early, the company can lose credibility and business because clients and potential clients may perceive the company, not the employee, as unreliable and not committed to the market. Even if a replacement employee can be sent out quickly, they will need to take time to establish themselves culturally and professionally, as you did when you arrived.

It has been estimated that the direct and indirect costs of an expat returning home early from a commercial posting can be more than £200,000 and rise to over £500,000.

One reason it can be difficult to return home early is that there may be no job to return to. Once you move abroad it is probable that someone will take over your old responsibilities full-time, or the position be made redundant.

If you have been abroad for some time and enjoyed the experience, you may want to extend your stay. However, your employer may want the benefit of your valuable international experience back in the home office to help develop other international ventures and manage them as they progress.

Alternatively your employer may want to localise the position (to save money), or has been planning to give someone else the chance to work abroad at the expected end of your posting. Many expats in Hong Kong have lost their jobs as part of the localisation process since the handover to China, and others have only been able to stay on one-year contracts, pending the recruitment of a suitable local replacement.

An employer's attitude towards your proposed change in length of stay will inevitably come down to what the company will perceive as commercial reasons and your proposal has a better chance of succeeding if it reflects that.

Tony Turton, of the International Human Resources Consultancy *Arnett Associates*, suggests the following reasons an employer would look favourably on a proposed change to the length of stay abroad.

---

1. If you went out with a specific task to complete, your employer is bound to feel let down if you ask to return before it is finished. But if the project is going well, you may be able to persuade the company that someone else could take it over — perhaps as a development opportunity for someone less experienced. It would help if you had a name or two to suggest. You could offer to stay during a handover period, although you will need to persuade your employer that the extra cost of running two expatriates is more than offset by the speed of your replacement becoming fully effective.

2. If things are going badly, an approach along the lines of 'let's cut our losses' may work — only don't expect your company to welcome you back with open arms.

3. If your assignment was more open-ended — managing an overseas office, for example — you may have agreed to an initial period of three or four years. In what circumstances would your company be pleased to bring you home early? One way would be to show that the office can run just as well without you (or another expensive expatriate) in charge. If you can develop your local staff to a point where they can take over the whole operation, you can come home — or move on — with a feather in your cap.

4. Another approach might be to convince the company that someone more junior (in other words, cheaper) could replace you — maybe not with your full responsibilities, but perhaps in support of the new local manager you propose to appoint.

The Outcome

Once you have decided what is best for you and your family you will need to work within all the constraints to come up with the best solution.

An early return prompted by you, for personal reasons, can outweigh the commercial objections of your employer (as far as you are concerned). You may consider that the happiness of you, your partner or your children is more important than your career or remaining in the current country. It may mean that you have to find a new employer, but that can have many advantages too that only become really clear after the move has been made. Many relocation consultants will advise an expatriate family to consider their most important needs first, and if that means the family needs to go home, then there is little alternative.

Alternatively, you may refuse to accept an extension of a posting, or contract, for similar personal reasons. Palma Pisciella was told that she would be asked to stay on for a third year (an extension to her two-year teaching contract), but she had already planned to go home. She had always said she would be abroad for two years, and then return home to her previous job, which she did.

One expatriate family planned two moves they had not initially considered, to new countries and new employers. In the first country the parents were unhappy so they looked for and found work in a country they liked. In the second one, though the family was happy, the only school available was unsuitable for their children.

The decision of whether to leave early, on the intended date, or to stay longer, needs to be made in the light of all factors and the important people involved. What is important to you and your immediate family should be the primary concern, not what is important to those who want to impose their will on you for their personal, commercial or financial gain.

RETURNING TO THE COUNTRY YOU USED TO CALL HOME

For Visits and For Good

It may seem strange to think about returning to where you come from before you even leave, but it needs to be done. Professional studies, as well as the comments of expatriates returning for holidays and the experiences of expatriates returning home for good (repatriates), show that returning home after living abroad can be more stressful than moving abroad in the first place.

Derrick Evans, a Canadian who worked abroad as an international schoolteacher, in Japan and Singapore, has repatriated twice.

I have repatriated a couple of times now and I always feel that the reverse culture shock is worse than the culture shock you experience when you're abroad. For some reason, you prepare yourself mentally for the surprises that life overseas throws at you, but you never expect to be surprised when you return home.

As the challenges of this aspect of international living become increasingly recognised, more companies are beginning to offer repatriation training, as well as expatriation training, to their employees; 70% of respondents to *Cendant Mobility*'s *International Assignment Policies & Practices 1999 Survey*, said they offered repatriation training.

Almost half of the companies who participated in the *Cendant Mobility* survey also tracked what happened to assignees after their repatriation, apparently because the companies believe that repatriation is an ongoing process that affects their employees for an extended period of time.

The issues that make repatriation stressful can seem to be obtuse to those who have never experienced them, but nevertheless they are very real.

While you have been living in a foreign country, no matter whether you enjoyed the experience or not, you will have seen and learnt many things, which means your attitudes to, and perceptions of, what is around you will have changed too. You will no longer be able to think and behave exactly as you did before you spent time in a foreign country and culture.

While you have been travelling you will have met people from diverse backgrounds, religions and cultures. Some of these will have become your friends and you can become used to your conversations revolving not around the local happenings of your immediate social circle and the city or town where you live, but the country, family and issues affecting the wider diversity of your multicultural friends. As Derrick found when he returned to Canada to attend teacher's college.

I simply felt like a changed person who had been forced into a life which outwardly appeared to have changed very little. I discovered that friends did not want to talk about my experiences, perhaps because they could not relate or perhaps because it made them feel as though they had accomplished very little in the same amount of time. For whatever reason, it seemed like I had to be the one to make the effort and take an interest in the lives of my friends and their everyday events.

While you have been abroad your relatives and friends will have carried on with their lives without waiting for you to come back. The second time Derrick repatriated to Canada he was keen to reintegrate better than he had the first time, and so made greater efforts to fit back into the lives of his friends and family.

After three years in Singapore, I experienced the same kind of repatriation shock when I returned to Canada, but this time I was a little more prepared. I knew that if I wanted to settle here, I needed to change my focus. I had to turn an international life into a local one. Often I felt like I could not relate to local concerns. What did I care about who had split up with whom or what a neighbour had said, when I was accustomed to talking about what governments in Southeast Asia were doing about the economy, the environment or poverty?

However, I knew that I would appear arrogant if I discredited the concerns of my peers. It was my job to readjust to Canadian culture, to re-assimilate. Changed, yet unchanged.

Outwardly, I appear to have made the transition smoothly. On the inside I'm dying to experience the sensory and mental stimuli that come with an expat life. I'm like a fish that has returned to the fishbowl after being allowed to swim in the ocean. The fishbowl is home, but the ocean is infinitely more interesting.

The small day-to-day happenings of family life and even some of the major traumas that happen are not always included in letters, e-mails and phone conversations, by accident, or because the correspondent does not want to worry you while you are so far away. This can mean that you feel left out of conversations on your return, when everyone else knows what is being referred to.

One expat did not find out about her mother's acute illness until after she returned home for a summer visit. When she asked how her mother could keep these things from her, such important family matters, her mother simply said, 'You don't live here now, what could you do? Besides, why worry you when you are so far away. I figured there was no sense in telling you about it until you were actually here'.

There are also the local news stories from your home town that do not make it to the BBC World Service, CNN, your host country's local TV news, or the newspapers that are available in your host country. You can be blithely unaware of the new expressway or supermarket, or the political and social changes occurring at home. Though in contrast, you may well be familiar with the politics and social problems that exist in the country that was formerly your home, and that few of your friends can even find on a map.

Events in the lives of friends and family in the home country, over the years that an expatriate is away, can mean that the friends and family change too. But these changes will be different to those that happen to the expatriate and may not seem so noticeable, or important.

Palma Pisciella moved back to Canada after two years in Turkey:

We believe that because our friends and family stayed behind and continued with their lives, as we would have done had we not left, they didn't seem to change as much as we changed. We left our familiar surroundings and having been placed in a completely new environment, we were forced to change in order to adapt.

These differences in the paths of change can cause problems for the repatriate, as Palma found.

When we returned to Canada, we found that we had less in common with our friends and family. It was difficult for them to relate to something they had never seen or experienced, so whenever we spoke of our time in Turkey, they were amazed but didn't know which questions to ask, and could not compare it to anything they had experienced. Likewise, when they reminisced about events and experiences that happened while we were away, we felt left out and even disinterested at times. It was clear that our interests and priorities were now different.

Other than the changes to your immediate circle of friends and family and the major national events you may have missed while you were away, there can be a host of other, smaller, changes that can be unsettling for returning expatriates. Changes to the bank notes and coins of your currency can leave you poking through your purse like you did the first few weeks you spent abroad, and have shop assistants staring at you as if you are stupid. Special offers in shops (that may never happen when you are abroad), store cards (that all the locals use) and changes to the local transport system (that you grew up with) can combine to make you feel like a foreigner in your own country. When you are a foreigner, people expect you to find things difficult, but when you sound like a local, people often seem to think you are stupid if you do not know the system.

The changes that happen to the expatriate and their family at home may be marked, even though they happened slowly over the years of separation. These changes, though they are not a problem in themselves, can cause problems because people often remember each other as they were the last time they met. Even during short home visits, expatriates can begin to notice that these changes are affecting their relationships as one expat found during her summer holiday back home.

I was at dinner with my friend and the conversation was just painful. My friend could not grasp why my interests had changed, why I didn't watch every new movie that had come out in the last three years. It was hard for me to explain that (1), I didn't go to movies any more and (2), that they didn't have a lot of the new movies where I was living anyway. This was way beyond her comprehension. She could not, for the life of her, figure out why I would want to live in such a place.

Conversations can be awkward when you are not familiar with the events people are talking about, or the subtle changes in social and political moods that occur over time. You may also find that the wide-ranging conversations of international interest you enjoyed so much no longer occur, and the interests of your family and friends can seem parochial by comparison.

These changes can manifest themselves as preferences and expectations for a lifestyle that may not be available at home. Helena Snedden cannot see her and her daughter, Kaylee, returning to their native South Africa, except for short visits.

I will never go back. When people ask if I miss the life, I have to be truthful. I miss the South Africa I used to know. It was a wonderful life back then, but so much of that was mixed with my childhood, the security, the lifestyle. That has changed, and I can't go back now. I do miss the climate, and the outdoor life, but even if South Africa goes back to being a wonderful place again, I still couldn't go back as it just wouldn't be the same. That was the past, and I have moved on.

You can also find that your friends and family have as little understanding of what you are talking about when you mention your experiences, as you have about theirs. And they may think you are being pretentious when you are casually dropping comments like, 'When I went to Bali for the weekend,' or, 'In Saudi we used to....'.

They may also have an erroneous view of life as an expatriate; that it is all exotic fun, with a big salary, a maid and no work. The limit of their interest in your life can be the food, weather and stories to reinforce the cultural stereotypes they have of your host culture. This can be the cause of much frustration and ruin home visits, as one expat finds when she returns home every couple of years. She is always asked the same questions by her family, 'Why don't you want to live in a real civilisation' and 'Why do you want to live with those backward foreigners?'.

There can also be the added complication that the longer you spend away from your home country, the stronger the tint on your rose coloured spectacles becomes.

You can forget all the hassles and aggravations you used to have at home, and concentrate on remembering your favourite restaurant, the scenery and the great shopping you used to enjoy. This can drop you into a hard dose of reality a few weeks after you return, when you find that life is not so good as you remember it. You may also have different expectations, and now want the exotic fruit you enjoyed in South East Asia, the sushi of Japan, or the incredible curries of the Middle East.

When Palma Pisciella and her husband Mario Antognetti returned to Canada they tried to take up the lives they had left behind two years previously, but found that they were unable to do so as their two years abroad had affected their view of home too much.

While we were in Turkey, there were those bad weather days (raining or cold and drizzly) when we had to go grocery shopping or make a necessary trip into town, but wished we had the comfort of our cars that we had left behind in Canada, and not the long, cold waits at the bus stop. Don't get me wrong, we enjoyed the fact that all of that walking to and from the bus stop and in and around the city put us in the best physical shape we've ever been in, but we had our miserable days too.

Mario and I loved Turkish food. It was simple and healthy, but we did miss good Chinese and Thai food, or the best pizza from the small Italian family restaurant in our neighbourhood. I never could get used to Turkish coffee so in answer to a desperate plea, my mother sent me a package of my favourite flavour. Soon after that she sent the recipe for home made pancakes and of course some maple syrup for the occasional weekend breakfast. There were just so many good things that we left behind at home.

The day before we left Turkey, I went into town to close off our phone line and pay our last bill. It took over three hours. I stood in one line after another to receive a stamp, or a signature, and would then be sent off into another line for another 45 minutes. It was torture and all I could think of was how much faster everything was back home. Why hadn't they figured that out here yet?

Approximately two days after we got home, I went to the shopping mall in my neighbourhood, anxious to stock up on all that was new. I lasted ten minutes and then had to leave. It was far too overwhelming. Everything we missed (the convenience, the wide variety of foods, clothing, etc.) was what scared me away. The commercialism was suffocating and all that was once familiar before we left had changed — expanded.

As we returned to work, Mario and I soon realised that the very things that we missed about life back home in Canada were the things that made our lives so much faster and congested. It was great having our cars again, but we both gained about ten pounds. Now, the workday is longer. We have more 'stuff' but less time to appreciate it.

Life was so much simpler and slower in Turkey. We had more than what we needed and plenty of time to enjoy it. We don't now. We have to consciously think about prioritising our lives so that we can make time for the most important things — the simple things. Like we did in Turkey.

In effect, what you encounter at 'home' is culture shock, or reverse culture shock as it is frequently called. There are two rather different parts of returning home from time abroad, holiday visits and repatriation.

Holiday Visits

Living abroad usually means you do not get to see your friends and relatives in your home country very often. Their visits to you can seem to be rare or non-existent. Maybe you are fortunate to have a few friends or immediate family members visit you, though you probably get plenty of letters asking when you are coming home next.

If you want to be sure of seeing family and friends it can be up to you to use your valuable leave-flights and limited vacation time to do so. Many families at home seem to feel that since it was you who moved away, you should be the one to travel to see them. This can be an onerous task, financially, physically and emotionally.

How long do you have for your vacation? How many friends and relatives do you want to see? Where do you want go, what do you want see and what personal administrative tasks (bank, dentist, etc.) do you have to complete? Often it can seem like there is little time left for you to have a holiday of your own and there is the likelihood that you will arrive back in your host country in need of a holiday.

Home visits can turn from an expected and anticipated holiday into a never ending round of visits, overlong stays with relatives in houses that are far too small to accommodate the normal occupants and you for weeks on end, or expensive hotels. Once you get home you may also have lots of people calling up to say, 'Come and visit us, we're not far from where you are'. But it hardly seems to occur to many people that you have just flown halfway round the world and the last thing that you want to do is spend another four hours travelling across country to go visiting for an afternoon.

Donna Young has found home visits difficult during her family's eight years abroad.

> *We generally end up staying in a hotel because no one wants all of us (can't really blame them, there are six of us) and many friends won't even change their social schedules to accommodate our rather hectic timetable. Everyone expects us to come, but once we're actually there, it seems like little effort is made to spend time with us except at their convenience. I felt constantly pressured to spend time with my parents. Which I guess becomes a bit of an issue of guilt i.e. we've taken the grandchildren (and us away) they miss us and they won't be around for much longer.*

However, the negative results of cramped accommodation, having to make weak excuses for not visiting people, or losing friends because you say 'No' rather grumpily whilst suffering from jet lag can be avoided. Start planning home visits well in advance. Take the initiative and organise the time to ensure that you have a holiday, meet family obligations and keep your friends.

Tips on Smoothing the Path of Home Visits

1. Before you tell everybody that you are coming back for a holiday make specific arrangements to see all the important people in your life; either in a group or separately as appropriate. Once these arrangements are made, other people will have to fit around you and you can comfortably say, 'I have plans on these dates already'.

2. Jointly rent holiday accommodation with immediate relatives, making sure it is large enough to comfortably house you, your family and all the grandparents, uncles, aunts and cousins you want to see at the same time. Meeting up on neutral territory also makes such get-togethers easier and makes it a vacation for those at home as well.

3. Plan time alone for yourself and your immediate family. An endless round of visiting can cause untold stress between spouses and between parents and their children. Make plans to visit places special for you, your partner and especially your children. Being able to remember where you come from and give your children some knowledge of your home country is important. This can be especially true if you spend a long time abroad, your children were born abroad, or they were very young when you first moved away.

4. Host one, or more, parties for extended family and friends. If possible

arrange a time and place before your trip, or at least tell everyone that a party will be held while you are home. That way you get to see many people and it puts the onus onto them to do the travelling. If your friends cannot make the effort to travel a relatively short way to see you, they cannot, in good conscience, complain about you not visiting them when you have flown halfway round the world.

5. Arrange a stopover on the way back to your posting, even for just a couple of days. Pamper yourself in a hotel, and relax in the knowledge that you are not going to get invitations you cannot easily refuse, surprise visits from strange uncles, or whatever other interruptions can spoil a holiday.

6. Stay in control, make your plans and stick to them (except when you want to change them). Being able to say, 'Sorry. We've already planned to...' is the best way to avoid upsetting other people and ensure you enjoy the home visit you are anticipating.

Repatriation

Repatriation is not something to be underestimated. Many repatriates say they found it as difficult, if not more so, as expatriating in the first place.

One British expatriate who repatriated from the US found that the UK was not living up to his expectations as the place that he thought it was. The problem, he stated, seemed to stem from the fact that he had got too used to the pace of life he enjoyed in the US and found it was very, very different from the pace of life in his home town. His resulting inability to readjust to his former lifestyle left him seeking out another posting back in the US.

The longer you spend abroad the harder it can be to return home as the ongoing experiences of international living continue to affect you. As discussed above, the experiences can change an expat significantly and that will affect how they view their own country and culture once they return home.

One family spent only twelve months away from the US and found that the family got straight back into their lives; they returned to familiar places, found their friends and the kids went back to the same school. In one year little had changed, either for them or those they had left behind.

However, the greater the adaptation to the host country, the more likely it is that the expat will consider some of the routines of that country as the normal way of doing things; as Palma and Mario found after two years in Turkey. The food items, the restaurants, the mannerisms, the social mores and customs and the lifestyle (of the host-nationals and expatriates) that you became used to during your time abroad will all change when you return home and you have to readjust.

Many repatriates also report that they were not expecting to find anything different about home when they returned (even if they knew a change had occurred) and were therefore unprepared for facing the reality of adjusting from their international life back to a domestic one, as Barb Davis found.

My family was a bit different, in that my mother died while we were gone. I find this is an all too common experience among expats. Many of us are of the age when our parents are elderly, and so we have the unfortunate experience of having to deal with their deaths from a distance. Although I came home for the funeral, I didn't experience the daily loss until I came home two years later. By then my father and sisters were somewhat accustomed to her absence, and I was dealing with it as a new experience.

Returning home can therefore be problematic on two fronts. The social changes to home that the repatriates are unaware of (or unfamiliar with in practice, if they knew about them in theory from friends and newspapers) and the changes to repatriates themselves that occurred while they were away.

While you are preparing yourself for the changes that will have occurred to your family and social settings, it is important to bear in mind the changes that may happen to your professional and economic position as well.

Frequent home visits during your time abroad can have the benefit of keeping you at least partially up to date with developments at home (and in the home office). Though not everyone has the finances or the inclination to travel from continent to continent every year, just to keep up with home. So, if you are not in the position to return home frequently while you are living abroad, it can be a good idea to approach repatriation as if it was a posting to a new country.

Research your home country, but concentrate on the social aspects to help you determine what has changed and reacquaint yourself with life in your home country. Read newspapers and magazines, both in print and online, so you can catch up on the current stories that people at home are reading about. This will then mean you are able to follow more of their conversations after your return. If available, watch television programmes from home on satellite television services, even if you would not normally watch them; everyone seems to talk about soap operas and chat shows even if they deny watching them.

Talk to other expatriates from home who are in your host country (especially new arrivals) so you can be reminded at first hand what life is like there. You may have forgotten what home was really like, the situation at home may have changed during your absence, or your family situation may have changed (marriage, new children, etc.) while you were abroad. Ask when rush hour is, which shops open on Sundays, how much the cinema is, the best mobile phone service to buy and the rules on car ownership, returning your pet and which school your children will be eligible to attend.

Try to get hold of money from your home country (especially if notes and coins have changed while you were away) so you can become used to the currency again.

Investigate the cost of regular commodities compared to when you last lived there, and try to work out what the cost of living will be. Readjusting to your home currency and adapting your spending habits can be as difficult upon a return home as it was on your first time abroad.

Once you return home, find other repatriates who can help you readjust, as they will be able to advise and sympathise with any issues you need help with. Meeting up with expatriates resident in your home country can also allow you to maintain many parts of the international social life you enjoyed whilst abroad and reduce the impact of returning to local life.

In effect, do much of what you did before you moved abroad. Refer to *Culture Shock*, for ideas on where to find the necessary information.

Saying Good-Bye before Repatriation

One significant issue for repatriates is saying good-bye to the people and places that have been the cause of significant personal, professional and emotional growth. The expatriate lifestyle has a profound impact on anyone that experiences it, and leaving that life can be very difficult.

Barbara Schaetti believes closure is one of the most important features of a successful transition.

The research literature on transitions is clear: successful adjustment to a new location depends upon bringing appropriate closure in the old. Some families may be uncomfortable saying good-bye and attending to other such closure activities. It's too 'touchy-feely,' they don't know what to do with the emotion that inevitably gets stimulated; they're too busy and can't afford the time it takes. In reality, families can't afford not to take the time. Inadequate closure can lead to anger, unresolved grief, later depression and other delayed reactions. (Schaetti, B., *Families on the Move: Working Together to Meet the Challenge.* Inter-Ed 23 p.75).

Saying good-bye is not always easy. Some expatriates use repatriation to run away from problems that they have encountered, or created abroad. One Third Culture Kid (see *Long-term Considerations*) expressed that he felt lucky to be able to leave at short notice since he, '...would have less explaining and cleaning up to do'. He would not have to repair broken friendships and would not have to work through problems. He could simply avoid them by leaving.

Barbara points out that expatriates will often, '...create conflict with their friends in an attempt to lessen the pain of loss when one of them is about to move'.

In not reconciling differences before departure, unresolved issues of failed relationships can come to the fore long after you repatriate and also result in the loss of friendships that you might regret losing after your return home.

An Explanation Intended for Family and Friends at Home

It can be difficult for a repatriate to explain to their family and friends the difficulties they face upon their return, without upsetting those people whose help they need the most. This section is primarily written for the people who stayed at home to read, to help them understand the challenges that repatriates face upon returning home, though repatriates may also find it useful for verbalising what they feel.

While your friends or relatives have been abroad their lives have, in many ways, probably been very different to what yours has been at home. Yet, in some ways it will have been just the same.

Yes, they have lived abroad, maybe somewhere exotic, maybe somewhere far away or maybe as close as the country next door. Yes, they may seem different, they may seem to have changed, but you probably seem different to them too. You have both lived your lives in the intervening months and years and maybe seen each other only intermittently.

You have gone to work, shopped, socialised and relaxed. You have seen things and done things that your returning friend/family member has not. There may have been marriages, births, deaths, celebrations, and trauma in your family that have been missed by the returning expatriate. They can feel that they have missed a significant part of your life, and can feel not only sad, but also guilty about having been away and missed these milestones of yours.

On their part, your family member/friend may have seen things you are never going to see, or even want to see. But now that you are back together, you and they will want to share your individual experiences and so get to know each other once again after the period of change.

When a repatriate starts talking about their weekends away, the people they knew or the country where they lived, they are probably not trying to show off, but are just talking about the life that was normal for them for a while. It may have been in a foreign country, but it was how their life was, in the same way that trips or holidays you take are normal for you.

Now that they are back home they also have adjustments to make in their life so that they can settle into the lifestyle you have been living while they were away. Life abroad is different and every country has its own ways of doing things, some of which will have rubbed off on your friends or relations while they were there.

It is quite likely they will have friends from the country where they lived and also other countries around the world, and will consequently have become much more interested in the events of those countries. They may want to watch the international news, and not the local news. They may even have found that they have a lot of sympathy for the people of a country that has a particularly bad name in your country. This new found interest does not necessarily mean they are less interested in their home country, but that their previous attitudes and views may have been changed by their exposure to other ideas that are not common at home.

While they have been away there will have been news stories and events in your country they may have missed, or only been vaguely aware of. This often happens when people live away from their home country, as it can be difficult to find good news sources abroad (how much do you know of what happened in the country that they lived in while they were there?). It does not mean they forgot all about you and home while they were away.

Also, they may not know the current trends in fashion, music or movies, as not all countries offer the cultural life available in your country.

Repatriation involves much re-adjustment to everyday life and learning about the social and professional changes that have occurred while the person/family was away, which can be stressful for the repatriate, their family, friends and colleagues. The repatriate needs help and understanding as they progress through the resettlement process, and the best sources of that help are sympathetic and considerate friends and relatives.

On a lighter note, Mike and Sarah van der Es, two long-term expatriates have supplied a list of things that expatriates have admitted to during their first weeks back home after living abroad.

---

1. Going the wrong way when driving home because the roads and junctions have been redesigned.
2. Taking the wrong turning off the new motorway in their home town.
3. Forgetting the differences between several methods of bill payment.
4. Forgetting how much bullying there is at local schools.
5. Being overwhelmed by the enormous choice in supermarkets.
6. Being shocked at how much is thrown away.
7. Being shocked at how nobody bothers to mend things, they just replace them.
8. Being confused by the complexity of the office drinks machine.
9. Being surprised how much time cooking, cleaning, grocery shopping and ironing takes when they have to do it all themselves.
10. Being amazed that the telephone and electricity almost always works.
11. Being amazed at how fast people drive everywhere in nice looking cars.

Resources

Print Resources
The Art of Coming Home, Craig Storti, Intercultural Press, ISBN 1-877864-47-1.

Online resources
http://globalnomads.association.com: A resource site for TCKs and their families.

www.expatexchange.com: An online community for expats, with associated experts to offer advice.

www.expatexpert.com: The website of expat writer, author and consultant, Robin Pascoe.

www.expatforum.com: Hosts online chat groups, including repatriation.

www.tckworld.com: A resource site for TCKs and their families.

Appendix A — Financials

There is a common perception among people who have never lived abroad that the expat life is one of wealth and luxury. Unfortunately, that is not always the case.

There are many perks and the salary can be good, but the financial costs can be high too, especially without careful planning. Among the financial concerns for expats are:

1. Traditional UK-style pension schemes are not usually available to non-residents.
2. Having money available quickly, in the country you want it, can be awkward and expensive to arrange if you are not prepared.
3. Your savings can be subject to secondary taxes if you leave them in the wrong place, or move them at the wrong time.

However, a prime concern for expats is having enough money in the country they are living in to be able to live comfortably, but still have enough money in a safe banking system to pay for mortgages, pensions, investments, schools fees etc. If you live in Singapore, Hong Kong or somewhere equally safe (in banking terms) you will not have too much of a problem managing your money. But would you feel so secure if you had all your money in Laos or a central African bank?

Before you leave home is the best time to plan your banking and investment strategy. You can do it once you are abroad but it can take much longer and it can be more difficult without the benefit of meeting your advisor face to face. Take advice from your company, returned expats, current expats you have contacts with, and most importantly your own bank.

The local economic conditions of your host country will affect how you want to be paid and how you manage your money. If you are going to live in a country with high inflation (some developing countries have inflation rates well over 100% per annum) you need to be sure that your salary keeps up with it. If your salary is to be paid in local currency, how often will it be adjusted? Or will you be paid an amount equivalent to a fixed rate of US$ or GBP, so that every month your local currency salary increases? If the local inflation rate is exceptionally high you should push to get your employer to pay you directly in a hard currency; US$ are common and easily convertible, though other 'hard' currencies may be used in countries that have specific ties to another currency.

If you do not expect to need all your salary to live on, or you have financial commitments in your home country, you might also want to have a proportion of it paid into an account outside of the country you are living in. This is especially useful if you have concerns about the stability of the financial system of the country you are living in. There are a number of offshore banking centres that are well set up to receive money from around the world and send it on to various other ones.

Even if a country does not have a high inflation rate, exchange rate fluctuations can cause financial difficulty for expats. A few years ago the US$ and the GBP£ were almost 1-to-1, making the US much more expensive than it had previously been for Europeans living in the US. Discuss with your employer who will bear any exchange rate risks before you go, when adjustments will kick in and how quickly they will do so after a fluctuation. After a major fluctuation has occurred is too late to start negotiations.

If your local, home-country bank is small, or does not have good knowledge of offshore banking services and international money management, look for another bank. The Channel Islands and the Isle of Man are popular banking centres for UK expats, while the Caribbean islands are popular for North Americans. Many large UK and US banks have offshore banking subsidiaries that can be convenient (and sometimes accept the regulatory practices of their parent country) for both existing and new customers. Online banking services are becoming more common, and can be very convenient for checking balances, moving money around the world and even managing your investment portfolio. Living the expat lifestyle can bring financial benefits if you are careful, but bad advice, wrong investments and greed can cause you to lose everything. High-interest scams and dodgy deals abound for the unwary, unless you are an expert, it can often be better to be safe than sorry.

Life as an expatriate is not always secure and predictable. Contingency planning can be a way of life in some countries and the financial aspect of the planning is important. If you have to leave your posting quickly, you need to be able to access your money easily and cheaply in the country you will end up in, so you can survive until you begin working again. One financial advisor suggested that expats should plan their financial strategy around the worst case scenario.

The worst case scenario being the immediate evacuation from the host country with nothing more than a suitcase. By having their savings in a safe and stable bank and easily accessible from most places in the world (and especially the country the expat would evacuate too), the expat will not lose everything and will be able to support themselves in the short-term.

Seeking expert financial advice is essential and being able to trust that your money is safe and well managed can go a long way towards minimising one more of the potential concerns of expatriate living. Personal recommendations and the use of reputable companies are important when choosing where to put your money and safeguarding your financial well being.

Resources

Financial

Brewin Dolphin Securities: 5 Giltspur Street, London, EC1A 9BD, UK (tel ++44 (0)20-7248 4400; fax ++44 (0)20-7236 2034).

Print Resources

Money Mail Moves Abroad, Margaret Stone (Editor), Kogan Page, ISBN 0749425873.

Resident Abroad magazine from the FT Finance offers financial advice for expatriates.

The Weekly Telegraph, a digest of The *Daily Telegraph*, especially for expats.

Appendix B — The Basic Features of Private Health Insurance

There are generally two major levels of private health insurance coverage:

Comprehensive Coverage: that includes in-hospital care including all services, the services of doctors, lab tests, x-rays and other scans, etc., plus the services of doctors, lab tests, x-rays and other scans in a non-hospital setting.

Basic Coverage: that is limited to care and services relating to in-patient hospital stays only.

Within the class of coverage bought there are also other variables such as:

1. The aggregate, annual, and other scheduled maximum claim limits (usually a maximum monetary value).
2. Deductibles and co-insurances (that part of any claim that the insurance provider will not cover).
3. Restrictions on where the medical care can be received (may specify or exclude certain medical establishments, cities, or countries).

Medical insurance policies can also be confusing due to the wording of specific clauses, leaving potential subscribers unsure as to exactly what coverage they would have if they sign up and are accepted.

Below are brief explanations of certain health insurance clauses, provided by Paul Wolf of *Innovative Benefits Consultants, Ltd.* (40 Homer Street, London W1H 1HL, UK; tel/fax ++44 (0)870-737 9000 ext 6129 or New York ++1 212-328-3030 ext 5854 or Singapore ++65 347 8333 ext 0303; info@ibencon.com; www.ibencon.com) who has worked in the insurance field for 20 years, the last eight of which have been with expatriates and other international clients. Over and above his comments below he states, 'There are no bargains out there, you get what you pay for'.

Applying for a Policy

Guaranteed-Issue Policies

It is easy to get coverage with one of these policies, applicants just have to answer a few easy questions and pay their premium. However, problems can start when claims are submitted, as proof may be requested that the complaint just treated was not a pre-existing condition at the time the policy was applied for.

Pre-existing Condition

Generally, a pre-existing condition is a medical condition which is being (or has been) treated, and any condition associated with it.

Treated generally means doctor's visits, tests, or even taking medication for the condition within the past one year, two years, five years, or anytime in the past (the time frame varies depending on the policy). It can also mean any condition which a 'prudent person' would have had treated, even if he or she did not know about it.

Any condition associated with it could mean, for example, a broken leg being deemed to be the result of brittle bones caused by cancer treatment.

If the insurer decides it is a pre-existing condition, they may deny the claim. Always remember, the larger the claim the more they are going to examine it very carefully, which is not what you want to go through when you have just incurred a claim for $10,000.

Fully Underwritten Policies

These policies ask very detailed health questions on the application form and may even ask for one or more doctor's reports. Based on all the information you supplied, the insurer may:

1. Accept the application with no exclusions or conditions.
2. Accept the application with an increased premium.
3. Accept the application with an exclusion for a specific medical condition.
4. Reject the application.

It makes good sense to disclose pre-existing conditions on an application form, even if the application does not ask about them; then the insurance company will be hard-pressed to deny a claim for a pre-existing condition if they did not exclude it when they approved the application.

Your Age

Some insurers automatically reduce benefits, charge extra premiums, or even discontinue coverage when clients reach a specific age, for example 60, 65, or 70.

Policy exclusions to be aware of:

Travel: Some policies exclude travel if it is specifically to get medical care. Others exclude care if travel is 'against the advice of a physician' or 'while you are on a waiting list for treatment'; in this case, treatment for that specific condition may not be covered while you are travelling.

Pregnancy and Childbirth: Some policies exclude one or both completely while others exclude them only for the first 12 months of the policy. Even if the pregnancy is covered, some policies automatically exclude the first 15 days of a newborn's life, while others cover only the first 14 days of life. In these cases, the baby must apply for insurance cover as a 'separate person'. Because many policies exclude birth defects, and congenital and hereditary illnesses, a newborn baby may not be accepted for coverage. Therefore, such policies may not be appropriate for those in their childbearing years — take a long, hard look and ask questions before you sign up for such a policy.

Chronic illnesses: Some policies specifically exclude, or limit, the coverage of conditions which are, or become, chronic (even after you purchase the policy). An asthma attack (acute) may be covered but not ongoing asthma problems (chronic).

Limited Coverage: Some policies limit coverage for any single accident or illness to, for example, the first 12 months of treatment following the onset of that accident or illness.

Organ transplants: Some policies exclude such procedures; others offer it as an additional benefit, and some include it as a part of the regular coverage.

Where you are: Some policies place no limitations on where you can get care while others limit the region of the world where they will cover you (and may charge different premiums based on the region(s) you select).

Home Country: Some policies limit the time you can spend in your 'Home Country', or even exclude it completely. For example, travel to/in the US may be limited to 30 or 60 days for US citizens, or anyone born there, regardless of their current citizenship. This could apply even if you go for a short visit and then, because of an illness or accident, need to stay longer. The policy may be cancelled or suspended when you reach the time limit, regardless of your health condition at the time.

Getting Claims Paid

Pre-certification: Many policies now require patients to get prior approval for a planned hospitalisation, with a penalty of reduced benefits if this is not done. They may be more lenient with emergencies, but still require notification as soon as possible after the emergency. Some may also limit the choice of hospitals or doctors you can use. Even if you do not need pre-approval, informing an insurer before a hospitalisation is a good idea since they can usually pay the hospital directly for your stay.

Non-hospital bills: In most cases, you must pay physicians, labs, etc. yourself and then submit those bills with proof of payment and await reimbursement from the insurer.

Submitting Claims: Some policies require a completed claim form, while others require only the original bill. In almost all cases, you should get the bill in English or supply an English translation, it tends to smooth the path to reimbursement.

Emergency Help

Almost all policies offer the services of an International Help Centre, 24 hours a day, seven days a week. The Centre can direct you to an English-speaking doctor and/or hospital and assist in the event of an emergency requiring medical evacuation. This is useful when travelling/living in a non English-speaking area, but can be used from anywhere in the world.

Medical Evacuation

This is a useful feature when in a country/region with a below par healthcare system. However, be aware that no policy offers evacuation just because the patient would prefer it, but only because the emergency could not be treated locally. The evacuation would be to the nearest major facility capable of providing a decent standard of care, and the definition of 'nearest' and 'decent' are decided by the Emergency Help Centre and the insurance company.

Paying Premiums

Premiums are normally payable for each person in a family, although some policies offer a family premium, and others offer 'free' coverage to pre-teen dependent children if one parent is covered. Premiums may vary with age and country of residence. Payment is usually by cheque or credit card and may offer a choice of currencies.

Renewing Coverage

Guaranteed renewability of an insurance policy is fundamental to the selection of a policy. If there is no guarantee to renew coverage regardless of your health condition at the renewal date — beware. Cancellation of coverage is not what you want to happen in the middle of a serious sickness or when you have a pre-existing condition.

Useful Addresses

BUPA International: Russell Mews, Brighton, BN1 2NR, UK (tel ++44 (0)1273-208181; fax ++44 (0)1273-866583; e-mail advice@bupa-intl.com; website www.bupa-intl.com).

Vacation Work publish:

	Paperback	Hardback
The Directory of Summer Jobs Abroad	£9.99	£14.95
The Directory of Summer Jobs in Britain	£9.99	£14.95
Supplement to Summer Jobs in Britain and Abroad *published in May*	£6.00	–
Work Your Way Around the World	£12.95	–
The Good Cook's Guide to Working Worldwide	£11.95	–
Taking a Gap Year	£11.95	–
Working in Tourism – The UK, Europe & Beyond	£11.95	–
Kibbutz Volunteer	£10.99	–
Working on Cruise Ships	£9.99	–
Teaching English Abroad	£11.95	–
The Au Pair & Nanny's Guide to Working Abroad	£10.99	–
Working in Ski Resorts – Europe & North America	£10.99	–
Working with Animals – The UK, Europe & Worldwide	£11.95	–
Accounting Jobs Worldwide	£11.95	–
Working with the Environment	£11.95	–
Health Professionals Abroad	£11.95	–
The Directory of Jobs & Careers Abroad	£11.95	£16.95
The International Directory of Voluntary Work	£10.99	£15.95
The Directory of Work & Study in Developing Countries	£9.99	£14.99
Live & Work in Saudi & the Gulf	£10.99	–
Live & Work in Japan	£10.99	–
Live & Work in Russia & Eastern Europe	£10.99	–
Live & Work in France	£10.99	–
Live & Work in Australia & New Zealand	£10.99	–
Live & Work in the USA & Canada	£10.99	–
Live & Work in Germany	£10.99	–
Live & Work in Belgium, The Netherlands & Luxembourg	£10.99	–
Live & Work in Spain & Portugal	£10.99	–
Live & Work in Italy	£10.99	–
Live & Work in Scandinavia	£10.99	–
Panamericana: On the Road through Mexico and Central America	£12.95	–
Travellers Survival Kit: Mauritius, Seychelles & Réunion	£10.99	–
Travellers Survival Kit: Madagascar, Mayotte & Comoros	£10.99	–
Travellers Survival Kit: Sri Lanka	£10.99	–
Travellers Survival Kit: Mozambique	£10.99	–
Travellers Survival Kit: Cuba	£10.99	–
Travellers Survival Kit: Lebanon	£10.99	–
Travellers Survival Kit: South Africa	£10.99	–
Travellers Survival Kit: India	£10.99	–
Travellers Survival Kit: Russia & the Republics	£9.95	–
Travellers Survival Kit: Western Europe	£8.95	–
Travellers Survival Kit: Eastern Europe	£9.95	–
Travellers Survival Kit: South America	£15.95	–
Travellers Survival Kit: USA & Canada	£10.99	–
Travellers Survival Kit: Australia & New Zealand	£11.95	–

Distributors of:

Summer Jobs USA	£12.95	–
Internships (On-the-Job Training Opportunities in the USA)	£16.95	–
Sports Scholarships in the USA	£16.95	–
Scholarships for Study in the USA & Canada	£14.95	–
Colleges & Universities in the USA	£15.95	–
Green Volunteers	£10.99	–

Vacation Work Publications, 9 Park End Street, Oxford OX1 1HJ
Tel 01865 – 241978   Fax 01865 – 790885

Visit us online for more information on our unrivalled range of titles for work, travel and adventure, readers' feedback and regular updates:

www.vacationwork.co.uk